# *Two Thousand Years of Jewish Life in Morocco*

HAIM ZAFRANI

SEPHARDIC HOUSE
NEW YORK

in Association with
KTAV PUBLISHING HOUSE, INC.
Jersey City, NJ 07306

Library of Congress Cataloging-in-Publication Data

Zafrani, Haèim.
Two thousand years of Jewish life in Morocco / Haim Zafrani.
p. cm.
Includes bibliographical references and index.
ISBN 0-88125-748-6
1. Jews--Morocco--History. 2. Morocco--Ethnic relations. I. Title.
DS135.M8 Z3213 2002
964'.004924--dc21

2002070238

Published by
KTAV Publishing House, Inc.
930 Newark Avenue
Jersey City, NJ 07306
Email: orders@ktav.com
www.ktav.com
(201) 963-9524
Fax (201) 963-0102

# About the Author

**Haim Zafrani,** Professor Emeritus at the University of Paris, was born in Essaouira, Morocco, in 1922. In addition to his work as a professor, he was chief inspector for Arabic, head delegate for scholarly activity of the Ittihad-Maroc and a member of the Royal Commission for Educational Reform. From 1962 to 1966, Professor Zafrani held the chair of Hebrew at the Ecole Nationale des Langues Orientales Vivantes (National School of Modem Oriental Languages). From 1976 until 1985, he was a member of the faculty of Slavonic, Oriental, and Asian Languages. At the time of his death on March 31, 2004, Professor Zafrani had been in charge of the University of Paris' Department of the Hebrew Language and Jewish Civilization since its creation in October 1969. He was also a member of two research groups at the University and at the National Center for Scientific Research (CNRS) (URA 1078 and SDI 6243), with authority to award doctoral degrees.

Professor Zafrani was a *Docteur d'Etat et-Lettres et Sciences Humaines* and also held a research doctorate in Oriental Studies, a master's degree in law and economics, a diploma in classical Arabic from the University of Rabat, Morocco, and a diploma in the Hebrew language from the Hebrew University, Israel.

From 1981 to 1988, Professor Zafrani headed the jury which awarded the *aggregation* degree in Hebrew and was named expert to the National Committee for the Evaluation of Universities in 1988. He was a member of the boards of the Institute of Semitic Studies (College de France), LACITO at the CNRS, the Society for Jewish Studies, and the *Revue des Etudes Juives* and was a member of the Asiatic Society.

Professor Zafrani was the author of sixteen books and more than two hundred articles on the Hebrew, Judeo-Arabic, and Judeo-Berber languages and on Jewish thought, literature, and languages in the

Muslim West and the Islamic world. His *Jewish Poetry in the Muslim West* was translated into Hebrew by the Ben Zvi Institute in Jerusalem. His *Two Thousand Years of Jewish Life in Morocco* has been translated into Arabic in Morocco (University of Rabat) and into Hebrew (Habermann Institute, Israel) and Spanish. It is currently being published in English in the United States. His work has been awarded two international prizes.

Professor Zafrani was a *Chevalier* of the Legion of Honor and of the National Order of Merit and a commander of the Academic Palms. He was also a corresponding member of the Royal Academy of Morocco and a fellow of the Institute for Advanced Studies at the Hebrew University of Jerusalem (1991–1992).

His Majesty King Hassan II of Morocco honored Professor Zafrani's writings by bestowing upon him the title of commander of the Ouissam Alaouite Order on September 10, 1997.

## OTHER HONORS ACCORDED PROFESSOR ZAFRANI

1985 Prix de l'Etat d'Israel Ben-Zvi (Israel)
1999 Prix du Grand Atlas de la Création (Morocco)
2000 de Vie Juive au Maroc
2001 Officier de la Légion d'Honneur (France)
2004 Commandeur de l'Ordre du Mérite Intellectuel, awarded by His Majesty King Mohammed VI of Morocco

*A tribute to Florence Amzallag Tatistcheff*
*with gratitude for her interest*
*and the attention she has devoted to*
*our work on Moroccan Judaism.*

# Contents

# Preface

## *Judeo-Maghrebian Consciousness and Collective Memory: The Dual Aspect of Moroccan Jewry*

The analysis that I have undertaken in this book is particularly concerned with the Jewry of the Far Maghreb, a limited region in the geopolitical area that encompasses the whole of the Arabic-Islamic world, where the Jews of what is known as the oriental Diaspora have lived for almost two thousand years. The evidence I provide on the Jewish societies of the Islamic West is worthy of note because of the way it can be transposed onto the other communities of the Sephardi and oriental world. These communities are indissolubly linked by a common fate, if not by a sociocultural identity and, originally, by the political status that the Islamic law of the *dhimma* accords to the "people of the book." For me, the Islamic West which I know is in the nature of a representative example: The same phenomena of civilization and culture can be seen in the whole of that Jewish world which has lived for more than a thousand years under the banner of Islam.

At the outset, I wish to state that Maghrebian and Moroccan Jewry, like any other Jewry, lives under the influence of rules and laws that have their sources in the Bible, the Talmud, and the halakhah, the latter formed of the contents of the various codes and other treatises of Hebraic law.

Maghrebian Jewry (historical Jewry, of course) maintains close links, favored relations, with universal Jewish thought and its various means of expression, at the level of Hebrew writing and classical and traditional literary creativity—the Jewish humanities, as it were. It must immediately be added that this Jewry is also the product of the Maghrebian land where it was born, where it was nourished, and where it has lived for nearly two thousand years. Over that period, in the close relationship of shared language and the similarity of psychological structures, there developed an active solidarity, a not negligible degree of symbiosis, even a religious syncretism, with the environment. This was so on the level of everyday life, as well as in its most important moments, birth, marriage, and death, and the rites and ceremonies associated with them, and also on the level of popular and dialectal oral literary creation. Thus was constituted a whole area of convergence, a zone of compromise, where a complex but authentic personality developed, an original and plural sociocultural identity. The Judeo-Maghrebian personality with its dual polarity, as it were, is characterized by a consciousness and a memory that can be observed on the level of history, wherein its destiny and its origins, the names of places and people are examined; on the level of the cultural landscape, wherein the manifold contributions of the Hebraic, Arab, Berber, and Castilian civilizations, intellectual productivity, and literary creativity are investigated; and on the level of social imagination, marked with the seal of religion and magic, which brings both together at the most solemn moments of life, in the ritual appropriate to each of the religious groups, so as to give the latter both its universal dimension and its local component.

Paris
March 15, 1982

*Two Thousand Years of Jewish Life in Morocco*

# Geographic Distribution of the Jewish Communities in Morocco[1]

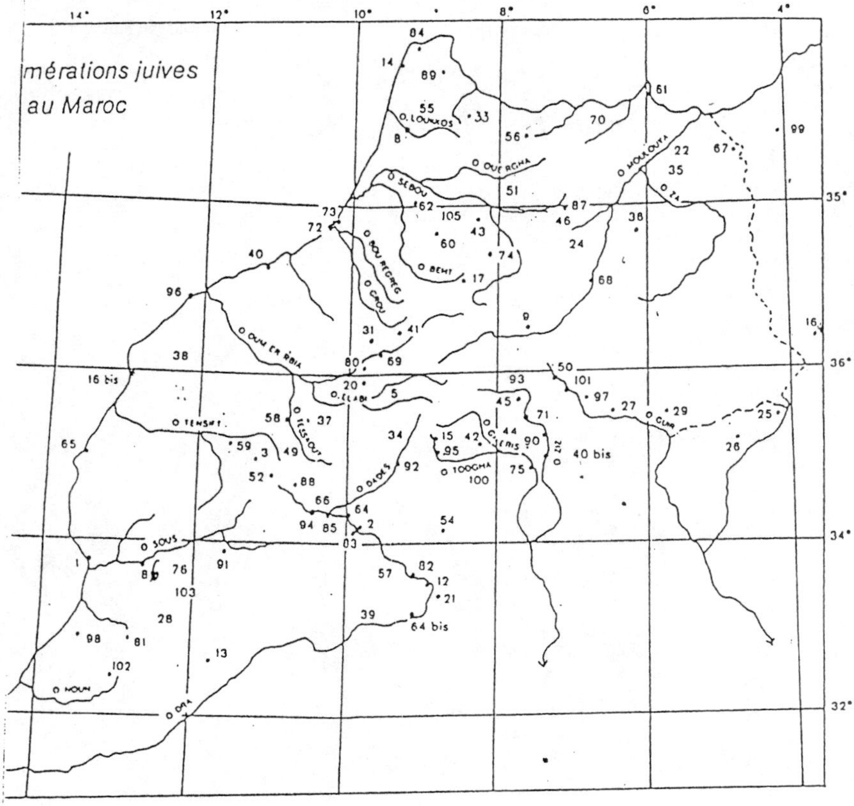


*Carte établie par H. Zafrani*

Only those communities cited in the book whose identification is more or less certain are indicated on this map. Those whose names are followed by an asterisk are not indicated in the map.

1. Agadir
2. Agidz (Agdz)
3. Aghmat
4. Aït 'Abd Kafra*
5. Aït 'Attab
6. Akhelluf*
7. Al-Gherfa*
8. Al-Ksar Kebir
9. Al-Ksabi
10. Al-Mesri (Al-Mashra')*
11. Amismiz
12. Amzerrou
13. Aqqa (Akka)
14. Arzila (Asila)
15. Asfalo
16. 'Aïn Sefra
16bis. 'Asfi (Safi)
17. Azrou
18. Beni-'Amir
19. Beni-'Ayyad
20. Beni-Mellal
21. Beni-Sbiḥ
22. Beni-Snassen
23. Beni-Snus*
24. Beni-Waraïn
25. Beni-Wunnif (B. Ounif)
26. Bessar (Colomb Bechar)
27. Bou-Dnib
28. Bou-Iḥya (Aït Yaḥya)
29. Bou-'Nan (Bouanane)
30. Bou-Routa*
31. Boujad (Bou-Za'd)
32. Bou-Zemla*
33. Chichaouen (Shawen)
34. Dadèas
35. Dar Mesh'al
36. Debdou
37. Demnat
38. Doukkala
39. Draa (Der'a)
40. Ed-Dar-el-Bayda
40bis. Erfoud
41. Ez-Zawiya (de Dila)
42. Ferkla
43. Fès
44. Gheris (Geris)
45. Gherslewin (Gerslewin)
46. Ghiyata
47. Gi-Iglan*
48. Glagla*
49. Glawa
50. Grama (Gourama)
51. Ḥayaïna
52. Iddr (Adr, Taddert)
53. Irara*
54. Izzaghine
55. Jbel
56. Ktama
57. La'roumiyyat
58. Mansour
59. Marrakech
60. Meknes
61. Melilia
62. Meshra 'Ar-Ramla (Sidi-Slimane)
63. Mezgida (voir 64)
64. Mezgita
64bis. Mḥamid
65. Mogador (Essaouira)
66. Ouarzazat
66bis. Mzab*
67. Oujda (Wajda)
68. Outat al-Hadj
69. Qaṣba di Tadla
70. Qdara
71. Qṣer-Es-suq (Ksar-el-Souk)
72. Rabat
73. Salé
74. Sefrou
75. Sijilmassa (Tafilalet)
76. Sous
77. Souk-Hras*
78. Tadla (voir Qaṣba di Tadla)
79. Tafilalet (= Sijilmassa)
80. Tafza (= Efza)
81. Tahala (Tafraout)
82. Tamegrout
83. Tamengoult
84. Tanger
85. Taourirt (de Ouarzazat)
86. Taroudant
87. Taza
88. Telouet
89. Tétouan
90. Tezwimi-l-Ma'adid
91. Tifnut
92. Tillit (Tiilit)
93. Ti'lalin
94. Timesla (Tesmasla)
95. Tinghir
96. Tit (Mazagan, Al-Jadida)
97. Tit-n'Ali
98. Tiznit
99. Tlemcen
100. Todgha
101. Toulal
102. Ufran (Oufran, Ifran)
103. Ulad Ḥassin
104. Utat d'Aït Zdeg (voir Outat)
105. Zerhoun
106. Ztat (Zettat)*
107. Zrigat*

# Chapter 1

# *Moroccan Jewry and Its Destiny*

## MAJOR HISTORICAL TRENDS

The Jewry of the Islamic West has its roots in a distant past. Historically, the Jews were the first non-Berber people to settle in the Maghreb, and they have lived there ever since. We have no epigraphic documents and scarcely any other evidence on the establishment of purely Jewish colonies on the African coast at the time of Tyre and Sidon. This world belongs to the realm of legend, and accounts relating to the period have only recently been collected. These accounts appeared in various places in the Maghreb, on the island of Djerba in Tunisia, in Tangier and Fez, in the Drâ Valley, and on the Saharan borders of the Maghreb. They tell of boundary-stones placed by Joab ben Seruya, the leader of King David's armies, who had come thus far in pursuit of the Philistines, whom some of the Jewish mountain peoples consider to be none other than the Berbers (it will be noted that the term *plishtim* of the Hebrew Bible is here translated as *braber*).

Valuable information on the Greco-Roman period exists in the talmudic and homiletic literature (midrash and aggadah), epigraphic and archaeological documents now available, and accounts by ancient and modern Jewish and non-Jewish historians who deal with this period, describing Cyrenaican Jewry, the Jewish revolt under Trajan, the accounts by Procopius, and so on. A Jewish community lived in the Roman town of Volubilis. A seven-branched bronze candelabrum has been found in the ruins of that city, as well as a fragment of a tombstone bearing a Hebrew inscription that says in part, *matrona bat rabbi yehudah nah*, "woman, daughter of Rabbi Yehudah, may [her soul] rest." The Jewish colony apparently continued to live there until the Arabs came. Arab historians themselves mention the existence in the Ẓerhoun, not far from there, of judaized Berber tribes at the time when Fez was founded in 808.

The Roman authorities generally seem to have been tolerant toward the Jews, who went tranquilly about their business, some of them benefiting from the abundance of civil rights. The Jewish or judaized population was increased by the settlement of new Jewish immigrants and also as a result of a fairly strong wave of conversions to the Mosaic religion among natives and foreigners. A talmudic saying by R. Yehudah in the name of Rav (Menaḥot 110a) gives some information on the period of Septimus Severus and his son Caracalla (193–217 C.E.): "From Tyre to Carthage [the faith of] Israel and its God are known; from Tyre to the west and from Carthage to the east, neither [the faith of] Israel nor its God is known." This seems to mean that proselytes were not always converted according to the requirements of the law (halakhah), and, in particular, that some of them were not circumcised.

The theory that the majority of Maghrebian Jews are of Berber origin is sustained by several historians, for whom the judaization of the Berbers has acquired the status of a fundamental fact. Others, such as H. Z. Hirschberg, question it: "It seems," he says, "that there is no solid basis for the theory of *judaized Berbers*, those who are said to have become Jewish in all respects and in this way to constitute the fundamental ethnic component of Maghrebian Jewry. . . . Decisive proof of the absence of any assimilation by sizable Berber groups is the absolute nonexistence of penetration by Berber languages into Jewish literature. There are, on the other hand, texts in Maghrebian Judeo-Arabic."[1] Without joining in the debate or dealing with the basic problem here, some of Hirschberg's assertions must at least be supplemented, if not challenged, on one specific point: the information he gives on the Jewish languages of the Maghreb and the cultural load they transmit. Our research in Berberophone Jewish circles in Morocco (mellahs in southern Morocco and the Atlas valleys) clearly shows that traditional teaching in these communities used Berber as

1. *Histoire des Juifs d'Afrique du Nord* (Jerusalem, 1965), in Hebrew, vol. 2, pp. 86 and 36.

the language for explaining and translating the sacred texts in the same way as other communities in the rest of the country employed Judeo-Arabic or Judeo-Spanish for the same purposes.[2]

We come up against a complete void and almost total silence in the sources for the period separating the Roman era from the beginnings of the Arab conquest. In this respect, the wondrous exploits and fabulous tales which misrepresent the history of the Kahena and star that Judeo-Berber queen and "priestess" who fiercely resisted the Arab invasion of the Maghreb must be relegated to the realm of legend.

It may be supposed that Christianity, Judaism, and paganism intermingled in pre-Islamic Morocco. Fourteenth-century chroniclers report that Idris I found Christian, Jewish, and idolatrous tribes at the time of his conquests. The Jews were admitted within the walls of early Fez by Idris II. Until the Merinides founded the existing mellah of Fez Jdid, the local Jews inhabited the area between the Quarawiyin and Bab Gisa, which still preserves the name of Fuduq-l-Iudi. The inhabitants of this area included some of the most famous Jewish scholars and writers of the tenth and early eleventh centuries. Rabbi Isaac Alfasi, born in Qual'at Ibn-Hammad in 1013, conducted a yeshîbâh at Fez, and still standing in the Old Town there is a partially ruined house, distinguishable by thirteen copper bells hanging from a balustrade, that is said to have been the residence of Maimonides when he lived in this city.

Marrakesh, founded in 1062 by an Almoravide, Yûsuf Ibn Tashfin, was forbidden to the Jews at first, and they continued to live in Aghmat-Ourika, 40 kilometers southeast of the town. But they were permitted to spend the day there for business purposes.

A commentary on the talmudic treatises of Bâbâ Qamma, Bâbâ Mesi'a', and Bâbâ Batrâ' was composed in Aghmat by Zechariah ben Judah Aghmati in 1190.

It was a Saadian king, Ahmed-Ed-Dahabi (1578–1603), who invited the Jews of Aghmat to settle in Marrakesh, and the existing mellah, situated close to the sultan's palace (Qasr-elbadî'), seems to date from this period. The South Moroccan capital was also, for centuries on end, a center for the spread of Jewish knowledge to the regions of the Sous, the Atlas, and the southern towns along the Atlantic coast.

As is well known, during the Golden Age of Spain, a time when

2. See *Journal asiatique* 1 (1964); *Revue des études juives* 1–2 (1964); *Pédagogie juive en terre d'Islam* (Paris, 1969).

Andalusia and Morocco maintained close relations, the Moroccan communities of Fez, Salé, Sijilmassa, and Der'a had large yeshîbot conducted by teachers who enjoyed an immense reputation in the Jewish world.

A considerable Jewish community lived in Sijilmassa, founded by the Beni-Wassuls in the ninth century. This town was renowned for its trade with countries on the banks of the Niger River in Central Africa, Egypt, and the Indies, and Jews had a major role in trade and the movement of commodities. Its rabbis maintained regular relations with their colleagues in Kairouan and Baghdad. There was a student from Sijilmassa at the yeshîbâh of Samuel ben Ali in Baghdad; and a rabbi who had originated in Fez, Salomon ben Yehudah Gaon, held the office of rôsh yeshîbâh in Palestine from 1025 to 1051.

A chain of agglomerations existed in the Oued Drâa Valley, where sizable Jewish communities had long been established. A man called Dunash wrote to Rab Alfas (Isaac Alfasi) from the town of Der'a to consult him on legal problems. Maimonides' *Iggeret Teman*, or "Letter to the Communities of the Yemen," provides important information on Moshe Der'i, the famous forerunner of the messiah, and mentions the names of several notables from Der'a who had settled in Fostat, in Egypt. The celebrated Arab geographer Yaqut (beginning of the twelfth century) emphasizes that most of the merchants in Der'a were Jews.

The Jews of Dar-al-Islam, the "Land of Islam," had the status of *dhimmi* imposed by the dominant religion. It was, of course, a degrading and often precarious status, but, taken all in all, it was a liberal legal status (providing a very high degree of legal, administrative, and cultural autonomy) as compared with the arbitrary position of the Jews under Christian rule in Ashkenazi lands. Moreover, the largely secular nature of the medieval civilization of the Arabic East and West allowed *dhimmis* (both Jews and Christians), as peoples of the book, to feel that they were heirs to a great and honorable cultural tradition. When they studied their own sacred texts, they regularly and unreservedly used the dominant tongue, Arabic, which was less closely attached to the ruling religion than was Latin to the Church of Rome or the Eastern Church. They abandoned their ancient common language, Aramaic, henceforth limited to talmudic (or kabbalistic) texts, and replaced it with the new language of civilization and culture of the Arab-Islamic world.

In the gaonic period (sixth to twelfth century), the Maghreb held an important place in relations with the Babylonian academies of Sura and Pumbedita (Iraq) and even with the one in Palestine. Evidence of its close ties with the centers of Jewish learning of the day is found in documents from the genizah (repository of documents) discovered in the old synagogue in Cairo at the end of the nineteenth century and partially known to us as a result of the work of S. D. Goitein. It contains responsa (legal consultations) of the gaonim, complete treatises or fragments of works on halakhah, business correspondence, and deeds executed and authenticated by notaries of the rabbinical courts that all add to what was already known of the Maghreb's exchanges with the Orient, the bulk of which is concerned with legislation. All this documentation bears witness to the antiquity of the Jewish settlements in the north and south of the Far Maghreb and to their rootedness in the country.

The results of this work also suggest that rabbis from the Maghreb were the teachers of Spanish Jewry. The first grammarians, linguists, poets, and authors of decisionary legal literature in that country, who are rightly considered the founders of the so-called Spanish school, came from Morocco in the tenth century.

Spanish Jewry at that time led an existence infinitely easier and more secure than the life of Jews anywhere else. Subject to a legal status which, when all is said and done, was liberal, the Jews of Spain played an important role in the flourishing economic life of the country, even in public affairs, and enjoyed a not inconsiderable share of the general prosperity. Affluence gave them the leisure to study and to achieve a high level of general culture, represented in that period by science and by Arabic-Hispanic literature. The acquisition of this knowledge by Jews exercised considerable influence on the development of Jewish thought and its various modes of expression, and contributed to their enrichment.

What must also be noted is the extraordinary freedom of movement and communication that characterized the Mediterranean world at this time and its concomitant cultural and socioeconomic unity. These are quite remarkable phenomena that in certain respects explain the high degree of autonomy of the Jewish communities. Its extent can be gauged from the following episode, mentioned in the postscript to a letter sent in 1016/17 by the Kairouan representative of the Jewish academies (yeshîbâhs) in Baghdad to Ibn Awqal, head of the African district that had its headquarters in Old Cairo.

According to the postscript, a Jewish merchant who was a native of

Baghdad had died at Sijilmassa (on the Saharan border of Morocco) at the other end of the Islamic world. The local Jewish authorities had informed the writer of the letter that the deceased merchant had left goods locally and had also entrusted merchandise to merchants from Kairouan.

The writer of the letter asked Ibn Awqal to require the Jewish authorities in Baghdad either to appoint a legal representative for the heirs or to communicate their names and titles (i.e., relationships to the deceased) to the *nagid* of Tunisia and the elders of Kairouan, who would undertake to handle the matter.

This simple correspondence confirms (if confirmation there need be) the well-known fact, noted elsewhere, that the non-Muslim communities comprised a state not only within the Islamic state but sometimes beyond its frontiers. It took several months to travel from Baghdad to Kairouan and from Kairouan to Sijilmassa; several frontiers separated the countries along the route and had to be crossed in order to go from the Maghreb to the Mashreq. No reference is made to the governments of the countries concerned. The affair relating to the patrimony of the merchant in question remains within the province of the rabbinical and lay Jewish authorities and is handled as an exclusively Jewish matter. Could there be more eloquent testimony to the eminently autonomous nature of a non-Muslim community in the Land of Islam?

As their misfortunes increased with the advance of the Reconquista, the Jews of Spain began to flow back, well before the edict of 1391, to the countries of the Maghreb which their ancestors had left a few centuries earlier. In 1492–97, successive waves of Spanish and Portuguese *megorashim* (exiles) arrived and settled, temporarily or permanently, in Berberie, in the Mediterranean and Atlantic ports and in cities in the interior of the country. They brought with them their Old Castilian language, their learning, the communal institutions prescribed in their *taqqanot* (rabbinical ordinances), their customs and costumes, their spirit of enterprise. All this made them, compared with the *toshabim* (native inhabitants), a dominant sociocultural group from which the intellectual elite and the bourgeoisie of notables were recruited. The latter played a role of quite considerable importance in the realms of commerce, finance, and diplomacy, the likes of which had never before devolved on a Jew in a Christian land or even in another Muslim country.

Although the arrival of the Jews expelled from Spain caused some disturbance in the life of the local communities, it was, above all else, a factor of considerable spiritual enrichment. For a long time the toshabim and the megorashim held conflicting views on certain points relating to the liturgy and the laws governing the ritual slaughter of animals for consumption; but in the end the newcomers took the lead in the communities where they had settled, particularly in the north of the country.

In the synagogue of the toshabim in the Mellah in Fez, they still use a siddur (prayerbook) that follows the customs of the former native inhabitants of Fez, the toshabim, as opposed to the megorashim. It is called *Ahabat ha-Qadmonim* ("Love of the Ancients") and was printed in Jerusalem in 1889.

A serious conflict broke out between the megorashim and the toshabim on a problem relating to the ritual slaughter of animals for consumption, and particularly over the conditions for the examination of the lungs of the animal whose throat had been slit. It ended in victory for the megorashim and the adoption of common regulations for the communities.

The *serarah*, the hereditary right to be appointed a rabbi or an officiant in the synagogue, which will be mentioned again later, was the monopoly of certain families originating in Spain, who added the Hebrew initials *samekh ṭet* to their names.

The initials *samekh ṭet* seem originally to have been an abbreviation for the Aramaic words *sefeh ṭab* (lit., "his end is happy") which are added to the name of a living person, enunciating the wish that he may continue to consecrate himself to the service of God until the end of a happy life, in order to merit the world-to-come.

These initials have also been interpreted as indicating the words *sefaradi ṭahor* ("pure Sephardi"), presumably a title assumed by some Spanish Jews. This interpretation seems dubious, whereas the first is confirmed when the ketubbâh (marriage contract) is read on the wedding day and the words *sefeh ṭab* are clearly enunciated each time the name of a living person is mentioned. The names of dead people are followed by the words *noho'eden* (literally, "let him rest in the celestial paradise"), the initials of which are *nun 'ayin*.

The families that monopolized the *serarah* are the ones from which most of the famous men of Moroccan Jewry were recruited: legal scholars, ambassadors, financiers, royal counselors, consuls, commercial attachés—men of learning and action. Their ranks include the names Ben Attar, Ben Danan, Aben Sur, Serero, Mansano, Berdugo,

Sarfati, Tolédano, Ben Ẓmirro, Cansino, Sumbal, Kalfon, Azuellos, Uzziel, Bibas, Coriat, Elmaleh, Azoulay, Meimran, and Palagi.

Moroccan Jewry also experienced persecution, extortion, and victimization. Although the two religious groups, Jews and Muslims, had unequal status, one dominant, the other dominated, they nonetheless co-existed in a fruitful political and religious collaboration, most of the time in peace and tranquility, except in the periods of passion and violence that marked difficult interregnums, the absence of power and authority, palace revolts, large-scale dynastic upheavals. Raids, pillage, and massacres occurred in the course of these periodic crises, and their victims included innocent people, Muslims as well, among the opponents of the regime that was established. The Jews paid a heavier tribute, and were in addition forced to convert or be exiled, an extremely rare event, when what was preached was *jahad*, or "holy war," in which case the political disturbances became complicated and changed into religious war, as happened after the advent of the sectarian Ibn Toumert in the twelfth century. The saddest drama took place when the Jewish populations were subjected to the authority of the Almohades. It was no less terrifying and its consequences no less vital for Maghrebian Jewry than the first Crusades and their sequel for European Jewry.

There is only sparse documentation on this event: the *kinah* (elegy) of Abraham Ibn 'Ezrâ, a few comments by Abraham ben David in his *Sefer ha-Qabbalah*, and two notes in *Shebeṭ Yehudah* by Salomon ben Warga. At Sijilmassa, 150 people chose death for the "sanctification of the Name" of God. Others embraced Islam; the first to convert was the *dayyan* (judge), who subsequently returned to Judaism.

Moroccan Jews retained bitter memories of the short reign of Moulay Yazid (1790–1792). They called this king *mezid* (meaning, in Hebrew, guilty of premeditated crime) because of his hatred for them. David Ḥassin (1730–1790), a poet and scholar who lived in Meknès at the time, wrote an elegy on the tragic events that plunged the Jewish communities of the day into mourning.

The rapid decline of the Jews in the lands of Islam was caused by political and economic factors that go beyond the framework of this book. The Jews lived under a dual yoke: the isolation of the country as a whole removed it from all aspects of Western civilization, and confinement in the mellah prevented productive contacts with the outside world. The Jews of Morocco were unaware of the ideological trends that were stirring European Jewry—the Jews of France, Germany, and Italy—like a tidal wave in the period of the Enlightenment.

European civilization and culture invaded the Maghreb at the end of the nineteenth century. They burst into a world where the Middle Ages had been perpetuated in the socioeconomic and religious structures. They penetrated the Jewish communities, first in Algeria, then in Tunisia and Morocco, through the medium of the French language, seen as the language of prestige, emancipation, and social preferment, especially by members of the bourgeois elites. Secularization and assimilation were the result of the French presence, which on a different count changed the face of these societies politically and economically. Nevertheless what should be noted is the resistance to the penetration of the Western world, and the mistrust of its culture among the spiritual leaders of a relatively large number of communities, for whom the *école nouvelle*, the "new school," the *escuela*, was *eshkullah* (Hebrew), that is to say, "all fire," leading straight to Gehenna.

After the creation of the State of Israel in 1948 and the achievement of independence by the Maghrebian countries, there was a massive emigration of entire communities, the majority to Israel, but also to France, Spain, Canada, and elsewhere. With this dislocation there disappeared the whole social system of these two-thousand-year-old societies, and their rich and original linguistic and cultural traditions.

## THE JEWS OF MOROCCO THROUGH THEIR OWN EYES

The self-image or internal perspective of the Moroccan Jews can be perceived in the cultural world they created, in their literary creativity understood in the broadest sense; that is to say, in their written and oral literature, whether in Hebrew or dialect, all of which draws its inspiration and source from a certain historicity.

The direct relationship of this literature with the neighboring world, with life and the realities of living, makes it possible to come to know the various Jewish communities of Morocco from the inside. It also makes it possible to obtain a better grasp of certain otherwise unsuspected aspects of their behavior, thought, and history that are not mentioned in the descriptions of the mellahs and their populace included by travelers in their narratives, or by certain diplomats and consular or commercial agents who very often blamed the Jews when their missions in the country failed.

### *Events*

The history of events proper, of matters concerning the whole country, the ruling dynasties, and the geopolitical landscape, is absent from the rare collections of chronicles written by a few scholars that have come down to us. In the nature of things, these memorialists were interested in the humble realities of everyday life. They wrote solely for themselves and for their closed circle, and did not allow themselves to be influenced by the same political and personal concerns as Muslim historiographers. Activities outside the community, even the relationships that must have existed between Jewish business circles and their counterparts in other ethnic or socioreligious groups, are not within the purview of these chronicles, which principally reflect the internal life of Jewish society.

The legal literature, comprising *taqqanot* (rabbinical ordinances) and responsa (legal consultations and decisions by rabbinical courts), furnishes the best material for knowledge of the socioeconomic organization, ritual, and religious life of the communities, but provides no more than a rare, occasional, and scanty indication of the history of events in Morocco and the world outside the mellah. Moreover, these indications consist of nothing more than chronological reference points introducing the account of a given situation or the circumstances of a legal dispute, or allusions to civil wars and to the economic crises that marked periods of famine and epidemic following years of drought.

Among the Muslim population, themselves victims of these recurrent and frequent scourges, the Jews were even more wretched, if not because of poverty, which some of them succeeded in overcoming, then because of the persecution, the day-to-day insecurity, the systematic pillaging and extortion they had to suffer as a consequence of unrestrained arbitrariness.

We give below a few samples of the evidence of this "self-view," unoptimistic to boot, which mention the conditions of life as well as some historical situations.

- The *taqqanah* of 1691 recalls "the misfortunes and calamities which have crashed down on the communities, the increasingly strong pressure of taxation, the hardships of life, the diminution of means of subsistence. . . . People who were formerly affluent can no longer help the poor of the town, whose numbers are growing ceaselessly. Not a week goes by without six or seven poor arriving from other towns in

Morocco. . . . In addition, emissaries from Ashkenaz and Poland bring messages from their countries and clamor for funds to ransom their captives. . . . The year 1722 [?] was a year of economic crisis and great famine; large numbers of heads of households no longer had the means to ensure their families' subsistence, not even the wherewithal to buy a crust of bread to feed their children."

• Two responsa refer to the famine of 5497 (1736/37). During the winter of that year, hunger impelled a family from Meknès to emigrate to the Doukkala, then to Susa and the Drâa.

• After the pillaging of Fez by the Oudaya in 1727, and particularly of Meknès by the Abids in 1728, appeals were made to the rabbinical court to judge legal disputes arising from the loss of property belonging to the partners in joint-liability businesses.

• A later document, dated 1791 and written at Rabat, contains this typical detail: "When the king died, silver and jewels were placed for safety in underground hiding places in anticipation of pillage."

• The *taqqanot* of 1605, 1607, and 1609 were drawn up following monetary manipulations that occurred in Morocco at the beginning of the seventeenth century in order to resolve conflicts caused by repayment of debts and liquidation of ketubbot (marriage contracts). One of these documents alludes to the seizure of the town of Fez by the king, Moulay Abdallah, on 18 Tammuz 5369 (summer 1609).

• The preamble to the ordinance of 1669 notes the entry of the sultan (Moulay Rachid) into Tetuán and his confiscation of property belonging to the powerful Naqsis family.

• "When the king reconquered the town of Tangier, representatives of the Jewish communities of northern Morocco brought him the customary gifts: the people of Tetuán came with 800 uqiyas [silver coins], those from Tangier with 200 uqiyas, those from Arzila with 100 uqiyas and a mule laden with wax, the inhabitants of Chichawen and Al-Ksar having stayed away. They were accosted by a servant of the sovereign who found these gifts most inadequate, enjoining the Jewish emissaries to increase the sum."

• The death of Moulay Yazid, a bloodthirsty sultan whose brief reign (1790–1792) left painful memories for the Moroccan communities, is described in a responsum of 1795, written in Rabat.

• Let us also note that the *haqdamot* (prefaces) to books of every type constitute a very valuable source of historical information.

• This is how Elyahu ben Amozeg, author of the preface to a collection of responsa and sermons, describes an episode he witnessed during the Franco-Moroccan dispute in the reign of Abd-Ar-Rahman ben Hicham, the ally of Abd Al-Kader (1844): "Like the doves of the valleys, the French ships swooped down on the town, discharging a rain of fire and iron on it. . . . savage hordes of Bedouin from the countryside crashed down on the city, sowing terror, taking hostages, pillaging and slaughtering the innocent Jewish populace."

• The author of the preface to another collection of responsa describes the disturbances that marked the period following the death of Moulay Hassan I (1894). He perceives events with great acuity and describes them with bitter humor: "Security of life and possessions, honor, all the acquisitions and values of human society hang by a thread finer than a spider's web in Morocco. . . . A happening in life which in the civilized world would not make a dry leaf tremble on its branch, here shakes the earth, sowing fear and panic in the populace. . . . Everywhere else, when a monarch dies, the heir-presumptive, or some other prince worthy of mounting the throne, is crowned in joy and gladness, and the advent of the new king is accompanied by popular celebrations. In Morocco, as soon as the news of the illness or death of the reigning sovereign spreads, we have revolution; institutions are shaken, savage and cruel Berber tribes rise up, block roads, make raids on towns, pillage, assassinate. . . . This is what happened when the pious and merciful king, Moulay Hassan, died. His son, heir to the throne, was very young; he was less than fifteen when he succeeded his father. The tribes refused to submit to his royal yoke . . . ; disturbances broke out and civil war was waged for almost four years. . . . To our misfortune and our distress, who do you think was the appointed victim if not Israel, the customary scapegoat? The Jewish populace was pillaged, virgins violated, large numbers of men and women massacred in towns and villages in the regions of Demnat, Al-Qel'a, Mesfiwa. . . . As soon as calm returned, there was the stern test of drought and famine. . . . A typhus epidemic struck cruelly at the town of Fez; from the beginning of Siwan to 15 Shebaṭ [1901] the mellah was engulfed in desolation; the plague claimed nearly three thousand victims, and only a few people were spared the illness, no more than three or four percent of the Jewish populace."

## *The People and Where They Settled*

### *Ethnic, Linguistic, and Sociocultural Groups*

When we did our fieldwork in the Islamic West some twenty years ago, we found three major sociocultural groups roughly corresponding to three ethnic and linguistic streams of variable importance: the Arabophone, Berberophone, and Spanish-language communities (the Jewish population at that time exceeded 250,000 souls). We are disregarding recent changes following colonization and the imposition of French and Spanish protection, which in any case concerned only a small fraction of the population.

The Jews belonging to the Spanish-language community were descendants of the former megorashim, "exiles" from Spain and Portugal. They had generally settled in the old Spanish zone of Morocco or in other locations on the Atlantic coast and in the interior, following various migrations. The Old Castilian language was preserved there as the traditional language of communication (*haketiya*), culture, and teaching (Ladino). They are to be found in Tangier, Tetuán, Arzila (Asila), Al-Ksar Kebir, Chichaouen (Shawen), and Melilia, as well as in Fez, Casablanca, Rabat, Salé, and Marrakesh.

The Arabophone communities are a combination of the descendants of formerly arabized megorashim and the great mass of toshabim, "natives." The latter are the autochthonous Jewish population, whose ethnic origin and first settlement in the Maghreb still pose a problem for history and to this day have found no satisfactory solution. This again is to a large extent a domain that belongs to the world of legend (see above).

The Arabophones people an area that covers the whole country, mountains and plain. Bilingual, sometimes even trilingual, they use dialects of their own together with other local languages, Judeo-Berber, or Judeo-Spanish.

In addition to their lively dialect and a folklore which is at least equal to that of their Muslim neighbors, the Berberophone Jews of the *chleuh* and *tamazight* lands, of the Atlas and Susa, had a whole body of traditional and religious oral literature, barely suspected by Jewish and non-Jewish historians and linguists. Unfortunately, none of this has been preserved, barring the few remnants collected in the course of our research and, most especially, the Haggadah shel Pesaḥ, or liturgy for Passover eve, a totally unpublished document found at Tinghir of the Todgha (Upper Atlas) in oral and written form. This has been the subject of linguistic, literary, and historical studies carried out in collaboration with Madame Pernet-Galand.

In the Todgha Valley (Tinghir), in the region of Tiznit (Wijjan, Asaka), Ouarzazat (Imini), Demnat (Aït Bu Welhi), at Oufrane of the Anti-Altas, at Illigh, and elsewhere, the Jews were generally bilingual,

Berbero-Arabophone, some exclusively Berberophone. In the past they formed small agglomerations, called mellahs, established there for one or two millennia.

Whatever their vernacular, Hebrew remains the principal language of all the Jewish communities of the country for the liturgy and traditional teaching.

### *Internal Migration and Geographical Distribution of the Communities*

The first thing that meets the eye is the great mobility of the Moroccan Jews within the frontiers of the country and also their regular and frequent movements toward the outside world. They can be observed leaving their native land quite readily to go to the Orient, Europe, or the Americas.

Jews easily crossed Morocco from north to south, and from east to west, from Tetuán to Taroudant, from Sijilmassa to Meknès and Salé, despite the difficulty of communications and, particularly for dhimmis and Jews, the almost permanent insecurity of the roads, which were transformed into death-traps during the anarchic periods of interregnum and civil war.

Some reigns, notable for the forcefulness of the ruling sovereign, were exceptionally calm and peaceful. Muslim chroniclers record that during the reign of Moulay Ismaël (1672–1727), "A woman and a Jew could go from Oujda to the Oued Noun without meeting anyone who asked them whence they came and whither they were going. . . . No robber or highwayman was to be found in all the Maghreb."

We also have the evidence of a Moroccan rabbinical source on this subject: "So long as our sovereign was alive . . . a great peace reigned over all the provinces of the Maghreb [Ma'arab = Morocco]. We went from here, from the town of Fez, to places situated at a distance of twenty days march and more, traveling in caravans which carried great riches; we encountered bands of "strangers" in large numbers, but no one dared open their mouth or let out a whistle, because his terror had crashed down on all the nations (*goyim*) and fear of him had fallen on them; he was, in truth, a great king, powerful, wise, and intelligent; he kept daily watch over the affairs of men. . . . But because of our countless sins he fell ill on the neomenia [new moon] of Ṭebet in the year 5487 of the creation and died on the neomenia of Nisan [in the same year 1727]."

Internal migration had a variety of causes. On this subject, as on many others, the *taqqanot* and responsa provide valuable information.

• The population of a rebellious town was sometimes forced to leave it by order of the king. Veritable transfers of populations took place, and we know that the Jews were not the only victims. Quite the contrary, these reprisals were more particularly intended to punish Muslim communities hostile to the *makhzen*. The forced removal of the Jewish inhabitants of agglomerations affected by these coercive measures, therefore, did not have a discriminatory character. On one occasion, they were even accompanied by special advantages or privileges for dhimmi migrants. In this context it is worth remembering the departure of the Jewish communities from the Ẓawiya of Dila' to Meknès and Fez during the reign of Moulay Rashid (1668) and the drain of the populations of Agadir to Mogador under Moulay Mohammed ben 'Abdullah (ca. 1765).

• In times of epidemic and famine, scourges that generally followed upon droughts, isolated individuals or compact groups from regions near and far can be found flowing toward the least-stricken areas to seek aid from their less unfortunate or wealthier brethren.

- "In 1738, the Jews left Meknès to escape the famine raging there and sought sustenance, first in the Doukkala, then, moving farther southwards, arrived in the Drâa."
- "The Jews from the town of the Beni Snus went to settle in Oujda during the years of famine that preceded the death of the king" (according to a responsum dated 1731).
- "In 1745, hunger and poverty prevailed in besieged Sefrou; Moses b. Hammu was forced to leave the town, where he no longer had means of subsistence; he went to Fez, where his wife refused to follow him, invoking the customary clause in the ketubbâh that the husband must not change residence without the consent of his wife."

• Pilgrimage was also a major motive for large-scale journeying across Morocco. Entire families sometimes undertook long and perilous journeys at fixed dates, generally at the hillula (see below), in order to fulfill a vow to visit the tomb of a saint, sometimes situated in an area very difficult of access. The Jewish travelers would most often disguise themselves as Muslims, the men wearing the *rezza* (turban), and the women, the veil. My own grandmother confirmed this in the tales she told me about the long excursions from Mogador to

Msakalla (Ain-Lahjar) in the south, to visit the tomb of the saint, Rabbi Nissim.

• Yeshîbot in certain spiritual centers of Moroccan Jewry were often attended by students who came from neighboring villages, or sometimes even from very far afield, to obtain a talmudic and halakhic education that would be given official recognition by semikhah, a "diploma of aptitude." They then returned to carry out rabbinical duties in their native mellah or took up permanent residence in a new location, where their families would join them.

Along the same line, people frequently went from one town to another to serve an apprenticeship to a craft. A document of 1701 indicates that "the man Makluf b. Yosef b. 'Atiya of the Tafilalet pledges to oblige his son to enter the service of David bar Jacob Botbol [of Fez] for eleven months, for a wage of fifteen uqiyas and instruction in the craft."

• People also took to the road to bring important legal disputes before the court of a large town or to consult an eminent rabbinical authority, for family reasons or, at least apparently (as the texts are not always explicit on this point), without any precise motive at all.

• "A family belonging to the Sevillan community of Debdou and owning considerable landed property (houses, groups of dwellings, fields and vineyards) was in Fez in 1752 to settle a matter of an inheritance" and seemed determined to stay there permanently.

• "A Jew from Tetuán, nephew of a certain Jacob Buzi of Fez, went to Taroudant, took a wife there, and had a daughter by her" (responsum dated 1728).

• The Kohen Sqalli family emigrated from Debdou around 1619 to settle in Dar Mesh'al.

• "A couple married in a village of the Tafilalet, where the two partners were born, and emigrated to Sefrou. The husband wants to return to his native province and take his wife back there, but she refuses to accompany him. . . . The court of Fez decides in favor of the latter on the grounds that 'the villages of the Tafilalet are not populated by a majority of Jews' [*sic*] and forces the husband to fix his residence at Sefrou or Fez, on pain of paying the amount of the ketubbâh" (responsum dated 1746).

• In a responsum of 1727 we read that "a man called Moses b. Isaac ben Hayun from the town of Sijilmassa states that the vicissitudes of life led him and his wife to the lands of the West. After living together for some time in the town [Fez], his wife returned to her native province, where he cannot join her because of the insecurity of the roads. . . . We authorize him to take a second wife in that town [Fez]."

The extraordinary mobility of the Jewish populace is essentially explained by socioeconomic considerations, the organization of professional activities, the requirements of trade and industry. Itinerant craftsmen, peddlers distributing in the countryside products imported from abroad or manufactured in the workshops of the large Moroccan towns, business agents charged by their partners with collecting domestic produce (cereals, wax, oil, almonds, gum sandarac, etc.), landowners (or simple mortgagees of cultivable land) watching over the work of their fields or orchards or personally participating in it—they periodically moved to places a long way from their usual residences, urban centers or rural mellahs. They penetrated deep into hazardous regions, into the territories of tribes that were running wild, in revolt against the central authority of the *makhzen*. These commercial travelers and migrants of every stamp were often the victims of unfortunate misadventures, acts of brigandage at the best. Their wanderings might also end tragically: in disappearances that left no trace, and in murders. The reverberations can be found in the responsa and decrees by the courts relating to the status of the *'agunot* (an *'agunah* is a wife "bound" to an absent husband; she remains unable to remarry so long as proof of death is not established).

We know about the *suwwaqa* and *duwwasa* and their seasonal migrations. Itinerant craftsmen, peddlers, and market-traders (?), they left their villages the day after Pesaḥ and returned home on the eve of Rosh Hashanah, taking to the road again after Sukkot to come back on the eve of Pesaḥ, bringing with them a variety of goods (barley, dried fruit, honey, clarified butter) and not much money.

On another count, a legal consultation dating from the beginning of the eighteenth century shows that Jewish merchants also traveled by sea from one town to another along the Moroccan coast. Thus, "Isaac Mendes usually took ship to go from Agadir to Salé . . . or to reach the countries of Edom [Europe]."

Responsa determining the fate of *'agunot* and statements collected by the courts and recorded in our texts in the dialect in which they were received from the mouths of the witnesses, generally Muslim, provide valuable information on the movements of Jews in the Moroccan countryside, the perils which threatened them during their wanderings, and also the help they sometimes obtained when they found themselves among Muslim protectors and friends in moments of danger.

• A document dated 1732/33, signed at Fez, reproduces evidence establishing proof of the death of Jewish travelers in order to free their *'agunot* spouses from their matrimonial bonds and permit them to remarry: "David ben Kamun and his son Jacob penetrate at peril of their lives into the territory of the Hayaina and Ghiyata for the needs of their trade. They are assassinated by brigands belonging to the tribe of the Ghiyata after courageously defending themselves against the aggressors."

• During a raid, a certain Moses ben Abraham Al-Karsani (or Al-Korasan) found a Muslim protector who expressed himself in the following terms: "The Jew [Moses] is one of us, he has nothing to fear from anyone and no harm will come to him; to raise a hand to him is to touch the apple of our eye."

• A responsum dating from the same period and bearing on the same subject (the status of *'agunot*) points to the presence of Jewish agglomerations in the northern provinces of Morocco, in the Beni-Snassen, Qdara, and the Jbel. Their populations went to Tlemcen, Melilia, and Tetuán to bring their disputes before rabbinical courts.

• A later text, dating from the end of 1842, gives the evidence of Moses ben Yosef and M. ben Mordekay establishing proof of the tragic death of Mas'ud ben Menahem Rebibo during a journey in eastern Morocco, among the Beni-Waraîn. The evidence is reproduced in an Arabic dialect that shows scarcely any linguistic features different from the present-day Jewish Arabic of the Moroccan south. The caravan he was traveling with had succumbed to thirst; the survivors, two Muslims, described the event to the two aforenamed witnesses. On the strength of their statement, the wife of the deceased was authorized to remarry.

*Geographical distribution of the Jewish communities.* What we have seen of the problem of Jewish migration across the Sherifian provinces has already provided some information on the geographical distribution of the mellahs within the frontiers of Morocco. Other documents from various sources can throw a little more light on the subject.

The 1728 rabbinical list comes from a formulary of rabbinical law entitled *'Et Sofer* ("Pen of the Scribe"), written by Jacob Aben Sur, a Moroccan author of the seventeenth to eighteenth century. It records the names of twenty-six places, each followed by the name of the river it stands on or of the neighboring waterway, a detail required for drawing up a certificate of marriage (*ketubbâh*) or divorce (*get* + ).

L. Massignon, using data provided by N. Sloush,[3] makes frequent reference to this list in his *Nomenclature des mellahs au temps de Léon l'Africain* and *Marmol*, or when he refers to the *Tableau méthodique des mellahs*, by Charles de Foucauld. H. Z. Hirschberg, in his *Histoire des juifs d'Afrique du Nord*, continued the examination and successfully solved the major problems of deciphering and identification. He quite rightly emphasizes its fragmentary nature and gaps, which, however, another document now available makes it possible to fill.

The following are the names of places inhabited by Jews in the order given in the 1728 list: Fez, Marrakesh, Tlemcen, Agmari (unidentified), Taroudant, Salé, Tafilet, Gherslewin, Gheris, Demnat, Aït Attab, Izzaghine, Al-Ksar-Kebir, Tafza (Efza), Debdou, Aït Abd Kafra, Meknès, Amismiz, Oujda, Taza, Butat (Outat al-Hadj), Bou-Iḥya, Beni-Ayyat (Beni-Ayyad), Tetuán, Sefrou, Azrou.

Information found in various handbooks makes it possible to complete the list of Jewish settlements in Morocco. But much more important is the advantage to be drawn from systematic exploitation of the Moroccan rabbinical literature that is still accessible, methodical investigation of the legal documents in our possession, particularly the *taqqanot* and responsa. These reflect the everyday life of individuals and communities and their living conditions, and echo their adventures and misadventures in the various places where they settled or during their frequent migrations.

Other sources of information, which are often neglected and whose importance is barely suspected, are the *haqdamot* (prefaces), the *haskamot* (forewords and permissions to print), and above all the lists of individual subscribers and communities that contribute to the cost of printing books (the *maḥaziqim*). The majority of authors take pains to draw up these lists in great detail, indicating the names of the donors in each place. Moreover, the donors set great store on being named in an "honors list" of this kind, not so much from vanity as from considerations of a magical or religious nature, however one prefers to describe it. It was the desire to see their names present in connection with a (Hebraic) written work, always regarded as sacred, and to have a share in the blessing and holiness that in these circles was attached to any rabbinical literary work in the belief that a voice from heaven had inspired its author.

3. *Archives marocaines* 6 (1905/6).

We have been able to analyze a fairly large number of documents of this sort in the course of our research. They have yielded an abundant harvest of information on the geographical distribution of the Jewish communities in the interior of Morocco and on its Algerian and Saharan borders.

We will only reproduce a few samples here to give an insight into the extraordinary dispersion of the mellahs, particularly those belonging to a world that unfortunately has been little explored. This is the area of the valleys of the Atlas in eastern Morocco and in the pre-Saharan zones where Jewish communities lived for centuries, if not one or two millennia. Today these communities have disappeared, their people having emigrated to Israel or scattered elsewhere.

We have taken the following list of subscribing communities from *Yosef Ḥen*, "a collection of sermons for all circumstances," by Yosef b. David Nahamyas, a rabbi whose memory is venerated by the Jewish populations of Marrakesh and southern Morocco. The book was printed in Tunis in 1915. We have omitted the names of individual donors from the list, which appears after the foreword: Telwat, Mezgita, Tamengult, Agidz (Agdz) Wa-Sellem, Dades, Tedgha (Todgha), Ferkla, Tafilalt, Al-Gerfa, Gi-Iglan, Ulad Ḥsin, Mezgida, Irara, Bu-Ẓemla, Glagla, Tezwimi l-M'adid, Ẓrigat, Qṣer Es-Suq, Te'lalin, Grama (Gurama), Tulal, Tit n'Ali, Utat d'Aït Ẓdeg, Al-Ksabi, Bu-Dnib, Bu-'nan Bessar (Colomb-Béchar), Beni-Wunnif (Ounif), 'Ayen Sefra, Al-Mesri (Meshra'), Bu-Ruta, Demnat, Beni-Mellal, Qasba di Tadla, Bu-Ẓa'd (Boujad), Mzab, Ẓtat (Ẓettat).

*Netibot Shalom* ("The Paths of Peace"), by Shalom b. Nissim Abisror, a contemporary author originally from Aqqa, is a compilation of homilies and novellae on the Pentateuch, printed in Casablanca in 1953. It contains a list of subscribers who lived in the following places: Der'a, Timsla, Akhelluf, La'rumiyyat. Bni-Sbih, Amzerru, Taroudant, Aqqa (the author emphasizes that this is his hometown), Ufran, Tiznit, and Agadir.

Note that the toponymic element is highly mobile, and the question of identification is very delicate (the varied ways in which different authors write, the almost total absence of vocalization of the diacritics necessary for the transcription into Hebrew of certain Arabic phonemes). Identification is relatively easy in the case of the places quoted in our lists. The names can be found on ordinary Michelin maps (Morocco 170–171) and on the maps of Morocco to the 200,000th in the *Répertoire alphabétique des agglomérations du Maroc*, published by the Service du Travail au Maroc in 1936. Also available are the caravan itineraries mentioned by certain authors, such as the one from Fez to the Tafilalet, which was called *triq as-sultan*, "the royal road."

*The Jewish kingdom of Tamghrut.* An elderly rabbi in Ashkelon (Israel), who emigrated from southern Morocco, supplied us with certain pieces of information about the communities of Ben-Sbih whence he came: Ktama, Glawa, Tifnut, and Tamghrut. Our informant, Rabbi Jacob ben Hammu, told us that Tamghrut was "the realm of the king of the Jews" (*blad es-seltan d-lihud*), Samuel ben Yosef, killed in a battle against the Muslims on the ninth of Ab. In this connection, he cited the existence of a legend called *qiṣṣa di brahim al-berd'i.* The story of the "Jewish kingdom" is widely known among Muslims too, and they gladly recount it. Another detail is worth noting: According to our informant, the day of the great market, *musem*, was fixed for a Saturday in order to prevent the Jews from following their customary activities or even circulating. The story is reported by several authors, among them J. M. Tolédano and P. Flamand.

*Great journeys and relationships with the outside world.* There seems to have been uninterrupted emigration from the time of the Almohade persecutions, and for a large number of megorashim from the Iberian peninsula, the Islamic West was most often only a halting place. It was just one stage on the long road to the Holy Land, where they were going to settle in order to found yeshîbot or to end their days. Over a period of four centuries there was a continuous movement toward the Islamic Orient, the eminently hospitable Ottoman Empire. Insecurity drove scholars and writers to flee to more clement climes, and they found refuge at that time in Western Europe, especially in Italy and Holland. They even settled on the other side of the Atlantic in the Americas.

Contacts were maintained with other world Jewish communities throughout the centuries by way of legal consultations among rabbis, commercial relations, and cultural exchanges, particularly the exchange of books. In the absence of local printing establishments, Moroccan rabbis had their manuscripts printed in Leghorn (Livorno), Amsterdam, Constantinople, Prague, Berlin, Karkow (Kharkov? Cracow?), or nearer home in Djerba. The prayerbooks, tractates of the Talmud, rabbinical legislation, and homiletic and kabbalistic (Zohar) literature that were needed were procured, semi-clandestinely, at exorbitant prices, from outside the country, despite all sorts of difficulties and despite measures imposed long since by the Church to prevent the free circulation of Hebrew books.

*Relations with the Holy Land; emissaries and alms collectors.* Relations between the Maghrebian diaspora and the Holy Land were closely associated with the thousand-year-old institution of the emissary/alms-collector rabbi. Itinerant representatives of the communities of Jerusalem, Tiberias, Safed, and Hebron, they scoured the Jewish world to collect gifts for their constituencies and spread Jewish knowledge, particularly the thought of Palestinian teachers, by teaching, preaching, and lending or distributing books obtained on their travels.

*Methods of collecting gifts.* One of the principal tasks of the emissary/alms-collector rabbi consisted of collecting gifts from individuals, religious brotherhoods, and foundations, as well as the quota set aside for him in the communal budgets; of receiving all bequests or donations and emptying collection boxes. He then had to send these funds, by the quickest and safest means, to the Palestinian community or institution that had commissioned him.

In the Moroccan communities the emissary/alms-collector rabbi was generally held in the highest esteem because of the love for the "ancestral land" felt there, a deep and spontaneous love drawn from the living sources of the faith. His prestige and authority can also be explained by his talmudic knowledge and by the aura of sanctity which, in the eyes of the masses, gave him the power to work miracles. The emissary/alms-collector rabbi was warmly welcomed everywhere. He was offered board and lodging. People gave to him generously, sometimes out of all proportion to the modest means at their disposal. Only rarely, in times of financial difficulty, did they dispute his right to make collections at his own discretion and sometimes to raise considerable levies on the scant resources of the community. He was, in effect, the representative of the Holy Land, and in its name he claimed the right of the Jews who lived there to the support of their brethren in the Diaspora. On the basis of the law and tradition, he proclaimed "the duty of every Jew to settle in the land of Israel; whoever cannot achieve this physically must fulfill it with his property, by ensuring the subsistence of those who are there; and that will count as if he were living there himself."

In periods of poverty, the Jewish authorities in the Diaspora sometimes countered this argument with the rabbinic adage that "the poor of your town take precedence over those of another town." The rabbis of Fez followed this course in 1691, "in order to limit the amount of gifts to two reals." They were reacting to "the frequent solicitations and excessive demands of emissary/alms-collector rabbis from Poland and Ashkenaz at a time when the local Jewish communities were themselves in great penury, despoiled by taxation and unable to give aid to the growing body of their own poor."

An earlier *taqqanah*, signed by the Castilian rabbis of Fez in 1603, set the conditions in which collections on behalf of two Jerusalem emissary/alms-collector rabbis could be carried out.

A few details are worth mentioning.

• In Morocco, the Hebron collecting boxes bore the name of R. Amram ben Diwan, emissary/alms-collector rabbi of that town, whose tomb at Asjen (near Ouezzane) was the object of a genuine cult. The boxes for Tiberias bore the name of R. Meir Ba'al Hanes, and for Safed, that of R. Simon Bar Yoḥay (buried at Meron, not far from Safed). These last two were great teachers of Jewish knowledge in the Roman period, two saints whose memory is venerated by the Jews of Morocco.

• Very often, two emissaries, one Ashkenazi, the other Sephardi, were sent to the same country. The Sephardi emissaries who visited Morocco were frequently natives of the country. They performed their mission in the country which they themselves or their ancestors had left, but it is equally possible to follow their wanderings in Africa and Asia. Two fascinating figures are worthy of note.

• Yosef ben Moses Maymaran, born in Tetuán, emigrated to Safed and was given his first mission to Arab lands at the age of twenty. He was the first emissary/alms-collector rabbi to penetrate Central Asia. When he arrived in Bukhara, he mingled with the Jews of the country and became their spiritual guide. He brought about a genuine revolution in that far-off community, which believed that it was descended from the Ten Lost Tribes. He taught them Hebrew, which they barely knew, and Jewish law and tradition, which they had almost forgotten, introducing them mainly to the Sephardi ritual.

• Raphaël Ohana, born in 1850, emigrated to Tiberias with his grandfather in 1865. At the age of thirty he left on a mission to Bukhara, following in the footsteps of his predecessor, Yosef Maymaran. In 1894, he is to be found in India and Burma, in Kurdistan. He then crossed all the eastern and western Arab countries. In 1897, he visited Morocco and at Meknès received an "imprimatur" for his book, *Ṭobat Mar'eh* ("Beautiful of Face"), a panegyric on Tiberias. At the end of this book there is a certain amount of evidence about his journeys in Central Asia, laudatory poems dedicated to the notables of the communities where he stayed, all dated 1876: Issakhar ben Judah Hanassi of Tashkent, Salomon Ḥayyim ben Aharon Quazi, also of Tashkent, Benjamin ben Simon of Turkestan. (He was also the author of several other works, including a treatise on medicine and magic.)

The itineraries of many other emissary/alms-collector rabbis of Moroccan origin took them, like their colleagues, wherever a Jewish community existed: D. Maymaran and E. ben Danan to India, A. Qoriat to Arabistan, H. Sh. Amar and the famous Rab Ḥida (Yosef Ḥayyim David Azoulay) to Western Europe, A. Maymaran to Ashkenazi countries, and so on.

Note too that when an emissary/alms-collector rabbi impressed the leaders of a community with his knowledge and authority, and his influence over the people, he might be permanently attached to their community's service as a senior magistrate or in some equivalent post. Examples include R. Raphael Ḥayyim Moshe ben Na'im at Gibraltar in 1881 and Moshe Hayy Elyaqim at Mogador and Casablanca around 1920.

*Rabbinic activities of the emissary/alms-collector rabbis; the spread of Jewish knowledge and Palestinian thought.* The emissary/alms-collector rabbis were at the origin of some *taqqanot* and contributed to the formulation of others, sometimes setting their signatures alongside those of the local rabbis to confer added authority on the text. When customs or practices differed (because law or tradition did not fix their exact form), the rabbis of the Diaspora sometimes turned to an emissary/alms-collector rabbi for a ruling, and he then would give the Palestinian version of the question. This became the rule. Often, too, it was sufficient to observe the emissary/alms-collector rabbi in a specific situation and imitate his actions.

It was essentially through the intermediation of emissary/alms-collector rabbis that the works of the kabbalists of the Safed school worked their way into Morocco, as well as Qaro's code and the halakhic writings of the great teachers of rabbinical jurisprudence, the books of sermons and of biblical and talmudic exegesis, and a copious body of literature exalting the preeminence of the Holy Land of Israel. It was under the influence of the preaching and teaching of emissary/alms-collector rabbis that Palestinian ways and customs were introduced into Moroccan ritual (kabbalistic prayers and invocations, night prayer, special liturgies). They were the agency whereby Sabbatian ideas, for which they were often the spokesmen, were disseminated in Morocco.

In their luggage, the emissary/alms-collector rabbis carried books published in the rest of the Jewish world. They sold them, traded them, offered them to generous donors, or lent them to those unable to buy them, who then proceeded to copy out all or part of them. They took away with them the manuscripts they found in the genizot or which local authors entrusted them with in order to have them printed in the Orient or Europe.

The emissary/alms-collector rabbis would honor their hosts by presenting them with a sachet of Palestinian soil which elderly people wanted to keep so that it could be thrown into their grave on the day they were buried. Palestinian magical inscriptions, amulets, and charms (*segullot* and *qemi'ot*) were also attributed more powerful qualities than protective objects distributed by locally practicing kabbalists. In Morocco, these *qemi'ot* were passed from hand to hand like precious objects.

*The Maghrebian communities of Palestine.* Over the centuries the flow of emigration to Palestine was never broken. It was generally fed by the movement of students sent to yeshîbot in the great centers of Jewish culture (Jerusalem, Tiberias, Safed) and of pilgrims who very often ended their days in the Holy Land.

A strong Moroccan colony grew up in Safed in the sixteenth century, headed by several scholars attracted by the kabbalist schools that flourished in Galilee at that time. Three of them are still famous: Yosef Ibn Tabul, a disciple of Isaac Luria, the founder of a new kabbalist school that bears his name; Mas'ud Azulay the blind (*saggi nehor*); and S. Abuhanna Ma'arabi.

R. Abraham Azulay, a native of Fez (1570–1643), the author of a kabbalistic tetralogy of major importance, settled in Hebron. R. Jacob Hagiz (1620–1674) founded a yeshîbâh in Jerusalem, with subsidies from the community of Leghorn, where he had traveled to have one of his books printed.

In the eighteenth century, around 1739, Ḥayyim ben 'Attar left Morocco to go to the Holy Land, accompanied by a group of disciples whose numbers increased at every stage of the journey. He stayed temporarily in Italy, where he had his *Or ha-Ḥayyim* printed, a commentary on the Pentateuch that became a classic of rabbinic exegetical literature. Then, thanks to the financial support of Italian donors, he went on to found the Yeshîbâh Kneset Yisra'el in Jerusalem, where he died in 1743, not long after his arrival in the holy city.

In the nineteenth century, in 1860, the number of immigrants rose to several hundred; in that year alone three hundred of them settled in Galilee. Living conditions in Ottoman Palestine were often hard at that time, and quarrels between communities of different origin were very frequent. Two letters dating from 1860, from the rabbis of Meknès to their colleagues in Tiberias, mention all sorts of discrimination against Moroccan immigrants, mainly in Tiberias, especially in the areas of teaching in yeshîbot and the distribution of subsidies to scholars.

Return to the native land, known in the present-day language of Israel as "descent," seems to have been exceptional. A letter dated 1823 sent from Tiberias mentions the case of a North African immigrant who, having "run through his property" in Palestine, returned to his country of origin completely penniless.

Wives quite often refused to accompany their spouses when the latter wanted to go to the Holy Land. The husband was sometimes forced either to give up the idea of the journey and of settling permanently in Palestine or to hand his wife a get and pay the amount of her ketubbâh.

### *Emigration to Other Countries*

Those leaving Morocco did not always have Palestine as their final destination. Some emigrants did not reach the end of that long journey, either through lack of funds or because they succumbed to the attractions of the countries they were passing through or for a variety of other reasons, including the desire to create centers of Jewish culture in communities regarded as "decadent." They stopped on the way and settled on the Mediterranean coast. This was the case with Simon Labi in Tripoli (sixteenth century), and with Mas'ud Alfassi and Aharon Pereṣ in Tunis and Djerba (eighteenth century).

Gifted with extraordinary mobility, Moroccan Jews found it easy to travel to Europe or the Americas. The greatest travelers, those who went "over the seas" (*medinot ha-yam*), were merchants or their agents, and, even more, rabbis. We need only mention a few typical examples of the latter here.

- Isaac Uziel, of Fez, a grammarian and poet, was appointed rabbi of the city of Amsterdam, where he died in 1620. His disciple, Isaac

Atias (seventeenth century), held the same office in Hamburg and Venice.

• Elyahou ben Amozeg, the famous Leghorn publisher of Maghrebian Jewish books, had to leave his hometown of Mogador and settle in Italy after raids on the city by Berber tribes, which the Prince de Joinville bombarded in 1844. His description of these events (which we cite; see p. 12) is taken from the preface to one of the Moroccan books he printed.

In the eighteenth and nineteenth centuries in particular, there was a dearth of rabbis in Italy. The communities of Leghorn and other towns recruited them in North Africa and the Orient; those in northern Italy called on rabbis from Ashkenazi communities.

*The African and European periplus of Yehudah Pereṣ.* In the autobiographical preface to his collection of sermons, entitled *Peraḥ Lebanon* ("Flower of Lebanon"), printed in Berlin in 1712, Yehudah ben Yosef Pereṣ, a seventeenth-century Sephardi rabbi from the Upper Atlas, tells of the long journey of his ancestors, who settled in Morocco, in the Dades, after their expulsion from Spain. He also describes his own wanderings in the Maghreb, the Orient, and Europe, when he and his family decided to leave the pleasant valleys of the Upper Atlas, the country which had given them asylum and where they had lived for more than two centuries.

While their unfortunate brethren sought refuge in towns along the Moroccan coast or in the interior, principally Fez, the Pereṣ clan, direct descendants of the Royal House of David, crossed the ocean and reached the shores of Africa. From there, it moved inland and settled on the other side of the stronghold of Adr (a Berber village in the Upper Atlas, the domain of the Glawa) in the kingdom of the sovereign of Marrakesh, from whom the family purchased the territory of Dades. The "children of Pereṣ" built houses there and led a peaceful existence, living off agriculture and stock-breeding, not mixing at all with strangers, and only taking wives from within the clan in order to preserve the complete purity of their race and royal lineage. They were fruitful and multiplied to such good purpose that the land they cultivated no longer sufficed for them to live together as brothers. They therefore acquired the neighboring domain of Tillit, which they bought from the king at a very high price. They still live there today, and their numbers include some great and illustrious scholars who are able to explain the law in its seventy facets and strictly observe the precepts of the Torah.

Yehudah ben Yosef Pereṣ left the Todgha Valley with a few members of his clan, with the aim of realizing the dream dear to the heart of every pious Jew, "to go to the ancestral holy land, the jewel of the earth." He reached Tlemcen but was forced to stay there for some time because of disturbances and a war between the king of Fez and the "chief of the tribes of Qedara." Reduced to poverty, the family crossed the Maghreb and reached Tunis, where its leader seems to have acquired some wealth through trade, and this enabled him to go to Italy, where he remarried to the daughter of a notable, Salomon Shema'yah of Lucena.

On his return from a journey to Egypt, more precisely to No-Amon (Alexandria), the ship he had boarded was wrecked, sinking off the coast of the Kingdom of Naples, a Spanish possession, where the Inquisition was then active. He thus fell between Scylla and Charybdis, or as he himself says, paraphrasing the prophet Amos (5:19): "As if a man did flee from a lion, and a bear met him; and went into the house and leaned his hand on the wall, and a serpent bit him."

He miraculously escaped the stake, after an audience at the royal court to which he was brought by a detachment of fearsome, battle-hardened soldiers, and where some surprise was shown that he bore the prestigious name of Pereṣ, reserved for famous families of Old Castile. He then went to Leghorn and from there to Venice, where life was hard for him and he earned his living by teaching and giving sermons. He left Venice and wandered through Europe, in quest of funds to pay for the printing of his own book, *Peraḥ Lebanon*, as well as one by Isaac Cavallero, his predecessor in the post of *darshan* (preacher) in the synagogue of the Ashkenazi community of Venice. The preface of his book also supplies some information on his wanderings through Europe. The author expresses gratitude to the communal leaders, rabbis, and notables who gave him hospitality and granted him generous subsidies during his travels: Samuel Tausk, head of the Prague community; Barukh Segal Austerlitz, president of the rabbinical court and rector of the Cologne yeshîbâh; Isaac Oppenheim and his son David of Prague. The *haskamot*, or "imprimaturs," of his book are signed by the rabbinical authorities of Poznan, Frankfurt-am-Main, Berlin, Neumark(t),

*The adventures of an eighteenth-century scholar from Agadir.* The wanderings and eventful life of Moses ben Isaac Ed-Der'y are a tissue of strange adventures and vicissitudes. He was born in Agadir in 1774, a year before its inhabitants were forced to leave the city by order of the king, Mohammed ben Abdallah, an Alaouite sultan who wanted to channel all trade with southern Morocco to Mogador, a city he had just founded, and therefore sought to punish illicit trade that was avoiding his control. Moses Ed-Der'y was brought up and educated in Mogador and then in Rabat-Salé. At the age of sixteen, he accompanied an emissary rabbi from Safed to London, where he was admitted to the Sephardi yeshîbâh Sha'ar ha-Shamayim. He married while in the English capital, but the match was a failure that inspired his *Ma'aseh Nashim* ("Female Adventures"), a book which has not yet been published.

For unknown reasons Moses Ed-Der'y left London and went to Amsterdam in 1802, where he attended the Sephardi yeshîbâh 'Eṣ Ḥayyim. There, in 1807, he was engaged to correct the proofs of *Tehillah le-Dawid*, a collection of poems (*piyyuṭim*) by David Ḥassin, a famous Moroccan poet from Meknès. In 1809, while in Amsterdam, Moses Ed-Der'y published his book *Yad Moshe*, a collection of fourteen sermons with a preface that provides biographical information about him. A wandering rabbi in search of the Ten Lost Tribes, he collected a number of texts relating to this theme and published them in Amsterdam in 1818, under the title *Ma'aseh Nissim* ("Book of Miracles"), which went into several successive editions in Hebrew, Yiddish, and English. The English version, which we have consulted, was printed in London in 1836 and is entitled *An Historical Account of the Ten Tribes, settled beyond the river Sambatyon in the East.* Its preface contains abundant biographical material that is worth mentioning.

The title page bears the legend "The Rev. Dr. M. EDREHI [*sic*], native of Morocco, Member of the talmudical Academies of London and Amsterdam, Professor of Modern and Oriental Languages, Private Tutor of the University of Cambridge, Author of the *Law of Life, Hand of Moses*, etc."

In the following pages, the author provides a mass of documents in English and French: letters of recommendation received in the course of his wanderings and in the manifold and varied offices he had filled in the course of his life, testimonials from eminent persons, references and certificates from various officials (members of the talmudic academies of the Portuguese Israelite community and the Ashkenazi community of Amsterdam, syndics, mayors, police commissioners). Then come tributes to his erudition and knowledge by professors at institutes and men of learning in Amsterdam, Leyden, The Hague,

Utrecht, Rotterdam, Arnheim, Nijmegen, Cleves, Cologne, Mainz, Strasbourg, Nancy, and Paris.

In Paris he knew "Baron Sylvestre de Sacy, Langles, member of the Institute, administrative curator of the Manuscripts of the Bibliothèque Impériale, administrator and prefect of the École Spéciale des Langues Orientale" (the certificate is dated February 2, 1814). The head of the Prefecture of Police "certifies that M. Moïse Ederhy, a Moroccan, has twice served the Prefecture of Police . . . as interpreter of Arabic languages for the interrogation of a Persian."

The king's secretary-interpreter for oriental languages presented him with a reference for services rendered to his administration (document dated February 2, 1817).

The commissioner of police for the fifth district of the city of Brussels certified that one Monsieur Moses Ed-Der'y had been living in that district for three years (January 1, 1821). The commissioner for the city of Paris, Feydeau district, testified that "one Monsieur Moses Edrehi [*sic*] from Morocco occupied a stall in the center of the bazaar, Boulevard des Italiens, that the bazaar fell victim to flames on the first of that month, and that all the goods in the stall of Monsieur Edrehi were completely destroyed, which reduced him to the saddest of situations, since he had no other resources" (Paris, January 5, 1825).

He then appears in Lyons, Marseilles, Geneva, Leghorn, Malta, Izmir, and Jaffa. He arrived in Jerusalem in 1841, ill and penniless, and died shortly afterwards.

## *Judeo-Maghrebian Onomastics*

### *The Names of the Jews of the Islamic West*

The names of the Jews of the Islamic West reflect the place and the time. They are related to the place of settlement and to history. They recall old and more recent origins. They bear witness to rootedness in the Maghrebian land and to the symbiotic life of its peoples in the diversity of their ethnic origins. But they relate also to their languages, their occupations and preoccupations, their psychological and sociocultural structures, the intellectual landscape and natural phenomena.

The names tell of the history of the group, the everyday life of individuals, relationships with co-religionists and members of other religious communities. They also speak of the group's migrations and removals near and far, in the same way that they outline the itinerary of the great movements of Jewish populations across the societies of the Mediterranean world and elsewhere.

*The "power" of names.* A person's name has a fundamental place in the life of Maghrebian Jewry. This is borne out by the genealogical scrolls of the great families, by the records kept by mohelim, the functionaries designated to perform circumcisions (all, to my knowledge, unpaid), containing the names of the boys they circumcised, and by the lists drawn up by the rabbinic authorities for writing marriage and divorce certificates, the register of deaths in which the names of "martyrs," victims of natural or accidental deaths, are recorded, and so forth.

I myself drew up onomastic lists when I was analyzing the legal and literary documentation I had to examine for my research on the intellectual life of the Jews of the Islamic West, more particularly the *taqqanot* and responsa. A systematic survey of the names of the signatories to these documents and of their correspondents, the parties involved in lawsuits, witnesses, and various other personages hovering around the court or referred to in the texts, constitutes another source of eminently valuable information on Jewish origin, the formation and composition of patronyms, names, first names, surnames and nicknames, whole series of which have now disappeared or been naturalized.

The full importance that the Maghrebian Jew attaches to the name he bears, the considerable role that this name plays in his life, and the religious and socioeconomic functions it fulfills can thus be seen inscribed in the onomastic documentation, some of which is now accessible, and some still unpublished (but which we had the opportunity to examine).

Awareness of the power of names probably comes from the power which rabbinic tradition, more especially mystical and kabbalistic literature, attributes to the ineffable name of God, and to the infinity of vocables deriving from angelology and demonology. Practical kabbalah, a science bordering on magic, utilizes subtle and varied combinations of names of angels to compose prayers, amulets, and talismans as protection against evil, to avert the evil eye and drive off danger, to incur the goodwill of supernatural beings or the powerful of this earth. Nor is there any hesitation in having recourse to the "impure names" of the beings who inhabit the lower world of darkness, the invisible universe of the demons whom practitioners claim to subdue and with whom they enter into communication by reciting the necessary mysterious formulas.

Names are the principal component of identity, and exact spelling of their different elements (first name and patronymic, even the surname) is required in the most important situations of an individual's life: birth, or rather circumcision, marriage, divorce, times of serious illness, and death.

On the day of the ritual of circumcision, the male child enters into the covenant of Abraham (*brit milah*) by the removal of the foreskin, of course, but also by solemnly receiving the name he will bear during his life. A girl is given her name at a much more modest, one might almost say optional, ceremony. Many rules govern the choice of name, varying with circumstances (commemoration of a national or local historical event) and also with the origin of the community to which the person belongs. The traditions in force among the toshabim are different from those scrupulously observed by the megorashim.

The marriage certificate (ketubbâh) bears the names of the future couple and their respective parents. Some families also inscribe the genealogical tree of the clan and tribe on it, going back to the eponym, the best-known or most respected ancestor, who lived several centuries earlier. Some families are said to be *meyuḥasot*, a term designating the legitimacy of lineage, nobility of birth, a certain degree of aristocracy customarily based on virtue and learning that are commonly attributed to "good families."

The writing of the geṭ (writ of divorce) is the subject of scrupulous care regarding the actual preparation of the certificate, the wording of formulas, and particularly the exact spelling of names and places. We have already seen in another connection the toponymic and historical interest contained in such a document, which has perforce to carry the names of the town and the nearest body of water.

A change of name is made in the case of serious illness and follows a very precise ritual. Remember also the mysterious dimension attached to this operation in biblical literature, the character of initiation that it received, the spiritual elevation conferred on the beneficiary. It even conveyed his attachment to the divinity, as in the case of the patriarchs Abraham and Jacob. For Abraham, this consisted of the insertion of the letter *h* of the Tetragrammaton (the ineffable name of God) into his original name, Abram; for Jacob, by the metamorphosis of his secondary name, which refers to the "heel" and the "ruse," into Israel, which suggests the authority and nobility conferred by association with God, El.

The religious function of a name is emphasized at the time of death, and its influence is exerted beyond the world of the living, the name of the believer remaining attached to him in the world-to-come. This explains the importance given to the section of the ritual that concerns the name of the deceased, and the liturgy associated with it: the *hashkabah*, a sort of requiem, and the reading, in the alphabetical Psalm 119, of the verses that begin with the letters of the first names of the deceased and his mother. This declaration of the name traditionally safeguards the individual's religious identity.

All in all, the Maghrebian Jew, like any other Jew, believes that the name he bears exercises a decisive influence on his career and destiny, in this world and in the world-to-come, and moreover, this conviction has its origin in talmudic teaching (Berakhot 7b).

*Form and structure, history and identity of names.* Examination of Judeo-Moroccan onomastic certificates immediately discloses a remarkable variety of languages. In order of frequency, there are dialects of Arabic and Berber, Hispanic dialects, Hebrew, Aramaic, even Greek, Latin, and Punic, with manifold combinations and transpositions of one with another and one into another. At the same time, it is possible to recognize the diverse origins of the Moroccan Jews, as well as the different stages in their settlement in the country from ancient times up to the present, their history, their social, economic, and religious life. It reveals how the Jews put down roots in Berber soil when the Phoenicians came along to found trading posts on the coast and the Romans to settle as colonizers there for several centuries. It discloses how the Arab conquest set its stamp, and very deeply so, on the life of the Maghrebian Jews, their culture and their language, without, for all that, in the slightest altering their active solidarity with world Jewry, their spiritual links with the talmudic schools in Palestine and Iraq. The Mediterranean world, under the banner of Islam, for more than seven centuries then enjoyed a unity of civilization and language that made for easier communications between East and West, for more fruitful exchanges of ideas and goods, more frequent and more regular movements of populations.

The richness of the ethnic and toponymical components of Judeo-Moroccan onomastics reflects a vast geopolitical area and the populations that inhabit it, innumerable sites and place-names from the Islamic East and West, more especially from Spain and the Maghreb, even from the rest of the European continent.

Let us investigate these names still further. They supply abundant information on the public offices, professions, arts, and crafts practiced by the Maghrebian Jews at different periods in their history, plus a mass of other information and sociolinguistic peculiarities: surnames (*kunya*), nicknames (*laqab*), pseudonyms and imaginary names (*takhalluṣ*), which in their turn became patronymic names; references to attributes, faults, individual physical characteristics and infirmities; to chance and fortune, to strength and power; to natural phenomena (sky, light, etc.), to flora and fauna; to clothing and adornments; to precious stones and metals; to music, to arithmology (names of numbers), and so on.

We need to add a few words about indications of filiation and an observation on the names Kohen/Cohen and Levi, and the compounds they form with other, less prestigious, names:

• A name is most frequently preceded by an indication of filiation. The Hebrew/Arabic *ben/ibn/eben*, alternating with the Berber *u* and *wa* or the Aramaic *bar*, all meaning "son of": u-Ḥayun (Ohayon), ben Ḥayun (Benayoun); u-Sa'dun (Oussadon)/ben Sa'dun (ben Sadon), u-Yosef/ben Yosef/bar Yosef.

• There are also examples of the use of indications of filiation in two different languages successively in the same name: Abraham ben David u-Yosef; Ḥayyim bar Jacob Ibn Ḥayun.

• A name can be prefixed by the Aramaic honorific title *mar* (pronounced *mor* by the Maghrebian communities), which produces the patronyms Mor-Yosef (Moryoussef), Mor'Ali (Morali and Morelli), etc.

• The genealogical Hebrew/Arabic indications *abu/abu/bu*, meaning "the father of, the author of, the man with," etc., are also recorded: Abisror, Abudarham, Buhaddana, etc.

• The kohen/cohen, descendant of the high priest Aaron and former servants of the Temple, has to watch over the purity of his caste and must not profane it by a matrimonial misalliance. If the rules commanded by biblical law and tradition are violated (Leviticus 21, Numbers 6:22–27, 18:15–16, etc.), the kohen surrenders his honorific title and takes a new name. In Morocco, we know that the Bettans and the Kessous are former kohens. It can happen that another patronymic is added to the name Kohen/Cohen to make the identity of its bearer more specific. This is the case with the Cohen-Scalis, the Cohen-Solals, the Cohen De Alocanas, and the Cohen-Alkhallases, among others. The same applies to the Levis: Levi-Soussan and Levi Ibn Yuli, for instance.

It remains to illustrate the Judeo-Moroccan onomastic phenomena by a series of family names and first names taken from one of the lists mentioned above. We regret that it is, of necessity, arbitrarily selective. We have used, in the main, the list drawn up by Jacob Aben Sur, a rabbinical authority from Fez (1673–1753), and have, as needed, added short explanations and, in some cases, modern transcriptions. These series of family names and first names will be found in the appendix to this chapter.

*An onomastic legend: Ẓa'afrani (Ẓafrani) and Ẓa'afran ("saffron").* The patronym Ẓafrani does not appear in the far from exhaustive list compiled by Jacob Aben Sur. This patronym, which is my own, is mentioned for the first time by M. Steinschneider and S. W. Baron.[4] Musa al-Ẓaf'rani (second half of the ninth century), called Al-Tiflisi, was born in Baghdad and settled in the town of Tiflis, then Armenian, where he founded the Karaite sect of the Tiflisides. This name is very widespread among the communities of the Mediterranean basin.

The story that follows is taken from M. Abraham 'Ofran (the modern Israeli rendering of the name Ẓa'frani), son of R. de Mordekhay Ẓa 'frani, clerk and copyist to the rabbinic court of Mogador (Morocco) in the 1940/50s, then in Israel. M. A.'Ofran tells that the family was originally named Al-Qayim. At a certain period in history, all the children of the male sex born into it inexorably died, until a thaumaturgical scholar advised them to soak the gown of the newborn child in water that had been steeped in saffron (Arabic and Hebrew *za'afran*) on the eve of the circumcision. After that, newborn sons ceased to die.

This rite is still de rigueur in the family today, a family of strictly observant intellectuals: M. Abraham 'Ofran is an executive of a bank in Jerusalem; his wife teaches physics at the Hebrew University (she is the daughter of the famous professor Yeshayahu Leibowitz). The custom of soaking the child's linen in "saffronized" water has been scrupulously observed for the circumcisions of the five boys in the family, which also includes two daughters.

## *Appendix*

### *Patronyms*

Abenṣur (toponym, Phoenicia, Spain)
Abihsera ("the man with the plait," a surname that became a patronym, the original name being Alfilali)

4. Steinschneider, *Jewish Literature* (Hildersheim, 1967), pp. 118, 180; Baron, *Social and Religious History of the Jews*, see index, s.v. "Zafrani."

Elbaz (toponym Tafilalet)
Abiqaṣiṣ/Abecassis (Hebrew-Arabic from "priest, elder, senior")
Abiṣror ("the man with the bundle"? 'the bearer of purses"?)
Abuhab/Aboab (Arabic, "distributor")
Abudarham (Arabic *dirham*, "piece of silver")
Aburbi' (Arabic, "spring"),
Abuzaglo/Buzaglo (Arabo-Berber, "the man with the pole")
Addahhan/Dahan (Arabic, "hammerman")
Adder'i/Ederi (toponym, Drâa)
Al'alluf/ Elalouf (Arabic, "to grow stout")
Al'allush/Allouche (Arabo-Berber, "lamb")
Al'anqri/Lancri (toponym Lancara)
Al'asri/Lasri (Arabic, "left-handed"),
Albalansi/Valensi (toponym, Spain)
Albarhanes/Baranès (ethnic from Branès)
Albaz/Elbaz (Arabic, "falcon")
Alfassi (toponym, Fez),
Alghrabli/Elgrabli (Arabic, name of a craftsman, "sifter")
Alghrissi(toponym, Gheris)
Alhaddad (Arabic, "blacksmith")
(Ben) Alhajj/Elhadj (Arabic, "pilgrim")
Alkarugi/Karutchi (toponym, Spain)
Alkeslassi (toponym, Spain?)
Alkharsani/ (?) (toponym, Khorassan)
Alkhriyyef/Krief (Arabic, "lamb")
Almdadsi/Addadsi (toponym, Dadès),
Alnaqqar (Arabic, name of a craftsman, "engraver")
'Allal/Benallal (diminutive of the Arabic 'Abdallah and Hebrew 'Obadiah)
Almedyuni/Médiouni (toponym, ethnic from the Medyuna)
Alqayim/Elkaim (Arabic, "the existing, the constant")
Amarillo (Spain, "yellow")
Amghar/Amgar (Berber, "the elder, the leader")
Amlal/Mellul (Berber, "white")
'Ammar/Amar (Arabic, "colonist, farmer")
Amozeg/Benamozeg (Berber, ethnic, "the son of the Berber")
Anahori (Hebrew, "light"),
Annaḍḍam/Niddam (Arabic, "jeweller, threader of beads")
Annaqqab/Nakab (Arabic, "examining inspector")
Annajjar/Najar, Anidjar (Arabic, "joiner")

'Aqnin/Wa'qnin/Aknin (Berber, derives from the Hebrew Jacob)
Arollo/Aroyo (Spain, from "river")
Arrwimi/Rouimi (Arabic, "the European")
Ashbili/Ishbili (toponym, "from Seville")
Ashshriqi/Cherqui (Arabic, "from the Orient")
Aṣṣabbagh/Sebag (Arabic, "painter")
Aṣṣayyagh (Arabic, "jeweller")
Aṣṣerraf/Serraf/Benazerraf (Arabic, "money-changer"),
Assouline (Berber, from "rock")
Assudri/Soudri (Arabo-Berber, "shawl")
'Aṭiya/Ben Atiya (Arabic, "gift" or ethnic from the Banu-'Atiya)
'Attar/Benattar (Arabic, "spice merchant")
Attedghi/Etedgui (toponym, from Todgha)
Awday (Berber, "the Jew")
Azzawi/Ẓaoui (toponym, "from Ẓawya")
Azznati/Ẓnati (ethnic, "from the Ẓnata").

Bahlul (Berber, "the simple, the fool")
Bargilon/Barchilon (toponym, "from Barcelona)
Ben) Barukh/Baruch (Hebrew, "blessed")
Barukhel/Barujel (Hebrew, "Blessed be God")
Benbénisti/Bénisti, Benveniste (Spain)
Ben David Uhayun (Hebrew, Berber)
Ben David Uyossef (Hebrew, Berber)
Berdugo/Verdugo (Spain, "executioner")
Bibas (Spain, "of life")
Ben-Bidukh/Bidukh (Berberized biblical name, Mordecai)
Biṭon (Spain, "of life")
Banon (Hebreo-Phoenician)
Buṭbul/Botbol, Abitbul (Arabic, from "drum")
Burgel/Abergel (Arabic, "one-legged")

Cabessa (Spain, "head")
(De) Castro (toponym, Spain)
Corcos (toponym, Spain)

Dabila/Davila, De Avila (toponym, Spain)
(Ibn) Danan (Hebrew-Aramaic, "judge")
Dayyan (Hebrew, "judge").

Faraj/Farji, Farjon, Frija, Farache (Arabic, from "good fortune and health")
Fhima (Arabic, "charcoal")
Franco (Spain)

Gabbay (Hebrew, "tax-collector")
Gabizon (Spain)
Gdalya (Hebrew)
Guennun/Ben- (toponym, Atlas)
Guigui/Ben- (toponym, Atlas)

Ḥadida (Arabic, "iron strip")
Ḥagiz/Ḥadjez (Arabic, "pilgrim")
Ḥajwel/Hatchuel (toponym, Spain)
Ḥaliwa (Arabic, "sweetness")
Ḥammu/Ben- (Arabo-Berber, ethnic, Atlas)
Ḥamrun/Ben- (Arabic, from "red, reddish")
Ḥarrar/Elharrar (Arabic, "working with silk")
Ḥarrosh/Haroche (Arabic, "harsh," surname)
Ḥassun/Ben- (Arabic, "goodness, beauty, strength")
Ḥayyim/Ben Ḥayyim/Abenhaïm (Hebrew, "of life")
Harrus (Arabo-Berber, from "to break, to devour," surname)
Ḥazzan (Hebrew, officiating minister, synagogal office)

Iflaḥ/Ben- (Arabic, "to succeed")
Ifraḥ/Ben- (votive name, Hebrew, "to flourish, to prosper")
Illuz/Ben- (toponym, Spain, Maghreb)
Ittaḥ/Ben- (Arabic, "to fall"?)

Karsiente/Karsinty (toponym, Spain)
Khalfon (Arabic, "to substitute, to replace")
Kessous (Judeo-Arabic, "former, broken," diminished kohen)

Labi/Ben- (Hebrew, "lion")
Laḥsen/Ben- (Arabic, "the best")
Laniado (Spanish, "salted fish")
Laredo (toponym, Spain)
Lumbroso (Spanish, from "light")

Melka/Malqui/Ben- (toponym, Malaga, Spain)
Mamane (toponym, Spain)

Mansano (toponym, Spain, "apple tree")
Marciano (toponym, Murcia, Spain)
Marcos/Marco (Spain, measure of weight)
Maymaran/Mimran (indeterminate origin, Aramaic, "our master"?)
Mragi/Maradji/Marrache (toponym, Spain)
Mergi/Mergui (Arabic, "from the meadow")
Miyara (toponym, Spain)
Monson (toponym, Spain)
Monsonégo (toponym, Spain)
Moréno (Spain, "brown")
Moyal/Ben- (toponym, Spain)
Mshish/Meshash/Messas/Ben- (toponym, Arabo-Spanish)

Naḥmyas (Hebreo-Spanish, from Nehemiah)
Nahon (toponym, Spain)

'Obadya (Hebrew, Bible)
'Oliel/Ben- (diminutive of 'Allal and 'Abdallah)

Parienté (Spain, "parent")
Pereṣ/Peretz/Perez (Hebrew, Bible)
Pilo (from the Greek Philo/Philon? from the Hebrew Yedidiah)
Pimienta (Spanish, "pepper")
Pinya/Penyer (diminutive of the Hebrew Pinḥas)
Portal (toponym, Spain, Portugal)

Qadosh/Kadosh (Hebrew, "holy")
Qamḥi/Qimḥi/Camhi (Arabic, "corn")
Qandil/Candil (Arabic, from "lamp")
Qaro/Caro (Spanish, "beloved, dear")
Qaṭan/Cattan (Hebrew, "small")
Qoryat/Coriat (toponym, Maghrebian, "city," or the diminutive of the Arabic *qirat*, "carat")

Rebboḥ (Arabic, "profit, success")
Rimokh/Ben- (indeterminate origin, frequent among exiles from Spain)
Rofe/Roffé (Hebrew, "doctor, healer")
Rosh/Ben- (Hebrew, "head")
Rosilio/Roziyo (toponym, Spain, or "red")

Saba' (Aramaic, from "satisfaction, plenty," or Arabic, "lion")
Ṣabbaḥ (Arabic, from "morning, of the morning")
Samḥun/Ben- (Hebrew, and Arabic, from "joyous, blissful, clement")
Sananès (toponym, from Sens, France)
Sarfati (Hebrew, from France)
Sasportas (Spanish, from "doors, the six doors"),
Sasson/Ben- (Hebrew, from "joy")
Serero/Cerero (Spanish, from "wax," name of a craftsman)
Ṣeruya (Hebrew, Bible)
Sha'anan/Ben- (Hebreo-Phoenician, from "to maintain, to support")
Shabbat/Bensabat (Hebrew, from Shabbat, "Saturday")
Sharbit/Charbit (Hebrew, "scepter"; or Arabic, "thick and fat")
Sheqrun/Checroun/Ben- (Arabic, "red, red-headed"),
Shetrit/Benchétrit (indeterminate origin)
Shim'oni/Simoni (Hebrew, from Simeon)
Shushanna/Soussana/Shoshannah (Hebrew, "lily"),
Slama/Salama (Arabic, from "peace")
Soriano (toponym, Spain)
Soto (toponym, Spain)
Sqalli/Scali (toponym, from Sicily, or from the Arabic, "golden thread")
Susan/Soussan/Shoshan/Ben- (Hebrew, town of Susa, and Arabic, "lily")

Tangi/Tanugi (toponym, Tangier)
Tapiero (Spain, name of a trade, "mason")
Taragano/Tarigano/Trigano (toponym, Spain)
Ṭaṭa/Ben- (Berber, female first name)
Tawril/Taourel (toponym, Spain)
Tazi/Ben- (toponym, Maghreb, from Taza)
Timsit/Timstit (toponym, eastern and southern Morocco)
Ṭobi (Hebrew, biblical character)
Tolédano (toponym, Spain, from Toledo)
Tolila/Ben- (toponym, Spain)
Torjman (Arabic, "interpreter")
Twati/Touati (toponym, from Touatot, southern Algeria)

Yaḥya/Ben- (Arabo-Berber, from "to live, he will live")
Yuli/Ibn Yuli (toponym, Atlas)
Yunès/Ben- (Hebrew, Arabic, "dove")

Waḥnish (Arabo-Berber, from "serpent")
Walid/Ben- (Arabic, from "father")
Waqrat (Berber, toponym, Maghreb)

Ẓaqen/Benzaquen (Hebrew, from "old, ancient")
Ẓekri/Ben- (Hebreo-Arabic, from Ẓechariah)
Ẓimra/Ben- (Hebreo-Aramaic, from "music")
Ẓiri/Ben- (ethnic, Maghreb)
Ẓmirro/Ben- (toponym, Spain)

*First Names*

*Men.* Most common are Hebraic first names of biblical or postbiblical (mishnaic and talmudic) origin. They will not be listed here except when sometimes Arabized or Berberized.

'Allal (see the list of patronyms)
'Ammor
'Amram ('Amram)
'Ayyush (votive Berber-Arabic first name, referring to life, equivalent to Hebrew Ḥayyim or Spanish Vidal, like moreover its foreign counterparts Wa'ish, Yaḥya, Ye'ish, etc.)
'Aziz/La'ziz, 'Azzuz (referring to love and affection, strength)
Ḥassan
Idar
Khlifa (votive name, "substitute")
Mas'ud/Messod, like Sa'dun and Sa'id (S'id)(votive first names referring to happiness, good fortune, etc.)
Salem, Sellam, Slimane (counterparts of Hebrew Shalom and Shlomoh/Solomon, etc.)

Diminutive surnames or Arabic-Berber equivalents of Hebrew are frequently found in the list of Jacob Aben Sur, and in the responsa and *taqqanot* that we have analyzed: Bakhkha, Bidukh, Dokho, and Ukhkha replace Mordechai; Meshshan/Messan, Moshe/Moses; Haddan and Haddush, Yehudah/Judah; Bihi and Brihmat, Abraham; Iggo, Jacob; Baba Lio, Makhluf; Issan and Isso, Yosef/Joseph; Ishsho, Yehushua'/Joshua; etc.

*Women.* Female first names have quite special importance. Preceded by the Arabic indication of filiation (*ben*) or the Berber (*u*), they form the basic element of the patronym, even more perhaps than those of men, in the mellahs of the Atlas or the south of the country: Ben Ṭaṭa, Ben Cota, Uḥanna/Ohana, etc.

Note, too, that it is by the first name followed by the mother's name that an individual is designated in the funeral liturgy, as well as in magical processes, the writing of amulets, talismans, etc.

Here we will list female first names belonging to the Romance languages (R), Arabic (A), and Berber (B), excluding Hebrew ones: Alba (R), 'Allu (B), 'Alya (AB), 'Aysha (A), 'Aziza (A), Buena (R), Clara (R), Cota (R), Donna/Doña (R), Estrella (R), Fadueña (R), Flora, Flore, and Florida (R), Franca (R), Freḥa (A), Gracia (R), Hennu (AB), Hermosa (R), Iṭṭo (B), Izza (B), Jamila and Jemmul (A), Ledicia/Laetitia (R), Linda (R), Lumbre (R), Luna (R), Maqnin/Macnin (?), Marzuqa (A), Mas'uda (A), Mliḥa (A), Mira/Amira and Maryam (A), Nahla (A), Najma (A), Nuna (R), Ora, Oro, and Orovida/Rovida (R), Paloma (R), Préciada (R), Qamra (A), Rahma (A), Raqus (?), Reina (R), Rosa (R), Sa'ada/Saada (A), Sete (?), Shuna (?), Sol (R), Sultana (A), Tammu (AB), Ṭaṭa (B), Yamna (A), Yaqut (A), Ẓahra (A).

### *Legend and Onomastics: Za'afrani (Zafrani) and Za'afran "Saffron"*

The surname Zafrani is not contained in the above list drawn up by Jacob Aben Sur, which is far from exhaustive. This surname, our name, is mentioned for the first time by Mr. Steinschneiders (*Jewish Literature*, Hildensheim, 1967, pp. 118, 180) and S. W. Baron (*A Social and Religious History of the Jews,* see index, s.v. Zafrani). Musa al-Zafri (second half of the ninth century), known as Al-Tiflisi, was born in Baghdad and settled in the then American city of Tbilisi where he founded the Karaite sect of Tiflissides. This name was quite common in all the communities of the Mediterranean Basin. The following history was recounted by Mr. Abraham 'Ofran (modern Israeli version of the name Za'afrani). The son of Mordekhay Za'afrani, a registrar and copyist in Mogador (Morocco) in the 1940s and 1950s and later in Israel, Abraham 'Ofran tells how originally the family bore the name of Al-Qayim. During a certain period of history, all the male children inevitably died until a scholarly healer advised the family to immerse the clothing of the newborn in water in which saffron (Arabic and Hebrew *za'afran*) had soaked on the eve of the circumcision. Thereafter, the dying of newborns came to an end. To this day, this ritual is strictly observed in the family, a family of intellectuals who are rigorously orthodox. Abraham ‘Ofran is an officer in a bank in Jerusalem, and his wife teaches physics at Hebrew University (She is the daughter of the well-known Professor Yeshayahu Leibowitz). The custom of soaking the baby’s clothing in saffron water has been scrupulously observed for the circumcision of the five boys in the family, which also includes two girls.

As we have seen earlier, first names may be changed in certain circumstances, but it seems to me that changes in surnames are very rare, if not unheard of.

# Chapter 2

# *Jewish Society and the Judeo-Maghrebian Social Imagination*

## CHILDHOOD AND ADOLESCENCE

### *Birth*

At all times, from the biblical period to the present day, birth, circumcision, and weaning have been the occasion for solemn ceremonies in Jewish communities. These ceremonies are of a fundamentally religious, even historical and national, nature. "And Abraham circumcised his son Isaac when he was eight days old, as God had commanded him" (Genesis 21:4); "And the child grew, and was weaned. And Abraham made a great feast on the day that Isaac was weaned" (Genesis 21:8). They are also the scene of a symbiosis, even a syncretism, where magic and religion meet, more particularly when they involve customs, rituals, and local customs that are common to the Jews and Muslims of the Maghreb.

In the Maghreb, among both Jews and Muslims, children (particularly of the male sex) are wanted and are anticipated with emotion, even anxiety. It is a primordial duty to perpetuate the race, and it is a prime concern that the name and the family continue to live on in a long and fertile posterity. Sterility is a curse, as are repeated miscarriages. That a childless man is a lifeless man and a barren woman a dead tree is repeated in a variety of ways in sayings and adages. It is therefore necessary to protect oneself from such misfortune by every sort of natural remedy (appropriate foods and the consumption of special potions) or, if necessary, by resort to the supernatural, to the intercession of Palestinian saints and local Muslim monks, to many practices, originating in variable admixtures of kabbalistic esotericism and popular magic. We have noted some of them in a collection of prescriptions originating from Marrakesh. The text is written in a Hebrew-Aramaic-Arabic jargon and concerns sterility, miscarriage, and "the woman who only gives birth to girls."

When a woman is pregnant, the news is immediately announced to her own and her husband's family and is met with demonstrations of joy. During her pregnancy the prospective mother is hemmed in by a network of prohibitions and precepts prescribed by custom and tradition. The period before delivery is customarily divided into three months of "craving," three months of plumpness, and three months of general fatigue. The first three months are considered the hardest and the most vulnerable precisely because of the phenomenon of the cravings, called *tawḥim*, and the unpleasant, even fatal consequences for the physique of the unborn child, or for his health and his mother's, or for the fate of the embryo if certain movements are made or if the cravings are not satisfied.

As the birth draws near, the "cutting of swaddling clothes" begins (called *taqti'-le-gdawer* in Fez, *taqti'-ettgamet* in Mogador), and the preparation of the talismans, amulets, charms, and magico-religious inscriptions embroidered on "the sheet of the woman in childbirth," called in Hebrew *shemirah* (from *shamar*, "to guard"). These are intended to put mother and child under the protection of God and the guardian angels, and to ward off evil spirits, most particularly the demon Lilith, created to exterminate boys during the first eight days following birth, that is to say, the period before they have entered into the Abrahamic covenant. Symbolic representations of animals, plants, and certain objects play an important role in the composition of the *shemirah*, especially fish, which are protection against the evil eye. This popular belief is also based on a talmudic text that associates the symbol of fish with a biblical passage concerning Joseph as the incarnation of fertility: "In the same way as fish who live in the waters and whom the waters cover escape the grip and the attacks of the evil eye, so is it with the descendants of Joseph" (Berakhot 20a).

When the woman (*ḥabla*) feels the birth pains, her husband sends for the midwife, the *qabla*, or "receiver," the experienced obstetrician, she of the lucky hands. The close female relatives, and often neighbors as well, crowd round the woman in labor, who has to cry out and appeal to God and the saints, while the women around her embark on other prayers and invocations until the delivery, most often fairly quickly and without great complications. The afterbirth falls out; the membrane of the fetus is treasured by the mother, especially in the case of a firstborn son, because it is thought to possess beneficial and prophylactic qualities, such as hastening the release of prisoners. The Judeo-Arabic term that designates it, *khlaṣ*, also means "deliverance."

Great is the joy when the baby is a boy; the *qabla* receives him crying *Barukh habba*, "Blessed be he who comes" (Hebrew) three times and passes him to the women, who ululate (*zgha-rit*). A girl is usually less well received and the congratulatory formula is *Mbarka mas'uda*, "Let her be blessed and fortunate."

If the delivery is protracted, the men say prayers; and if the pains are excessively prolonged, a special liturgy is used. It consists of the recitation of the *'Akedah*, a poem belonging to the ritual of the Days of Awe (Yamim Nora'im), Rosh Hashanah and Yom Kippur, and recounting the tale of the binding of the patriarch Isaac, who was then delivered by an angel who stayed the knife of his father Abraham on the altar of sacrifice. During this period the woman in childbirth cries out, her hands pulling on a cord knotted round the bed- or doorpost.[1]

A recipe noted in our collection from Marrakesh, designed to hasten the happy conclusion of the confinement, consists of putting an inscription under the tongue of the woman in childbirth. It is formed of four Hebrew letters, *alef*, *mem*, *nun*, and *ṭet*, a sort of magical square, a cryptogram originating from the vocabulary of practical kabbalah and integrating the names of angels or the words of a biblical verse. The object must be withdrawn from the mouth immediately after the delivery.

### *Taḥdid*

Among the rituals that accompany birth, more particularly the birth of a boy, is *taḥdid*, which involves the use of a strip of iron (*ḥdid*), a

1. Compare the ritual L. Brunot observed in a Muslim environment in Rabat, which consisted of "knotting the woman's kerchief to the minaret of a mosque and raising prayers on the patient's behalf." In a Christian country, "one of the most frequent ways of making the confinement easier consists of ringing the bells. In olden days, the woman's belt itself was tied to the bell of the parish church, and it was rung three times." Sebillot, *Le paganisme contemporain*, quoted by L. Brunot.

metal that plays an important role in certain beliefs and ceremonies common to the Jews and Muslims of the Maghreb.[2] But *taḥdid* belongs both to religion, with a liturgy of its own, and to magic, with the ceremonial actions that accompany this liturgy, the two being designed to protect the child of male sex. He, it appears, is more vulnerable than a girl during the seven days that proceed his entry into the covenant of Abraham and the circumcision that he must undergo, which saves him, because his life is constantly threatened during this period, especially by the demon Lilith.

### *Lilith Conquered and Disarmed*

When midnight sounds, doors and windows are closed, and while the ritual is taking place, an old sword or a broad knife is passed over the walls and the hermetically sealed entrances to the room containing the new mother (*nfisa*).[3] The metallic object is then placed under the pillow of the child snuggled up against his mother.

Like so many other Judeo-Maghrebian rituals, this is simultaneously a manifestation of the popular local imagination, an active solidarity with the autochthonous Maghrebian and Arabo-Berber cultural landscape, and an expression of loyalty to universal Jewish thought, to a collective memory the origins of which go back to historical and prehistoric times, the biblical memory itself. To both alike, sacrifices are made.

In any event, the ceremony commences with the verses from the Holy Scriptures that tell the story of Noah, relating the episode of the ark, where all the living creatures that were to escape the flood find refuge: "And they that went in [i.e., into the ark], went in male and female of all flesh, as God had commanded him [Noah], and the Lord shut him in" (Genesis 7:16). At the precise moment when the reading of the text ends, all the doors, windows, and other openings to the room are closed, preventing the "other" (she who is not named, Lilith, the unnamable) from entering.

The ritual of *taḥdid* and the legends accompanying it are extant

2. We hope that our description of the quite unique ritual of *taḥdid* will make its significance understandable. It is no longer practiced in modern times. The phenomenon is mentioned once or twice in ethnographic studies of the Mahgreb, but as far as we know, no analysis worth recording has ever been made.

3. *Taḥdid* is also the act of drawing the boundaries of an area, fixing the frontiers of a place where a stranger cannot enter; in this case, Lilith.

everywhere in the Mediterranean Jewish world, in both the Islamic East and the Islamic West. Evidence of this, if evidence is needed, is provided by a story we heard a few years ago from a visionary painter, Joseph Manor, an Israeli Jew of Iraqi origin living in Paris. His grandfather, he told me with an air of conviction, had gotten the better of the demon Lilith, who was responsible for the death of Jewish children of the male sex in Baghdad, and had seized her deadly sword. This sword he had entrusted to his family, who ever since had carefully treasured it. According to my informant, the hero of this combat in which Lilith was conquered and disarmed was a great master of practical kabbalah, familiar with mysterious esoteric texts, who frequently effected miraculous cures. We have encountered many examples of this type of hero, at one and the same time a miracle-worker learned in the rabbinical sciences and a simple healer, in Morocco, Mogador, Marrakesh, and elsewhere.

The liturgical part of the ceremony continues with the recitation of other appropriate scriptural texts: Genesis 48:16 and 49:22 (extracts from Jacob's blessing), Psalms 91 and 121, Numbers 6:22–27 (the Priestly Blessing), and Proverbs 3:24. It ends with music and song, melodies of Hebraic expression (*piyyuṭim*), ballads and ritornellos, *qṣayed*, *ghnayat*, and *'arubi* in dialectal Arabic, and Berber or Castilian songs, depending on the ethno-linguistic group concerned.

There is only space here to discuss some of the most significant short sequences.

Jacob's legendary blessing is the fragment addressed to Joseph and his sons, Ephraim and Manasseh; it is repeated three times: "The angel who hath redeemed me from all evil, bless the lads; and let my name be blessed in them, and the name of my fathers Abraham and Isaac; and let them grow into a multitude [lit., let them multiply like fishes] in the midst of the earth. . . . Joseph is a fruitful vine, a fruitful vine by a fountain; its branches run over the wall."

The text of Psalm 91 is a protective reading par excellence, used in practical kabbalah in the making of *shemirot* (prophylactic inscriptions) and *qemi'ot* (talismans), integrating the words that form its verses into cryptograms and magical squares, in the form of gematria and notarikon. The following are a few typical verses: "He [God] will deliver thee from the snare of the fowler, and from the noisome pestilence. . . . Thou shalt not be afraid of the terror by night, nor of the arrow that flieth by day; of the pestilence that walketh in darkness, nor of the destruction that wasteth at noonday. . . . There shall no evil befall thee, neither shall any plague come nigh thy tent."

Psalm 121 in particular says: "The Lord is thy keeper; the Lord is thy shade [i.e., tutelary guardian] upon thy right hand. The sun shall not smite thee by day, nor the moon by night. The Lord shall keep thee from all evil; He shall keep [guard] thy soul."

The tenor of the Priestly Blessing is well known. The following are two of its components: "The Lord bless thee and keep thee; the Lord make His face to shine upon thee, and be gracious unto thee."

Proverbs 3:24 consists of this simple wish: "When thou liest down, thou shalt not be afraid; yea, thou shalt lie down, and thy sleep shall be sweet."

We quote the prelude-refrain of one of the most popular *piyyuṭim*, followed by the first stanza:

> *Prelude*
> Blessed be you all, the congregation of My worshippers,
> And blessed be the name of the Lord!
>
> *1st stanza*
> May the boy born to us be for a good sign!
> May he grow and flourish like a well-watered garden!
> May he rise, may he succeed, may he escape distress!
> May this be God's will, and let us say Amen!

Lastly, here are a few couplets from one of the many Judeo-Arabic songs dedicated to the midwife, *ghnayat al-qabla*:

1. *Ya qabla ya susiyya*
2. *Kull ma seddit swiyya*
3. *Nqum nhar as-saba' nkherrzek maksiyya*
4. *Ya qabla ya maqbula*
5. *Ya mbashshra ya mimuna*
6. *Bashshertni ya 'tik al-khir*
7. *Na'tik haja maṭmuna*

1. O midwife [lit., receiver]! O woman of Sous!
2. All the yarn I have prepared to weave with is but little.
3. I will rise up on the seventh day and send you forth clad in a flowing garment.
4. O midwife! O sweet and pleasant woman!
5. O bringer of good news and of good fortune!

6. You told me the good news, may [God] give you good fortune (and prosperity).

7. As for me, I will give you something precious.

The vigil, begun early in the evening, is extended beyond the ceremony of *taḥdid* by a long session during which the women, under the guidance of a professional storyteller, tell stories, appropriate legends, while the lengthy and meticulous preparations are made for the circumcision and the festivities that accompany it. *Taḥdid* thus becomes *taḥdith*, "to tell original tales, to converse."

### *Circumcision: Ceremonial, Legend, and Poetry*

The ceremony of circumcision, which as a general rule takes place on the eighth day after the birth, is a solemn religion occasion and a family celebration. It is accompanied by demonstrations of joy, festivity, and rejoicing which, among both rich and poor, glorify the entry of a boy into the world.

The ceremony is usually celebrated in the parents' home, in the mother's room, decorated with ornaments from the sefarim (Torah scrolls) borrowed from the synagogue and with multicolored hangings.[4]

The circumcision proper, the removal of the foreskin, is known as *milah* in Hebrew and *khtana* in Arabic. It is also called *ṭaharah*, "purification," and *ziyana*, "improvement," in a Muslim environment, where it is carried out when the child is between seven and nine years old. The mother offers her son for the ritual amputation, the sacrifice of circumcision, in order to spare him the total sacrifice of death. The *sandek* (sponsor), a role generally entrusted to a grandfather or sold by auction for the benefit of the community's poor fund, is seated on the chair of Elijah the prophet (*kissé Elyahu*). He holds the child between his knees while the mohel, official circumciser and voluntary practitioner, performs the operation, sucks the blood away from the sacrifice, and sprinkles the affected organ with rum or brandy, stopping the bleeding with a balsamic dressing (the *balsamon*).[5] The child's

4. It can also take place in the synagogue where the father prays.

5. Beneficent qualities are attributed to the blood of circumcision, as shown by the following rite, in which, as in most other rites, both social-imaginary and legal-religious elements play a part. It is reported by Rabbi Yosef Benaïm in his bio-bibliograpical dictionary, *Malke Rabbanan*. "One of the sages of Sefrou, Rabbi Isaac Hakkohen, known as Rabbi Yishaq *mul-al-milah* [i.e., master of circumcision], is buried at the foot of the well-known mountain near the town. He has been renowned as a great saint from time imme-

father gives the appropriate eulogy, thanking God for having permitted him to "bring a new member into the covenant of Abraham." After the traditional blessing over wine and aromatic plants, usually dried rose petals, the name is given.

The choice of first name obeys a certain number of rules, variable according to tradition, and different depending on ethnic origins. Among the megorashim, the descendants of the generation exiled from the Iberian peninsula, the child will bear the name of a grandfather who is still alive. This is forbidden to the toshabim, "natives," who only assign the name of a deceased grandfather or other elder.

The ceremony of circumcision, like the performance of any other rite, is of necessity accompanied by a special liturgy that incorporates appropriate *piyyuṭim* chanted by those present. The Jewish cantors and troubadours of Morocco, over the centuries, have devoted a considerable number of poetic compositions in Hebrew and of *qaṣa'ed* in Judeo-Arabic to the celebration of *berit-milah*. One of the pieces written for this solemn occasion by Jacob Aben Sur (seventeenth to eighteenth century) is very popular. Added to Maghrebian synagogue ritual at a very early date, it is sung to a lively tune and a fast rhythm when the father of the newborn son is called up to the Torah on the Saturday preceding the circumcision. It consists of four very short quatrains, in iso-syllabic meter:

Let our community rejoice!
Let our congregation be glad!
For unto us a son is born,
Unto us a son is given, unto us a son is given.

The supreme God, whose seat is in the heavens,
Will shower this child with His blessings;
And grant him, too, the privilege of entering,
The covenant of our father Abraham.

His Creator will grant his wishes,
And he will spend his days in happiness;
He will go up to the land of delights,
With all the Israelites, our brethren.

---

morial, and in periods of drought the people of Sefrou go to the place where he is buried and spread a linen handkerchief soaked in blood from a milah over his tombstone, reciting psalms and penitential prayers to ask for rain." Herman Hesse devotes a whole chapter to a figure of this type in his novel *Das Glasperlenspiel* (translated into English as *The Glass Bead Game* and as *Magister Ludi*).

May his father today, to the strains of the song,
Go up to read from the Torah;
And may he bless the name of our God,
In respect and dignity.

The ethical and religious aspects of circumcision, its social and ethnic significance, the ritual operation itself (*milah* and *peri'ah*, i.e., the tearing and folding back of the skin to reveal the crown of the phallus) form the dominant themes of the other compositions in this series. They find their inspiration and their literary and linguistic substance in the Bible, the Talmud, the Midrash, and the halakhah. The expression of these ideas in this poetry, designed to be sung at public and joyful ceremonies, underlines its didactic and pedagogic nature. It also demonstrates the desire to hallow every deed, every gesture that accompanies this striking religious occasion in Jewish life. The following extracts are the prelude and the second and third stanzas of a piece which testifies to this:

*Prelude*
You have marked us with your seal, Almighty God!
May your name, our King, be praised forevermore!

*2nd stanza*
We will cut the uncircumcised skin with sharp knives,
According to Your wish, O living God, maker of all creatures,
In order to perpetuate the covenant contracted by our loyal and faithful fathers,
And to weaken the maleficent force of our (evil) inclinations.

*3rd stanza*
We will cut the tender membrane with diligent hand
In order to reveal the flesh of the full crown,
To redouble energy by enhanced purity.
Such is the sign of the covenant You have sealed in our flesh.

On the thirty-first day after birth, the redemption of the firstborn male (*pidyon ha-ben*) takes place. As a ransom to the Kohen, a descendant of the priestly line of Aaron, the father offers his wife's jewelry (gold, silver, precious stones); he takes them back shortly afterwards, on payment of a sum of money destined for the community's charity chest.

This is another ritual of a socioreligious character. Moroccan poets have also devoted compositions to the ceremonial that accompanies this celebration. These evoke the biblical texts that prescribe the consecration of the firstborn male and the obligation to redeem him (Exodus 13, Numbers 3 and 23).

In the case of a girl, the giving of the name (Arabic *tsemya*) is much less solemn. In Hebrew, the ceremony is called *zebed ha-bat*, "the offering of the daughter." It is the occasion for a short ritual accompanied by a collation, demonstrations of joy, and appropriate *piyyuṭim*, including the one that is sung on the wedding day, composed by a Moroccan poet. It begins as follows: "Graceful doe, sweet maid, / In you perfect beauty and our forebears' mythical strength unite."

For both boys and girls, the father or grandfather inscribes the name and date of birth on a page of a daily prayerbook or a Pentateuch (there is as yet no registry office). The date employs the usual Jewish computation, which counts from the creation of the world, and is only in force in Jewish societies in the Islamic West.

## TEACHING AND EDUCATION

### *The Basis of the Teaching Tradition*

The basic principles of all Jewish teaching are found in the Written and Oral Law. During the biblical period education meant the socialization of the individual, preparing him to be a member of the community like everyone else, impregnated with the spirit destined to form a distinct nation, and motivated by the ideal of virtue and piety laid down by God in the following terms: "Ye shall be holy; for I the Lord your God am holy" (Leviticus 19:2).

It was only after the return from the Babylonian Exile, in the mishnaic and talmudic periods, that the Pharisee teachers and the scholars of the law who followed them laid the foundations of an educational system.

Ezra initiated readings from the Five Books of Moses to gatherings of the people (cf. Sukkah 20a). The men of the Great Synagogue operated by preaching, and houses for study and meeting places for scholars were founded for this purpose (Pirke Abot 1:1, 4).

After the destruction of the Second Temple, the spiritual leaders of Judaism tried to save the doctrine and the law from perdition. They stated that one of the first duties of every individual was to acquire a good education, and that the major responsibility of the community was to provide it. They decided on measures that would encourage this instruction and formulated a plan for a general educational program. A talmudic text ('Avodah Zarah 36) goes so far as to say that "Since the destruction of the Temple, God Himself devotes the fourth quarter of his time to teaching children."

A knowledge of Judaism penetrated deeply into the Jewish masses. The smallest Diaspora community, wherever destiny had pitched the Jew, in Iraq, the Yemen, the Maghreb, had its bet ha-midrash. And the Jewish teaching tradition, inscribed in the Bible and the Talmud, was passed from school to school through time and space down to the present generation of rabbis.

### *Idealistic Conceptions of Teaching*

After the first decision-making rabbis had codified the pedagogical heritage of the talmudic and gaonic periods (see Maimonides' Hilkhot Talmud Torah), other medieval Jewish thinkers pondered these problems, formulated theories, constructed systems. They drew their inspiration from the basic sources of the tradition, but also borrowed from the philosophical theories of their contemporaries.

Naturally, these systems were never applied to the letter. The ideal of a high level of education, as advocated by a twelfth- or thirteenth-century Jewish philosopher, could only apply to a small elite in a position to devote a lifetime to study. A typical ideal teaching program can be found in *Ya'ir Natib*, written in 1250 by Rabbi Yehudah ben Samuel ben Abbas, who lived in Spain and Morocco. Another rabbi of Moroccan origin, a contemporary of Maimonides, Rabbi Yosef ben Aqnin, discusses the "qualities of master and pupil" in the same spirit in his *Ṭibb an-Nufûs* ("Medicine for Souls").

### *Traditional Schools*

The traditional Jewish school in the Islamic West, which still existed not so very long ago, was a replica of the earliest schools, its roots going back to the beginnings of Jewish settlement in the Maghreb or at least to the Arab conquest.

In the schools of the Mahgreb, education was largely concerned with the socialization and integration of the individual into the community. One might almost say that the circles concerned with these goals quite frequently had no conscious conception of education. It was respect for tradition that governed life in the community. The child was educated by contact, example, orders, and prohibitions; by apprenticeship in tradition, adjustment to customs and practices, revelation of beliefs and rites and, lastly, introduction into the adult group by the initiation ceremony. Add to this very simplified outline the knowledge acquired at school, for the most part intended to give children, particularly boys, the means to participate in a religious service, and we have everything that goes to turn an individual into a member of a community, someone with the shared mentality and rooted feeling of belonging to a group, with a sense of the cohesion and solidarity of the members of that group.

### *The Child in the Family*

As soon as a child becomes aware of the life around him, he finds himself in an environment governed by a collection of actions and practices closely linked to the commandments of the religion. It is in the home, in the midst of the extended family, with grandparents and all the close relations often living together in the same group of dwellings, that his initiation into traditional Jewish life begins. Nothing separates children and adults. The child becomes acquainted with an established order, with laws and customs that he is called on to observe scrupulously, by imitating his elders, whom he respects and fears.

The child is trained in the family at least as much as at school. The teacher's influence only complements the education begun and continued in the home environment, and his function consists of teaching the child to read from the Torah.

It is in the home that the child receives his moral education. It is the mother who inculcates the basic virtues of charity, respect for other people's property, love of the Holy Land. It is not the task of the school and the teacher to teach the prayers; the child acquires a perfect knowledge of them from his parents' example and daily religious observance.

In certain special cases, orphans for example, the role of grandparents, uncles, and aunts can be considerable.

Education, properly speaking, does not stop at the school gate. In the evening, the child or adolescent finds his father or grandfather at home anxious to complete his Jewish education, to prepare him for the ceremony of his religious majority (bar-miṣwah) and, as he grows and develops intellectually, to introduce him to certain studies excluded from the school curriculum, particularly reading the Zohar, the mystical exegesis of the Torah, which is passed on individually to the disciple, often a chosen son.

### *The Al-Kuttab Ceremony*

In the communities of the Todgha (Upper Atlas) valleys, as soon as a boy reached the age of five, his parents had two concerns: to teach him the Torah and to choose a wife for him, in accordance with a talmudic instruction. On the eve of the festival of Shabu'ot, which commemorates the revelation on Mount Sinai, it was the custom to organize a miniature marriage (*ḥuppah biz'ir'anpin*). The boy and a girl of the same age who was intended for him were joined to one another in a genuine wedding ceremony followed by festivities. After morning prayers, Shaḥrit, the men went to the boy's house. The rabbi drew the letters of the Hebrew alphabet in honey on a clean piece of wood, asked the boy to lick them off, and said: "In this way the words of the Torah will be sweet on your palate" (cf. Proverbs 24:13).

Brunot and Malka mention this ceremony in their *Textes judéo-arabes de Fez.* Apparently only one of the two components was preserved in Fez: the pledging of the children to each other. According to our informants from Todgha and Mhamid-Al-Gozlan, on the edge of the Sahara, it primarily concerned the symbolic marriage of the child with the Torah.[6]

## *Elementary Teaching*

"The essentials of teaching are done in the synagogue, by the synagogue, and for the synagogue." This formula, which S. D. Goitein used in connection with the Yemen, to a large extent characterizes Jewish elementary teaching in Morocco. The function this teaching is assigned is not to prepare the young for life. Its aim and contents must respond to a single imperative: correct participation in worship, initiation into a tradition, into a system of negative and positive command-

6. At Béni Ounif, located on the Algerian-Moroccan Saharan border, the letters of the alphabet were written on an egg that the child was given to eat.

ments. The prayers in the synagogue are not read exclusively by the officiating minister; they are shared out between members of the congregation, as are the *piyyuṭim* on festivals and Sabbaths. The worshiper called up to the *sefer* is required to himself read the section of the Torah allotted to him (everyone is supposed to know how to read from the *sefer*) or to recite the Hafṭarah (the reading from the Prophets), with its Aramaic and Judeo-Arabic, Judeo-Spanish, or Judeo-Berber translation, depending on the region in which he lives.

Reading and reciting the sacred texts from memory and, as a secondary consideration, explaining and understanding them, are therefore the key to, and the fundamental condition of, the Jew's participation in the worship of God, who in this way demands a long apprenticeship and substantial knowledge.

The intimate relationship between teaching and liturgy is again manifested in the annual distribution of the material studied in the seasonal curriculum.

### *The* Ṣla: *School and Synagogue*

In the old mellahs of the large cities and in the more modest urban and rural agglomerations, in the shadow of the pre-Saharan *ksour*s or in the Atlas valleys, premises are reserved for teaching: a large building in the towns, a narrow room in the villages. This is the school, called the *ṣla*. The term designates both the place of prayer, the synagogue, and, as well, any other building where traditional teaching is done, even a private accommodation rented for the purpose by the teacher, or his own home. However, it should be noted that the synagogue very often does duty as a school, which further strengthens the interdependence between liturgy and teaching. This phenomenon and the same confusion of terminology can be found everywhere in the Islamic world.

In the Yemen, synagogue and school are called by the same name, *knis*, and the term *msid* ("koranic school") is no more than an adaptation of *masjid* ("place of prayer, mosque"). In Berber lands it is the *timezgida*.[7]

7. The word *ḥeder*, borrowed from the Ashkenazi vocabulary, came into use very recently, but we find it more convenient than *ṣla*. Linguistic convenience has also often led us to employ present-day pedagogical terminology, but we must emphasize that these are nothing more than comparative meanings and of relationships at comparable levels.

### *The Teaching Premises*

Classes may be conducted in any room of a house, upstairs or downstairs. The narrow windows are closed in winter, open in summer. The sun is an intruder there. The children—there can be as many as a hundred to a hundred and fifty of them in some mellahs in large towns—stifle in an airless atmosphere. Pale and sickly, suffering from scabies or trachoma, they sit in groups on the alfalfa or straw mats covering the beaten-earth floor. Only rarely are there a few rough benches, bookshelves, or lecterns. The teacher crouches on a small mattress against a wall near the door, observing everyone. Now and again he moves round the groups, a figure in a black *djelaba* and blue kerchief with white spots, brandishing a stick or cosh. A large earthenware jar covered with a small board and containing the day's supply of water stands in the corner of the room. A cup or bowl hangs from a nail above it. Oil lamps or candles, recently replaced by petrol or acetylene lamps, are lit when night falls.

In a Marrakesh ḥeder during the dog-days, children and teachers have a fan, a cardboard box nailed to a stick, which is waved continuously. In another ḥeder, the pupils take turns at "ventilator" duty. They struggle to rhythmically swing a rectangular mat hung from the ceiling over their comrades' heads.

This is the image of the synagogue-school that previous generations knew. There is every reason to believe that it had existed virtually unchanged for centuries, identical in time and space, with slight variations from one mellah to another.

Books are rare and expensive. Four or five small heads can often be seen bowed over the same Ḥumash, or Pentateuch, around its lucky owner, doing their utmost to read the right way up, the wrong way up, and sideways. The shortage of books will later force the students to copy out in advance the text of the *din* or *gemara*' to be studied.

### *Compulsory but not Free*

The child enters the ḥeder at the age of three, four, five, or six. He begins learning the alphabet at four, and must continue to study at least until the age of religious majority, fixed at thirteen. The responsibility for this falls on the parents or, in the case of orphans and paupers, on the community.

A *taqqanah* signed by the rab of Meknès, R. Jacob Aben Sur, in the month of Iyyar 5481 (1721), condemns parents who withdraw their children from ḥeder to apprentice them to brush manufacturers (*qrashliyyin*), and formally prohibits artisans from taking children into their service before the age of bar-miṣwah (thirteen years).

The parents (or the community, as the case may be) are obliged to make a payment to the ḥazzan or rabbi, called *sharṭ*. This is not, says the Talmud, "for the teaching he gives [since teaching is, in principle, done for free], but for supervising the children" or "as compensation for the time he withdraws from his normal occupations." In addition, in some southern Moroccan mellahs, he receives the "teacher's bread" on Fridays (a tradition also noted in the Yemen).

### *The Status of the Teacher*

The post of ḥeder teacher is not subject to regulation. What is more, it commands no great respect, probably because very often the teacher is a nobody who lacks innate teaching ability and has never had any professional training. It is a "profession of poverty" (*mlekhet 'oni*), said a rabbi from Meknès. Moreover, it is not unusual to see a teacher changing careers when he has the opportunity. He moves on from teaching the *prasha*, the text of the Pentateuch, to become a cloth merchant, brush-maker, tailor, shoe repairer, or apprentice jeweler.

The teacher's salary barely enables him to lead a decent life. Consequently, he is almost always forced to resort to marginal or secondary work: small-scale trade in paper, in ink of his own manufacture, in amulets or talismans. He may serve as a ritual slaughterer of poultry or cattle. He makes the thongs for tefillin (phylacteries) or fringes (*ṣiṣyot, ptilim*) for prayer shawls. Sometimes he is a *payṭan* (singer of *piyyuṭim*), or a *sofer* (notary and public scribe).

Nevertheless, the status of the scholar, applicable to ḥeder and yeshîbâh teachers, has been the subject of rabbinical decisions by Moroccan decisors. These mainly concern problems related to the exemption from taxation that scholars enjoy, and other questions pertaining to the recruitment of teachers and their right to retain their posts, regulating the competition between teachers in the same locality, the contribution of the "state treasury" to rabbinical salaries, regarded as illegal, and so on.

*Teaching Methods*

At the elementary level, instruction basically consists of teaching the child to read so that he can participate in the synagogue service as soon as possible. The process is as follows: the mechanical attainment of the ability to read letters, vowels, and words, followed by intensive practice in reading a sacred text.

Correct reading of the liturgical texts of the Bible involves a perfect knowledge of the "finer points" (*diqduqim*) and the "accents" (*te'a-mim*) of the Torah. The cantillated reading of the scroll of the law, in which neither vowels nor cantillation signs appear, is one of the fundamental components of the service. The child is gradually brought to this point by repeating and memorizing. The congregation is constantly on the lookout to ensure that the cantillation is meticulously correct, and roughly points out any errors committed by the reader, who must repeat the portion of the verse that he has recited incorrectly.

The teacher begins to explain the texts when the weekly scriptural reading is studied. This is the *sharh* or *tafsir*. It is confined to a simple translation in the local language, a juxtalinear translation, basically fixed by a centuries-old unwritten tradition passed on by word of mouth by successive generations of rabbis.

Although the translation was originally intended to make the meaning and import of the text comprehensible (and to a certain extent this is still its function), it is not always understood by the pupil, for its language is often quite far removed from the spoken language. This is a common phenomenon in the most important Arabophone communities, and it occurs almost as frequently with the Judeo-Spanish translations in use by the communities of the former Spanish zone of Morocco, and with the Judeo-Berber translations of the old Jewish tribes of the Atlas and the Saharan borderlands.

The Aramaic translation (Targum Onqelos and paraphrases of the Prophets) was also originally intended for understanding the sacred texts. It has been maintained by tradition, although it lost this role at the end of the first millennium of the common era (see the letter of Yehudah Ibn Quraïsh of Tahert to the Jews of Fez, tenth century). It does not form part of elementary teaching, but for pious men it is the fulfillment of an obligation based on the rabbinic command *shnayim miqra we-aḥad targum* (reading every verse of the pericope twice in Hebrew and once in Aramaic).

Writing is not regarded as indispensable to elementary study and is only taught very late. Then it is the cursive script of Andalusian origin (*neṣṣ-qlam*), found in the ancient communities of Turkey and Greece, and used by adults for family or commercial correspondence. Rashi script is reserved for reproducing literary documents and for copying out texts for study: because of the scarcity of books, the student copies out chapters of the *Shulḥan 'Aruk*, the Mishnah, or the Talmud. This copying process serves three purposes at once: books are acquired, the student remembers their contents better, and he learns the elements of the sofer's craft.

### *Discipline*

The pupil is regarded as a subject who must acquire certain mechanical skills, gain a certain amount of knowledge, and be subjected to certain rules. The first means employed is constraint. Fear of corporal punishment and other coercive methods, such as certain humiliating practices, force the child to pay attention, exert himself, and study.

However, some teachers adopt less severe discipline, especially in the case of young children, handing out sweets or other rewards to increase the appeal of an education that in its own right is not appealing.

In addition, some effort is made to find alternative means to threats. For instance, as a device for encouraging and stimulating achievement, students who do well may earn the right to go up to the *sefer*. Similarly, competitions are regularly organized between older pupils in the town's *ḥedarim*.

Nevertheless, corporal punishment, physical correction, still remains the general rule. The teacher moves around the room, the birch over his shoulder. The pupil caught red-handed not paying attention, chatting, or for any other reason, receives a rain of blows. Often, too, the teacher uses a long stick (a cane four meters long, in the specific case of a certain ḥeder in Casablanca), so that he can reach all the pupils ranged in rows in front of him, and shake them up when necessary.

A whole gamut of punishments is sanctioned for serious misdemeanors: *taḥmîla*, *falaqa*, *qarma*.

*Taḥmîla*. The culprit is held down by two of his comrades while a third deals him a predetermined number of strokes with the birch on the soles of his feet. The teacher sells the right to wield the birch by auction (evidence gathered by R. D. Bouzaglo at Settat).

*Falaqa.* A cord is fixed to the ends of a thick cane. The culprit's ankles are squeezed into the half-circle formed by the cord and the wood, while the thirty-nine strokes of legal flagellation (*malqut*) are dealt to the soles of his feet.

*Qarma.* A piece of wood is cut to fetter the culprit's feet and prevent him from running away. This punishment is used for pupils guilty of truancy.

The teacher who inflicts such punishments is not acting out of cruelty. Nor is he inspired by a desire to reduce his class to obedience or to dominate. His discipline is based on the teachings of the tradition to which he is obliged to conform and on local customs. In Spanish-language communities, they say: *la lettra con sangre entra*, "The letter [i.e., teaching] is only absorbed through blood"; the equivalent adage among Arabophone Jews is: *l-ḥarf ma yedkhel gîr b-eḍ-ḍerb*, "The letter is only absorbed through strokes with the birch."[8]

The pupils fear and respect the teacher. They kiss his hand when they arrive and when they leave. When they enter the ḥeder, they have to hand over the contents of their pockets to him: money, goodies or toys; these are given back to them when they go home.

### *Testing by Oral Interrogation*

As the teaching is basically, if not exclusively oral, written exercises are unknown. The only way to make sure that the students remember the lessons and have memorized the knowledge taught is by means of *tasmî'*, a method of testing based on oral interrogation.

For beginners this involves "reciting the *planche*" (i.e., a text written on a board) while standing on one leg. After the child reads it in the ordinary manner, the master makes him read it backwards, crossways, and jumbled up, his index finger running along the line. Every mistake earns a blow on the hand.

## *Bar-Miṣwah*

Elementary teaching culminates in the ceremony of *bar-miṣwah*, its completion thus coinciding with the religious majority. The adoles-

8. Even Paul Valéry seems to deplore teaching without tears: "It [the mind] is overwhelmed with effortless amusement, and even teaching without tears" (*Oeuvres*, I, 1386, Pleiade ed.).

cent is now bound to fulfill the obligations commanded by the law and, like an adult, is responsible for his actions and participates in synagogue worship with the same rights and duties as his elders.

The religious majority is customarily fixed at thirteen (Pirke Avot 5:26). However, intellectually mature individuals sometimes achieve it much earlier. Two Moroccan rabbis state that they were bar-miṣwah at the age of seven and eight respectively. In fact the scholars of the Talmud (Sukkah 42) authorize the father to place tefillin on his son as soon as the child is capable of looking after them.

On the day of the ceremony, the adolescent has to conduct the service and give a *darush*, a genuine sermon, beginning with a *mliṣah* (a prologue in rhyming prose) and developing into a long dissertation on a biblical verse, supported by talmudic texts and illustrated by homiletical stories. This sermonic presentation demands serious preparation, because the young man has to know it by heart.

During the preliminary festivities, which take place six months before the ceremony, the first steps are taken. The future *bar-miṣwah* (*mûl et-tfellîn*) recites the first lines of his sermon under the watchful eye of the rabbi, for whom this is the occasion to collect a few coins which the guests place on a tray by way of an offering known as *ghrama*.

The ceremony proper is celebrated in the synagogue on a Monday or Thursday, two working days when the Torah is read and tefillin can be donned. At a family gathering the evening before, henna was placed in the hollow of the child's hand. Now he is dressed in beautiful clothes. Covered by the tallit and crowned with tefillin, surrounded by an escort of young boys carrying large lighted candles, he arrives at the synagogue, after the procession has moved through the streets of the mellah. He conducts the service, goes up to the *sefer*, and recites his sermon. The close relatives (the women are also there in the section of the building reserved for their use) throw sugar, rice, almonds, and dates to the congregation. The *bar-miṣwah* is led back to his seat by those present, who are served fritters, tea, and dried fruit. There is singing and dancing; the Andalusian orchestra plays until the next morning.

The child has become an adult (*boger* or *mebuggar*) in the eyes of the law, and as such he participates in synagogue worship with the same rights and obligations as his elders. There are now two paths open to him: he can start an apprenticeship and begin to earn his living, or he can continue his studies at the yeshîbâh if he has an inclination. Whichever he chooses, he is not illiterate (there is no state of real ignorance even among the most deprived Jews). "Nowhere else in the world amongst other nations is there a child of thirteen capable of demonstrating so much religious knowledge."

### *"Higher" Education: The Yeshîbah*

Rabbinical judges (*dayyanim*), religious functionaries of various kinds, scholars who have no specific communal or cultural office, those for whom the Torah is not a livelihood and want a more advanced education than is given at the ḥeder—all these have to devote several years of their youth, if not their whole lives, to acquiring the knowledge indispensable to the exercise of their office or to their consecration as *talmide-ḥakamim* (scholars).

This education is given at the yeshîbâh, which is almost always either a religious foundation or an establishment created by a decision of the communal committee.

#### *Teachers and Students*

The teachers in the yeshîbot are rabbis renowned for their knowledge and virtue. They occupy a better material position than the ḥeder teachers. Their salaries are more substantial and much less unreliable. Their erudition qualifies them to serve as *darshanim* (preachers), a position that is quite generously paid in some cases. They may also be *payṭanim* who engage in singing and poetry, or calligraphers and engravers who design beautiful ketubbot (marriage certificates) or sculpt rich epitaphs. They may also act as *sofer*, *shoḥet*, or *mohel* (scribe, ritual slaughterer, and circumciser, respectively), duties that are not entirely honorary. Sometimes they go into business partnerships with merchants.

The yeshîbâh students, who often come from quite far off, have secure board and lodging with a *ba'al ha-bayit* (householder), a merchant or craftsman for whom it is a duty and an honor to offer hospitality to the *talmid*, a stranger in the town. The student also receives financial assistance. Teaching is, in principle, free, and the books for study, when there are any, are supplied by the body responsible for the yeshîbâh.

The relationship of the disciple to the teacher is stamped with absolute respect and veneration. The disciple is the servant of his master and owes him all his time outside the hours of study.

### *The Content of the Teaching*

The teaching in the yeshîbâh follows two distinct lines, depending on two different approaches. The first is material, pragmatic, assigning an important place to explanation of the *din* (law), with an eye to the action and practice of carrying out the positive and negative commandments. It is nourished by the literature of the *posqim* (rabbinic decisors).

The second approach is formal, intended to develop the student's intellectual acumen and accustom him to practice pure dialectic (*pilpul*), thus giving him the opportunity to reveal his aptitude by the discovery of a *ḥiddush* (original interpretation, new idea, or at least an original argument).

Our yeshîbâh teacher at Mogador, like other reformers, urged his best pupils to give priority to exploration of the sea of Talmud, to personal quest of the halakhah in the sources of the gemara. He had no great esteem for the study of the codes; they were good enough for the small fry. The great majority of Moroccan rabbis do not seem to have shared this attitude toward the secondary sources. Of course, study of the Talmud was held in high honor in the yeshîbâh, but it was the *Shulḥan 'Aruk* and the works of other *posqim* that were referred to, very often even on the occasion of a legal consultation.

The choice of a *masekhet* (talmudic treatise) to study for a term or a year depends on local traditions. It is often left to the teacher's discretion. The completion of the study of a talmudic tractate is marked by a closure ceremony called a *siyyum* during which the best students recite a *ḥiddush* or are tested in front of the notables and the rabbinic authorities, the whole thing ending in a joyous celebration.

The rank of rabbi, *semikhah l-rabbanut* (comparable to the Muslim scholar's *ijaza*) was publicly conferred by means of a blessing (*berakhah*) with a hand laid on the head, according to the preface to a book written at the beginning of the twentieth century. But in this field, too, certain old families possessed a monopoly, the *serarah*, which is discussed elsewhere.

*Teaching Methods*

Here we come face to face with ancient and medieval conceptions of education, the "rote school" reviled by modern teachers. The traditional teaching methods held in high honor in the Christian, Muslim, and Jewish schools of the Middle Ages have survived till our day in the ḥeder and yeshîbâh, just as they have in the *msid* or *medersa*. These methods consist of forming automatic mental reactions and intellectual habits in which repetition and memorization play a considerable part.

The participation of all the bodily organs during the recitation of the sacred texts, as commanded by tradition, involves gesture and speech at one and the same time. *Ma'aseh Efod*, a grammar by a fourteenth-century Hispano-Maghrebian writer, Profiat Duran, states: "The child must move all his body when he learns. Why? In Exodus 20:15, it is said, apropos the revelation of the Torah on Mount Sinai: 'The people . . . saw it, [and] they trembled [lit., swayed].' In addition, the cantillation itself aids memorization. . . . This melodical reading brings joy and the desire to learn to the person who applies himself to it, awakens the powers of the soul and stimulates them; what is more, it makes it easier for the memory to retain what is learned."

Study at the yeshîbâh level is conducted in the same spirit. Memorization of the passage in the Talmud or halakhah often precedes everything else. The master understands that comprehension can assist memory, and thus he comments on the text, employs talmudic dialectic, uses all the resources of discussion, hair-splitting. But memory has the last word: the student must memorize all the arguments that accompany the study of the *sugya* (the Aramaic term designating the subject dealt with) and has to reproduce them in the form in which he receives them. In so doing, he is remaining faithful to the methods of his ancestors in the yeshîbot of Babylon or Eretz Israel sixteen centuries earlier.

As the amount of knowledge to be remembered is considerable, particularly on questions of *halakhah psuqah*, "law and rabbinical jurisprudence," the teacher resorts to refined mnemonic techniques. He sagely formulates the material with a view to its easy acquisition by the student. The use of acronyms and abbreviations (*notarikon*) and writing out certain codes in verse or rhyming prose (tractates relating to the laws of *sheḥiṭah* [ritual slaughter] in particular) makes it easier to remember the ideas studied.

### *The Education of Girls*

The divergent points of view on the subject of the education of girls held by scholars of the law are well known, and also the general opinion that has prevailed in Jewish communities as a whole. As girls are not subject to the obligation to participate in worship, the essential object of education, they are exempt from learning either the Written Law or the Oral Law. Until marriage, often at a very early age (ten or twelve), their education is carried out entirely within the family, by relationships and contacts with other women.

With some rare exceptions, girls do not learn to read and write. They watch over the household tasks. Theirs will be the responsibility for kashrut in the household, the task of ensuring respect for the laws and traditions relating to the proper maintenance of a Jewish home. They will be almost exclusively entrusted with putting into practice a large number of commandments, such as those relating to Shabbat (lighting the candles, among others) and to the ritual and dietary prohibitions of the major festivals (especially Passover).

Women are not forbidden to practice a profession. The skilled dressmaker or embroiderer, often surrounded by apprentices, works for a Jewish or Muslim clientele(making dresses, embroidering in gold or silver thread on cloth or leather, or doing broderie anglaise on small wooden frames). Female professional singers and storytellers are invited to family celebrations, and female professional mourners to funeral vigils. Women are also matchmakers, and we have seen how honorable, as well as indispensable, the role of the midwife (*qabla*) is in Maghrebian societies.

Illiteracy does not exclude women from participation in the spiritual life of the home, and their role in the education of their children is sometimes considerable. Many indeed are the women who have deserved the description *'eshet ḥayil* ("woman of worth"; see Proverbs 31:10).

The woman is the soul of the home, its calendar and its pendulum. Like "wise" men and pious scholars, some women observe the unbroken six-day fast called *ta'anit hafsaqah* in Hebrew; the Judeo-Arabic term *settiya*, "period of six days," used to designate it, is more meaningful. What it actually involves is total abstinence from food and drink for six consecutive days, including the nights. The fast commences at dawn on Sunday and ends when Shabbat comes in at sunset on Friday evening, with an appropriate ceremony and special liturgy. I personally knew an old lady of very modest means, a washerwoman by trade, who observed the *settiya* regularly. She set aside a good part of her wages for the purchase of her shroud and the site of her grave in the Mogador cemetery.

The creation of educational institutions for girls called *em habanim*, "mother of children," at the beginning of the twentieth century was made possible by the mothers of families in Fez, Meknès, and Sefrou and the initiative of a Russian rabbi, R. Ẓe'ev Halperin, passing through Morocco.

Women are not illiterate in every part of the Mahgreb. Young girls in Tangier and Tetuán do, in fact, receive an education which enables them to read the Hebrew text of the prayers and the Judeo-Arabic translation. Women have been seen gathered on a patio, devoting Saturday or festival afternoons to reading *Me'am Lo'ez* (a monumental compilation in Ladino, written by R. Isaac Kuli and first published in Constantinople in 1730).

Thus one must not envision the Maghrebian Jewish woman as a sort of perpetual minor. In the framework of a male-dominated society, she is not as unobtrusive as might at first sight be thought.

In a civilization where old age on its own confers rights, the elderly lady is one of the people whose advice is sought and often taken. There are even occasions when she is seen acting as confidante and counselor to the wife of the governor of a large town, in Fez, Meknès, Marrakesh, and Mogador, even to the queen-mother in the royal palace in Rabat.

### *Continuing Education Through Homily and Preaching*

The study that begins in childhood and adolescence is carried on till a mature age—all one's life in the case of a confirmed scholar.

Jewish communities offer a sort of continuing education through the preaching on holy days (Sabbaths and festivals), night-time sessions when Bible, Zohar, and musar (rabbinical ethics) are studied, and *piyyuṭim* (vocal music combined with poetry) sung either in the synagogue, in the framework of craft or merchant guilds, or in specialized fraternities.

The vocation of the spiritual leader of the community, whether he be a dayyan, a yeshîbâh teacher, or even a craftsman or a merchant whose learning and virtue have qualified him for such a responsibility, is to instruct the adult congregation. His teaching is given in the form of sermons (*drash*) to the people gathered in the synagogue on Saturday or festival afternoons, which are never solely devoted to rest and family life. The preacher (*darshan*) explains and comments on a text, and illustrates it with anecdotes, stories, and legends (aggadah and midrash). His aim is not profound study but popularization. He does not claim to bring the talmudic discussions of the yeshîbâh to an unprepared public.

The preacher is sometimes a foreign rabbi or a representative of the *kolel*, one of the itinerant emissary rabbis, accredited messengers from the Palestinian academies (yeshîbot) and communities, that we have already mentioned.

### *Nocturnal Teaching*

Nocturnal education heads the list of the community's cultural activities (the connection with religion and worship is obvious). Moroccan rabbis, like all scholars of the law faithful to talmudic and midrashic tradition, attribute the greatest virtue to intellectual work accomplished at night and to the fulfillment of the duty to study during the long night watches.

Instruction in this tradition include Tractate Sanhedrin 94b, which gives an allegorical interpretation of Isaiah 10:27: "The oil of Hezekiah [i.e., the night-time study by the light of an oil lamp encouraged by Hezekiah] has broken the yoke of Sennacherib." The Midrash interprets Leviticus 24:2 and Exodus 27:20 as a commandment valid for all generations and for all places of worship (the light of the oil lamps must never fail so that study is never interrupted, even at night). Maimonides, in his *Book of Knowledge*, states: "it is only during the night that man acquires the major part of his learning. Therefore, whosoever wants to deserve the crown of the law must watch that he does not waste any of his nights in sleep . . . but devotes all of them to study of the law and to words of wisdom."

In Morocco, systematic courses on Bible (especially texts from the Prophets, which there is no time to learn in ḥeder or yeshîbâh), the *Shulḥan 'Aruk*, and the Talmud are usually given in the first third of the night. Members of confraternities called Ḥebrot Rabbi Shim'ôn bar Yohay devote the final third of the night to reading the Zohar after the *tiqqun-ḥasot.*[9] Other groups meet during the last hours of the night, before the Shahrît prayers, to listen to lessons on musar given by the rabbi, who reads, translates, and comments on one of the books dealing with this discipline.

The teaching of *piyyuṭim* (liturgical, even profane, songs) is confined to specialized confraternities (*ḥebrot*) led by teachers of renown (*payṭanim*) who are singers and composers. Song-loving worshipers gather round the teacher and his disciples for long vigils which generally take place during the three or four hours before dawn on Saturday mornings in a large synagogue in the town. The names of the cantors of the generation that has just died out include R. David ben Baruk Iflaḥ, R. David Elqayim, R. Ḥayyim Afriat (Mogador), R. David Bouzaglo (Casablanca), and Nessinn Neqqab (Fez).

The *payṭan* sings at circumcision, bar-miṣwah, and wedding ceremonies, as well as on festival days, in the synagogue or in the homes of wealthy notables, and lives off the gifts given him on these occasions. It is no negligible source of income.

If, during the night, adults, young and old, participate in vigils with the Zohar and *piyyuṭim*, in courses on the Talmud and *dinim*, or listen patiently to lessons on musar, then during the day too, in off-peak hours or after the souk, it is not unusual to see study groups gathered in a merchant's or craftsman's shop and overflowing into the street. They will be discussing a point of halakhah, debating a talmudic question, or commenting on a text. A talmudic tractate, a shorter *Shulḥan 'Aruk*, a *mqeṣṣiya* (a common Judeo-Arabic name for the Bible) have their places on a rack or under the counter and are consulted when the need arises. Pious men always have a psalter within arm's reach and devote any spare time, however brief, to reading the songs of David.

During my last visit to Mogador, in August 1963, I was present at a talmudic discussion in which a butcher, a grain broker, and a rabbi participated. It took place in the shop of a lumber merchant during the afternoon of a working day, when the butcher had closed his business and was making the rounds of his customers to collect what they owed him.

---

9. The *tiqqun* + *haṣot* is a special liturgy made up of psalms and elegies. Its theme is the destruction of the Temple in Jerusalem and the bitterness of the exile.

### *Apprenticeship to a Trade*

To teach your son a trade is a commandment of the law, and rabbinic literature is rich in teachings on this theme.[10] A child generally learns his father's trade: jewelery, joinery, tailoring and clothing manufacture, the production of combs to card wool, and so on. If a boy intends to go into business, he starts with a small case of goodies which he sells on the street or else accompanies his father or a close relative to the regional souks.

Apprenticeship lasts a long time. The apprentice learns the craft by watching the craftsman work. When he knows the ropes, he opens a shop if he has the wherewithal, or continues to serve his master in the same workshop. Teaching and apprenticeship are intimately linked in some fields but conflict in others. It is in the tradesman's shop or office that the tools of arithmetic are learned (addition, subtraction, multiplication, but only rarely division), as well as the conversion of money, the writing of correspondence, and occasionally, but very seldom, the rudiments of Arabic (reading commercial certificates or documents). On the other hand, the spiritual leaders are always on the watch for premature apprenticeship and its pernicious repercussions on school attendance.

Apprenticeship to a trade does not prevent the pursuit of study. As has been seen, young men and adults continue to learn at night, on Saturdays and festivals, as well as in any spare time throughout their working lives.

A great Moroccan scholar, R. Yosef Messas, who died in Israel a few years ago after having served as chief rabbi of Haifa, told me about the teaching of his colleagues in ḥeder and yeshîbâh. Half regretfully, half derisively, he added, paraphrasing Isaiah 29:13, "Their teaching is only a lesson learned by rote, made up of man's commandments."

Be that as it may, this teaching is everywhere. It ensures the education of spiritual leaders for the community. It preserves for Judaism generations of Jews who are loyal to their faith and attached to the ancestral tradition. It prevents the poverty-stricken Jew from floundering in the obscurantism of illiteracy. The cultivated or learned Jew has a spiritual life that consoles him for the disappointments of a hard

---

10. Since one must not derive material benefit from knowledge acquired at the bet ha-midrash school, it is necessary to learn a trade to provide for one's needs (Pirke Abot, and tractates Berakhot and Kiddushin of the Talmud).

life and very often fills his existence with light and joy. The superficial observer never grasps the existence of these emotions. Foreign visitors have barely a suspicion of their presence. But they make the citizen of the mellahs say, with the psalmist of yore: "This is my comfort in my affliction, that Thy word hath given me life" (Psalms 119:50).

## *The Period of Change and Reform*

Beginning in the last decades of the nineteenth century, while the ancient ḥeder and the old yeshîbâh pursued their accustomed course, the Alliance Israélite Universelle (AIU) initiated and expanded its projects in Morocco. It introduced the French spirit and French teaching methods, a laicism and secularization that gave rise to some reservations at first and caused distress to rabbis and Jews attached to ancestral tradition, but which everyone adapted to eventually.

Even more, the communities were stimulated by the example of the modern AIU school, or reacted to it, by opening a certain number of institutions (talmud-torahs) organized more rationally than the antiquated ḥeder. As originally conceived, these were intended to provide a revived form of traditional education on a full-time basis, but their syllabuses gave progressively more time to secular subjects. In the same period, a Jewish women's institution, Em-Habanim was spreading to the large towns.

After the Second World War, two American Jewish Orthodox organizations, Otzar ha-Torah and Oholei Yosef Yitzhak, the latter better known as Lubavitch, anxious to ensure the continuity of traditional teaching, which was losing ground to the modern school, created a network of schools throughout Morocco. These give priority to sacred studies and very often, in the mellahs of the Atlas or the Saharan borderlands, are the sole substitute for the old ḥedarim and preserve the same appearance.

Attempts at change and reform are to some small extent penetrating the yeshîbâh, which, however, is attracting fewer and fewer young people, seduced by the new life outside the ghetto. Despite measures by the authorities to arrest their expansion, Zionist ideas are filtering into the mellah, as shown in the spread of modern Hebrew and its literature.

The Council of the Communities has founded the Institut des Hautes Études Rabbinique in Rabat to educate judges and clerks for the rabbinical courts and other servants of the cult. What we are seeing here now is a regeneration of Hebraic and religious education. This is a result of the efforts of the AIU and its leaders in creating the École Normale hebraïque in Casablanca, intended to provide teaching staff for the remodeled discipline. Here, the student-teacher receives solid Hebraic training and a general education recognized by official diplomas in order to carry out his new duties.

When Morocco regained its independence and Moroccan Jews resumed contact with the classical Arabic language, they rediscovered a new humanity, enriching it with knowledge of the sister Hebrew language and its teachings and by the universal humanities which they are acquiring on the benches of the remodeled school.

## MARRIAGE

### *Major Trends in Family Law*

The toshabim ("natives") applied the old talmudic law, supplemented and adapted by local custom. After the arrival of the megorashim (Spanish and Portuguese exiles), it co-existed with the law defined in the Castilian *taqqanot*, which gradually entered Moroccan Hebraic jurisprudence. This itself evolved, taking into account the demands of the environment and the contribution of the *Shulḥan 'Aruk* (Joseph Qaro's sixteenth-century code), which codified and unified the manifold, often contradictory, decisions of earlier jurisprudence. Eventually, "Castilian" law came to prevail in all the communities of Moroccan Jewry whatever their origins. Recently, the Council of Moroccan Chief Rabbis adopted a series of ordinances standardizing matrimonial and testamentary regulations (1947–55).

### *Betrothal*

A request to marry (*shiddukhin* in Hebrew, *khotba* in Arabic), followed by a betrothal ceremony (Hebrew *'erusin*; Arabic *mlâk* or *rsîm*), is given concrete form by gifts (*sablonot*) that the man, who is binding himself by a formal promise of marriage, offers his future wife. These gifts consist of seven golden bracelets known as the *semaine* (French for "week," indicating a set of seven objects), a ring set with precious stones, and some silk kerchiefs. In addition, the "betrothal tray" contains five sugar-loaves, henna, perfumes, sweets, dried fruit (almonds, nuts, dates, figs).

The betrothal follows customs and conventions which, if violated, give rise to conflicts that the juridico-religious authorities are called on to settle. The following specific examples of such issues are taken from communal registers dating back over the past four centuries:

- A male, rejected some time after the betrothal, was only able to recover a fraction of the *sablonot*, valued at fifty ounces of silver in the money of the kingdom of Fez.
- A girl's parents wanted to separate her from her betrothed in order to marry her to someone else. This attempt was condemned by the judge, who threatened its authors with the *ḥerem* (anathema).
- The breaking of an engagement was allowed only for serious reasons that could cast a slur on the family's honor: conversion to Islam by a member of the family, for example.
- A boy and a girl, both minors, were promised to each other in formal betrothal by their parents. When the boy grew up, he did not like the girl very much. The promise of marriage was adjudged null and void by the rabbinic court of Fez.
- If the fiancé died before the marriage, his parents or close relations recovered the betrothal presents and any other pledge attached to the promise of marriage.
- It is customary in Jewish and Muslim Maghrebian society for the parents of a boy to name his future wife, and the youth must usually fall in with their choice. If the young man's wishes do not conform to filial piety, this gives birth to conflicts of the sort decided by the Fez court. The girl's opinion is not asked, however, and she must almost always bow to her parents' decision.
- The request to marry is made by the suitor's father. He speaks directly to the father of the girl if the families are acquainted, but most often a professional third party is commissioned to make the approach: a professional matchmaker, who may be either a man or a woman.

Other societies far removed from the Maghrebian world have similar customs. Milan Kundera describes some of these in his book *The Joke*:

> The groom was never the subject of the wedding. He was its object, He was not getting married. He was being married. . . . He was not to speak or act. The patriarch acted and spoke for him. But not even the patriarch. It was age-old tradition that men experienced one after the other, inspiriting them with its comforting flow.

During the betrothal period, the couple must not meet or see each other, the girl not being allowed to show herself in the street on any pretext. It is the families who make the preparations for the wedding: the girl's trousseau, the quantities of jams and preserves that are stored away in bottles and jars, and so forth.

## *Traditional Jewish Marriage and Muslim Ṣadâq*

Marriage, as an institution of religious law, is sanctified by the marriage blessing and by the ritual formula that accompanies the groom's handing of a coin or some other valuable object (an item of metal jewelry) to his bride. These are two aspects of the same ceremony, the same rite that solemnly consecrates the couple's legitimate and legal union. The sanctification of the marriage is then made by the Kiddush, the seven blessings over wine, and the consecrated formula, *Hare 'at meqqudeshet li beṭabba'at zo ke-dat Mosheh we-Yisrael*, "By this ring you are sanctified to me according to the law of Moses and of Israel." The union is made real by the consummation of the marriage, generally described by the Hebrew term *nissu'in*, derived from a Hebraic verb meaning "to carry" the bride to the conjugal home.

Marriage involves a contract that comprises a certain number of provisions, primarily intended to protect the woman's financial interests. The contract can also be a means for the couple and their families to choose one of three different matrimonial models: *ṣadâq*, traditional, or Castilian.

The ketubbah, or marriage contract, fixes the amount of the legal dowry to which the *addition* and the wife's contribution are added (see below). If the husband predeceases the wife or if there is a divorce, the full total of the sums written into the ketubbah revert, in principle, to the wife, who also holds a legal mortgage on her husband's possessions to the amount of their value.

Under both the traditional and the Castilian system, the ketubbah could be modified, by common consent, by adding extra clauses, generally in order to better protect the woman's interests.

The parties concerned could replace the Jewish marriage contract, the ketubbah, with a contract known as the *ṣadâq* from the term for the marriage settlement made by the husband. The *ṣadâq* was concluded before a Muslim court made up of a *qadi* and his two witnesses to a deed (*'udûl*) or simply by these last two. There is evidence that this practice still existed at the end of the sixteenth and the beginning of the seventeenth centuries in the Jewish community of Fez. The *taqqanot* of 1585 and 1603 state that "the father-in-law can require of his son-in-law that the document of *ṣadâq* be concluded before a civil [Muslim] court if the son-in-law is a violent person of low repute. The amount of the *ṣadâq* is left to the court's discretion."

The traditional system, which continued to be applied by the toshabim, was the legal system common to the Jewish world. It was based on the ancient talmudic law adapted to local customs and later to Qaro's code.

### The Castilian Matrimonial System

The Castilian system is the body of rules of law governing the conjugal or family unit in matters of personal status and possessions that the megorashim had known in their country of origin.

The original nature of the Castilian system lies in two eminently important provisions, two innovations foreign, as it were, to the traditional talmudic system in force in the autochthonous communities. They signified a considerable improvement in the position of the wife and children in the family: on the one hand, the creation of a statutory joint estate between the couple on the dissolution of the marriage by the death of either partner, and on the other, the prohibition of polygamy.

The rules that governed the statutory common estate were applied the moment succession was open, that is, on the death of one of the couple. The common estate was then liquidated, a complex operation that warranted appeal to the rabbinic authority to draw up an inventory of the possessions in existence on the actual day of death. These were then divided according to the procedure set down in the Castilian *taqqanot*.

### Monogamy, Bigamy, and Polygamy

Polygamy is permitted by talmudic law, within certain limits; and toshabim, by virtue of their matrimonial system in accordance with this law, could have more than one legitimate wife. However, well before the arrival of the Spanish emigrants, the families of brides-to-be began seeking to obtain safeguards from the intended husbands against the option allowed by law of marrying a second wife. A clause was very often added to the ketubbah forbidding the husband to take a second wife without the consent of his wife. In fact, bigamy was limited to the specific case when the first wife was barren and there was occasion to apply the requirement of levirate, the obligation that the law of Moses places on the brother of a dead man to marry the childless widow in order to secure him descendants (Deuteronomy 25:5).

Note that polygamy is generally regarded as a concession to customs and practices, something to be tolerated. Legislation has always had a tendency to restrain its practice.

The Castilian ordinances, dating from 1494, made the prohibitive clause referring to bigamy binding, usually linking it with another provision that bound the husband to obtain the wife's agreement to a change of residence. In the Castilian ketubbah, these provisions were formulated as follows: ". . . the aforesaid husband is forbidden to contract any other marriage for so long as his marriage to his above-named wife shall last, and to leave this town to reside in another without her consent, on pain of being forced to hand her the *geṭ*+ [writ of divorce] by paying her in cash the total amount of her marriage settlement fixed at the sum of ______. The present contract is made and accepted by the two partners named below under the Mosaic system known as the Castilian system."

The megorashim seem to have applied this system without any difficulty for almost a century, and bigamy disappeared, at least in those circles. Before long, however, the system met with resistance from public opinion (probably influenced by local customs and the practices of toshabim still attached to the traditional system), and in 1593 those who objected to the Castilian system succeeded in obtaining a reversion to toleration of bigamy on certain conditions. These conditions were extended in 1599 when a new measure permitted bigamy in cases where the husband's first wife had not born male children.

The rabbinate's opposition to greater concessions in favor of bigamy led the sultan to intervene, misled by a few influential Jewish notables who accused the rabbis of transgressing talmudic law. A royal edict authorized Jewish subjects to practice bigamy (and even polygamy). The rabbinate complied on the basis of the principle that "the law of the land is the law." But the injured wives threatened to renounce the religion.

A new appeal to the palace, led by a delegation of rabbis and members of the *ma'amad* (community council), persuaded the sultan to restore rabbinical authority in matters concerning personal status. The edict does not seem to have been repealed, but it remained without practical effect. A compromise was drawn up in the form of a *taqqanah*, dated 1600, which left the rabbinical court the option of consenting to new deviations from the prohibition on bigamy, "allowing the husband to take a second wife if the physiological condition of the first makes all cohabitation [sexual relations] impossible or if there is certainty that she is no longer able to bear children, even if there are already children of the male sex."

The violation of the status of the dhimmis (Jewish tributaries) which the sultan's interference in this matter constituted, is almost unique in the annals of the Moroccan community. And it was fear of seeing a dangerous precedent created that prompted the factions in this dispute to come to terms.

Thus the ordinances of 1494 and 1497 absolutely prohibiting bigamy fell into disuse. The rabbinate was, for practical purposes, obliged to ratify accomplished facts, resorting to compromise or using legal contrivances to justify situations that openly deviated from the earlier provisions of the *taqqanot castillanes.*

Later legislation provides many examples. For instance, bigamy was permitted if the first wife was barren, in order to make the practice of the levirate possible; in cases where a husband, finding himself a long distance away from his first wife, could not join her for serious reasons (e.g., blocked or unsafe roads); and if the first wife was ill, making conjugal relations impossible.

The toshabim were not obliged to bow to the Castilian *taqqanot* and by virtue of their own system retained, at least in theory, the freedom to take as many wives as they wished. On this subject, a document mentions that "the inhabitants of the land, *toshabe ha-'areṣ*, customarily repudiated their wife when they found one who was more beautiful, and took a second wife even when they had children born of the first."

Cases of polygamy (three or four wives) are rare; there is, however, evidence of polygamy in the seventeenth century in Fez, where it came to the knowledge of the rabbinic courts in connection with the division of an inheritance.

### *Marriage Rites and Ceremonies*

The ceremonial rhythm of marriage is punctuated by highlights. They reach their peak on a Wednesday, the day of the "seven blessings," with a ritual containing a thousand and one "actions," quite a long ceremony, and festivities that last for three or four weeks, eight days at the minimum. The brilliance, luxury, and ostentation of the latter vary with the means and pretensions of the families.

The dual proceedings of ketubbah and qiddushin are the hallmark of Jewish marriage the world over. But here, in addition, there is a whole collection of observances, practices, and customs, a system of sacred or symbolic rites belonging to a magico-ritualistic space where all Maghrebian societies, whether Arabo-Berber or Judeo-Muslim, meet, without distinction as to ethnic or religious origin.

This is a cultural landscape, an anthropological "commons," where all autochthonous, aboriginal mankind finds itself at one in fear of the mysterious world of demons, the realm of supernatural powers. The fact is that the time of marriage is considered eminently critical and dangerous, like all periods of passage in life. And the newlyweds are thought to be very vulnerable, threatened by all sorts of evil spells, sorcery, malevolent magical processes, most particularly the dreaded knotting of the aiguillette, the *itqaf* or *ribat*, "stoppage" or "closure," a binding ritual intended to induce sexual potency and the consummation of the marriage.

The couple must therefore be protected by talismans and amulets, *shemirot*, "magical inscriptions," similar to those that protect mother and child at birth. On the positive side, *berakhah*, happiness and success (the *baraka* of Arab-Muslim societies), has to be attracted to the young couple. This is the aim of the many and varied rites, always connected to music and singing and dancing, which strengthen their magical nature: *qaṣida* and *'arubi*, ballads and ritornellos, in Arabic or Berber; *cantigas* and *canciones* in Hispanophone communities of Castilian origin; and most especially, *piyyuṭim*, Hebraic epithalamia, integrated into the marriage liturgy and sung in the synagogue or at services held in the home of the newlyweds.

Here we can give no more than a very brief description of this long and complex ritualism, based on a few significant reference points and some striking features. The task is made no easier by the fact that its components vary from one town or mellah to another.

The ceremonies begin on the second Sabbath before the Wednesday of the actual wedding. This Sabbath is called *sebt er-rsîm*, "the Sabbath of appointment" or "the Sabbath of the sign," very probably because on that day the bridegroom and "sultan" (Berber, *asli*) appoints his guard of honor, or "viziers" (Berber *islan*, plural of *asli*), who are also called *baḥurim* (Hebrew) and *'azara* (Arabic), terms meaning "young men, bachelors."

The following Thursday is the day of the *azmumeg*, a Berber word of unknown etymology, applied to a ceremony in which an egg is broken over the bride's head. The liquid runs down her untied hair. Those present take turns soaking their hands in a bowl of henna and put the scented paste on the young woman's head. A piece of calico is then attached to her hair which has to be kept in this state until the following Tuesday, "bath and henna day."

The next Sabbath is usually called *sebt l-islan*, "the Sabbath of the king and his viziers," marked by a gathering of the betrothed couple and their unmarried friends. In Mogador, the *islan* is also the monetary gift offered by the family and friends to the bridegroom's parents. This day is sometimes called *sebt ar-ray*, the "Sabbath of deliberation, of counsel."

The following Monday is the day of "taking the oath," *nhar es-sbu'a* or *nhar el-qenyan* (these are the hebraic terms *shebu'ah*, "oath," and *qinyan*, "legal acquisition, act of acquisition"). The ketubbah, the solemn contract, which requires the services of a sofer (notary) representing the rabbinic authority, is written and accepted before the marriage ceremony. The ketubbah acts as both the *qinyan shṭar* and the *qinyan sudar*. The first is the acquisition by a notarial deed (*shṭar*), a document which the bridegroom personally hands to his bride, and which the parents guard with care. At the same time, the interested parties pledge themselves by *qinyan sudar*, a symbolic act of acquisition: the betrothed couple declare that they accept the conditions written into the ketubbah by "grasping" a *sudar* (handkerchief) held out by the notary. Holding the handkerchief in this way makes their union an actuality.

This symbolic act can be replaced or embellished in various ways. In Fez, the bridegroom is girded with a piece of white fabric, knotted round his waist seven times, which his betrothed wore on her head the day before, specifically called *nhar eṭ-ṭerf le-byed*, "day of the piece of white [cloth]." Other societies have similar "actions." Jacques Soustelle, for instance, mentions that among the Aztecs the young man's coat and the girl's bodice are knotted together.

The amount of the ketubbah is fixed by the *taqqanah* of 1497 at a minimum of twenty ounces (*uqiyas*) of silver divided according to custom into the *tosefet*, the "addition" to the legal dowry, the *mattanah*, a gracious "gift" from the husband, and the *nedunya*, the woman's contribution (trousseau and others), over and above the two-hundred-zuz marriage settlement for a virgin and the hundred-zuz marriage settlement for a widow or a divorcee. (The zuz was a silver coin, a reminiscence of biblical and immediately postbiblical times, equal to a quarter of a shekel and worth about 3.5 grams of silver.)

There was no upper limit to this sum. It varied depending on the bridegroom's wealth, the demands of the future wife and her family, the period when the wedding occurred, and the economic situation.

A judge of the Fez court at the end of the seventeenth century, Jacob Aben Sur, mentions that some families had gotten into the habit of writing fabulous sums into the ketubbah out of vanity: 5,000 ounces at Fez, 15,000 at Salé, 18,000 at Tetuán. The rabbinate often warned the parties concerned about such practices, which often caused serious disputes when the ketubbah had to be liquidated. Not so long ago (in the 1940s and 1950s), the sum of the ketubbah was often reckoned in millions of francs.

A sacrificial rite accompanies the ceremony of the taking of the oath. The traditional cow is brought onto the patio with much pomp, decked out in feminine finery: silk kerchief, jewelery, ribbons, flowers, and so on. The animal is ritually slaughtered by the shoḥeṭ. Its flesh will be used to prepare the many dishes to feed the numerous guests.

The "bride's bath," which represents the crucial purification rite, takes place on the Tuesday afternoon, in the communal baths reserved for ablutions of this type in the mellah. This is also the occasion for magical practices intended to protect the bride from demonic powers jealous of her happiness. The oldest of the women who accompany her throws an offering to the *shedim* (demons) into the water: jam from a dish, a glass of wine, a comb and cosmetics. The bride's head is washed and everything that falls from it—hair, henna, bits of egg—is mixed together with sugar and corn, squeezed up in white calico, and stuffed into the nuptial mattress. When the bride returns from the bath, her hair is dressed, she is clothed, made up, perfumed, and heavily decked with gold and silver jewelery. She is now ready for the great ceremony known as the henna, which takes place on the Tuesday evening, *lilt al-ḥanna*, "the night of henna," or *al-lila la-kbira*, "the great night."

On the Wednesday comes the solemn celebration of the marriage, *al-'ars*, by the "seven blessings" (*sheba' berakhot*) and by the public reading of the ketubbah. This is the day when the bride moves into the conjugal home. The ceremony takes place, on pain of nullity, in the presence of ten adults of the male sex (the minyan, or quorum, required for public prayer) one of whom has to be a rabbi, a judge, or a member of the *ma'amad*.

> Whomsoever marries only in the presence of two witnesses will be fined a sum left to the discretion of the nagid [lit. "prince," i.e., head of the community] and judges; he will be imprisoned, Sabbaths and festival days included, until he consents to hand the new bride a *geṭ*. If the parents agree to give him their daughter as wife, he must still institute the union that observes the law.

There is also provision for sanctions against the two witnesses: corporal punishment and heavy fines (50 ounces of silver).

Until quite recently, rabbinic courts constantly condemned these "furtive" marriages and battled against the stubbornness with which certain circles persisted in following the talmudic prescriptions, very liberal in this area, that facilitated the maneuvers of suitors tempted to take surprise advantage of a young girl's trust with the complicity of two unscrupulous witnesses.

After the bath of purification (*ṭebilah*) and a special liturgy led by a cantor in which *piyyuṭim* predominate over the usual ritual, the bridegroom puts on his ceremonial dress, a traditional costume consisting mainly of baggy cloth trousers (*serwal*), an embroidered waistcoat decorated with silk buttons (*bed'iyya*), and a long cloth jacket (*zokha*) tied at the waist with a silk belt.

The bride is enthroned on the *talamon*, or "marriage seat" (from the Spanish *talamo*, "armchair"; the custom was imported from Spain by the megorashim), made up, perfumed, adorned with gold and precious stones. She is resplendent in her ceremonial garb, the grand and sumptuous outfit known as *al-keswa la-kbira*. Its striking features are the gold-embroidered velvet tucker (*ktef*), the garnet or green velvet bodice, decorated with gold braid and silver buttons (*ghonbaj*), a velvet skirt of the same color (*zeltita*) adorned with gold braid and concealing several petticoats (*sayat*), a wide, stiff velvet belt embroidered with gold and beads (*ḥzam* or *mḍamma*), gold-embroidered slippers (*serbil*), full sleeves of embroidered silk voile (*kmam et-tesmira*), a crown-shaped headdress laden with pearls, emeralds, rubies, and gold coins (*khmar* or *swalef*), a long, fine silk scarf, which holds back her hair (*festul*), and a white or green silk kerchief (*sebniyya*) covered by a light white veil (*elbelo*, from the Spanish *velo*) over her face.

The families of most newlywed couples in the mellahs do not have such a costume at their disposal. Wealthy families lend them to others for the occasion.

A rabbi or a learned member of the family publicly reads out the ketubbah, written on new parchment and illuminated by a skilled scribe who is also something of an artist. Someone else recites the seven blessings. The bridegroom (*ḥatan*) drinks wine over which a blessing has been made and hands it to the bride (*kallah*) to drink, then breaks the glass in memory of the destruction of the Temple in Jerusalem. There follows a circumambulatory rite known as *haqqafot*, consisting of going round the patio seven times. Then the bride is carried in procession to her new home to spend the first night, called *lilt ar-raḥa*, "the night of rest."

The bridegroom is required to fast until evening, when he shares the ritual meal with his wife. The meal, specially prepared for the two of them, consists of pigeons stuffed with almonds and raisins and heavily spiced.

The day after, *nhar eṣ-ṣbaḥ*, the "first morning" of married life, is an important day in the couple's life. If *ṣbaḥ* literally means "morning," it also describes the linen spotted with blood, the irrefutable proof of the virginity, the "purity," of the new wife, her honor and her pride. The same word is also used for the wedding gift in cash that the newlyweds receive from friends and close and distant relatives on that day.

The ceremonies, always accompanied by festivities, continue on the following days: "the Sabbath of the new husband," *sebt la-'ros*; "the day of the binding," *nhar ar-rabṭa* (the man ties the *mḍamma*, "belt," to the woman, treading on her toes).

On Wednesday, "the day of the fish," *nhar al-ḥut*, the seventh day of the marriage, the bridegroom goes out for the first time, making his way, after morning prayers, to nearby gardens with his guard of honor, close family, and friends. But in the evening a very significant ceremony takes place around two shad or some other fish: whichever of the young couple finishes dismembering the fish first will gain the upper hand in the home (however, the test involves some "cheating" intended to spare the legitimate sensitivity of both competitors).

On "the Sabbath of repentance," *sebt en-ndama*, the guard of honor stages a short play parodying the marriage; and the *tonaboda*, from the Spanish *tornaboda*, "return from the wedding," is marked by the bride's first ritual bath since her marriage. It constitutes the closure of the wedding ceremonies and of the period of rejoicing that accompanies them.

### *Epithalamia: Marriage Poetry and Songs*

The Hebrew marriage songs reproduced here belong to an ancient poetic series with evocative titles borrowed from the Bible and, very paradoxically, from the Book of Jeremiah, the prophet of lamentation but also of consolation. They are the "rejoicings" of the newlyweds; "the voice of mirth and the voice of gladness, the voice of the bridegroom and the voice of the bride" (Jeremiah 7:34). A piece with a chorus, very widespread among Maghrebian cantors and also in anthologies in the Islamic East and West, is reminiscent of the scenario of the Song of Songs. We recorded a musical version of it in 1957, finely performed by a famous Moroccan cantor, Rabbi David Bouzaglo. It begins with this melodious line:

> This is the time of love, my betrothed, come into my garden.
> The vine has flowered; the pomegranate is budding.

Like most hebraic poetry written for a specific occasions—the compositions sung at circumcisions or dedicated to the bar miṣwah—the basic themes of the epithalamia that celebrate the marriage of the newly weds, the *ḥatan* and *kallah*, reflect the wish to instruct.

Furthermore, they are closely connected with the liturgy specific to the marriage ceremony and the various events that accompany it. There are a considerable number of marriage poems and songs composed by Moroccan poets, probably because of the length of the festivities and the many rituals that punctuate the week following the marriage blessing, when the newlyweds are isolated and forbidden to leave the home.

The anthology of Jacob Aben Sur, a Moroccan poet from Fez (seventeenth to eighteenth century) contains twenty-three marriage songs, collected under the title *Le-Birkat Ḥatanim*, "for the blessing of the newlyweds." Most are *reshuyot*, "prologues" intended to flank parts of the grace after the meals, the various liturgical sections of Shaḥrit and 'Arbit, the morning and evening services, and, particularly, each verse of the lesson from the Bible reserved for the bridegroom (Genesis 24:1–7). Hymns accompany him as "he goes up to the *sefer*."

One of the latter, a poem of the *muwashshaḥ* type, extols the pleasures of married life in the following terms:

> Your soul will always delight in rich (and savory) foods,
> Wheat from Minnit, honey and fine dishes.

Also worth mentioning in this series are a poetic prologue, the first verse of which, its author claims, was composed in a dream, and a long mystical poem, dedicated to the bride, which represents her beloved sometimes as the Torah, and sometimes as the Community of Israel united with God, as in the symbolism of the kabbalah. The text that introduces this composition is already very significant in this respect.

> It is the voice of my beloved.
> He comes like a husband running to meet his new bride;
> He speaks of the marriage covenant to the heart of the young girl, the virgin of Israel.

An epithalamium with an instructive aim in mind, written "for the marriage procession," must also be noted. The custom of first carrying out the legal sanctification of the marriage at the home of the bride's parents before conducting her at nightfall to her new husband's house comes from an old tradition that seems to belong essentially to megorashim families originally from Spain.

Whether or not this be so, the "transport" of the bride in procession is subject to a strict ceremonial and obeys precise rites. The slow advance is accompanied by music and singing. When the newlyweds belong to a family of notables or rabbis, the ceremony assumes an eminently solemn nature, and the honor of taking the bride over the threshold of her parents' house falls to the leading magistrate of the rabbinical court.

The procession chants numerous wedding songs, including hymns long since fixed by the liturgy and melodies in Castilian or Judeo-Arabic, borrowed from local traditions, which during the course of time have enriched marriage folklore. An epithalamium composed for the occasion by a well-known local poet is sung by its author and his disciples.

The epithalamium that we quote here is a literary composition of this type. It was composed by Jacob Aben Sur, who was a poet but more importantly the spiritual leader of his community (president of the rabbinical court of Fez) and, in this capacity, guardian of the law and tradition. He made his *piyyuṭ* an outburst of rhyming sentences exalting the great ethico-religious values of Judaism. It is an edifying discourse, listing the commandments that the wife must hereafter observe in her new home: the rites of purity (ablutions and ritual baths), the blessings over the lights on the Sabbath eve, the symbolic consecration of the dough by the removal of the *ḥallah* (the portion due the high priest in the time of the Temple in Jerusalem), the virtues of modesty and discretion, charity and goodness, the duty to help the needy who come knocking at the door, and so on. By following these commandments she will deserve to be given a progeny of scholars who will inherit the divine blessing.

As we have already given its substance, it would be superfluous to reproduce this didactic poem here. Instead, we have chosen to print almost the whole text of the beautiful poetic composition whose first two lines have already been quoted. Allegorically dedicated to the Torah and the Community of Israel, it is also chanted at the naming of a newborn daughter, the blessing of the marriage, and on Simḥat Torah, the festival of "Rejoicing of the Law," which occurs on the ninth day of Sukkot.

Graceful doe, sweet maid,
In you perfect beauty and our forebears' mythical strength unite.
Rise up, for the hour of your light and glory is come,
Rise up, rejoice and sing airs of gladness.
Rise up, don your royal diadem.
Dress in scarlet and delights
In brocade and linen tunics, finely sewn.
Of all maids,
You are the fairest, beyond all praise; majestic,
You are bound by the chains of your ancient love.
Every virgin will acclaim your happiness,
To the sound of drum, harp, and flutes.
What say you, girls, of my lover? To my lover
I belong, and he desires (and loves) no other.
You are cinnamon, fragrance of essences, fine marble (or flax) from
  Tarshish,
Emerald and mother of pearl sparkling with glowing fire,
Your eyes shine forth swords and spears.
Your teeth are crystal and your cheek [lit., your temple] a slice of
  pomegranate.

And your body is most beautiful,
Like a palm tree! O you, you are the most magnificent rose!

The Andalusian musical tradition was also used in Moroccan Jewish society. Loved and appreciated, it was adapted to the music of the *piyyuṭim*, to Hebrew-language poetry, both liturgical and designed for the major moments of family life: circumcision, *bar-miṣwah*, and, obviously, marriage ceremonies. We will come back to the relationship between music and poetry and the musical traditions of the Jewish Mahgreb in the discussion of intellectual life in Chapter 5.

## DIVORCE

The marriage bond is dissolved by the death of one of the partners or by a written repudiation, the *geṭ*, which in principle is only available to the husband.

In the interests of women and morality, efforts have been made over the years to limit by various means the exercise of the unilateral and *ad-libitum* right of repudiation which traditional rabbinic legislation confers expressly on the husband. Nevertheless, this right still remains prohibitive, and the grounds for repudiation that the husband—rarely the wife—can invoke cover a very extensive range from the most serious to the most trivial.

• Adultery is the most serious cause. The woman is forbidden to her husband, obliged to hand him the *geṭ*, "repudiation document"; she is also forbidden to her lover, who is subject to a fine and also faces the major threat of excommunication if he approaches the same woman again.

• Refusal to cohabit, a secondary cause of divorce, has several aspects:

1. The wife refuses sexual relations, sometimes pleading that she is the victim of a spell, or abandons the conjugal home; if the man is the guilty party, the divorce is pronounced at his expense, that is to say, he has to hand over the *geṭ* and pay the full amount of the ketubbah.

2. Physical malformation is also regarded as grounds for repudiation and so too, obviously, is sterility. The legal time-lag of ten years is reduced to seven or even five years. Note that the wife can obtain a divorce if the husband is impotent.

3. Decisions are contradictory in cases where the wife refuses to

follow her husband. A wife who refuses to follow her husband when he is forced to seek a livelihood in another town is obliged to do so, despite a clause written into the ketubbah stipulating that "the husband must obtain his wife's consent to any change of residence." In two other cases, on the other hand, when a wife refused to emigrate to Palestine with her husband, she obtained not only her get but the whole or partial settlement of her ketubbah.

Some extreme cases have already been cited—like the husband who repudiates his wife because he finds a more beautiful one or because she neglects her domestic duties.

The law of *yibbum,* the levirate, is applied in Moroccan society. In accordance with the biblical commandment, it compels the brother of a man who dies without issue to marry his widow (Deuteronomy 25:5).

*Ḥaliṣah* ("unshoeing") is in some ways an alternative solution to the levirate, often encouraged by jurisprudence. In principle it is the procedure that the law imposes on a brother-in-law who refuses the levirate, a prescription dating from the biblical period (Deuteronomy 25:9–10): "Then shall his brother's wife draw nigh unto him in the presence of the elders [of the town], and loose his shoe from off his foot, and spit in his face; and she shall answer and say: 'So shall it be done unto the man that doth not build up his brother's house.' And his name shall be called in Israel The House of him that had his shoe loosed."

Although it is relatively easy, repudiation is subject to many formalities, on pain of nullity. These sometimes result in long delays, capable of making the husband reflect and revise a hasty decision that may have resulted from a minor disagreement or passing fit of anger. Meticulous precautions are taken when writing the *geṭ,* in preparing the document, the statement of the formulas, the exact spelling of the names. This extreme strictness is necessary in order to eliminate any possibility of the divorce being nullified once the certificate is written and handed to the woman. In fact, if the woman remarries, and the divorce certificate freeing her from her first marriage is vitiated by a flaw, the second marriage is considered adulterous and the children born of it pronounced illegitimate.

On the occasion of a divorce, under both the traditional and Castilian systems, and on the death of the husband, under the authority of talmudic law, the liquidation of the ketubbah sometimes raises many problems, despite the coercive strength of the written certificate. The customs and practices which also affect this matter need to be taken into account.

Two related questions will be mentioned very briefly: the status of the ʿagunah and the apostate (called *mumar* or *meshummad* in Hebrew).

An ʿagunah is a wife "bound to an absent husband," missing during a journey, most frequently the victim of a mishap which has cost him his life. It is impossible for her to remarry as long as proof of death is not established.

The problem of ʿagunot created by the husband's probable but unprovable death was particularly acute in a country like Morocco, because of the insecurity of the roads. When a husband had to embark on a long sea voyage, he left his wife a provisional writ of divorce (conditional *geṭ*). Thus if he had not returned by a predetermined date, his wife could remarry.

Moroccan rabbis, like their colleagues in other Diaspora communities, have always applied the rules concerning proof of death liberally, in such a way as to permit the first marriage to be dissolved and the "presumed widow," whose fate is often considered worse than death, to remarry.

In the texts in our possession, this proof is almost always based on the "spontaneous" evidence of a Muslim, taken and recorded by the court in the dialect in which it was given.

There is frequent mention of cases of conversion to Islam in the jurisprudential literature of the Moroccan rabbis.

The procedure adopted in questions of inheritance consists of transferring the renegade's share to the most distant relatives. In addition to this discriminatory treatment, the "islamized Jew" is presumed dead to his family; no mourning is observed when he dies, "his close family wear white clothes, drink wine and rejoice in the ruin of the enemies of the Lord."

Almost from the beginning of the common era, every generation of rabbis has come up against the problematics of apostasy. This issue led Saadya Gaon (Egypt and Iraq, tenth century) to differentiate the two notions of religious adherence and ethnic origin. In respect of the religious law and its implications (participation in worship, validity of evidence, etc.), the apostate is no longer a Jew. But, taking into account his membership in an ethnic group (notably defined by his maternal filiation), he remains subject to the laws relating to personal status (marriage and divorce). The distinction is a subtle one and solves a number of problems that are often very delicate.

## DEATH

### *Religion and Magic*

Deaths occurring accidentally or after an illness are the occasion for a considerable number of practices and rites, as well as for a religious ritual in accordance with the rules and commandments of the halakhah (Jewish law) as found in the various codes, most especially the one in force in Maghrebian and Mediterranean societies, the code of Yosef Qaro, the *Shulḥan Aruk*. In addition to the universalist Jewish denominational, religious, and legalistic aspect, this body of ritual has much in common with comparable rituals borne of the indigenous social imagination of local folklore and magic, with a cult and ceremonial where Arabo-Berber, Jewish, and Muslim populations, with similar mental structures, meet, discover, and recognize one another. In the privileged area of death, as in such areas as birth and marriage, a cultural symbiosis, even a syncretism, is apparent on the religious terrain, which is translated into the same beliefs, the same actions, the same magical formulas, sometimes the same cries and the same laments, when it is specifically death that is concerned.

On another count, the beliefs and ideas about death are those conveyed by Jewish biblical or rabbinic writings (Talmud, midrash and legends, Zohar, etc.) or by popular and dialectal oral tradition, a large part of which belongs to the collective memory of the Semitic and Mediterranean world which has gathered together many and varied versions of them, modeled most frequently on a written tradition.

Moreover, it is not always easy to separate the various ingredients that make up this cult of death. Its complex structure makes it barely possible to distinguish the purely legalist component from the other elements drawn from magic and folklore, inherited from manifold customs and practices of varied origin.

Remember too, that death is a very important problem for the individual in Jewish thought because it marks the evaluation of his life, the Day of Judgment and the settling of accounts (*yom ha-din, yom din we-ḥeshbon*). It is the time when the nature of one's eternal existence will be once and for all decided, whether one will be damned for eternity or saved. Nevertheless, death is not the essential problem, since it is secondary as compared with redemption and salvation. Death is a time of deep emotion, and also of great exaltation, for the believer detached from the things of life, from the banality of earthly existence. For him, it is a door opened onto a new world, the world-to-come (*'olam habba'*), the road to the bliss to which every believing religious human being aspires.

## *Death Throes and the Time for Confession*[11]

### *Self-Scrutiny and Repentance*

"Before the supreme moment, the dying man must make a complete self-assessment, repent in order to die innocent, recall the words of King Solomon: 'All go unto one place: all are of the dust, and all return to dust' (Ecclesiastes 3:20). It is the time to deliver his soul in love to the Holy One, blessed be He, to obey the will of his creator, to remember that he is no better than the forefathers, that the soul is leaving darkness for light, servitude for salvation. . . . At the moment when the man takes leave of this world, his actions pass before his eyes one by one and say to him: 'You have done this or that, in such and such a place, on such and such a day'; and the man answers yes and signs, as it is said: 'Every man signs with his hand, acknowledging his actions' (Job 28:7, paraphrased); he accepts the divine sentence and gives reason to God for this."

### *To Die in a Kiss*

To die old, at a venerable age, is a blessing. To die young, or in the prime of life, is a misfortune and a curse (on this subject, compare the biblical texts of Genesis 15:15 and Isaiah 38:10). Man dies because of original sin, that of Adam eating the forbidden fruit. He also dies because of his personal sins. However, the rabbis quote the names of dead heroes and saints who died without having committed sins because of the serpent's poison (primordial).

---

11. Apart from our personal experience and evidence, the discussion of death also includes information, mainly concerning ritual, borrowed from *Naḥalat 'Abot* ("The Heritage of the Fathers"), published in Leghorn in 1898. This is a collection of liturgical texts for the days of mourning and an account of the funeral rites practiced in Morocco by a Mogador rabbi, Isaac Qoriat.

People die in various ways, peacefully or violently, after a long or short death-struggle, each according to his merits. There is "death in a kiss" (*mittah be-neshiqah*; it is like a hair that is removed from a glass of milk or like a drop poured from a pail of water; to pass from life down here to the life of the hereafter without suffering; thus die righteous men, the *ṣaddiqim*; thus did Moses die, "by the mouth of God" (Deuteronomy 34:5).

*Entering Paradise with Open Eyes*

It is the lot of the righteous to be recalled to God while still alive, going into death with open eyes or, as a Judeo-Arabic adage from Morocco says, "entering paradise with open eyes." In Islamic society, those so blessed are the barber who circumcises children, purified by this Abrahamic rite, and the man who puts the bread into the oven and who has freed his soul during his lifetime by exposing it to the flames of his stove. In Jewish society, too, it is the lot of humble folk who have fulfilled pious duties and followed hard trades.

*The Shadow and the Dream*

To lose one's shadow, to dream of parents and friends, even to dream of a scroll of the law (*sefer torah*) are premonitory signs of approaching death and at the same time herald the entrance of the angel of death.

A *gissa,* a hagiographic poetic piece in Judeo-Arabic collected at Tinghir (Upper Atlas), which we have published elsewhere, displays a certain number of ideas and beliefs, all sorts of notions dear to the hearts of kabbalists and even to the authors of the halakhah. These correspond very well to the mentality of the Jewish populations of the Atlas communities (and of the Maghreb, in general), that is, their local traditions and folklore: the world of death and its myths; paradise and the heavenly court; the saints' extraordinary powers of intercession; funeral rites; the duty to teach the Torah to one's children; obligations between colleagues. The author has found all these ideas expressed in texts which he knows well, namely Zohar I, 217b–218a:

> R. Isaac was sitting at the door of R. Judah's house one day, plunged in deep sadness. R. Judah came out and, finding him in this state, said to him: "What is so much [i.e., so burdens you] today?" [R. Isaac] replied:

"I have come to ask three things of you: when you are studying the Torah, if it so happens that you quote some of my words, you must attribute them to me and make mention of their author; you will do my son the honor of teaching him the Torah; every seven days you will go and pray at my grave." R. Judah asked: "Where did you get the idea that you are about to die?" The other replied: "My soul left me on each of these [past] nights, without my being given sight of a dream as previously; much more, when I bow in prayer, I do not see my shadow on the wall; what it means, therefore, is that the messenger has left to proclaim [my death], for it is said: "he moves like a phantom" (Psalms 39:6) and: "Our days upon earth are a shadow" (Job 8:9). R. Judah said: "I will do all that you ask of me on condition that you save me a place by your side in the other world; thus [we will be neighbors] as we are in this one." R. Isaac wept and said: "Do me the favor of never leaving me." Then they went to the house of R. Simon, whom they found engaged in study of the law. Raising his eyes, R. Simon saw R. Isaac; the angel of death was running and dancing in front of the latter. He went to take R. Isaac's hand and said: "I command that whosoever is accustomed to enter will enter; whosoever is not accustomed to enter will not enter." R. Isaac and R. Judah entered; the angel of death was forced to stay outside. R. Simon looked at R. Isaac and saw that his hour had not yet come. He still had until the eighth hour of the day.

He sat him down and they studied together. R. Simon said to his son Eleazar: "Sit at the door and speak to no one, and if anyone wants to enter, you will entreat him on no account to enter." Then he said to R. Isaac: "Have you seen the image of your father today [in a dream]?" For thus, so we are taught, a man's father and his close relatives return to his side at the time he leaves this world; he sees them, recognizes them, as well as all those with whom he was connected here below: all of them will gather around him and accompany his soul to the place that is reserved for it. R. Isaac replied: "So far I have seen nothing." R. Simon immediately rose and said: 'Lord of the Universe! R. Isaac is well known to us, he is one of the seven eyes here below.[12] I am holding him, leave him with me." Then a voice surged up and said: "The throne of the master [R. Isaac] is close to the wings of R. Simon. Here, he is yours, you will bring him with you on the day when you come to sit on your throne." R. Eleazar then saw the angel of death depart, saying: "There is no room at all for the master of great works in the place where R. Simon bar Yohay is." R. Simon said to his son: "Come and support R. Isaac, I see he is afraid." R. Eleazar came in and grasped [the hand] of R. Isaac, while R. Simon returned to his study of the law.

12. These are the seven comrades of zoharic legend, symbols of the seven eyes that watch over the world.

R. Isaac slept and [in a dream] saw his father, who said to him: "My son, your lot is goodly in this world and in the world-to-come, for amongst the leaves of the Tree of Life in the Garden of Eden, a large tree is rising 'powerful in both worlds' and that is R. Simon bar Yohay. It holds you [i.e., shields you] in its branches." R. Isaac asked him: "Father, what is my lot down here?" The father answered: "For three days, they have 'covered' your room, keeping the windows open in order that you should be lit from the four sides of the universe [the four points of the compass]. I rejoice at the sight of your place and I say: 'Your lot is goodly; however, your son has not yet learned enough Torah.'" R. Isaac says: "Father, how much time am I granted [to live] in this world?" The father answered: "That I am not allowed [to say]. That is something that is never revealed to man. But at R. Simon's *hillula,* it will fall to you to set his table."

This is an appropriate place to mention another zoharic idea:

When a man's hour of judgment draws nigh, a new spirit enters him, and as a result he perceives things he was not able to perceive before: the Divine Presence (*shekhinah*); he then departs the world, as it is written: "man shall not see Me and live" (Exodus 33:20), that is, during life; but it is permitted at the hour of death.

All these legends relating to death and the angel of death are known in Morocco. The rabbis use them to illustrate their sermons and their lessons on Talmud and musar (ethics), and they circulate in the local dialects. It is known that good deeds quell the anger of the angel of death. However, immediately he receives orders from God, he is free to remove, indiscriminately, good and evil alike.

### *The Town Where Death Does Not Enter*

In the famous city of Luz, often mentioned in the Bible, the angel of death had no power, and when one of its inhabitants reached a venerable age, he left the town to fade away and die outside its walls.[13]

---

13. A similar legend is known in Ireland. Luz has been identified with Beth-El in the land of Canaan, then with a town in the land of the Hittites, and with Lizan in Kurdistan. The legend is told in the Talmud (Sotah 46b), the Zohar (II, 151b), the Midrash (Genesis Rabbah 69, commenting on Genesis 28:19), and elsewhere. It must also be noted that the term *luz* means "almond" in Semitic languages but in Hebrew also designates a vital organ, most particularly the cervical vertebra, considered indestructible. When the time comes for the body to be resurrected, it will start from this bone, called the "Jew's bone"), which resists all decay in the grave, according to a legend passed on by the Midrash (Leviticus Rabbah 18, Ecclesiastes Rabbah 12:5), the Zohar (I, 137a; III, 122a), and medieval Jewish, Christian, and Muslim writings on theology and medicine.

The master of the great works is often forced to bow to the will of the masters of tradition. It can even be observed that he has a certain familiarity with some of them but defers judgment on others. R. Simon ben Halafta says: "Death cannot seize him who is engaged in study of the Torah." Teaching and study are a shield against the power of the angel of deatḥ. R. Simon b. Yohay says: "When the Israelites accepted the Torah, the Holy One, blessed be He, gave them a sword engraved with the Great Name [of God]. While it was in their hands, the angel of death had no hold over them." Psalms 19:18 says: "The law of the Lord is perfect, restoring the soul." Although a sentence of death is irrevocable once it has been pronounced, whosoever is charged with carrying it out very often encounters difficulties. It is said that the patriarch Abraham refused to allow the angel Michael to take his soul. Moses refused to deliver up his to Samaël. The angel of death only succeeded in overpowering R. Hiyya by the ruse of disguising himself as a beggar. Sometimes God has to intervene to overcome the resistance of famous talmudic heroes. Joshua ben Levi, for example, snatched the sword away from the angel of death, and God, through the intermediary of a *bat-qol,* the heavenly voice, had to call to him: "Give him back his weapon, the sons of man have need of it." We have mentioned the same type of story in the ritual of birth: the deeds of the master of kabbalah who got the better of the demon Lilith, responsible for the death of Jewish children of the male sex in Baghdad and seized her deadly sword, entrusting it to his family who have treasured it ever after.

Legends based on well-known Jewish sources are mingled with others of Arabic origin or belonging to a cultural substratum common to both societies. According to one: "Forty days before death, a leaf falls from the Tree of Life, standing beneath God's throne, into the arms of Azraël [the angel of death in Muslim homiletic literature], thus heralding the death of a human being." Another tells: "When a righteous man dies, Azraël appears before him, accompanied by a legion of good angels bearing the sweet perfumes of paradise, and ensures that the soul leaves the body like a drop taken from a pail of water." It is also said that when people indulge in excessive lamentations or weep inconsiderately for someone's death, Azraël stands at the door of the house, calling: "Why these lamentations and these tears? I am only the messenger of God, the executor of His orders. If you rebel against Him, I will return to this house and take another of you."

## *The Brotherhood of Loving-Kindness and Truth*

There is no community without a benevolent association organized to carry out the following pious duties: to be present in the house of a dying person in order to help him until the supreme moment, to watch over, wash, and dress the corpse, to lead the funeral procession and arrange the burial, and, when necessary, to provide the consolatory meal. Moreover, all of this is done in accordance with the commandments of law and custom. The association is generally called the *ḥebra kaddisha,* or "holy brotherhood." It may also be called the *ḥebra* of Rabbi Shim'on (i.e., Shim'on bar Yohay, traditionally attributed with the composition of the Ẓohar), or again *ḥebrat ḥesed ve-emet,* "the brotherhood of loving-kindness and truth."

## *The Final Profession of Faith*

Comes the time for the soul to "depart." The dying man confesses his sins, verbally, "from his lips," or mentally, and in his heart, without women and children being present to disturb the solemnity of the moment with their tears and cries. There follow the farewells to the dying man, the exchanges of forgiveness, the last wishes expressed, the blessing of the children. After his hands have been washed and he has said the customary blessing, his head is covered with the ritual prayer-shawl (tallit) and he declares, "The everlasting God is truth; His Torah is truth; Moses, His prophet, is truth, the words of the sages are truth; blessed be the glory of His reign, for ever and ever." Then comes a special liturgy made up of extracts from the Book of Psalms and Ezekiel (the first chapter, dedicated to the fulgurating vision of the divine throne), penitential prayers, and so on.

The dying man is presumed to be alive in every way. Therefore, says the author of *Naḥalat 'Abot,* until his "soul has departed" his jaws must not be bound, his orifices not closed, the pillow not removed from under his head, he must not be stretched out on the bare floor, nor a vase of water or a grain of salt placed on his stomach, nor his eyes closed, in the same way, professional mourners must not be called in, etc. Whosoever acts otherwise, is considered to have committed homicide. Similarly, the keys of the synagogue must not be placed under his head to hasten death. However, the death throes must be prevented from lasting too long, and every obstacle to a gentle death, "an unhindered departure of the soul," removed—such as too much noise from a nearby wood-cutter (*sic*), salt placed on the tongue, crying and weeping. In certain rural societies, he is stripped of his jewelery and amulets, of everything binding and wrapping him, the *djellaba*, which has "seven openings like hell" and the pillow which "keeps the soul earthbound." It is proper for those present to form a close circle around the dying man at the moment when he surrenders his soul, so that no breath from without can reach him, and a night-light or candle is lit at his head. It is also customary to keep his weeping parents and close relatives at a distance, and to open the windows of the death chamber. This is the way that the demons and cohorts of spirits who accompany the angel of death come in; but it is also the route by which the soul of the dead man departs to reach the vault of heaven, escaping from the body with the last breath, flying, it is said, like a bird, a fly, or a bumble bee.

The members of the *ḥebra* keep vigil, waiting for the supreme moment. They are experts. They are aware of certain signs about the eyes and lips, certain rattles which herald death, and they alone decide the moment to pronounce the profession of faith, the Shema' Yisrael, "Hear, O Israel, The Lord is our God, the Lord is one," the short prayer that proclaims the oneness of God.

It is an impressive scene! Those present, the watchers of the *ḥebra,* close family, and friends, gravely and solemnly repeat the ritual formula, with sobs in their voices, punctuated by the ominous rattle of the dying man, until the last moment, until the last sigh. What pious Jew does not want to hear, with his last breath expiring on his lips, the word *eḥad,* the "one" *of the* Shema' Yisrael, as did Rabbi Akiba, the great scholar of the law and martyr of Israel, who died, tortured by the Romans, for the sanctification and glory of the Name.

The eldest child closes his dead father's eyes, as did Joseph for his father Jacob, as it is said: "Joseph shall put his hand upon your eyes" (Genesis 46:4). The Zohar offers a mystical interpretation of this act: "closing the eyes on this world and having a glimpse of the world-to-come and of its great light, at the very last moment of life" (Zohar, III, 169a). Among some groups it was a custom to insert soil from the Holy Land into the mouth of a deceased woman who lost her children during her lifetime.

The assembled company break out in lamentations as soon as the last breath is drawn and the soul departs: the women weep, cry, tear their faces. This is a survival of the "bloody mourning" that Frazer mentions in connection with Hebrew and other Mediterranean peoples and civilizations, who expressed grief when a parent or friend died by slashing their faces, mutilating their bodies, rending their clothes. These practices were later forbidden as barbaric and pagan: "You are the children of the Lord your God; make no incisions in your flesh . . . for the dead" (cf. Leviticus 19:28).

### *Spilling Water and Rending*

The body is stripped of clothing, placed bare on the floor, and covered completely with a sheet. It may also be isolated by a sheet hung between two walls; the looking-glasses and mirrors, if any, may be covered with a cloth, or simply turned to face the wall.

Penitential prayers are said, prolonged by the reading of psalms, hymns, and laments, the Thirteen Principles of the Faith, and a special liturgy called Sidduq ha-Din: the statement of acceptance of the divine sentence with the formula, "Righteous art Thou, O Lord, and upright are Thy judgments" (Psalms 119:137). Finally, the eulogy: "Blessed art Thou. . . . Thou who art the judge of truth," which accompanies the act of rending, *qeri'ah,* symbol of the break (in some way a repetition of circumcision), the permanent separation which the brethren of the *ḥebra,* past masters in ceremonial, signify to the family of the deceased.

These are rites of separation practiced by the Arabo-Berber societies of the Maghreb. The soul leaves the body that it inhabited, as it must leave, without regret, close relatives, friends, the world of the living, and all the possessions acquired on earth; to join the world of the dead and be "gathered to his father's kin," as was said in biblical times (Genesis 25:8 ff).

In Judaism, the act of rending, like all the other rites associated with death, is strictly defined by talmudic legislation and the various codes (those of Maimonides and Joseph Qaro in particular), and described in minute detail in the summaries which record local practices and customs. The same is true of another significant act consisting of pouring down the drain all the water found in the house of death and those abutting on it, even all the water in the alley or neighborhood.

This water, customarily stored in earthenware jars or other container or vessels, is rendered unusable and must be immediately replaced by new water, freshly drawn from a spring or well (*dine shefikhat mayim*). Various reasons are given to explain this act. It is a way of "spreading" the news of the death in the neighborhood without the need of speech, of words charged with menace and imminent danger; the angel of death is prowling in the vicinity. But the basic reason, adopted by several rabbinic authorities, is that the same angel of death washed his bloody sword in the water of the house where he struck and of those nearby, letting fall poisoned droplets, laden with death and mourning. Care should be taken not to touch it, and all the more so not to use it.

While some of the brethren from the *ḥebra* make preparations for the funeral, others—the watchers, properly speaking—have to stay with the dead man from the instant he surrenders his soul till the moment the earth of the grave covers him. Forming a close circle so that no breath of outside air can reach him, they endlessly repeat a mystical prayer and a kabbalistic meditation intended to keep away the evil spirits which prowl around the corpse. This is a very ancient poetic piece, attributed to the tanna, Neḥunya ben Haqana. It consists of forty-two words divided into seven metrical lines ending with the rhyme *ra*. The words are said to represent the forty-two letters of the great Name of God, who is called on here to protect the soul of the deceased. In addition, the second line contains an acrostic of the letters forming the sequence *qr'stn,* a formula entreating God to "tear Satan," that is to say, to revoke his indictment. The piece begins as follows: "May you unbind the sheaf by the power and greatness of your right [hand]."

## *The Funeral*

### *The Duty to Bury the Dead*

The author of *Naḥalat 'Abot,* Rabbi Isaac Qoriat, states that to deny proper burial to a dead person is to deal him the most humiliating insult. Biblical law demands that even the criminal condemned to death and executed be buried, as well as the enemy killed in battle. This duty is incumbent on the close relatives and the whole community, and the cemetery is a communal place and institution. Someone who finds a corpse in a deserted area or on "foreign" (i.e., not Jewish) soil is obliged to bury it without the slightest delay, without even taking time to seek help in a nearby inhabited location. This is the case of *met miṣwah.*

Placing a body in the earth, talmudic texts say, certainly prevents its material deterioration, but is also equivalent to the expiation of sins.

According to a midrash (Pirke de-Rabbi Eliezer 21), Adam and Eve learned the art of burying the dead from a crow. Elsewhere it is said that "two *pure* birds buried Abel, assassinated by his brother Cain."

Burial must take place on the same day as death, as long as that day is not a Sabbath, in which case it is postponed until the morrow. Rab Ḥida (Ḥayyim Yosef David Azulay), an eighteenth-century rabbi of Moroccan origin, who was born in Jerusalem and died in Leghorn, earnestly recommended that burial follow immediately on death, "even at the risk of burying a person alive." His grounds for this was a mystical doctrine taught by the kabbalists to the effect that any delay causes terrible suffering to the dead person and could be the cause of great misfortunes for all mankind.

The cemetery is a sacred place. It is euphemistically called *bet ha-ḥayyim,* "house of the living," but it is usually referred to by the Judeo-Arabic term *me'arah,* "grotto," which recalls the ancient places and procedures of burying the dead in the Holy Land and in the Maghreb. The grave is dug quite deep and its sides are lined with planks (in Mogador) or bricks (in Fez). Certain sites are reserved for rabbis, notables, and their families. There is a patch for the "excluded," suicides and prostitutes: The grave-digger spins his pick-axe over his head and throws it at random; the outcast is buried where it lands, without ceremony, in haste and shame.

### *Preparation of the Body*

The corpses of pious men are subjected to a simulation of the four capital punishments, a rite of expiation intended to spare them the torments of Gehenna. It is gravely and solemnly performed by the brethren, who prepare themselves for it by ablutions. The simulation is accompanied by a special liturgy, itself preceded by the mystical meditation which consecrates every action in life that must be accomplished "with a view to joining the Holy One, blessed be He and His Presence (*shekhinah*), in fear and love, with the purpose of unifying the name of God . . . in a perfect union."

The modes of torture by stoning (*deqilah*), fire (*serifah*), slaughter (*hereg*), and strangulation (*ḥeneq*) are simulated in turn. One of the brethren throws seven stones, one at a time, at the dead person's heart, repeating three times: "Thus is done to the man who rebels against his Creator"; the others reply, echoing him: "Misfortune is ours on the Day of Judgment, misfortune is ours on the day of punishment."

The dead man's nostrils are lightly burned by letting drops of melted wax from a lighted candle spill over them. A rope is attached to his feet and he is jostled and dragged a few cubits to simulate slaughter. Strangulation is simulated by squeezing his neck with the same rope or with a strip of cloth. Like the first, each ensuing operation is accompanied by invocations, elegies, and laments. Then the brethren move away from the corpse, stepping back nearly four cubits. They pause a moment, then return to his side and proclaim: "You are our brother, you are our brother, you are our brother. From the moment that you accepted the sentence, you have been absolved and pardoned, cleared of all anathema and exclusion."

The procedure for preparing the body, the rite of purity expressed by the Arabo-Hebraic term *taharah*, is then carried out with the same gravity and solemnity, but with different prayers and appropriate incantatory formulas. However, the divine name Adonay does not figure in these; it is replaced by the usual term, Hashem, "the name."

The washers, men and women, *roḥasim* (in Hebrew) and *ghassalin* (in Arabic), carry the corpse on trestles and perform various ablutions and lustrations in the order directed by law and custom, and according to a complicated ritual. They use, alternately, hot and cold water, soap, rose-water and orange-water, and branches of myrtle and thyme, scrupulously cleaning all the orifices. They employ a predetermined number of utensils (pots and boilers), seven for certain ablutions, taking care not to pass them from hand to hand but to place them on the floor before a colleague picks them up and uses them. The nails are cut and the parings collected so that nobody steps over them or treads on them. The nail parings of the dead, like those of the living, are thrown straight down the drain, lest they be put to magical use or any other operation of sorcery.

The body is dried with clean sheets, then dressed. The various items of clothing are usually made of linen or cotton fabric. The corpse is dressed in them according to the prescribed ritual and in a precise order: the head-dress, called in Arabic *'arra-qiyya*; trousers of a certain type, *sarwal*; an undergarment, *quemzza;* a jacket, *qeṣṣot*; a turban-headband, *'amama*; the ritual prayer-shawl, the fringes of which have been intentionally tied up or rendered unsuitable for prayer (*ṣiṣit*); and an over-garment, sewn up all round, which constitutes the real shroud (*ujeh le-kfen*).

Two other rites should be mentioned at this juncture, one specifically Jewish, the other bearing the stamp of the Maghrebian Judeo-Muslim and Berber-Arabic cultural symbiosis.

When dressing the dead person, it is the custom among Jews to place his thumb in the hollow of his hand in such a way that, with his other fingers, it forms one of the names of God, or rather one of His attributes, *shadday*, "All-Powerful," formed from the letters *shin* (three down-strokes), *dalet* (one), and *yud* (a point). The hand is also stretched out to signify that he renounces all earthly goods.

In Muslim societies, the corpse's sex organs are covered with a piece of his burnoose during the preparation. This bit of clothing is kept as a relic, in the belief that the dead father's virile potency and *baraka* have found refuge in it. Treasured in the family, it is placed on the heads of daughters on the nights their marriages are consummated in order to pass on the paternal *baraka* to them. The corresponding Jewish practice, observed in several families we knew in Mogador and Casablanca, consists of tearing the dead man's last shirt and dividing the pieces among the members of his family, who treasure them, in order that each receive his share of the blessing of the deceased father or grandfather.

Another custom, still practiced in Tlemcen in the 1940s, was condemned in the following terms by R. Yosef Messas, a Moroccan rabbi who acted as judge in that town at the time:

> There was yet another abomination. When two consecutive deaths occurred in the same house in the same year or the same month, the funeral was not held on the second occasion until a cock had been slaughtered on the threshold of the house or in the center of the courtyard, and while the men brought out the mortal remains, the lintel and the two doorposts were sprinkled with the bird's blood. The cock was then consumed exclusively by the family of the deceased or neighbors in the courtyard. There, too, I have advocated a change in custom. To make allowance for their fear of death, I decided that the cock should no longer be slaughtered and that they should be satisfied with reciting the formula of *kapparah* (substitute sacrifice): "This is the ransom of the people of the house, their substitution and their redemption," and the cock should then be given to the poor.

### *The Funeral Procession*

The body is put in a coffin covered with a black sheet or with the djellaba that the deceased wore during his lifetime.[14] This is the *mittah*

---

14. A woman's coffin is covered with her white shawl or a sheet of the same color.

(Hebrew), the "deathbed" which the *kattafim* will carry on their shoulders (*ktaf*) to the cemetery, taking good care that the dead man leave the house of death head first, followed by close relatives and friends. The respect due to the dead requires that the "deathbed" lead the procession. Everybody seeing the procession pass must follow it (*miṣwat lewayah*) for at least four cubits (a Jew also has to perform this duty when the dead person is a *goy*) lest the words of Proverbs 17:5 be said of him: "Whoso mocks the poor blasphemeth his Maker" (that is to say, God Himself).

The passing of the funeral procession is announced by the sounding of the shofar (ram's horn). One by one the shops along the way close and the crowd of followers swells until the arrival at the cemetery. The progress of the procession is punctuated by the cantillated reading of the alphabetical psalm (Psalm 119, consisting of twenty-two eight-line verses in the sequence of the Hebrew alphabet, all the lines in each stanza beginning with the same letter), first in full, then by composing the dead person's first name, his mother's name, and the letters of the acronym *qr'stn,* "expulsion and removal of Satan." Then the mystical meditation already mentioned is recited: "Let it be Thy will, to unbind the sheaf by the power and greatness of Your right [hand]." This is followed by Psalm 91, highly regarded by talmudic and esoteric tradition for its powers of protection against demons and sorcery. The Song of Songs may also be recited, as well as the chapter on the "woman of valor" from Proverbs (31:10–31) and *kinot* (elegies).

The presence of women, whether preceding or following the procession, is not recommended by the author of *Naḥalat 'Abot,* who recalls that local custom forbids it and that it was prohibited by an emissary rabbi from Jerusalem. According to the Zohar,

> There is a risk that the presence of women in the procession will bring misfortune to the world and mankind, because the angel of death likes the company of women and can be seen among them singing and dancing. Men are tempted to look in that direction; the angel seizes the opportunity, goes back up to heaven and brings accusations before the throne against the man who succumbed to temptation.

Note, however, that women often disregard the prohibition. In ancient times, professional mourners customarily led the procession, singing laments and beating drums (Jeremiah 4:4), and this custom has been preserved in some oriental societies to this day.

The rabbinic authorities in some towns, particularly Fez, forbid the son to accompany the procession. He has to precede it to the cemetery. In connection with this, it is said in Judeo-Arabic: *Ikun f-ennedduy menzzera' dyalo widuz mnora gnazto,* "May [the son] be ]cursed]! He is his progeny and he walks behind his coffin?" The explanation given is that the children who might have been born of the father's lost "seed" would be jealous of those who are present in the procession.

When the procession arrives at the cemetery, the *miṭṭah* is set down at the entrance, in a room assigned to a special ritual, called *bet ha-midrash (*house of study). It remains there during the funeral sermon (*drash*) given by a rabbi or a *talmid-ḥakham* (disciple of the wise).

*Circumambulatory rites and the pursuit of demons.* The circumambulatory rite of *haqqafot* begins immediately after the sermon. The coffin is circled seven times by processions made up of ten people, holding hands in a close circle and reciting a special liturgy. The author of *Naḥalat 'Abot* says that this is a *tiqqun* (rite of atonement) intended to make evil spirits take flight, for it is said: "Around him [the dead man], the ungodly prowl" (alluding to Psalm 12:9).

### Pieces of Gold

The *miṭṭah* is carried to the grave. The honor of lowering the body is sold by auction if the deceased person was a rabbinical figure or a man renowned for great piety. The sums collected are paid into a fund for the poor or some other charitable cause. A few pieces of gold are thrown into the four corners of the grave, recalling an episode in the life of the patriarch Abraham described in the following text: "But unto the sons of the concubines, that Abraham had, Abraham gave gifts; and he sent them away from Isaac his son, while yet he lived, eastward, unto the east country" (Genesis 25:6). In Fez, the jealousy of potential progeny is again taken into account. In this case it is represented by evil spirits who have to be appeased by a part of the family patrimony (*ha l-irusha dyalkum*). "Here is your share of the inheritance," they are told in Judeo-Arabic. Also said is *ka idahhbu es-sitanim,* "They drive out the satans," a play on the word *dahhaba,* which in local parlance means both "to cause to take flight" and "to cover with gilt."

### The Underground Passage to the Holy Land

The body, placed in the grave, stretched out on its back and insulated by planks, is covered with earth (everyone present throws in a handful), mixed with a little sand brought back from a pilgrimage to the Holy Land or presented by an emissary rabbi visiting Morocco. Relevant in this connection, is a theme much discussed in homiletic literature and the Zohar,[15] and integrated into the popular imagination of the masses, who link it to various stories and legends.

This theme is derived from the belief in the resurrection of the dead, which will necessarily take place in the Holy Land. Bodies buried in the Diaspora roll underground to the ancestral home, and there, when the moment comes, after the Day of Judgment, they will receive their souls and be resurrected. An unpublished document in the manuscript collection of the Bibliothèque D. Sassoon contains evidence that corpses were exhumed and transported from the Maghreb to Palestine.

Once the mortal remains are buried, those present return to the bet ha-midrash. There then takes place the ritual of Sidduq ha-Din, "submission to the divine sentence," the reading of the *hashkabah,* the requiem, or prayer for the repose of the soul of the deceased, and the recitation of the Kaddish for the dead, which is said at a distance from the grave, because it is believed that the dead person wants to escape his fate and calls out: "Wait for me, I am coming with you." The distance is maintained lest anyone hear this, for whosoever hears his voice will die within the year.

"*Your limbs shall be as fresh as grass.*" Before leaving the cemetery, the mourners pluck blades of grass and throw them over their heads to show their grief, but also to express their hope in the resurrection and the coming of the messianic age, for it is said: "And your bones shall flourish like young grass" (Isaiah 66:14), "and may they blossom out of the city like grass of the earth" (Psalms 72:16). They wash their hands, not drying them on a towel but leaving them dripping to dry of their own accord. This, says a midrashic text, is to put to flight the spirits which fasten more stubbornly to impurities on hands. But, adds the author of *Naḥalat 'Abot,* it is also to confirm and testify that "our hands have shed no blood" (alluding to Deuteronomy 21:7) and that we are in no way an accessory. Some people also wash their faces while repeating the verse: "And the Lord God will wipe away tears from off all faces" (Isaiah 25:8). When there is no water or when it is in short supply (as in the case of a caravan in the desert, for example), a prac-

15. Midrash and aggadah (Song of Songs, Aramaic paraphrase, Tanḥuma, Psiqta Rabbati, etc.); Zohar (Midrash ha-Ne'elam, I, 113b).

tice borrowed from Muslim society is employed, consisting of carrying out the ritual ablutions by rubbing the hands with sand (*tayammûm*) or earth (*'istijmâr*).

### *The Consolatory Meal*

Returning to the home of the deceased, the bereaved family is served with their first meal, consisting of raw eggs and black olives. Everyone present, friends and close relatives, joins in the tears and condolences, broken by the laments of the professional mourners (*nuwwahat*). Thus they observe the ancient command: "It is better to go the house of mourning, than to go to the house of feasting; for that is the end of all men, and the living will lay it to his heart (Ecclesiastes 7:2). They are also bidden to console the stricken in these terms: "The Almighty will comfort you amongst all the mourners in Ẓion and Jerusalem, and in Jerusalem will you be comforted" (alluding to Isaiah 66:13).

A custom is observed at this consolatory or condolence meal (*se'udat ha-bra'h*) that seems to go back to a very ancient time. The mourners are passed their food by hand, contrary to the practice at an ordinary meal, when the master of the house breaks the bread after the ritual blessing and places the pieces on the table so that everyone can help themselves. Tradition explains this practice with reference to a painful period in Jewish history, described in Lamentations 1:17: "Ẓion spreadeth forth her hands [in prayer]; there is none to comfort her." Food must therefore be passed only by hand to a man tried by mourning.

A candle or an oil night-light burns in the death chamber. It remains lit until the end of the year of mourning. It is then taken to the synagogue, where its flame is periodically fed. This is the soul of the deceased, which remains in the home among his family for a year.

The author of *Naḥalat 'Abot* notes a practice at Mogador consisting of placing a bowl of water next to the candle or night-light. The basis for this, he says, is inexplicable, and he condemns it as a practice foreign to Judaism, like the customs and practices of the biblical Amorites (*darke ha-emori*). This practice has already been mentioned; there is evidence of it in Arabo-Berber circles.

### ***The Period of Mourning***

The time of mourning is divided into three successive periods. The first lasts for a compulsory seven days, and the second for a compulsory thirty; the third can continue for seven, nine, or eleven months, depending on the customs in force in the family or on the social or rabbinical status of the deceased. Each of these three periods is marked by a series of prohibitions and an appropriate ritual. They terminate in a threefold commemoration consisting of a liturgy suitable to the occasion, accompanied by sermons, prayers, and funeral eulogies (laments and elegies), a special meal, offerings and charitable donations.

In this connection, the Mogadorian author of *Naḥalat 'Abot* recalls the substance of a talmudic text (Mo'ed Katan 27b):

> Rab Yehudah, in the name of Rab, says: "Whosoever persists [in mourning] his death is mourning another death. . . . Do not indulge in excessive moaning and lamentation; do not exceed the bounds: three days of tears, seven of lament and funeral prayers; at the end of thirty, wash and press your clothes, cut your hair. Furthermore, the Holy One, blessed be He, tells you: "You cannot sympathize with his fate more than I Myself do." What there is every reason to observe is that the son say Kaddish for the repose of his father's and mother's souls, so that they merit entry into the Garden of Eden. . . . It would also be fitting that a quorum of ten sages give pious readings for one hour a day in the house of the deceased, during the year or at least during the thirty-day period (Psalms, Mishnah, Zohar, etc.).

## *The Great Mourning*

The great mourning applies to the seven days that follow the death, a period of isolation, marked by a large number of taboos and prohibitions. These affect the exercise of one's profession (business or handicraft trade), washing and dressing, the wearing of shoes (one walks barefoot or in espadrilles), sexual relations, food (no meat is eaten, no wine drunk; but on the other hand, abundant *maḥya* [brandy] is consumed); the mourners' food is provided by third parties and prepared outside the house of death. A man wearing mourning must not don tefillin (phylacteries) during prayer, study Torah, or read from the halakhah, Mishnah, or Talmud, with the exception of the biblical Book of Job, a few chapters of Jeremiah, and *kinot* commemorating the destruction of the Temple in Jerusalem. Seated on a mattress or carpet, or even on the bare floor (some say on an "upturned bed") in the left-hand corner of the death chamber, the hood of his black djellaba pulled down over his head, he must not exchange comments or greetings, even the word *shalom,* with visitors. He must let his hair and beard grow, and must not leave the house except to go to the synagogue on Shabbat and to the cemetery.

According to Rabbi Isaac ben Sheshet Perfet (Ribash), a fourteenth-century Hispano-Algerian author, the custom of visiting the cemetery during the seven days which follow death is borrowed from the Muslims of the Maghreb.[16] However, this custom has acquired the force of law and is scrupulously observed by all the Jewish communities in Morocco. It is practiced by their Muslim neighbors, accompanied in both cases by the distribution of charity.

The first commemorative ceremony is held on the eve of the seventh day. In Hebrew this is *peqidat ha-shabu'a,* "the septenary remembrance"; the Judeo-Arabic term *mesmara,* itself coming from the Hebrew *shamar,* "to guard, to watch out," is more familiar. This is an evening of readings (Bible, Mishnah, Zohar, etc.), followed by a collation to which the brethren of the *ḥebra,* the rabbis, and all present are invited. They take away *ka'ka',* a type of jumbal (a cake made of sweet dough in the shape of a crown), for those not there. The following day, after a visit to the cemetery, there is a ceremony marking the ending of the septenary period of mourning, accompanied by rites of purity (washing, dressing, and ritual bath).

Similar commemorative rituals are conducted on the thirtieth day and after the period called the "year," although it only lasts seven or eleven months. These are the *peqidat ha-shloshim,* "thirty-day remembrance" (in Arabic, *ash-shhar*) and the *peqidat ha-shanah,* "one-year remembrance" (in Arabic, *al-'am*). They consist of evenings of readings, rites of purity (bath, haircut, etc.), ritual meals, visits to the cemetery, placing of a funeral stele (the "stone," *al hajra,* as it is more familiarly called), and the distribution of charity. It is customary on this occasion, in both Jewish and Muslim circles, to make a special donation to the children at the school (*sla*); this offering, known only by the Arabic term *ma'ruf* (gift), consists of a distribution of fritters or couscous.

## *Other Ideas and Beliefs*

The ceremonial for the mourning period, like every other Jewish ceremonial, is fixed by the rabbinic authorities and inscribed in law and

16. Ribash (Rabbi Isaac Ben Sheshet), responsa, no. 158.

custom. And, of course, it draws upon rabbinic, midrashic, talmudic, and zoharic literature. Notwithstanding, it also drives some of its substance from the local cultural landscape, from the world of legends, beliefs, and ideas belonging to the Maghrebian and Mediterranean environment, and from a more universal terrain.

The Bible states that Joseph mourned for his father for seven days (Genesis 50:10), that to demonstrate grief the bereaved placed ashes on their heads, that mourners sat amid ashes, wore sackcloth, and so on (Joshua 7:6; Jeremiah 16:6, etc.).

According to the Talmud, the seven days of mourning were even observed before the Flood. It is also said that for the first three days the mourner is like a man threatened with death by a double-edged sword hanging over his head: from the third to the fifth day, the deadly sword rises up before him in a corner of the room; from the seventh to the thirtieth day, it moves backwards and forwards in front of him in the street; and for the whole year, the family runs the risk of falling victim to it.

As far as the spirit of the deceased is concerned, the Zohar, the great repository of mystical doctrines, declares that the spirit of the righteous remains bound to his body for thirty days, whereas the spirit of the ordinary man remains attached to him for twelve months, the duration of its passage to purgatory.

According to a talmudic text (Shabbat 152b), "the soul prowls above the grave until the flesh is completely reduced to dust." Muslims hold that the soul wanders for three days around the house of the deceased, and for forty around the grave.

At the end of these two periods prayers are said, charity distributed and the offering is made of the *ma'ruf*, "meal intended for the *tolba* in the schools and for the poor of the mosque and cemetery." Among the Muslims, too, no cooking is done in the house of death, but only for the three days following the death, instead of the seven the Jews observe; and it is the close relatives and friends who send in the necessary food to the members of the bereaved family.

### *The Redemptive Power of Kaddish*

The part played by the Kaddish prayer in the soul's post-mortem itinerary, its accession to the Garden of Eden, and its repose at the foot of the heavenly throne has already been mentioned.

The word *qaddish* is the Aramaic equivalent of the Hebrew *qadosh,* meaning "holy." It designates a vital element in Jewish liturgy, a public doxology (hymn to the glory of God) necessarily recited in the presence of a minyan, the quorum of ten adult worshipers, who reply Amen.

Except for the finale and a few responses in Hebrew, the Kaddish prayer is composed in Aramaic, the vernacular of the Babylonian communities. It exalts, magnifies, and sanctifies the Name of the Eternal, entreats the rapid arrival of the Messiah, the advent of the Kingdom of God, redemption, and universal peace. But there is hardly any reference to the destruction of the Temple in Jerusalem (by the Romans), which would indicate even more ancient origins. Several versions of the Kaddish exist, all of them containing one section in common, but augmented according to circumstances by additional elements, particularly in the rabbinic Kaddish (Qaddish de-Rabbanan) and in the mourners' or orphans' Kaddish.

The 'Otiyot de-Rabbi 'Akiba, a midrash[17] dating from the gaonic period (i.e., the High Middle Ages), says:

> When the Messiah comes, God will be seated in paradise and will give a commentary on the new Torah in a sermon before the assembly of saints, pious men, and angels. At the end of the sermon, Zerubbabel will rise and recite the Kaddish in a voice which will be heard from one end of the world to the other, and all mankind will reply Amen.[18] Every soul, those of Jews and those of gentiles (*goyim*) will also say Amen. At that time God's mercy will awaken, and He will give Michael and Gabriel the keys to Gehenna. The forty doors of Gehenna will open at the archangels' command. . . . All those redeemed from hell will emerge and be led to paradise.

*Rabbi Akiba and the wood-cutter.* According to a later aggadic legend (Seder Eliyahu Zuta), Rabbi Akiba saved the soul of a dead man from the punishment of Gehenna by teaching his son to how to recite Kaddish.

> One day R. Akiba met a spirit [a soul] which appeared in the form of a man carrying wood on his back. The wood was intended, the man said, to feed the fires of Gehenna, where he himself was burned daily as a punishment for the maltreatment he had inflicted on the poor dur-

17. Ẓerubbabel led the exiles back from Babylon to Judea, after the decree of Cyrus authorizing their return (539/38 B.C.E.).

ing his lifetime, when he had been a tax collector. He would only be spared this terrible torture, he added, if his son could recite Kaddish before an assembly of worshipers. Learning from this that the man had completely neglected his son's religious education, R. Akiba went off to seek out the boy, found him, and undertook to teach him the read the Torah; one day the boy was able to rise and recite Kaddish publicly, thus saving his father from the fires of hell.

### *The Anniversary*

The Yiddish term *yahrzeit,* pronounced *yarsyat* in Judeo-Maghrebian society, designates the anniversary of the day of death. The custom of commemorating the death of loved ones is very ancient. During the talmudic period (third to sixth centuries C.E.), the anniversary of the death of a father or a teacher was marked by fasting and study. The ritual called *hazkarat neshamot,* "the remembrance of souls," was carried out. But the custom of observing the *yahrzeit* to honor the memory of close relations was probably born, and practiced most punctiliously, in Germany in the Middle Ages. The oriental and Mediterranean Jews adopted it, preserving the Germanic designation, both in their local languages and in the halakhic literature (codes and collections of jurisprudence), that fixes the ritual of this ceremonial.

The ritual of *yahrzeit* took on a mystical dimension with the appearance of the kabbalistic doctrines of Isaac Luria and his disciples of the Safed school in the sixteenth century. The recitation of the Qaddish Yatom, or orphan's Kaddish, the mystics teach, helps to give relief to the soul, assists its passage from Gehenna to the Garden of Eden during the eleven months following death.

The *yahrzeit* Kaddish each year raises the same soul to an ever-higher heavenly sphere. This annual ceremony is not only a commemoration, a simple remembrance ceremonial; it celebrates the mystery of the soul's ascent to the divine throne whence it was formed and its establishment in the eternal beatitude to which it has always aspired.

Several rites mark the *yahrzeit:* fasting and the recitation of Kaddish and a *hashkabah* (requiem), the reading of a special liturgy comprising selected texts from the Bible, the Mishnah, the Zohar, a chapter from the Code of Maimonides (the one devoted to the laws of sacrifice), hymns and prayers. A candle or night-light is lit; this is a very important act, for the wick of a burning candle is like the soul in a man's body, and "the spirit of man is the lamp of the Lord" (Proverbs

20:27). It is customary to go to the cemetery to visit the grave of the deceased and to give charity. On the eve a meal of remembrance is consumed in the company of the brethren of the ḥebra kaddisha, indigent scholars, and the poor.

### *The Hillula*

The anniversary of the death of Moses is celebrated on the seventh day of Adar. That of Rabbi Shimon Bar Yohay, to whom is traditionally attributed the composition of the Zohar, is commemorated on Lag Ba-omer (thirty-third day of the *'omer*), or on the eighteenth of Iyyar, and that of Rabbi Me'ir, "master of the miracle" (*ba'al ha-nes*), on the fourteenth of the same month. The commemorations of the deaths of these two Palestinian saints have become occasions for festivities and illuminations at the actual sites of their graves in Meron and Tiberias, as well as in every Mediterranean community. In Morocco, local saints and santons, all manner of miracle-workers, and famous Maghrebian scholars ('Amram ben Diwan, David Ad-Dra', David Al-Ashqar called Moulay Ighghi, etc.) are also commemorated by seasonal pilgrimages and by a festivity known here and elsewhere as *hillula,* remarkable for its theatrical and spectacular aspects.

The hillula is a sort of movable feast, both religious and secular, comparable to the Islamic custom of *moussem.* A rite takes place on the site of the presumed grave of a rabbi and saint. Pilgrims generally perform this in accordance with a vow made on the occasion of an unusual event or with a voluntary promise made to the rabbi to visit his grave occasionally or at a definite time. The rituals of the hillula and the pilgrimage are made up of special liturgies combined with a great deal of jollification. Prayer and the cantillation of psalms are accompanied by copious meals, abundant libations of brandy and wine, dancing, singing, large bonfires. These popular celebrations based on folklore verge on heresy and are very often condemned by rabbinate, which, however, is powerless to prevent them from taking place.

The hillula celebrations have also occasioned rich literary creativity in Hebrew and local dialects. The hagiographic poetry here provides examples of the two graded levels of Jewish knowledge: Hebraic scriptural knowledge embodied in poetic compositions written for special occasions, and verse poems in Judeo-Arabic or, more rarely, Judeo-Berber. The long *qaṣâ'id* or *qiṣaṣ* which are sung tell of the saint's extraordinary life, a life marked by legendary events, miraculous interventions, prophetic signs and visions. The shorter pieces consist of one or two verses, laudatory, bacchic, or individual thanksgivings, and are generally improvised. They are sung while carrying out one of the two acts bought at a special auction sale: the right to light an oil night-light, candle, or taper dedicated to the saint or rabbi, and the right to rise and drink a glass of brandy in his honor and in thanksgiving.

Mystical doctrine, and the Zohar in particular, considered the day of death to be a feast day (*yoma de-hillula*), and the author of a biblical text (Ecclesiastes 7:1) says that "the day of death is better than the day of one's birth," which the Midrash interprets as meaning: "Death tells of the praiseworthy life of the dead. . . . It is like a boat that enters port loaded with merchandise" (Exodus Rabbah 48). Elsewhere, it is said: "And the great of every generation must die to make way for their successors."

## *The Cemetery and the Cult of the Dead*

The hillula is celebrated in the synagogue, but certain ceremonies and festivities take place in the cemetery. It is also visited on Mondays and Thursdays, and on the eves of Rosh Hashanah and Yom Kippur, with good care being taken not to go to the same grave twice on the same day.

According to the author of *Naḥalat 'Abot,* the graves of the dead are visited on the eves of Rosh Hashanah and Yom Kippur because "On that day, God is preparing to judge the world. The souls of the dead implore divine mercy for the living and tell them in a dream the decision concerning them, once it is decreed by the heavenly court." The living, therefore, go to the cemetery to pray to the dead so that they will intercede on their behalf.

Invalids and barren women sometimes stay in the cemetery, near the graves of local saints and santons, in little rooms reserved for the purpose. They spend three to seven days at a time there, praying and entreating to be cured or for their wishes to be granted.

For Muslims, the cemetery is usually a place to take a walk; women and children go there on Fridays to drink tea and chat. On the twenty-seventh day of Ramadan, and even more on the festival of 'Ashura, a general lustration of the graves is carried out, literally flooding them. There is nothing about this to suggest the sadness of visits by the bereaved and the Christian Day of the Dead.

Asking the dead to intercede seems to be a very ancient practice, going back to biblical origins. According to a scriptural text, as seen through the medium of the Oral Law, when Caleb arrived at Hebron he visited the Cave of Machpeleh, where the patriarchs were buried. He prayed to escape the plot hatched by the scouts sent into the land of Canaan by Moses, an expedition in which he himself participated. (For this episode, see Numbers 13 and Sotah 34b.)

A reverse relationship can also occur, with the dead taking the initiative and showing a desire to communicate with the living. Several stories tell of visits by dead persons to close relatives; and visits by a deceased husband to a wife to pledge her to do certain things are very frequent. In addition, the dead seem to take a keen interest in the daily lives of the living, in their earthly concerns and occupations. A talmudic text tells how Rabbi Ḥiyya went to the cemetery in the company of Rabbi Jonathan. On the way, he noticed that this latter had the fringes of his tallit (ritual prayer shawl) unknotted, hanging out over his clothing. He reproved him for this, telling him to gather them up and put them back inside lest the dead say: "Tomorrow they are going to join us, and today they are mocking us."[18]

A contemporary author expresses the relationship between dead and living in other terms, saying, in substance, "that after having crossed the doors of death, the soul breaks free and returns to regard the world behind it," and adding that "the dead live on in us if we choose to keep them alive."[19]

*Judeo-Muslim pilgrimages.* The same grave can be a place of pilgrimage for both Jews and Muslims, a compromise zone, the scene of manifestations of cultural symbiosis, even religious syncretism. It may seem surprising to find Jews and Muslims seeking the intercession and protection of the same saints and santons, indulging in the same practices and acts, making the same offerings, using the same invocations, the same formulas of prayer. Both leave their visit to the same saint dreaming of the abundant benefits that the success of their pilgrimage will bring, returning home with new faith and hope, at the very least.

### *Funeral Eulogies and Orations*

Moroccan elegiac poems of the seventeenth and eighteenth centuries are generally collected in anthologies under the title *'Et Sefod*, "the

18. See also our *qiṣṣa* from Tinghir in the Todgha, pp. 91–93, above.
19. Saul Bellow, *Humboldt's Gift* (Harmondsworth: Penguin Books, 1978), pp. 197 and 327.

time of lamentation and tears." These compositions deserve attention primarily because of the considerable part played by balladry in funeral rites and the important place occupied by the *kinnah* (elegy) in the liturgy of the seven days of mourning and the three major commemorative ceremonies. In addition, the contents of the poems themselves and the comments that their authors write in their headings make this type of literature a valuable source of information about people who are no more and the circumstances of their deaths, a not negligible biographical and historical document.

The funeral eulogies composed by Jacob Aben Sur and the accompanying headnotes reflect Jewish life in his time in Fez and Meknès. They are a source of information about relationships with the Islamic environment and the central and local authorities, about the lay dignitaries who governed the Jewish community, and the senior magistrates and rabbis who legislated and watched over the moral and spiritual health of its members. As part of his duties and in his capacity as a leading judge of the Fez court and an eminent preacher, Jacob Aben Sur was often called on to give funeral sermons.

On a fundamental level, these elegies are real funeral orations and homilies. The expressions of grief and regret, the listings of the virtues and titles of the deceased, are linked to meditations and reflections on the problems of faith, variations on the theme of death, truisms on "the ephemeral nature of life and the fragility of the world, on the transcendent nature of the body compared with the immortality of the soul, on the delights of the world-to-come reserved for the righteous and sages who sit, crowned with glory, at the foot of the heavenly throne."

The pieces reprinted here, with their headnotes, belong to the poetry in Hebrew and are generally short.

> On Friday, 19 Adar 5449/1689, the perfect sage, the excellent teacher, the leading magistrate of the court of the town of Fez, Rabbi Judah 'Uzziel, may his memory be blessed in the world-to-come, was called to appear before the heavenly Academy. In this *kinnah* I have paid homage to his illustrious memory. I sang it to the tune of bitter laments.

My heart quivers and I tremble with sadness;
Bitterly, I grieve and I lament.
I cry my affliction in the bosom of the assembled community.

God [lit., Rock], in His anger and vexation has held out His hand.
That is the reason I was seized with fear and trembling when the pride of Judah was destroyed.

Crown of venerable men and sages, treasury of delights,
He knew the letter, symbol, allegory, legal significance, and mystical meaning [of the texts].
In smooth words he taught his knowledge to the people.
The excellence of his virtues is immeasurable and their number countless.
Righteous he remained throughout his life, engaged in the service of the faith and the law.

A light has gone out, alike in brilliance to the golden splendor of the sun.
He cleaved to God in action and in thought . . .

Jacob Aben Sur dedicated several elegies to the memory of a contemporary rabbi, Menaḥem Serero. One of them, he says, was sung when the coffin arrived at the Great Synagogue, where the deceased scholar had prayed and taught. Here it must be pointed out that displaying a coffin in a synagogue is a practice unknown to the ritual of the Jews in Morocco. This was an exceptional situation which, to my knowledge, is not mentioned anywhere else, and I myself have never witnessed it. On the other hand, it is a common Muslim practice to display the mortal remains in the mosque before burial when the deceased is a high-ranking political or religious figure.

This elegy begins with the following couplet written in Aramaic:

It is fitting that you tear out your hearts
O [members of] this holy community!
For it is through your sins
That a venerable scholar is dead.

In a moving lament, Jacob Aben Sur mourns the death of his two sons, Yosef and Menashe, which occurred in the month of Shebat 5462/1702 following the demise of their brothers Re'uben *Rabbah* and Re'uben *Ẓota* (Big Reuben and Little Reuben). Fate raged against this "aged oak" who survived sixteen of his children. Their loss filled his life with mourning. He poured out his grief in moving elegies. In this one, a verse piece with a chorus, he weeps bitter tears over the four successive tragedies; his *tamrur* (lament-form) is reminiscent of a *kin-*

*nah* for the Ninth of *Ab* attributed to the eleventh-century Cordovan poet Isaac Ibn Ghiyyat, which begins as follows: "Driven from the house of their delights . . ."

Aben Sur's composition begins with this appeal:

My brethren, comrades, beloved friends.
Feel for my grief, for my hands dropped with weakness,
That day when the prince of executioners, like a beast of the fields,
Came to take my two children.

In two *kinot,* Jacob Aben Sur delivered a funeral eulogy for R. Barukh Tolédano, a native of Meknès who had settled in Jerusalem, in the Holy Land, where he died on 10 Tebet 5472/end of 1711.

He left his home,
His country and his native land,
Fulfilled the wishes of his Creator,
In love and humility.
Agile as a deer, he hastened
To go with zeal,
To the town of charm and holiness,
To the land of the mountain and the hill.

A series of seven elegies celebrates the memory of some notable Jews of Fez and Meknès who were shot or burned alive on the orders of Moulay Ismail. The headnote for one of these laments is given below, followed by its chorus.

To Judah Aben Sur, my cousin, a burnt offering reduced to smoke in the flower of life, died for the sanctification of the Name, Friday, 11 Tammuz 5472/1712, at Meknès.

You, faithful men of my community!
Gather and assemble.
And mourn the victims of the flames, the fire lit by God.

On the same day, 11 Tammuz 5472/1712, Isaac ben 'Amara, an honorable merchant of Fez, was consigned to the flames. His son Aharon suffered the same fate the following Sabbath.

The first couplet of the funeral eulogy that honors their memory is reprinted below:

Men of brazen faces surrounded them with bundles of branches,
Dragged them to the stake,
Thrust them into the flames,
Heaped bitter words upon them.
Nothing was spared of their flesh.
They proclaimed [despite all], the unity of their Creator,
And the truth of his judgment.

Finally, Jacob Aben Sur eulogizes one of his disciples. The headnote reads:

On the afternoon of Friday, 6 Elul, the scholar Moshe ha-Kohen and his brother Shem Tob ha-Kohen, the two sons of Rabbi Nehemyah ha-Kohen, were tortured and put to death.

The lament begins:

Chant a chorus of laments!
[Mourn] the death of a man of faith,
Of a prince among priests [variation: of the race of the strong].

# Chapter 3

# *The Moroccan Jewish Community*

## STRUCTURE

### *Megorashim and Toshabim*

Moroccan Jewry comprised two ethnic groups of different origins, languages, and cultural levels, with different rites and, more particularly, social concepts and customs, living side by side with separate institutions. In time they merged their communal activities on the local level, and leadership passed to the immigrant element of Spanish stock, which soon emerged as the dominant influence in the sphere of economics, and even in rabbinical knowledge.

In the available texts, the two groups are described as *qahal qadosh ha-megorashim,* "the holy community of the exiles," and *qahal qadosh ha-toshabim,* "the holy community of the native inhabitants."

The term *baldiyyîn,* "natives" (in contrast to *rumiyyîn,* "Europeans") is used to describe this second group in an ordinance in Arabic dated 1550.

The question of the relationships between the exiles and their native co-religionists is fairly complicated. The conflicts between the two communities concerned the dietary laws, the liturgy, personal status, taxation, and similar matters.

We know that there were marranos in the Maghreb, and especially in Fez, from a few responsa that also throw light on the community's attitude toward them. Although they had returned to Orthodox Judaism after their arrival from Spain and Portugal, attempts were made to prevent them from holding public office in the community and to remove the privileges attached to the name of Kohen from those who bore it. This opposition to the influence of the marranos and to their integration into the community came primarily from the toshabim. On the other hand, their former Castilian brethren helped and supported them.

Note that families of Spanish origin who had been living in Morocco before the expulsion of 1492 regarded themselves as toshabim, as compared with their co-religionists, newly arrived from Spain and Portugal (e.g., the Ibn Danan, Ben Rimokh, and Gagin families).

### *Christian Prisoners and Black Slaves*

An ordinance signed in Fez and dating from 1603 makes a passing allusion to the presence of Christian prisoners in Jewish homes in the mellah. A few rich merchants must have kept some in their service, using them as domestic servants or for less humble, specialized tasks, while awaiting their eventual ransom. The ordinance in question prohibited the buying or selling of alcoholic drinks to gentiles, but made an exception for prisoners: "Whosoever owns a non-Jewish prisoner whom he has purchased with his money, is permitted to give him wine and brandy to drink on condition that he takes them in his master's presence."

We also know that Maghrebian Jews owned non-Muslim slaves, and that they acted as intermediaries when Muslim prisoners in Christian lands were released and when Christian prisoners on Islamic soil were ransomed. Moreover, the services of Jewish bankers were used in relations with Europe.

In the Moroccan south, notably in Mogador, up to the beginning of the twentieth century, a few Jews owned black slaves. These were almost exclusively women, called M'Barka or Ghalya, and were generally presented by the *kaid* to his intimate friends and courtiers. They adopted the way of life and religious practices of the families they lived with, becoming full family members and exercising a real influence on the children. Problems often arose as to where to bury them when they died, although some did officially convert to Judaism.

Whatever their origin, Islam accorded Jews the legal position it reserved for "people of the book": The Muslim community tolerated them on its soil and, in principle, guaranteed to "protect" them. This was the status of *dhimmis*, governed by *fiqh* (Muslim law). Within the limits of this status, the Jewish communities enjoyed a wide degree of administrative and cultural autonomy: they organized themselves in their own way; and had their own courts and finances; they ensured that facilities for worship, welfare, and education were available to their members; they determined matters of personal status and even the application of Jewish law, and had the power to enact compulsory regulations for their members in matters of taxation and public order.

## *The Community Council*

### *Rabbis and Notables*

As in every Jewish society, the aristocracy (i.e., the ruling class) was in principle recruited from the cultured elite, the only true value and the only hierarchy being based on learning. Thus, the people chosen to participate in the administration of the community, in the framework of the Community Council, the *wa'ad ha-qehillah* or *ma'amad*, were drawn from the following categories:

• The official rabbis (*ḥakhamin*) and judges (*dayyanim*), who held the powers of decision in legal matters and were the guardians of doctrine and tradition. They were supplemented by a category of religious people, designated as *ḥakheme ha-hesger*, members of the brotherhood of "hermits," to support their authority in exceptional circumstances.

• The notables, who could themselves also be fine scholars, represented a sort of plutocratic oligarchy which, as a general rule, served the public good zealously and devotedly. But there were also occasions when it took advantage of its wealth and influence to rule the community harshly, demanding privileges and committing abuses which the rabbinate was forced to condemn.

In the available documentation, the notables bear various honorific titles which seem to correspond to levels in the social hierarchy or to fixed functions: *rashe ha-qahal*, "leaders of the community"; *tobe-ha-'ir*, "excellencies of the town," who were limited in number to seven; *tobe bet ha-knesset*, "the betters of the synagogue" (or its benefactors); *nikhbede-ha-kehillot*, "honorable or respectable bourgeois"; *yehide ha-qahal* and *yehide-segullah*, "elected or chosen members of society, those who enjoyed special standing"; *anshe ha-serarah*, "ruling class."

The "members of the council," *anshe ha-ma'amad*, were recruited from this class of society. Together with other agents, they carried out a certain number of public duties, generally voluntarily: the levying and distribution of taxation, collection and administration of charitable funds, administration of synagogues and religious foundations. They were the *parnasim* (administrators), *gizbarim* (treasurers), *peqidim* (civil servants), *mukaddemin* (officials), *memunnim* (agents occasionally assigned to specific tasks).

It was the notables too who appointed the community's highest dignitary. Although the texts freely refer to him by the flattering title of *nagid,* and sometimes even as *nasi'* (prince), he was none other than *shaykh al-yahûd,* "doyen or leader of the Jews." He was even called "prince of princes" in an ordinance of 1603. But common parlance up to the present day generally uses the Arabic term *shaykh al-yahud* or simply *shikh.*

### *The* Nagid

The legal assistants were the notary clerks (*sofrim,* "scribes"), whose main functions were to supplement the magistrates when necessary, and write and sign the legal certificates and ordinances of the *ma'amad,* on the responsibility of the judges and communal leaders. "The sofer is a scholar who is required to have a perfect knowledge of legislation and procedure, especially in matters of matrimonial law. However, the presence of a judge is necessary at the time the document is written." The court had bailiffs (*shlihe bet din*) at its disposal and could if necessary call on experts to arbitrate, such as the senior members of the craft guilds (Arabic *'amin,* plural, *'umânâ*).

The communities were usually free to choose their magistrates.

Legal authority was conferred on anyone who possessed a thorough knowledge of rabbinical learning, the only guarantee of being able to speak in the name of the divine law. Moreover, it was not necessary to bear the title of magistrate to administer justice. The parties to a dispute were free to appeal to the "wisdom" of a rabbinical authority of their own choice, even one who was not a *dayyan,* to settle their quarrel and "make law and justice prevail between them." The decision had force of law for the parties concerned, and the rabbinical courts generally respected its decisions.

This procedure had something in common with the arbitration by experts (*berurim*) to whom the judges themselves submitted certain lawsuits relating to commerce or crafts.

The leader or doyen of the Jews, the *nagid,* was the medium of communication between the Jewish community, on one hand, and the official authorities of the country or town (the sultan, governor, officials of the *makhzen*), on the other. He was entrusted with duties relating to public order and levying taxes. He was responsible for the strict implementation of the decisions of the *ma'amad,* over which he most often presided, and the execution of the judgments pronounced by the rabbinic courts. This personage frequently played an important role at the royal court (e.g., personal adviser to the sovereign, statesman, ambassador, purveyor to the army).

It can be assumed, as a general rule, that to achieve the rank of *nagid,* government support and the consent of the notables and rabbis had to be obtained. The order in which these two stages occurred depended on circumstances. Whatever the case, it must have been a very complex process, sometimes immersed in intrigue, corrupt practices, and bribery. Several ordinances and responsa reflect the conflicts within the community at the time when a *nagid* was appointed, and on some occasions the rabbinate rose up in protest against a *nagid* whose nomination was obtained against the wishes of the *qahal,* or who was guilty of malpractices committed in the exercise of his office.

Although the *nagid* had extensive powers and enjoyed privileges which sometimes placed him above the common law and exempted him from the restrictive measures that some *taqqanot* imposed on the community, he was also the first victim of policy reversals and of arbitrariness and greed on the part of the rulers. In times of serious crisis, his lot was scarcely enviable, and the community was bound by contract to compensate him for any material loss he suffered in the exercise of his duties.

Oral information that we have received on this dignitary of the Jewish community of Morocco corroborates the ancient sources on many points. Shikh Smuyal (Samuel Elbaz) of Casablanca still had a retinue of *mokhaznis* in his service at the beginning of the twentieth century, before the French Protectorate. They helped him to enforce order in the mellah and defend his co-religionists against Muslim incursions, using cunning to prevent conversions and bring recent converts—toward whom he was merciless—back to their former faith. He protected the widow and the orphan, and freely championed the poor against the greed of a moneyed aristocracy in search of privileges and promotion, particularly in matters relating to the distribution of taxation (information obtained from M. Armand Elbaz, grandson of this Casablancan *nagid,* and confirmed by other sources).

### *The Ordinances*

The *ma'amad,* with the *nagid* usually presiding, administered the community by ordinances (*taqqanot, haskamot*). These covered a vast area of the lives of the congregation. They were generally permanent but could be temporary, in which case the period of validity was specified. Details contained in several texts provide information on the procedure for drawing up and promulgating ordinances, the public proclamations whereby the *qahal* was informed of their content, and the penalties incurred by contravening them.

The *taqqanah* of 1550 gives the following description of this ceremonial (note that as it is addressed to the "community of natives," *qahal fas al-baldiyyîn,* it is written in Arabic):

> . . . We have drawn it up for the benefit of the *qahal,* by order of the *qahal* and before the leaders of the holy community of toshabim. . . . We have written it in the presence of the sage (*ḥakham*) and the seven notables of the city; we have transcribed it in the Book of Records of the community, which is in the possession of the *qizbar.* Before signing it, we have read the text before the *qahal* assembled in the synagogue on Shabbat, while the Sefer Torah [scroll of the Law] was still on the *tebah* [officiant's dais]; the *qahal* then gave its approval.

The decisions of the *ma'amad* were sometimes solemnly proclaimed on the public highway, accompanied by the sounding of the shofar (*taqqanah* of 1716).

Once promulgated, the ordinances were put into immediate effect, and the members of the community were obliged to observe them, "they and their descendants after them, for ever more" (permanent *taqqanot*) or "during the period of their validity" (temporary *taqqanot*). They were imposed on pain of *ḥerem* (excommunication), a formidable weapon which the community could use against delinquents; subjected to a religious and social boycott which in itself already entailed very serious moral and material repercussions. This ban was accompanied by other penalties, such as corporal punishment, *taṭwif* (ignominious exposure of the delinquent), imprisonment, and fines, executed by the *nagid* in accordance with the rulings of the rabbi-judges and the *ma'amad.*

The *nagid* was sometimes "permitted" to hand delinquents over to the secular authority of the *makhzen,* which executed the most severe punishments. The rabbinic court could also take action to expel an undesirable member of the community, forbidding him access to the mellah.

One *taqqanah,* dated 1730, prohibited the disclosure of its terms to non-Jews, on pain of anathema. It concerned the exemption of sales of liver, "food of the needy," from the *siga* tax, and fixed its price at a reasonable level. It must be added that *taqqanot* drawn up by the *ma'amad* of one locality were not applicable in another. The *taqqanah* of 1603, for example, specified that "it only has force of law in the city of Fez and two parasangs beyond its limits."

### *Courts and Magistrates*

Within the limits of the administrative autonomy that the statute of "protection" (*dhimma*) granted them, the Jewish communities had free exercise of justice and their own courts. The power of these courts extended over a vast area of the public and private life of the community: strict observance of the legal and ritual rules of the religious law *strictu sensu;* determination of personal status. In questions of civil law (contracts and obligations, disputes over property or business). They heard every lawsuit between one Jew and another. Moreover, the state authority referred Jewish litigants—usually plaintiffs—to their own jurisdiction:

"By order of our master the king, may his majesty be exalted, and the judge (*shofet*), may God fortify him, disputes between Jews can only be judged by the magistrates of Israel" (ordinance of 1603).

The magistrates were *ex officio* members of the *ma'amad* and participated in all major decisions concerning religious practice and communal administration.

Sentences imposed by the rabbinic courts were implemented by their own bailiffs (*shaliyaḥ bet-din*), by the *nagid,* the secular arm of the spiritual authority, or even by government agents.

#### *Organization of Judicial Power*

Justice was administered by the *bet-din,* "house of justice," or rabbinical court. It was presided over by "one" (*bet-din shel yaḥid*) or several judges, generally "three" (*bet-din shel shalosh*), called the "great court" (*bet-din ha-gadol*), and sometimes more. The principal judge, called *ab bet-din,* presided over the "great court."

Some matters were beyond the competence of the court with a single judge, notably certain serious questions concerning personal status.

### *The Non-Jewish Justice System*

The first concern of the Jewish authorities, whether rabbis or laymen, was to avert any outside interference in the affairs of the community and any violation of the autonomy granted it within the framework of the *dhimma*.

The Islamic regimes, on the whole, respected the general principle of autonomy and, apart from certain extralegal interventions, which all in all occurred only rarely, the governmental authorities meddled very little in Jewish legal affairs. The only case officially recorded in Moroccan rabbinic annals is the episode we mentioned in connection with bigamy (see p. 76 above).

Nonetheless, in Morocco, as in most Islamic lands, the rabbinate took precautionary measures motivated by a wish to assert the specific character of the Jewish communities and the supremacy of the law which governed them, a desire to protect the congregation's moral and material interests, and a distrust of Muslim justice. They only tolerated deviation from the general rule of prohibitions in predetermined, and very exceptional, circumstances, and used the threat of that fearful weapon, the *ḥerem,* against members of the community who appealed to Muslim jurisdiction of their own accord and invoked the koranic law in their litigation.

As has already been noted, the practice of *ṣadaq,* which replaced the Jewish contract of the ketubbah by a marriage contract concluded before a Muslim court, still existed in Fez at the beginning of the seventeenth century. In the same *taqqanot* which record this practice, as well as many responsa, the attitude of their Moroccan authors to the power of non-Jewish courts—a power which was, moreover, limited to actions in civil law and restricted by many reservations—was often dictated by circumstances. Recourse to non-Jewish justice was sometimes prescribed, sometimes tolerated, sometimes formally prohibited.

Thus any transfer of landed property, any operation concerning real estate in general (sale, mortgage or bailment), previously concluded before a rabbinic court and signed by Jewish clerks, had to be confirmed by a second certificate written by an agent of the civil justice and placed in the hands of a trustworthy third party (Jewish) . . . (*taqqanah* of 1603).

In 1736, a Fez court, referring to the previous *taqqanah,* authorized recourse to Muslim justice in a dispute concerning an estate, specifically stating that "the certificate must remain in the hands of a Jewish third party until such time as the rabbinic court considers it opportune to return it to the creditor." This would apply particularly in a case when "the debtor stubbornly refused to honor his liabilities." Rabbinic legal annals mention many other cases of this type.

*The crime of denunciation.* The legal literature frequently associates the topic of denunciation with the theme of recourse to non-Jewish jurisdiction. But the legislation applying to informers was more severe and made no allowances in its extremely harsh condemnation of "the man who denounces a co-religionist and delivers him into the hands of a gentile. . . . [The informer] is required to redress the wrong he has done his victim and must in particular pay him all sums he has expended, fines and bribes, in order to obtain his release." This is the substance of a decree by the Meknès court in 1728, and of a fairly large number of legal decisions spread out over the past four centuries.

### Other Rabbinic Functions

The high dignitaries of the community (the *nagid* and members of the *ma'amad*) and the rabbi-judges, too, when they possessed a certain level of personal wealth, in principle carried out the duties entrusted to them on a voluntary basis, free of charge.

The legal assistants (clerk-notaries, *sofre bet-din*) and synagogue officials, such as the *shoḥeṭ* and the *mohel,* appointed to carry out ritual slaughter and circumcision respectively, the *shaliyaḥ ṣibbur* (officiating minister), and the *shammash* (synagogue beadle), the schoolteacher, and the *sofer* (scribe) might all receive a modest payment from community funds. But the bulk of their income came from payment for their work. Life was hard for all of them, with the exception perhaps of the clerk-notary, although they enjoyed benefits in kind (like the *shoḥeṭ*) and tax benefits (exemption from poll-tax, freedom from communal taxation), which were, moreover, periodically challenged. Very often several religious duties were carried out by the same person, who was also obliged to practice one or several other trades to make ends meet.

Although plurality of functions existed for the majority of offices, a distinction was still made between the *sofer* (scribe) and the *sofer bet-din* (clerk-notary). He was responsible for copying on parchment the *sefarim* (Torah scrolls), the tefillin (phylacteries), and the mezuzot (parchments bearing the scriptural lessons Deuteronomy 6:4–9 and 11:13–21 that were enclosed in a case and fixed to the right-hand door-post).

The salary of the chief rabbi and senior dignitary of the large Jewish metropolis of Fez was no more than 12 *metqal*s at the beginning of the eighteenth century.

In 1610, a *taqqanah* fixed the rate of pay of a clerk-notary for writing a certificate at half an *uqiya* and 5 *muzuna*s.

In 1698, a *shoḥeṭ* received one *prutah* per head of poultry ritually slaughtered. On the subject of the ritual slaughter of chickens, Rabbi Yosef Messas says with a touch of humor that this poor man's trade was all the less profitable because the rich man, who ate chicken, did not pay for it. In a fit of mirth, he added maliciously: *'asir we-khelleṣ*, "to be rich and pay!"

The authors of an ordinance of 1722 deplored the great poverty of the scribes and the prevalent unemployment in that profession, mentioning the considerable fall in rates of pay for their work: for a Sefer Torah, it had fallen from 250 to 80 uqiyas; for a pair of tefillin, from 90 to one; and for a mezuzah, from two to one tmen (or one-eighth of an uqiya). They referred to this situation in order to decide to grant fiscal immunity to the clerk-notaries and scribes, who had earlier formed a corporate association (*ḥebrah*) to call for the benefits of this measure.

### *Rabbinic Monopolies*

Magistrates and synagogue officials were generally recruited from an intellectual aristocracy made up of a small number of families who to all intents and purposes led the Moroccan communities for 450 years. They exercised a sort of spiritual and temporal leadership, an authority termed *serarah* in Hebrew, controlling, by virtue of hereditary privilege and without the participation of others, *shehiṭah*, the administration and the unpaid or burdensome operation of the synagogues, the right to hold the office of *sofer* or *dayyan*. In Fez, this role was played by the Ibn Danan, Sarfati, Serero, Aben Sur, and Ben 'Attar families; in Meknès by the Berdugos and Maymarans.

The arrival of new scholars in an area, the personal rivalries between rabbis, the opening of a new synagogue or yeshîbâh, even a ḥeder, sometimes the challenging of *serarah* itself, gave birth to conflicts, lawsuits which echo through the responsa. A frequent question is: Does possession of a *serarah* (i.e., office) give its holder a real right, or does he enjoy a legal presumption (*ḥazaqah*) over the position he occupies, and can he bequeath it to his son or to a close relative? In almost every case the decisors reply in the affirmative, most frequently on the basis of the general principle of the heredity of *serarah,* which Maimonides himself codified in his *Mishneh Torah.*

A legal consultation on this subject dating from 1728 and signed J. Aben Sur declares: "Whosoever has deserved to be appointed to an office (*serarah*) retains the benefit of it for himself during his lifetime and for his descendants until the end of the line."

The same phenomenon can be found among Muslim elites in Morocco. E. Levi-Provençal says in essence: "The title of scholar is hereditary; the same names recur at intervals of two or three centuries . . . ; a few great families have monopolized knowledge, from father to son in the course of generations; they have supplied lines of scholars whose present descendants enjoy the principal of their reputation."[1]

In this connection, note that the Muslim elites included several Jewish families, islamized at various periods in the history of Morocco, who mostly retained their original patronymics (e.g., Kohen, Sqalli, Bennis, Bensheqrun).

## *Communal Institutions*

### *The Synagogue*

The synagogue was the natural rallying point of the *qahal:* the house of prayer, the center of education and culture (ḥeder, yeshîbâh, adult education via night-time study and homilies), the meeting place of the *ma'amad* and congregation to publicly decide and proclaim ordinances, to pronounce or lift excommunications, and so on.

Religious objects, such as the Torah scrolls and their adornments, the hangings which covered the holy ark and the officiant's seat, the candelabra, the night lights, the oil and the candles were provided by religious donations.

---

1. *Historiens des chorfa,* p. 11.

A synagogue obtained the major *miṣwot* (the right to go up to the sefer for the reading of the Law or to carry out part of its income from the sale by auction of certain ritual acts), *nedarim* (occasional donations), and *rentas* (six-monthly contributions) paid by worshipers who wanted to reserve the right to perform a miṣwah during the period which separated two consecutive major festivals, Sukkot and Pesaḥ, for example.

After a sum had been set aside for the upkeep of the premises, the synagogue's revenues were divided between the holder of the *serarah* (or *ḥazakah*) attached to the synagogue in question, the *shaliyaḥ ṣibbur,* or officiating minister (who sometimes held both offices), and the *shammash.*

### Heqdesh *Property and Charitable Works*

As a result of purchase, donations, or legacies, the community owned property intended for religious or charitable use, called *heqdesh,* "sacred or consecrated property," also called "the property of the poor. This was property held in mortmain, and there were very limited possibilities for transferring it. Thus heqdesh is similar to *ḥbâsr* (classical *ḥubus*), a term designating the property of Muslim religious foundations.

A *taqqanah* dated 1700 states: "The community of Fez was forced to mortgage its heqdesh property in order to help its members who had been reduced to poverty by extralegal taxation extorted by the king's son."

The existence of well-managed welfare funds made it possible to provide for the needs of the poor in cases of economic distress or famine. A document dated December 1613 asserts that "more than sixty gentiles died of starvation every day, but, thank God, not a single Jew perished."

The charity fund was fed by the fines, sometimes very heavy, which the *nagid* or courts imposed for infringement of the ordinances, and by indirect taxation (see below). Apart from fixed contributions from their members, the welfare societies received donations and legacies. Taxes were removed from certain commodities, reserved to the poor.

The "poor of the town" had a prior right over the charitable funds of the community to which they belonged. There is a very significant *taqqanah* on this subject.

In 1691, in reaction to "the frequent solicitations and excessive demands of emissary rabbis from Poland and Ashkenaz," the community of Fez, which was itself plunged in deep distress, regulated the collections carried out by the emissaries and limited the amounts.

### *Education*

The work of teaching and education devolved on the family and also on the community, which supervised the strict application of a certain number of rules and provisions, and which financed a few Talmud Torah establishments. For the functioning of these institutions, see the discussion above in Chapter 2.

## *Taxation*

### *Direct Taxation*

The Moroccan Jewish communities, as "protected" collectivities, were subjected to strong fiscal pressure. There was, in the first place, the *jizya,* the legal poll-tax, a typical ingredient of the status of *dhimmi,* raised annually per capita and affecting all adult males. But over and above this, the treasury required the community to make all manner of extralegal payments, arbitrary sums at fixed dates or for exceptional reasons. Added to this were confiscations, fines, forced labor, bribes, and the "gifts" or "presents" which made up the *hyiya,* consecrated by custom. "At the great Muslim festivals . . . , a delegation brought the sultan and the governor of Fez the community's good wishes and presented the customary presents: golden bracelets, fabrics, silk kerchiefs, to a value set in proportion to the wealth of the families."

The Jewish communities were obviously powerless in the face of the fiscal oppression practiced by the "protecting" power, and groaned under its weight. This is reflected in the complaints which fill the prologues to the *taqqanot* and responsa dealing with this question. Yet their leaders, cleric and lay, who were responsible for the payment of the tax and its collection, strove to distribute the burden as equitably as possible among the congregation, taking into account certain imperatives of rabbinic law. This was their major concern, as is shown by several texts full of information on what today would be called tax evasion, on operations relating to the basis of the tax, its rate, and the method of collecting it.

The tax evasion of the day emanated from the efforts of certain influential notables to escape the yoke of taxation by the "influence" (*'inaya*) they enjoyed in government circles. As a consequence, the burden fell on the less wealthy or poverty-stricken section of the population.

The mechanics of the tax (i.e., the taxation imposed by the state, which can be described as a direct tax, as distinct from the indirect taxes on expenditures levied by the community to cover its own needs) were fairly simple. What was difficult and often controversial was estimating the value of the taxable assets—in this case, the taxpayer's wealth.

The usual procedure, and the one which the rabbinate supported, consisted of entrusting the drawing up of registers to collectors, elected or appointed by the *ma'amad,* who were adept at assessing the wealth of the members of the community and their ability to pay taxes.

Other methods of estimating wealth seem to have been dismissed by the bulk of the authors. This applied to the systems of fiscal confession and of forfeitures for which wealthy people, who wanted to avoid part of the burden of taxation, had a marked preference.

Whatever the procedure employed, the amount of the assessment was in direct proportion to the amount of wealth, and a rate, fixed by a *taqqanah* and valid for a given period, was applied to it. However, there was one specific exception to the rule of proportional taxation. In fact, the texts generally made a provision for a deviation for "the greatest wealth," which was taxed at the same rate as the level immediately below it. This measure was sometimes explained by the wish to turn away the evil eye from the most wealthy. But it was primarily intended to screen them from the cupidity of the rulers and demonstrate the solidarity of the communal group with its wealthiest leaders, a theme that most texts specifically stress.

### *Indirect Taxation*

The category of indirect taxation includes all the taxes that the community levied in order to cover part of the collective burdens which devolved on it, and, in particular, to help the needy. This system of taxation, similar to the modern sales tax, was called *sììa* (from the Spanish *sisas,* "tax on goods"), and sometimes also *'ezer,* a Hebrew word meaning "help." The system probably originated in Spain, continued in use among the exiles in the host country, and was finally adopted by the "native inhabitants."

At first it was levied on meat and then extended to other foodstuffs, to domestic consumer goods, then to all commercial transactions. A "farming out" system was usually adopted for its collection. The community negotiated with one or more individuals who contracted to pay it a lump sum recoverable from the consumers. Sometimes, too, the agents of the *qahal* collected the sum directly or levied it in kind on merchants.

The proceeds from the tax on slaughter were the main source of the welfare fund. Together with a tax on kosher wine, it is still one of the communities' principal sources of income today.

According to a *taqqanah* dated 1649, a levy of two pounds of flour was made on every shop once a week for the benefit of the poor, and one old uqiya of oil, soap, butter, and honey for the same purpose.

### *Fiscal Immunity*

Jews employed in the king's service enjoyed freedom from taxation. This principally applied to the *nagid*, who could also, if he so wished, take advantage of special privileges and exceptions from certain ordinances.

But this issue essentially concerned all synagogue officials and especially members of the rabbinate. As they were in some sense interested parties, they, like their colleagues in the Jewish world in every generation, devoted copious writings to justifying the maintenance of an ancient prerogative inherited from Temple days. They adopted legislative measures at various times via a large number of ordinances and responsa in order to safeguard its strict implementation or to extend it to a larger and larger number of categories of "scholars" bearing the title *talmid ḥakham.*

## *Policing of Customs and Sumptuary Laws*

In the narrow confines of the mellah, the Jew's public and private life was subject to strict supervision by his co-religionists and by the community. No infringement of the ethico-religious discipline which governed the collectivity escaped the vigilance of the *muqaddemim,* who denounced and punished reprehensible actions in the name of the rabbinate and *ma'amad.* This condemnation and control helped to maintain a high level of morality, in accordance with the precepts of traditional Judaism.

Of particular concern was the observance of morality and purity in married and domestic life. This did not prevent a few "misguided" individuals" from stepping out of line, departing from the path of musar (*ethics*) and din (law). Some responsa, for example, mention cases of debauchery and concubinage, adultery and prostitution, which the rabbinic authorities severely condemned. But lust was not always at the origin of departures from accepted behavior: They were sometimes forced on their perpetrators by the precarious conditions of Jewish life or simply by poverty.

• "During the period of drought, a woman of Tetuán prostituted herself to a gentile and gave birth to a daughter whom the parents of the gentile claim as one of theirs in order to raise her in the Muslim religion" (evidence given in 1750).

• "A woman gave herself to a gentile so that her daughter would be spared during the pillaging of the Meknès mellah" (end of eighteenth century).

Drinking bouts in the mellah, in which Jews and non-Jews sometimes joined, facilitated debauchery and corruption. This led the rabbinate, in agreement with the governmental authorities, to control the trade in alcoholic beverages, forbidding Jews to sell them to their Muslim or Christian neighbors or to serve them to gentile guests.

A *taqqanah* dated 1602 says:

> Meeting by order of his majesty the king in the house of the *nagid,* Abraham Roti, and with the permission of the *nagid,* Moses Halevi, the rabbinical authorities confirm an ancient *taqqanah* which forbids any Jew to sell wine or brandy to anyone, Jew or non-Jew, man or woman, Idumaean, Israelite, Parsi, renegade, European (*'ilj*), or Jewish convert to Islam (*meshummad*) as from today and during the next ten years, on pain of excommunication, anathema. . . . The same punishments apply to anyone who gratuitously serves them to non-Jews or who allows the latter to indulge in drink in his presence. . . . Whosoever owns a non-Jewish prisoner whom he has purchased with his money, is permitted to give him wine and brandy to drink on condition that he does so in his master's presence.

Another ordinance, dated 1617, made in the presence of the *nagid* by order of the governor, also prohibited dealing in wine or brandy. But both *taqqanot* made provision for exemptions on the part of the *nagid.*

The texts which yield the most information of every sort, equally valuable for jurists, ethnologists, and linguists, are the sumptuary regulations. These dictated restrictions on expenditure on the occasion of family celebrations. They forbade the wearing of certain jewelery and the display of valuable finery. Legislative measures of this kind, generally dictated by ethico-religious considerations, also expressed a concern not to expose property and people to the envy and cupidity of "outsiders." Composed in Hebrew, Arabic, and Castilian, they contain an infinity of hitherto-unpublished detail regarding dress, women's jewelery and finery, ceremonial, the customs and rites which accompanied marriage and other family celebrations, circumcision, and so on. It is most regrettable that the authors of the many works that describe these ceremonies were completely unaware of this documentation.

Look at the following text, dated 1688, for example:

> Because of circumstances [e.g., fiscal pressure, economic stagnation, other communal misfortunes], the rabbinic authorities, the *ma'amad* and the *negidim* condemn the practice of sumptuous meals served on the occasion of family ceremonies . . . and take the following measures, applicable, on pain of fines, to both rich and poor, these latter borrowing at usurious rates in order to follow custom and imitate their wealthier co-religionists. . . . Whosoever is accustomed to organize the festivities called *al-khtayem* [a ceremony marking the end of a cycle of teaching at a ḥeder or yeshîbâh, comparable to the Muslim *khatma,* celebrating the completion of reading the Koran], for his children on the eve of Shabu'ot, is only permitted to make one single meal, which must exclude chicken, pigeon, and poultry of any sort. This also applies to meals for weddings, circumcisions, redemptions of the firstborn, etc. . . . It is also forbidden to send poultry dishes for the *sbut u-'shawi* [meals on the "Saturdays and evenings" of the marriage week], with the exception of dishes intended for the newlyweds and eaten exclusively in the intimacy of the home.

Even more instructive is the ordinance dated 1618 on the same subject: "the wasting of money on meals and banquets on the occasion of family celebrations."

> In these hard times, when each day brings its share of curses and calamities, when the majority of the populace is bowed down under the burden of taxation and payments of every sort, we see both poor and

rich indulging in excessive expenditure on the occasion of [family] celebrations, giving increasing numbers of banquets to which the "nations" (*goyim*) come and pillage and steal, sometimes under the defenseless and impotent eye of the master of the house. . . . Whatever the occasion—betrothal, marriage, circumcision, redemption of the firstborn, etc.— none but close relatives of the betrothed or newlyweds, or of the father of the newborn son must be invited to celebrations, limited to a single meal. . . . Non-members [of the family] must only be invited if the [legal] quorum [of ten adult men] is not made up. . . . Only the future bridegroom and possibly his closest relatives, if such there are, will be invited to the first meal given in his honor, commonly called *dekhla* ["entry"], in the home of his fiancée's parents. None of the dishes prepared for the meal must be sent outside, from one house to another, be it through the window or passed through the verandah. . . . On the day when the husband-to-be (*ḥatan*) has his hair cut in honor of his chosen, he must only invite his close relatives and those of the *kallah* [bride] to the collation prepared for the occasion. In addition, he must not ask any women other than his mother, his future mother-in-law, his sisters ,and those of the *kallah* to make *al-k'-ak* and *al'qâdâ* [special pastries], none of which must be sent outside the house, be it via window or verandahs. . . . The practice of *taqyil* [celebratory sessions] is henceforth abolished. The customary meal will no longer be made on the Sabbath before the marriage, in the house of either the *kallah* or the *ḥatan,* nor the meal that the latter serves to his guard of honor toward the evening of that day, which is commonly called *qâ'â.* Also forbidden is the collation that the *ḥatan* customarily gives during the marriage period on the occasion of the *ribṭâ* [the ritual girding of the bridegroom with the piece of white fabric which the bride wore on her head on the Sunday before the marriage week]. . . . The fish meal which the new bridegroom customarily serves at the end of the nuptial period must be restricted to the closest family, even excluding the guard of honor. The *ḥatan* is forbidden to send the *kallah* the collation called *miryindá* [from the Spanish *merienda,* "to taste, lunch"] on the Sabbath before the wedding, the usual presents on the ninth and tenth of the month of *Ab,* and the gifts which it is customary to send her on the day when she is bled. One and only one woman will be instructed to carry the *al-hiniyyâ* [tray of henna, from the Spanish *alhẽna*] to the house of the *kallah* for the needs of the marriage rites, and it must not be accompanied by either sweets or drinks, except for honey and butter. . . . The sending of pastries, meat dishes, and other food of this nature to the house of a woman in childbirth during the week after her delivery are henceforth prohibited, apart from what she receives from her closest relatives. . . . Let us add that after the marriage ceremony (*qiddushin*), the new bride is bound to cover her head with a silk kerchief; in addition, she must only return to the house of the *ḥatan* at nightfall. . . .

Any infringement of this *taqqanah* is punishable by excommunication and a fine of a hundred ounces to be paid directly to the tax collector.

A certain number of ordinances are concerned more particularly with the excessive use of finery and jewelery by women, and proclaim the need to place restrictions on it.

> Meeting in the presence of the *nagid* during the last ten days of the month of Sivan in the year 5364/1604, the perfect sages are examining questions which concern the *qahal* and note the damage caused to the community by women who go out covered and adorned with golden jewelery and precious stones called *khalkales* [rings], *tazras* [Berber chains], *'aqud d'al-jufar* [pearl necklaces], exhibiting themselves to the eyes of the people whose desire and envy they excite. . . . Henceforth, no woman, married or virgin, will wear the above-mentioned jewelery . . . except for pearls decorating earrings. Wearing a silk headband is permitted on condition that it is no more than an eighth of a cubit wide. But the veil (*khmâr*) which covers the bride is henceforth prohibited, as well as the jewelery which dresses her face, called *dlâyil,* particularly items made of gold and pearls. . . . [Female] undergarments will no longer be cut from brocade and lace, except for the collar and gorget.

Sometimes, too, the spiritual guides of a community publicly denounced certain practices. This was the case with customs which Rabbi Yosef Messas, a native of Meknès, noted among the Jews of Tlemcen when he was summoned to act as rabbi and judge there from 1924 to 1940. He records them in autobiographical notes which I published in my book *Pédagogie juive en Terre d'Islam,* in 1968.

> I found among them [the Jewish inhabitants of the city] an unfortunate practice, bearing the stamp of absolute heresy. When an individual rented a house or shop, he did not occupy it until he had placed a small pile of henna, the measure of a handful, in the four corners of the premises on the evening before he moved in, and had lit four candles on each pile. He then called on the demons who inhabited the place, imploring them to give a willing reception to the new tenants, the "neighbors" who were preparing to come and lodge with them. Then he closed the house with a key and went away. The next morning, he

returned with a black cock, and a *shoḥeṭ* slaughtered the beast in the center of the building, whether private dwelling or shop, sprinkled its blood in the four corners, and said: "So have we carried out the sacrifice [of this bird], we have sprinkled you with its blood, you, our good neighbors who live here, in order that you will graciously accept as neighbors those who come to live with you today, in this place."

They then prepared a dish of couscous with the slaughtered cock. The whole family ate of it; the neighbors were given a taste; a small quantity was thrown into the well and the cesspool.

A cock was not enough when someone built a new house. He had to sacrifice either a black billy goat or an ox of the same color, depending on the means at his disposal: "the rich man, his ox; the poor man, his goat." When I learned of this, I began by making sure it was accurate; then I immediately convened a great assembly, the community of worshipers, in the main synagogue in the town on a Shabbat, after the Shaḥrit prayers; I gave a long sermon, informing my audience of the gravity of the sin: "They are sacrificing to demons who are not God." The words I spoke bore fruit.

I raise this subject in a sermon once a year.

Another scourge, comparable to the previous one, affected this community. When a patient suffered from an illness for a long time, when a woman was subject to miscarriages or lost children at birth or at a very young age, or in any other unfortunate situation, a meal was made to summon demons and solicit their favor. The Arabs of the country called this sacrificial ceremonial *nasra/nashra.* A couscous was prepared with the flesh of a cock cut into tiny pieces. All the members of the family were invited. The meal was eaten at sunset in the evening. Large dishes were prepared. Women who specialized in exorcism and incantations threw their contents down the town drains or on the dung heaps.

I have severely condemned such practices and harshly admonished their authors. In this case, too, my speeches have had an effect.

Jewish wedding in Spanish Morocco. R. Benazeraf family.

A learned man praying. American Jewish Joint Distribution Committee.

Young Jewish woman in Debdov, eastern Morocco, early twentieth century. Collection of M. Zerbib.

Rabbis in Essaouira (Mogador) on the way to the *meshwar* (pasha's residence). Collection of M. Zerbib.

Jewish musicians. Collection of M. Zerbib.

Entrance to the Jewish Quarter, Meknès. Collection of M. Zerbib.

Eugène Delacroix, *Jewish Wedding in Morocco*. National Museum, Paris.

Bride wearing the traditional Jewish wedding dress (*berberisca*). Al-keswa Alkbira-Belisha family.

Jewish Cemetery in Tetouan. Collection of M. Zerbib.

Jewish coppersmiths in Marrakech. American Joint Distribution Committee.

Jewish merchant and a Muslim customer, Amizmiz, Marrakech region. American Joint Distribution Committee.

Eugène Delacroix, *Two Jewish Women at the Water Fountain*. National Museum, Paris.

Jewish Agricultural School, Marrakech. American Joint Distribution Committee.

Interior of home of a wealthy Jew in Fez.
Collection of H. Zafrani.

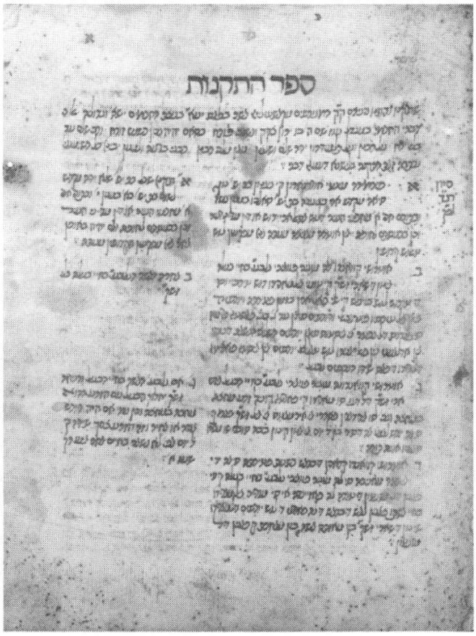

ספר התקנות

*Sefer ha-Taqanot* ("Registry of Ordinances") of the Castillian rabbis, Fez, 1494. Texts in Spanish and Hebrew from eighteenth-century manuscripts. Collection of V. Klagsbald. Original in Abensur Library, Fez.

Ketubbah. Essaouira (Mogador), Morocco, 1918. Collection of H. Zafrani.

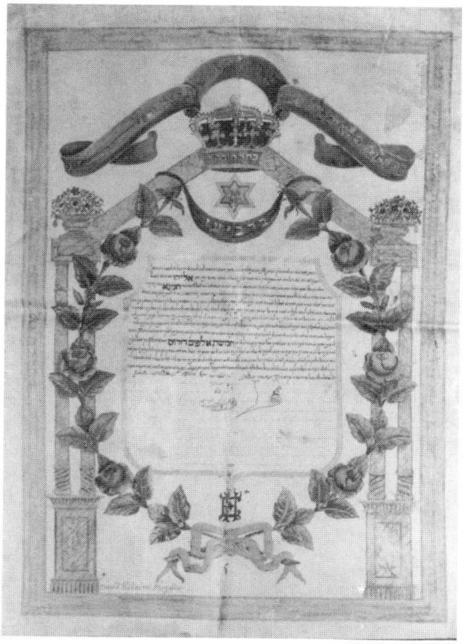

Ketubbah. Essaouira (Mogador), Morocco, 1909. Collection of H. Zafrani.

Excerpt from *Et Sofer* ("Pen of the Scribe") by Jacob Abensur, Fez, 1673–1753. Bibliothèque Nationale, Paris.

Teaching Hebrew at the Heder (ṢLA). American Joint Distribution Committee.

Teaching Arabic in a traditional Jewish school in independent Morocco. American Jewish Joint Distribution Committee.

# Chapter 4

# *Economic Life*

The main sources used here are the unpublished documents already utilized elsewhere in this book, namely the *taqqanot* (ordinances) and responsa (legal consultations, court decrees). These constitute a whole body of legal literature inherited from Moroccan judges and rabbis, and give, as it were, an inside look at their communities.

Other authors, outside these communities, have also supplied useful, but marginal, information on the Jewish contribution to the development of urban life, and the economic and political role of a few families of notables.

## *Communal Socioeconomic Structure*

The socioeconomic structure of the Moroccan Jewish communities varied with time and place, and any attribution of uniformity to it is certainly unwarranted. Moreover, primary, actual historical, documentation on this subject is practically nonexistent. What is known from the literature and specifically the Jewish archives mainly consists of incidental comments, chance remarks, circumstantial details of a secondary nature, solely the material that that was indispensable to drawing up and writing a legal text, a responsum or *taqqanah*.

What is more, *taqqanot* and responsa principally reflect the internal life of Jewish society. Although activities outside the community, even the business relationships its members might have with other ethnic or socioreligious groups, are not totally absent from this literature, they barely fall within its province. It only yields very sparse and fragmentary information—on the occasion of a lawsuit concerning an inheritance, for example—about the important role of Jews in the

Moroccan economy and their not negligible influence on the actual commercial and artisanal structures of town life.

The documentation, the *taqqanot* that governed the community, and the legal discussions of the responsa, which aimed to settle the day-to-day disputes between individuals, therefore, basically refer to the organization of economic life within the mellah, where the conditions of existence of the Jewish community were shaped and developed.

Examination of these texts yields a glimpse of the socioeconomic structure of the Jewish communities of Morocco.

The spiritual and temporal leadership of the community was in the hands of an oligarchy descended from old aristocratic families, mainly of Andalusian origin (megorashim), although a few had sprung from the ethnic group of former "inhabitants" (toshabim). It was these circles that usually produced the eminent scholars of the law, the *negidim* (notables), who sometimes rose to top-ranking official positions, the men who controlled credit, large-scale internal and external trade, or financed local craft, purveyors to the royal armies, capitalists and arbitrage bankers.

Nevertheless, this plutocratic bourgeoisie only formed a tiny minority of Jewish society. These brilliant careers were the lot only of isolated individuals who rose above the generally very modest level of their co-religionists. This contradicts the widely held opinion, and the impression created by certain documents (Jewish and non-Jewish), which suggests that the privileged few were representative of the whole Jewish populace.

It must be added that the positions of these individuals, however eminent they might have been, were extremely unstable, fragile, and often ended in disaster. Great wealth was a trap for its possessors, a noose which the holders of secular power had only to tighten to strangle. Those high dignitaries who reached the peak of opulence and influence were, in their capacity as Jews, at the mercy of the evil whims of the rapacious lust of the governing classes, who had no hesitation in stripping them of their property, sometimes even to the extent of poisoning or assassinating them.

According to a responsum dated 1727, "The *nagid* Samuel was arrested by the authorities and imprisoned; his sister had to pay the sum of two thousand ounces [of silver] to obtain his release."

Another responsum, dated 1704, reproduces a letter in Arabic that a Jewish notable from Meknès, Abraham ben Barukh Toledano, sent from prison to his brother Ḥayyim asking him to pay a ransom of four hundred *metqals* to Moulay Ali (son of Sultan Moulay Ismail).

The tragic fate of some Jewish dignitaries is witnessed by the *kinot* (laments, funeral eulogies) written in their memory. These works include the *kinot* in which the poet Jacob Aben Sur, an eyewitness, commemorated the Jewish notables of Fez and Meknès who were shot or burned alive on the orders of Moulay Ismail. The following dedications were written at the head of some of his pieces:

> To Judah Aben Sur, my cousin, a burnt offering reduced to smoke in the prime of life, died for the sanctification of the Name, Friday, 11 Tammuz 5472/1712, at Meknès.
>
> On the same day, Isaac ben 'Amara, an honorable merchant of Fez, was consigned to the flames; his son Aharon suffered the same fate the next day, Shabbat.
>
> On the afternoon of Friday, 6 Elul 5474/1714, the scholar Moshe ha-Kohen and his brother Shem Tob ha-Kohen were tortured and put to death.
>
> The famous *nagid* . . . Abraham Maymaran drank a suspicious beverage administered by one of the Muslim doctors in attendance . . . and died on 15 Tebet 5483/end 1722.

The vast majority of the working populace lived off small-scale trading, crafts, peddling, religious functions (teaching and occupations related to the religion), and agriculture in some rural areas.

In addition to this productive socioeconomic class, creating the means of existence of the community and with which the ensuing examination of the texts is primarily concerned, there was the large world of the poor and needy, whom the community was obliged to help by personal charity and from public welfare funds financed by special taxation.

## *The Tools of Economic Life*

### *Money*

We have laboriously tried to reconstruct from the responsa and *taqqanot* the monetary system utilized by their authors.

The monetary units mentioned are listed below:

Gold and silver: *metqal*
Subsidiary silver units: *uqiya, tmen, muzuna* (the Hebrew terms *ma'ah* and "white" [*laban*] and the Spanish *blanquilla,* were also used)
Copper subsidiary coins: *fels* (Arabic, plural *flus*), *pruṭah* (Hebrew).

The sources mention other monetary units as well and use certain notations to indicate the nature, origin, and form of the coins, and to specify their exact value, which varied depending on economic fluctuations, in terms of other coins or in subsidiary units of the same coin: the gold dinar, the real, the ducat, the *pondion* (Aramaic), the *kikkar* (Hebrew) or *qenṭar* (Arabic), which was worth a thousand *metqals*. The expressions "old money," "heavy money," and "square coins," in Hebrew, Arabic or Spanish, also occur.

*Monetary Manipulations*

The legal literature makes mention of considerable fluctuations in the relationship between the various standards (gold, silver, and copper) in Morocco in the early years of the seventeenth century. These gave rise to disputes that the rabbinic authorities had to decide when a ketubbah was settled, or between debtors and creditors. It was to settle financial disputes resulting from what the sources call "a rise in the price of money" that they enacted legislative measures of a general nature in the form of three *taqqanot,* in 1605, 1607, and 1609.

> On the sixth of Shebaṭ in the year 5365 of the creation [i.e., the beginning of 1605], it was publicly proclaimed, by order of our lord, the king, in all the towns of his kingdom, that the gold *metqal,* weighing twelve *pondions*, and which was previously exchanged for six *uqiyas*, will henceforth be worth seven and a half *uqiyas*: that the silver *ma'ah* (*muzuna*), weighing eight *pondions*, and which previously exchanged for twelve *pondions*, will henceforth be worth fifteen *pondions*. . . . This measure has given birth to quarrels between creditors and debtors, the creditor claiming the extra value of his credit, and the debtor wishing to withhold it. . . . For major reasons relative to the public interest, we have decided to exonerate the debtor from payment of this extra value following the change in the exchange rate, except in the case where a clause in the loan contract expressly specifies that the debtor pledges to

repay, in number and weight, the gold or silver coins received, should they increase in price by order of the king. . . . The *taqqanah* only applies to credit dealings that took place after the month of Kislev 5343 [end of 1582].

The second *taqqanah* begins by mentioning a change in the parity of money which preceded the previous one and actually took place in the month of Kislev 5343 (end of 1582), when the metallic (or silver) currency was first revalued: "the gold *metqal* had risen to 6 *uqiyas*, by order of the king, and the silver *ma'ah* (*muzuna*) to 12 *pondions*." Then comes the real purpose of this second *taqqanah:* "Today, on 3 Iyar 5367 [1607], the king has decided on a new rise in the price of money, fixing the rate of the *metqal* at 10 *uqiyas*, and of the silver *ma'ah* (*muzuna*) at a quarter of an *uqiya* or 20 *pondions*."

This decision remained in force for about two years until the neomenia of Adar I in the year 5369 (1609), when the rate of the *metqal* fell from 10 to 8 *uqiyas*, following a palace revolt. On 18 Tamuz the same year, after Moulay Abd-Allah had taken Fez, the *metqal* regained its value of 10 *uqiyas*. The rabbinic authorities then decided to rescind all *taqqanot* issued following the monetary manipulations of 1582, 1605, and 1607, and replace them with the *taqqanah* of 1609 (Ab 5369). It decreed that "henceforth the consequences of any change in the parity of money will be borne equally by creditor and debtor, the difference in the exchange rate on the day of the loan and its repayment being divided between the two contracting parties in half."

The role of Jewish craftsmen in the official production of coinage (smelting and refining the metals, striking the coins) will be discussed below, in connection with texts relating to Jewish industries.

### *Weights and Measures*

The value of the units of weight and measure varied from product to product and from one town to the next. These systems of measurement are made even more complex by the frequent use in the ordinances and responsa of talmudic terminology, for which the equivalent in the local dialects is not always easy to find.

Weights: *kikkar* (Hebrew) or *qenṭar* (Arabic); *rṭel*, sometimes replaced by *litrah* (plural, *litrot* and *litrin*); *uqiya*

Capacity: *kor* (plural *korin*), *paniegas*

Length: *'ammah* (in the wholesale trade, fabrics, linen, and cloth were dealt in by the piece, and a few items of clothing by the unit of measurement)

The qenṭar was used to measure the weight of both solids and liquids: sulphur, wax, honey, milk, oil, leather, tobacco

The *rṭel* was equivalent to one pound; one hundred *rṭel*s made a *qenṭar;* the *litrah* was the Roman measure of weight, *libra* or *litra,* found in talmudic texts.

The relationship between the *uqiya* and the *rṭel* was variable: 1:16 and 1:8.

The *kor* was a talmudic measure of grain, used for barley and corn. I personally think it is probably the *saḥfa* (see below).

The Spanish term *paniegas,* which denotes the contents of a sack or load, is employed for corn. Other measures of capacity were the *mudd* (bushel) and the *saḥfa,* which was equivalent to 60 *mudd*s, for grain; and the *qella* (jug), with a content of about 10 liters, for oil.

The Hebrew term *'ammah* (cubit), used for the Arabic *qala* or *dra'* (55–56 centimeters), was used to measure cloth.

*Prices and Salaries*

The prices of foodstuffs varied with the season. But the largest fluctuations in prices, notably in the price of cereals, followed climatic variations and the political situation. They showed considerable increases in periods of drought, and hence of shortage or catastrophic famines, or during problematic interregna. They experienced falls of the same magnitude the moment the first rains heralded abundant harvests, or as soon as disturbances and insecurity came to an end.

In 1731, for example, "the minimum price of 24 loads (*paniegas*) of corn in that year when life was expensive, was 36 *metqal*s." In 1750, "the current price of 100 *kor*s of barley rose to 220 *uqiya*s" and of a *kor* of corn to 22 *uqiya*s and 4 *tmen*s. In 1552, in a time of drought, a *sahfa* of corn cost as much as 6 ounces. But after the rain, it was sold at two and half ounces. In March 1606, famine was so acute that a quarter *qab* [*mudd* ?] was worth 19 ounces. In 1611, a *saḥfa* of corn cost 40 ounces; in January 1612, 60 ounces; around the end of 1613, 20 *metqal*s, and in January 1614, 300 ounces. In 1651, a period of famine and instability, a *mudd* of corn cost 5 dirhems in Fez.

The legal texts referring to trade in local and imported products are a rich source of information.

• Sulphur was sold at Salé in 1728 at 102 *uqiyas* for a *qenṭar*, "above the normal price because the boats were late."

• "The purchase price here in Barbary of the fifteen silk overcoats (*ksi*) which R. Isaac sent to F. Abraham in Gibraltar, came to 530 *uqiyas*, according to the statements in the account-books, which also record the price of 18 "round cushions" at 140 *uqiyas*, "their value here in Barbary."

• Two pieces of fabric, of a color called *paño*, of mediocre quality, were valued at 350 *uqiyas* each, and 67 pounds (*litrin*) of cochineal were taken on account for two bars (or ingots) of gold (text dated 1720).

• Ten pairs (or pieces) of fine linen from Cambrai were bought for a thousand *uqiyas* in about 1720.

• At Rabat, the price of tobacco from the Doukkala was fixed at 30 *uqiyas* a quintal (*kikkar*), and the price of hashish at 80 *uqiyas*. The prices of Meknassi tobacco and Slawi and the imported variety, called *tobacco*, had to follow market prices at Meknès (text signed in Rabat in 1802).

In another field, a responsum of 1749, dealing with a question relating to a mortgage, mentions that the monthly rent for a room on the ground floor of a house in Tetuán, situated outside the *judería*, was an old half-*uqiya* "in silver of good alloy." On the subject of rentals, the rabbinical authorities almost systematically rejected—particularly when premises for housing were concerned—landlords' claims for increases, even when justified by a general rise in prices.

A text dated 1705 mentions that the entrance fee to the "purification bath" did not exceed one silver *muzuna* at that time.

The preceding chapter contains some rates for services and salaries (the remuneration of senior magistrates, legal assistants, scribes, and synagogue officials) revealed by the examination of other texts. Still other documents mention the amounts of fines for infringements of rabbinic ordinances, some fiscal assessments, and rates of taxation.

### *Trade*

Trade in various commodities was mentioned earlier in this chapter. Several documents give further information on the products traded and on the commercial activities of the Moroccan Jewish communities.

Large-scale commerce was in the hands of an oligarchy which had capital at its disposal, contact with the makhzen, and means of obtaining economic information through international correspondents. It monopolized the export of local products (e.g., cereal, hides and skins, wax) and the import of various commodities, particularly textiles.

These wholesalers were very tough in their business dealings with their co-religionist small retailers, shopkeepers in the mellahs, and the market-traders (*suwwaqa*) who peddled their shoddy goods around the countryside, where they also collected local products on behalf of their partners or associates in the towns. This is the profession known as *taduwwast;* the man who practiced it was the *duwwas,* "itinerant merchant."

That the sums involved in these dealings were often considerable can be seen from an account book that a Fez rabbi examined in 1735, where the debits relating to the same person came to 20,000, 51,000, and 30,000 *uqiya*s successively.

### *Grain and Cereals*

Grain merchants marketed the produce of their own lands (the agricultural activities of Moroccan Jews are discussed below). But the main source of supply was grain purchased in the souks or from harvests pledged them by countrymen as security on an advance of funds, as well as grain received in payment for advances.

A document dated 1708 mentions that "two partners went to the Doukkala to buy cereals . . . after the harvest, during the summer, in order to resell them in winter, generally before Passover, when prices would be higher."

Cereals were exported or stored for local consumption; individuals made their own arrangements, keeping them in cisterns or storerooms specially adapted for "reserve foodstuffs." They were also sometimes imported. A responsum dated 1751 notes a "cargo of corn loaded on to a ship [coming from Portugal], sold by S. ben Dellac to the pasha of Tangier, to whom it had to be delivered, and which his partner, Y. ben Ẓaqen, diverted to Tetuán."

### *Cloth*

The cloth trade was a flourishing activity mentioned in a great many responsa. Some of them have already been cited, recording transactions in several kinds of imported fabrics, listed in notarial deeds or account books: damask linen, called *damasquito* (Spanish *damasquino*) and *damasco doble* ; *m l f* (?) "linen" and *fustan,* "fustian," imported from Gibraltar; *bernata,* "heavy linen material, blue-black in color," pieces of "Cambrai linen," a woolen fabric called *calimaco,* "fine Cambrai linen," Holland cloth (*ulanda, cambric*).

### *Beeswax*

Refining and trade in beeswax were very widespread in the principal Moroccan towns where Jewish traders had a monopoly. Cakes of wax were exported and the distilled dregs provided some of the brandy drunk in the mellahs. A responsum written in Fez and dated 1714 mentions an agreement between a large-scale wax merchant, Sh. T. Hakohen, and J. Bibas, one of his agents. Bibas contracted to deliver to his partner 107 *qenṭar*s of wax at the price of 70 *uqiya*s a *qenṭar.* In order to make his purchases on the Tangier, Salé, and Tetuán markets, Bibas had to obtain a special permit from the king, which was handed to Sh. T. Hakohen by the intermediary of the governor.

Two other later responsa (1793 and 1794) involve the division of an inheritance consisting of the right to use a press (*al-m'asra*) where cakes of wax were produced.

### *Tobacco*

Monopolies on the marketing of tobacco (*saka*) were acquired by several Jewish merchants, after paying fees levied by the royal treasury. The transfers of this monopoly, bidding for it, and the various transactions relating to this trade gave rise to disputes that came before the rabbinic authorities (decrees of a Salé court, dated 1802).

### *Hides*

Hides, salted and dried by Jewish labor were dealt in locally before they were exported. In Mogador, until recently, these processes were still done in a place called a *mensher,* (exposure area) in an outlying district of the town.

A responsum (Fez, 1706) states that "the aforenamed Salomon Ibn Danan and Aharon ben Amozeg have contracted to pay Moses Masiyah the sum of 5,600 *uqiya*s in old silver money of good alloy on 15

Sivan 5463/1703 or to deliver to him in payment of their debt, 200 *qenṭar*s of cowhides, making four hides per *qenṭar*, of true and healthy quality, negotiable on the Idumaean [Christian] market in Tetuán."

### *Olive Oil*

"In certain rural areas, like Sefrou, it is a common practice to buy plantations of olive trees. . . . Last year, David bought an olive grove for the price of four quintals of silver; when he had picked the olives and extracted the oil, he stated that he had suffered a loss of one and half quintals (*qenṭar*) of silver" (responsum dated 1718).

The texts also mention dealings in ostrich feathers and "precious stones from distant lands." The trade in gold and precious metals will be discussed later.

Worthy of note is a document dated 1719, written in Meknès, which contains an order for a *guitarra* (guitar), and the importation of a "new edition of Maimonides' Code and commentaries."

### *Crafts*

In the division of labor between Jewish and Muslim craftsmen which seems to have been established at an early date, certain trades were specifically reserved for the Jews, particularly those which most involved the handling of valuable precious metals like gold and silver, gemstones, and high-quality pearls.

### *The Mint*

In the days when the sultans coined money in Fez, a Jewish workforce was employed at the mint, working with Christian craftsmen under the direction of a Muslim *'amin*. A text dated 1751 states:

> The king entrusted *dar es-sekka*, that is, the house where money is produced, to Christian merchants, leaving them to recruit employees at their will. The Christian merchants engaged three Jews, Joseph, Moses, and Mordecai, to cast and stamp the money. . . . The three Jews agreed in a partnership contract, bearing the date of 23 Adar 5506/1746, a copy of which was placed in the hands of the Christian merchants, to share the proceeds of their work at the mint equally, each of them remaining free to practice the "craft of the hammer" [gold-beating, i.e., into thin

> sheets], in his free time and to keep all he might earn thereby for himself.

The *taqqanah* of 1750

> forbade any Jew to produce gold dinars and silver coins or to cause them to be made by a co-religionist or non-Jew, whether in the mellah, in Fas-al-Jdid or in Fas-al-Bali, the process having to be carried out exclusively on the responsibility of the *'amin,* Si 'Abd-Al-Qader Aj-jwahri or any other *'amin* appointed to coin money. . . . It is also forbidden to send gold and silver to another town for the same purpose or with a view to marketing these metals on the exchange. . . . The present *taqqanah* will remain in force for five years, at the end of which time other arrangements will be made if circumstances permit, and if dinars and silver coinage have recovered the status as precious metals which they had in the days of Moulay Ismael, may God have mercy on him.

This decision was motivated by a concern to spare the community the losses and disputes caused by "the circulation of money of bad alloy which did not give the right weight or pure metal when cast."

### *Jewelry*

Jewish jewelers, whether in Fez or Mogador, had a reputation for skill and taste which was not belied for centuries. One of the most attractive figures of eighteenth-century Moroccan Jewry, Judah ben 'Attar, "was a talented gold- and silversmith, who lived off his trade, refusing payment from communal funds for his services as senior magistrate and president of the rabbinical court in Fez."

The texts refer to jewelers by the Hebrew term *ṣorfim* or use the Arabic words *dahhabin* for those who work with gold, and *sekkakin* or *sayyaghin* for silversmiths.

It is an established fact that the Jews brought their capacity for order, activity, and initiative to the craft guilds: The Jewish *mo'allem* carried out commissions with more dispatch and more taste than his Muslim colleague. This assessment was particularly true of jewelery. In addition, the value and variety of the jewelery made by Jewish craftsmen in Morocco was well known. "The Jewish community paid [the king] as tribute one fowl and twelve chickens in artistically worked gold," reported an eighteenth-century French traveler.

### *Gold and Silver Thread*

One of the most flourishing Jewish industries was the production of thread made from precious metals and the various types of work done with this valuable raw material. The sources call it by the Hebreo-Arabic term *mlekhet assqalli;* the employers and workers who practiced the craft were *sqalliyyin.*

The Jews seem to have brought this craft with them from Spain. The patronym Kohen-Sqalli is still very widespread in Morocco, where families that have borne it for centuries think it is of Sevillan origin. R. Yosef Messas tells of the tradition that the Kohen-Sqalli family was descended from the craftsmen who wove the high priest's vestments from golden thread in Temple times. He heard this from the rabbis of Fez, to whom it was passed down by their ancestors. The patronym Sqalli is also borne by Muslims, particularly in Fez, who probably are descended from converted Jews.

A *taqqanah* of 1744 protected poor and isolated craftsmen in the gold thread industry against associations of employers and merchants, formed illegally without the permission or knowledge of the rabbinical courts. The *taqqanah* condemns collaborations of more than two employers or craftsmen, and the concentration of capital and means of production in the hands of small, powerful, and unscrupulous syndicates, made up of "those whose salvation and desire consists of piling up an embankment and building a trench in order to swallow up the unfortunate on earth and the poor among men" (the text here is a paraphrased pastiche of verses from the biblical books of Samuel, Ezekiel, and Proverbs).

It must be said that the gold-thread industry was in the hands of a limited number of employers who were not necessarily members of the profession. As they very often had relatively large amounts of capital at their disposal, they acted more as merchants and financial backers than as technicians, and hired experts in the craft to work with the customer's material. Work on commission was the general rule and practice in the majority of cases.

### *The Gold Trade*

The gold trade was carried on by "money-changers," called *serrafiyyin* (Arabic) or *shulḥanim* (*Hebrew*) in the sources. It is mentioned in the *taqqanah* of 1750 examined above and in a responsum dated 1727, which regulated the method of apportioning among the members of the guild the taxes and payments which they had to meet by virtue of their profession and "which the king, the princes, the officials, and the councilors of the country imposed on them. The amount of the assessment was fixed in proportion to the capital invested and the size of the turnover."

Dealings in gold jewelery and precious stones are mentioned in a document which describes a dispute about the quality of a gold dagger set with precious stones, worth a thousand *metqals.* A governor had bought it from a jeweler with a view to presenting it to the king at an audience, in order to be forgiven for an offense.

A document dated 1723 shows that it was not only coins that were marketed on the money exchange, but even more readily, "scrap" (*alfajra*), metal in bars or coins which had been clipped or cut into pieces.

### *Other Jewish Industries*

The sources contain information on other trades practiced by Jewish craftsmen: work in brass by coppersmiths (*ṣeffârîn*), spinning and weaving, dressmaking and the production of valuable finery by trimmers and tailors, called by the Hebrew term *ḥayyaṭim;* production of combs to card wool by *qrashliyyîn.*

Jews also seem to have been masons. Evidence of this is the Hebraic word *ha-bannay* ("the mason") attached to a genuine patronymic in the name Yishaq bar Dinar ben Shemmul ha-Bannay in a responsum signed in Fez in 1731. Another text from the same period mentions "a custom of the town of Fez acknowledging a debt to every Jew who contributed in his capacity as mason to the building of a house on a piece of land belonging to a gentile."

Other documents contain evidence that Jews practiced other manual trades: the production of belt buckles, niello on stirrups, and iron work; they were wood-turners and cartwrights. Apart from tailors in the clothing industries, there were craftsmen who made skullcaps or chechias, women's slippers embroidered with gold or silver (*shrabel*), experts in working silk (*tahrart*), lace, buttons, belts, and so on.

### *Guilds*

The Hebrew of the documents uses the term *ḥebrah* to designate trade guilds. The same word serves equally to describe the various charitable associations and the confraternities of readers of the Zohar and the Psalms. In the context of economic activity, the word *ḥebrah* indicates a grouping of craftsmen practicing the same trade or merchants belonging to the same business, obeying a certain number of professional rules, fixed by custom and tradition, responding as a group to the charges imposed by the authorities and to the payments due the community by virtue of the profession, under the supervision and responsibility of the *'amin,* their leader and official representative, to whom the rabbinic authorities often appealed, in his role as expert and arbitrator, to settle commercial and industrial lawsuits that required his intervention.

Membership in a guild was free, at least in principle. It was, however, necessary to have sufficient knowledge of the trade to meet customers' demands, and to possess a small amount of capital in order to open a stall or shop. It must be added that the Jewish guilds in Morocco, like their Muslim equivalents, had nothing comparable, as far as structure and functioning are concerned (rigid regulations, internal hierarchy, cohesion, etc .), to the guilds of medieval Europe.

We know about a few of the guilds from the texts. The moneychangers' guild was mentioned in the texts examined above (*taqqanah* of 1750 and responsum of 1727); the tailors' guild (*ḥebrat ha-ḥayyaṭim*) appears in a legal decision fixing the method of distributing the *sokhra* (special levy assessment) among the parties concerned (Fez, 1749).

A document dated 1722 shows the guild of scribes (*ḥebrat ha-sofrim*) demanding tax exemption for its members. An eighteenth-century manuscript refers to a rabbinic ordinance dealing with the "oath taken by members of the guild of coppersmiths."

Little information is available on the organization of other professions into guilds apart from remote and vague allusions. In connection with the procedure for drawing up ordinances, for example, it emerges that members of guilds were sometimes consulted before decisions which concerned them were proclaimed: butchers (*taqqanah* of 1600), moneychangers (*taqqanah* of 1750).

One other aspect of corporate life must be remembered: the guild was not exclusively a professional grouping; it was also the framework for intensive religious and educational activity. "The scribes regularly devoted part of their time to the Torah, in addition to lessons in gemara [Talmud] which they followed after the dawn prayer every morning with the sages at the yeshîbâh" (text dated 1696, Fez).

Craftsmen and merchants belonging to other guilds also made it their duty to devote certain fixed times of the day and night to study of the Bible, halakhah, Talmud, and Zohar, as has been stressed in an earlier chapter in connection with questions relating to teaching (study circles, night-time teaching, etc.).

### *Localization of Trades*

Trades were grouped topographically in the mellah: For example, the money-changers' market (*shuq ha-shulḥanim*), the area where precious metal thread, the major industry of the district, was worked (*suq as-sqalliyyin*), the leather-workers' quarter.

Rabbi Yosef Messas, in his *'Otsar ha-Miktabim* ("Collection of Correspondence"), devoted some thirty years to a very complete toponomastic study of the Meknès mellah. It contains a detailed list of the names of roads and lanes, traditional souks, and buildings characteristic of Moroccan town planning or peculiar to the mellah and corresponding to the needs of Jewish life.

> Setting out from the gate of the mellah, one meets in turn, on either side of the main road: shops selling spices and haberdashery, fish, fruit and vegetables; the premises of the *dahhabin* (jewelers), a bookshop, grain merchants, cobblers (*kharrazin*), butchers, the lane of the cisterns where grain is stored (*mṭâmer,* singular *maṭmora*), a *funduq* where transient animals and people find lodgings, the lane of the synagogues, the lane of the ritual purification bath (*miqweh ṭaharah*), and the lane of the cemetery, the road of the *'attarin,* "spice and perfume merchants," the premises of the public house (*ṭberna*) . . . ; the abattoirs (*al-gerna*), the Moorish bath, a small prison where the rabbinic authorities, with government consent, lock up perpetrators of religious offenses, and which is guarded by an armed Muslim official; the premises of the beeswax press. . . . All in all, 250 buildings comprising almost 1,200 dwellings, shops, and warehouses, to which must be added 300 stables and cowsheds and six ovens, all kept by Jews. The whole area is surrounded, at the four cardinal points, by high, wide walls.

Professional needs sometimes led Jewish craftsmen and merchants to visit souks in Muslim districts. This emerged in the case of the men who worked in the Fez mint, and the moneychangers who went to Fas-Bali and Fas-Jdid to carry out transactions. Jews also owned a few shops there. Until recently, there were still streets outside the Mogador mellah proper almost entirely made up of shops owned by Jewish craftsmen and merchants: *Souk-jdid* (linen and calico), *Souk al-ghzil* (woolen yarn and haberdashery), *Al-khaddâra* (fruit and vegetables), *Al-gazzâra* (butchers), *Al-'aṭṭâra* (spices, sugar, tea, tobacco), *As-ṣeyyâgha* (jewelers); *Al-haddâda* originally grouped the iron and hardware trades; at present, it only contains large-scale dealers in sugar, tea, and wood.

### Policing the Markets

The *mohtaseb* was responsible for the economic order of a whole urban agglomeration but does not seem to have exercised his powers in the Jewish quarter, which in fact enjoyed a very wide degree of autonomy. Prices there seem to have been freely established, probably taking account of current prices in the *medina*, the native quarter of the town, and competition inside the mellah. The *nagid*, the rabbinical authorities, and their officials were sometimes called on to intervene and fix the prices of specific commodities, supervise the legality of transactions, prevent fraud, or prohibit boys being apprenticed before their religious majority, so that they could remain in elementary school until the age of thirteen. This prohibition was mentioned in the chapter relating to teaching. Several legislative provisions testify to their readiness to intervene.

The *taqqanah* of 1730, for instance, fixed the price of liver at one *muzuna* for two rtels; this commodity, exempt from communal taxation (*sisa*), was reserved for the poor, who did not have the means to buy meat. Note that it was forbidden, on pain of anathema, to disclose the terms of the *taqqanah* to non-Jews, because of the moderate price of the commodity in question.

In order to detect cases of usury and to anticipate maneuvers intended to evade the prohibition on lending at interest, a *taqqanah* dated 1602 "forbade clerk-notaries to write documents relating to certain commodities (corn, wax, butter, honey, olive oil, and silk) for anyone who is not known to trade them."

A *taqqanah* dated 1649 severely condemned "people who mix different qualities of flour in order to sell it at the price of the best, because the market inspector only fixes the price of the corn sold by weight, not the price of the product leaving the mills. . . . For this reason, two officials are appointed to expose these practices and to punish the perpetrators with fines and imprisonment."

Defrauding the customs is mentioned in a legal text referring to a quarrel between a wholesale merchant and his agent. The agent had succeeded in withholding from the customs inspector a commodity imported on behalf of his employer. This was viewed in a different light by the rabbinical authority, obviously accustomed to such practices, which was apparently tolerated because of the fiscal pressure on the Jewish community from other directions.

### *Agricultural Activities and Rural Property*

European authors writing about the Jews of Morocco make almost no mention of agriculture and stock-raising as economic activities pursued by Jews. If they do break the silence on this subject, it is only to state that "Jews possessed neither lands nor gardens."

However, the itinerary of N. Slousch's mission to the Moroccan Atlas in 1914 took him "through a village, Mansour, consisting of twenty-five farming families," and André Chouraqui mentions that "several small communities exist in the Moroccan South who have practiced agriculture from time immemorial."

The Israeli historian H. Hirschberg, most often citing the responsa of the gaonim or documents originating from the Cairo genizah, reports that "the Jews of the Maghreb farm small rural properties by the sweat of their brow . . . earning their living by working the land and raising cattle . . . pursuing agricultural occupations although these are considered socially disreputable." The studies of Moroccan Jewry by David Corcos also contain some—but very little—information on such activities.

Certainly, very few Jews went into agricultural occupations, mainly for security reasons but also on social and economic grounds, and perhaps through repugnance for hard physical labor, which was too demanding and unprofitable. It should be noted that the long days of work in the fields scarcely allowed the Jewish farmer to reserve even an hour a day for study—the time fixed by the rabbis as a minimum. Insofar as the postulates of the doctrine decreeing that as much time as possible should be devoted to study might have been applied to everyday life, they drove the Jews even further toward other professions, particularly trade. Nonetheless, there was a Jewish presence in the Moroccan countryside. Since there was no impediment to the exercise of the right of ownership, Jews owned and worked land, living off its produce, side by side with their Muslim compatriots, and most often in a profitable partnership with them. The legal documents and evidence analyzed below are far better proof of this than the fragmentary and disparate pieces of information mentioned above.

- The inventory of a bequest, known from a decree of the Fez rabbinical court, includes, inter alia, "premises, fields, and vineyards." In all probability, they must have been situated in the Debdou region, as Aharon ben Yosef Sqalli, one of the parties concerned in the lawsuit, was a native of that town. But the decision fixing the method of division was made in Fez in 1758.
- An earlier legal decree concerned a Jew who "rented the property of a gentile, plowed, sowed, harvested, bound the corn into shocks, and carried out all the work in the field and vineyard."
- Another text, dating from the beginning of the nineteenth century, mentions a Jew who "marketed" the cereal production of his field.
- A item of contemporary evidence is a decision by the Meknès rabbis which stipulates that "the field belonging to a gentile . . . must not give rise to a privilege deriving from the usual rights of settlement and presumptive domicile in order to avoid over-bidding." The author of the decree notes, however, that "the hard work in the fields, the rent of the farm that has to be paid in kind, and the various expenses which make farming unprofitable, are increasingly turning Jews away from agriculture."
- Lawsuits arising from legislation on landed property, and especially in regard to privileges and mortgages (e.g., possession, prescription, antichresis), were the subject of many other legal consultations.
- According to evidence taken down locally some twenty years ago, in the Todgha Valley, "rich Jews were landowners. They owned fields, vineyards and large numbers of palm trees."

An older document, the preface to a collection of homilies printed in Berlin in 1712, tells the history of the Pérèṣ family mentioned in an earlier chapter of this book. They emigrated from Spain in 1492 and settled in the Atlas valleys "in the kingdom of the sovereign of Marrakesh [*sic*], from whom the family purchased the territory of Dades. The 'children of Pérèṣ' built houses there and led a peaceful existence, living off agriculture and stock-breeding."

### Related Questions

#### *Disputes About Business and Real Estate*

All these economic activities, whether commercial, artisanal, agricultural, or concerning real estate and landed property, naturally gave rise to lawsuits. These the rabbinic authorities had to settle every day, assessing and judging them in accordance with rabbinic law, as laid down in the Talmud and codes, and adapted by custom and the prevailing local practices in civil cases, and in greater detail in legislation relating to property law, regulating the status of property and obligations.

Disputes only involving Jewish litigants were relatively easy to deal with. The situation became more complicated when a non-Jew was a party to the dispute, either as a full partner or as an executor in his own right or as a third party, indirectly involved in the dispute, whether through a written contract or verbal convention. In fact, business relations with gentiles were very common, as the Muslim public comprised the majority of customers, purchasers, borrowers, and sometimes lenders. When disputes of this kind went beyond the competence of Jewish courts, they were taken before Muslim jurisdiction.

But the rabbinic authorities still had to consider the implications for relationships among Jewish protagonists, and assess the legal effects and consequences affecting the interests of rightful claimants (third partners, heirs, etc. ) or the whole community, sometimes held to be collectively responsible in certain disputes.

The relationship between Jewish courts and Muslim jurisdiction, and more especially the recourse by Jewish tributaries (plaintiffs?) to Muslim law and its representatives to settle certain disputes, was mentioned earlier when legal organization was discussed.

All disputes between Jews and Muslims were, of course, settled by Muslim courts (pasha or cadi as the case might be). In civil cases or those concerning real estate, when disputes were between Jews, the pasha only intervened if the rabbis did not succeed in bringing the parties to an agreement ; what is more, he only acted as a secular arm and in no way interfered with the substance of the case.

The examples which follow show how the Moroccan rabbinical authorities acted in some of the real situations that came before the courts most frequently or on which they were most often consulted. The cases concern lending at interest and the organization of credit, deeds of partnership, disputes over real estate, and what in Hebrew legal terminology is called *ḥazaqah,* a concept which covers several situations and, as such, defines a specific method of purchasing and retaining a property, the legal prescription, a right to settle (or the right over premises, the right to enjoy possession of a property, etc.).

### *Lending at Interest*

The formal prohibition and ethical condemnation of lending at interest are written into the scriptural texts and their talmudic commentaries, as well as into the prescriptions of the Koran and the *fiqh* (Muslim law).

In later centuries, the rabbinical authorities theoretically abided by this ancient prohibition. But they did accept the distinction between moneylending proper (moneylending incorporated in a verbal agreement or a written contract), which the Written Law forbade, and the "subtleties of usury," which postulate the nonexistence of a preestablished agreement between lender and borrower. The legislation here does not have the peremptory character of the prescriptions which regulate stipulated usury. They assume that the borrower "spontaneously" gives a profit to the lender, as a quid pro quo for service rendered, or that the lender derives direct advantage from the property that the debtor has given him as security for the debt.

Talmudic discussions on lending at interest, usually in the realm of real estate, were generally extended to cover business, industry, and banking. But here the strictness of the principles was even more at variance with fundamental economic requirements. Thus merchants strained their ingenuity to discover means of circumventing the laws on lending at interest, even succeeding, to a greater or lesser extent depending on the case, in getting jurists to approve their legal subterfuges and adapt the law to make certain forms of usurious transactions legal.

A Jew unable to borrow from a gentile would sometimes turn to a co-religionist for capital, using a non-Jewish neighbor or partner as an intermediary. Although traditional legislation proclaimed this illegal, it was still widely practiced. The same applied to certain modified versions of the *mohatra* contract.

The most common subterfuge, which rabbinical legislation approved with least reservation, was the commercial contract on commission, a sort of mixed-liability company or profit-sharing partnership: It showed the lender as a silent partner with a share in the profits, but the lender's profit could be fixed in advance and his losses reduced to a minimum. This type of agreement thus became an ordinary contract for lending at interest.

Aware of the gravity of the offense (civil infringement prejudicial to another person and violation of a basic prescription of the religious law and ethics), Moroccan judges and consultant rabbis, like their colleagues in other Diaspora communities, strove in their *taqqanot* and responsa to track down maneuvers intended to circumvent the prohibition on usury. They denounced artisanal and commercial transactions (various varieties of antichresis, mixed-liability companies, and deeds of partnership) traditionally suspect as regarded usury, and restricted them to forms which local practices and custom had legalized.

One example of the attempts to track down maneuvers designed to circumvent legislation prohibiting usury (fictitious sales and various forms of *mohatra* contract) has already been seen in the ordinance dated 1603 which ordered clerks of the courts to refuse to write notarial deeds relating to certain commodities (wax, honey, butter, olive oil, silk, etc.) for anyone who was not known to usually trade in them.

Also reflecting this concern was the ordinance of 1607 which regulated improper use of the exceptional legislative provisions in favor of property belonging to orphans. The *taqqanah* condemned the exorbitant conditions that creditors illegally imposed on debtors: payment of high monthly rent (not ascribable to their debt), often above the rentable value of the premises, during the period of the mortgage; and the requirement of a guarantee by a third party who undertook to liberate (buy back) the property at a given time.

The *taqqanah* stipulated that rent should not exceed the fair price fixed by the official appraiser appointed by the communities, and that neither landlord nor tenant should be asked for a guarantee as security against rent. However, the ordinance confirmed the clause permitting the creditor to receive a pledge against the security of his capital.

How the Fez rabbis settled financial disputes consequent on the changes in the parity of money in 1605, 1607, and 1609 has been discussed in the section on monetary manipulations, which also analyzed the general legislative measures they took, in their concern for equity, to settle the disputes which such operations usually caused.

A responsum dating from the end of 1723 has already been mentioned in relation to the gold trade. It contains references to hidden transactions of lending at interest in connection with moneychanging and industrial activities (gold and silver work). The moneychanger gave a certain sum in current coinage to the borrower. The borrower contracted to refund a larger sum, no longer in coinage but in gold bullion. The loan was thus converted into a *purchase* of metal and avoided the legislation forbidding usury. Rabbi Judah ben ‘Attar used very harsh language to stigmatize "this practice which is spreading like a wound," intended solely to "cover the sight of the sun with a sieve." Notwithstanding, moneychangers and other businesses and craft guilds did not abandon this practice, any more than the *mohatra* contract and similar subterfuges.

Note too the prohibition on loans geared to the value of commodities or precious metal. "The repayment of a debt must be made as follows: Whosoever borrows money or goods will refund them at their price fixed at the date of borrowing; no new assessment is necessary, whether the price has risen or fallen" (decree of the Fez court, 1735).

Mention must also be made of a few texts concerning usurious loans on harvests, and some real or fictitious business partnerships. At the beginning of the twentieth century the Jews of Fez still had agents called *sowwaka* who took products manufactured in Fez or imported by the native inhabitants to Berber lands, and brought back livestock. The Jews of Sefrou played an important part in this trade, which was based on a long-term credit arrangement at regularly changing rates.

### *Ḥazaqah*

The Hebrew word *ḥazaqah* derives from a verb which, in its causative-declarative form, means "to seize, to possess, to presume." It defines a concept encompassing a large number of ideas, including, in particular, a method of purchasing, possessing, and retaining a property. The situations involved are too complex and the law governing them too specialized to be studied exhaustively here. It will suffice to describe its underlying motives and a few actual cases which convey the concerns of the Maghrebian Jewish minority society.

The wish to prevent overbidding, eliminate fraudulent transactions prejudicial to the interests of the community or to one of its members, and above all, guarantee the security of the collectivity against suspect or dangerous neighbors inspired the rabbinic authorities to take precautionary measures based on biblical and talmudic texts.

- As with the *serarah,* the offense of "violation of the property of another person" was invoked.
- Various types of *ḥazaqah,* guaranteeing certain privileges or charges, were created on the basis of several rabbinic judgments.

Thus, on pain of ḥerem (excommunication) it was customarily forbidden to any Jew to rent a house or shop belonging to a gentile when it had already been rented by another Jew. The first occupant possessed a *ḥazaqah,* or right of possession, which it was illegal to deprive him of without his consent. This practice was instituted in a *taqqanah* applied in Europe as early as the tenth century.

In order to condemn a Jewish landowner guilty of selling or renting an estate situated in the Jewish quarter to a gentile, and at the same time to grant a right of pre-emption to any other Jewish landowner in the vicinity, the sentence of the ḥerem for such an offense was proclaimed in the following terms: "You have sheltered a lion on the bounds of my land" (Baba Qamma 114a).

A special type of *ḥazaqah* appears in certain responsa dating from the seventeenth and eighteenth centuries. It is called *ḥezqat yishshub* in Hebrew and *ḥezqat al-gulsa* in Hebreo-Arabic, comparable to "right of settlement," the *jalso* of Muslim legislation.

The attention to the *ḥazaqah* is, of course, explained by doctrinal considerations and the concern, common to all Diaspora communities, to preserve their identity and protect the interests and security of their members. But local conditions and the special relations between Jews and Muslims must be added in this case. The narrowness of the mellahs, and the restrictions on settlement elsewhere by Jewish merchants and craftsmen, were, for the Moroccan rabbinic authorities, additional reasons for continually applying the institution of the *ḥazaqah,* whether based on law or local custom, in the numerous disputes concerning property.

For example, an ordinance dated 1603 states:

> The *ḥazaqah* remains vested in whomsoever is forced, by need or violence, to sell his real estate to a gentile. . . . This practice is in accordance with a former *taqqanah* which we think it good to supplement in this way: The *ḥazaqah* is retained by whosoever yields his property to a gentile who, in his turn, sells it to a Jew. . . . When a Jew's land is offered for sale by the civil courts because of debts and is bought by a Jew or gentile, the first owner retains the *ḥazaqah* on the land; for this, he must draw up a judgment of distraint in the legal forms.

A responsum stipulates: "Major excommunication is pronounced against whosoever rents a piece of land without the knowledge of the holder of the *ḥazaqah.* This decision is in accordance with the *taqqanah* of our forebears." However, the ordinance of 1603 adds that "the tenants of *heqdesh* ["consecrated" property, i.e., the property of the poor and of religious foundations] cannot claim any sort of *ḥazaqah.*"

Various texts are concerned with the very delicate situation of the Jews who embraced the dominant religion, Islam, and were outlawed from the community. A document from the beginning of the eighteenth century fixes the status of the *mumar* (apostate) in respect of the institution of the *ḥazaqah:*

> The apostate retains the benefit of the rights he inherited or acquired himself while he had the status of a Jew. If he sells his real estate to gentiles or to an apostate like himself after his conversion, the *ḥazaqah* remains attached to the property and, on his death, will pass to his close relatives entitled to receive his heritage. . . . Every *ḥazaqah* that he might have possessed in his capacity as a Jew and has sold after his conversion remains vested in his close relatives if the purchaser is a gentile; Jewish purchasers retain the benefit of it.

Another document, dated 1731 and signed at Fez, states on the same theme: "An islamized Jew sells his real estate to a Muslim. . . . The Jewish holder of the *ḥazaqah* attached to this property claims the realization of this right. The court responds favorably to his request"

# Chapter 5

# *Intellectual Life: Culture and Religion*

## THE AIMS OF LITERARY PRODUCTION

Our studies and research, extending over a period of more than twenty years, aimed to shed light on the cultural heritage of Jewry living in Islamic lands, heir to the Judeo-Arabic Golden Age. What emerged was the religious and intellectual effervescence and the atmosphere of optimistic spirituality that prevailed in these forgotten communities. Yet they generated a literary output that made a not inconsiderable contribution to the formation of the cultural heritage of their countries of origin or adoption, on the one hand, and to Jewish humanities and knowledge on the other.

Our writings on Jewish thought in the Islamic West—those already completed, in process of completion, or in the planning stage—testify, or will testify, precisely to the activity of the Jews of those countries in the privileged realms of written knowledge (legal thought, poetry, mystical literature, exegesis, homiletics) and the oral transmission of popular learning (dialectal literary creations in Judeo-Arabic and Judeo-Berber).

The primary aim of this output was to ensure the safeguarding of the intellectual and spiritual heritage bequeathed by Castilian and native ancestors. The Maghrebian communities were living under the dual yoke of the isolation of the country itself, withdrawn from all

Western civilization, and of confinement inside the mellah, which prevented productive contact with the world outside. Yet, for the past four dark centuries of Moroccan history, they knew instinctively how to protect the treasury of culture entrusted to them—like glowing embers under the ashes—so that they could revive, reactivate, and fertilize it when better times came. Despite unstable or unequal conditions of existence, often preoccupied with the religious or even the physical survival of their communities, assailed by every sort of danger, including internal divisions and forced or voluntary conversions, the spiritual leaders, both laymen and clerics, the *ḥakhamim,* "scholars and sages," strove constantly to study, propagate, and teach the law and tradition.

Note that in centuries when intellectual production was poor (the sixteenth to nineteenth centuries), compared with the effervescence and prosperity of the Golden Age, spiritual works reflected a culture polarized on faith and religion.

The second aim of this intellectual activity was closely linked to the first. It not only interpreted the universal values of Judaism, but it was also the mirror in which the community looked at itself. It was the means of expressing a world hitherto very little explored, a socioeconomic and religious environment, an original Jewish society that evinced a model of solidarity with the other Jewish communities of the world, despite its own isolation and its own hardships.

## THE *TALMID ḤAKHAM*

### *The Education of the Scholar*

The education of the learned Jew and his intellectual itinerary have already been mentioned in an earlier chapter on the problems of education and teaching. That chapter examined the basic principles of the Jewish teaching tradition in the biblical, talmudic, and gaonic periods, set out the idealistic conceptions of teaching, and gave a detailed description of the traditional Jewish school in Morocco. Our survey extended from the elementary teaching of the ḥeder to the "academic" education of the yeshîbâh, also mentioning the "continuing education" by means of preaching on holy days (Sabbaths and festivals) and in night-time study sessions regularly devoted to the Bible, halakhah, Talmud and Zohar, musar (rabbinic ethics), midrash (homiletics and legends), and *piyyuṭim* (poetry associated with music and singing), either in the synagogue, in the framework of craft or merchant guilds, or in specialized confraternities.

Of course, the ḥeder and yeshîbâh teaching had all the shortcomings of traditional medieval pedagogy. It was bound by the educational conceptions of the "receptive school," and its methods, esteemed by Christian, Muslim, and Jewish educational institutions in the Middle Ages, survived in the ḥeder and yeshîbâh of contemporary Morocco. As in the *msid* and *medersa,* teaching was dominated by excessive use of memory, the value placed on *hifẓ,* "training in mnemonic techniques," and on *nuqul,* "reference points." The aim of the studies undertaken in childhood and adolescence, continued to a mature age, and lasting a lifetime in the case of the confirmed scholar, was the long and difficult assimilation of traditional knowledge and mastery of rabbinical dialectics and casuistry. The acquisition of these "humanities" tended to perpetuate a scholastic and formalistic academism. The scholar became a lawyer specializing in halakhah, a scholar of biblical and talmudic exegesis, a preacher (*darshan*), a kabbalist, and a talented or mediocre versifier, concentrating on rhyme in his poetic compositions (*piyyuṭ*) or assonance and alliteration in the diverse texts he wrote in artistic prose (*mliṣah*).

The scholar who aspired to renown as a writer followed the usual intellectual route leading to a literary genre corresponding to his basic interests. He gathered together the fruits of his scholarship or the results of his experience into one or several collections, making it almost a sacred duty to leave posterity one or several *ḥibburim,* "compositions, dissertations," which faithfully reflected rabbinic knowledge and its casuistry. It could be a work on halakhic doctrine or jurisprudence, a collection of responsa or homiletic dissertations, a mystical commentary on the Zohar or liturgical texts, *ḥiddushim,* biblical and talmudic "novellae." Often too, it was a *diwan* containing poetic writings, his own and those gleaned from various anthologies of *piyyuṭim* or memorized during Sabbath vigils and study sessions. To this must be added the oral literature expressed in local dialects. To a large extent it served (directly or allusively) as an aid to the teaching and communication of other traditional rabbinical disciplines. It was also the favorite stage for the enactment of religious, popular, and folkloric life.

### *Knowledge in the Service of the Law*

The teaching given in the ḥeder, yeshîbâh, and other institutions, the knowledge acquired at a mature age, the whole of the scholar's culture and the literary production which reflected it, were in the service of the law, whose divine origin made it the object of deep and constant study. Intellectual life was polarized on an ideal composed of both legalism and spirituality. The ultimate intentions of the literature engendered in these circumstances and in such an environment were entirely religious. Without claiming to mark the boundaries, which would in any case be illusory, between the world of legislation and the other areas of Jewish thought, we have shown the predominant role that study of the Talmud and halakhah played in yeshîbâh teaching and the education of the scholar (*talmid ḥakham*). The halakhah was, in fact, constantly called on to regulate the life of the Jew in the direction that the Torah intended, to organize every detail of his existence, so that he would be provided with the means to attain eternal salvation. Hence the extreme care expended on every level of religious education and instruction.

### *The Oral Transmission of Knowledge*

The oral transmission of knowledge is one of the favorite procedures of traditional teaching. It is also one which circumstances, the isolation of the Maghreb and the conditions of existence of Moroccan Jewry, contributed to maintain during the past centuries.

Books are very expensive working tools. Hebraic printing (and Arabic also, apart from a few lithographic editions from Fez) was nonexistent in Morocco until the establishment of the French Protectorate in 1912. It was very difficult to import books. They had to be brought clandestinely from Europe, especially Italy, at prohibitive prices, because the Church often clapped an embargo on Jewish writings, and their free circulation was forbidden.

Teaching is communication in the full meaning of the word. Instruction is initiation, and personal transmission is more important than anything else, particularly when esoteric knowledge (the mystique of the kabbalah) is involved. In the beginning, oral transmission was considered the only permissible method, and the transition to written literature only took place very gradually, with misgivings and reservations, in order to correspond to the need to definitively fix the texts.

### *The Prestige of Knowledge*

No one was unaware of the importance of learning and the predominant role of knowledge. The only true worth and the only undisputed social hierarchy was based on scholarship. Once acquired, scholarship conferred privileges that might appear excessive in certain cases (not inconsiderable material advantages and exemption from taxation, whatever the state of the scholar's wealth).

In addition, the scholar enjoyed an undeniable moral influence, sometimes going beyond the spiritual field and reaching a mystical dimension: the intellectual schoolmaster was endowed with esoteric authority; every rabbi of renown was surrounded by the aura of the *ṣaddiq* (intercessor), and ended in an odor of sanctity.

Graves of rabbis, metamorphosed into miraculous saints and santons most frequently after death, were the subject of general veneration and a genuine cult. They were places of regular pilgrimage (*ziyara*) at times of various commemorations and ḥillulas. Scholarship could thus become a source of hereditary power. The aura of sanctity, and the supernatural power attached to it, was regarded as transferable from the miracle-worker to his descendants, who sometimes abused it. We knew two families who enjoyed such extreme prestige only a few years ago: the progeny of Rabbi Ḥayyim Pinto, a halakhist and kabbalist rabbi at the beginning of the nineteenth century, buried in the old cemetery in Mogador, and the descendants of Rabbi David ben Barukh Hakohen (eighteenth century), buried in a village upstream from Taroudant, in the Sous.

The same phenomenon is found in Maghrebian Muslim society, and also the same debates between orthodoxy and the popular manifestations of the religion, which verged on heterodoxy, even heresy, and which both the official rabbinate and Islam vainly condemned. J. Berque writes in his *Al-Yousi*:

> There is no shortage of mystics, true or false, there. They have immense influence over the people whom they hoax and fleece. However, the credulity of the masses is such that they vow veneration to the *sufi* and his descendants. Thus a sort of nepotism of sanctity is created which Al-Yousi denounces . . . as ridiculous. This is primarily observed among the sons of an ascetic. The first-born tries to don his father's divine status, with which to pursue disciples.

The rest of the text is very racy and describes a commonplace everyday situation in Jewish and Muslim societies.

In the Jewish world in general, and the Maghrebian Jewish world in particular, it will be noted that scholarship was not the prerogative of one class, like the clerics in medieval Christian society or the *ulemas* and *fuqahas,* scholars and jurists, in Islamic lands. Nor was it elitist in the sense of being reserved to a predetermined social category, a moneyed aristocracy, or dignitaries and notables distinguished by their special duties in communal leadership or administration.

### *Scholar Craftsmen and Businessmen*

The scholar-craftsman, who did not make a profession out of his knowledge but practiced a trade to earn his living, has already been mentioned. Such a one was Rabbi Judah ben ʻAttar, one of the most attractive figures in seventeenth-century Moroccan Jewry. He was a talented gold- and silversmith who lived off his work, refusing payment from the communal coffers for his services as senior magistrate and president of the Fez rabbinical court. But there were also scholar-businessmen who pursued a dual quest: for knowledge and wealth. This pursuit of the synthesis of *torah u-mlakhah,* "study and livelihood," was very widespread in the Jewish world from the beginning of the Babylonian exile and the development of the Mesopotamian yeshîbôt (second century C.E.), and played a crucial role in the exchange of ideas and commodities. This model of the wise man also existed in Islam; he was a typical product of the Golden Age of medieval Judeo-Arabic civilization, where the free circulation of knowledge was linked to that of goods, the products of trade and industry.

Moroccan Jewish society in the sixteenth to eighteenth century offers several examples of notables and *nagidim,* "princes of the community," who were both businessmen and fine scholars, learned in halakhah and poets.

Khlifa ben Malka was one of those strong rabbinic personalities who hold a leading place in the collective memory of the Moroccan South and whose fame and renown sometimes went beyond the Jewish framework.

Khlifa ben Malka was a wholesale merchant, exporting local products and importing European merchandise, a talmudist and poet, who lived principally in Agadir, between the end of the seventeenth and the beginning of the eighteenth centuries, and died in an odor of sanctity. His grave, situated in the old cemetery of the upper town of Agadir (Talborjt), is a place of Judeo-Arabic pilgrimage. This is also the case with the tomb of his Muslim counterpart, a local female saint, Lalla Sefia, who is claimed and revered by the Jews of the country.

Very little is known about the man himself, other than through his cult, a lawsuit heard before the Jewish magistrates of Agadir and Meknès, and, in the field of rabbinic literature, a few unpublished fragments of one of his works, which have now disappeared. Entitled *Kaf Naqi* ("Clean Hand"), it was dedicated and addressed to a correspondent in Amsterdam, Rabbi Isaac ben Salomon Yeshurun, with whom the author maintained both commercial and friendly relations. The work was a collection of glosses on almost the whole corpus of poetic pieces used in Sephardi ritual worldwide. The glosses were combined with commentaries on the masoretic rules and their usages in the traditional reading of the Bible by the Maghrebian populations. The title of the collection is explained by the contents; the author says that it was inspired by various scriptural texts that all use the word *kaf* ("hand") to define the diverse aspects of the liturgical "act."

### *The Elite and the Masses: Israel and Jacob*

Although the whole community had a right to education and access to knowledge, it is no less true that the concepts of elite and mass were current in Jewish society, and also in the surrounding Muslim world, with a meaning and content that referred more to the intellectual and socio-religious field, and also extended to the realm of a mystical spirituality at a higher level.

In this context it is relevant to recall the description of the structure of the Moroccan Jewish community in an earlier chapter. There, the ethnic distinction between the immigrant group of megorashim and the toshabim denoted a discrimination between an intellectual aristocracy proud of its Castilian origin and the unpolished mass of native inhabitants, generically called *baldîyyin,* as opposed to *rumîyyin,* "Europeans."

A text, essentially inspired by kabbalah, that a poet of the seventeenth to eighteenth century, Moses Aben Sur, wrote as a preface to his *diwan,* conferred privileged status on the wise man, the scholar, and the poet. It makes a distinction between the popular masses and the intellectual and spiritual elite made up of the *talmide-ḥakhamin,* which it calls *Yisrael,* and to which it attaches the idea of authority and nobility. Not, of course, that the masses were devoid of virtue, but they were at a lower level in the hierarchy and the text refers to them as *Ya'aqob,* related semantically to *'aqeb* ("heel"). However, this distinction between the elite and the masses was mitigated by the community's deep feeling of unity and by the fact that the ignorance and illiteracy current in other societies was absent from Jewry.

Maimonides himself was not free of this prejudice and did not resist the temptation to talk about his co-religionists in the Maghreb and the Orient with a certain amount of derision. He contrasted them with the Jews of Spain, to whom he attributed a well-known intellectual superiority, going so far as to advise his son to shun the company of the first and seek the society of the second, "our beloved brethren of Andalusia." It should be added that this attitude on the part of the famous philosopher and master of halakhah was inspired by the intellectual decline and precarious position of Maghrebian Jewry following the Almohade persecutions.

The demarcation is less subtle in a Muslim environment, where, according to J. Berque,

> the *'samma* is set against the *khassa* as the common people are set against the elite, the layman against the initiate, the illiterate against the *tâlib,* "scholar." These three discriminations dominate the thought of the day. . . . For centuries on end, in North Africa, the social reality that scholars saw seemed to them to postulate this convenient division into two categories of individuals.

## WRITTEN WORKS IN HEBREW

The discussion of written literary works encompasses all the disciplines and genres of Jewish thought that are pursued by learned Jews throughout the world.

There is no intention here of drawing up an inventory of Moroccan Jewish literary output or of embarking on even a brief methodical examination of the cultural heritage of a two-thousand-year-old Jewry, its relations with the world and the religion. At the very most, the aim will be to shed a little light on a sector of Jewish thought abandoned to historical oblivion, and to bring the major trends in this thought, its diverse genres and its modes of written and oral expression, out of obscurity.

We must begin, however, by dispelling the myth that the Maghrebian diaspora of the last four or five centuries was not represented in the world of Jewish thought, and in particular that it was absent from the literary and poetic scene, although we do not intend to plead its cause or essay hazardous assessments.

## *Judges and Halakhah: Juridical Thought*

### *The Hegemony of Law*

What must be emphasized from the start is the direct interest of the legal literature, particularly the responsa and rabbinic ordinances. Irrespective of the problems of doctrine and sources that it can elucidate, the legal literature embodies what might be called the socioeconomic environment of the law. The direct relationship of this literature to the world, to life and the realities of existence, make it possible to know the Jewish communities of Morocco from the inside and to obtain a better grasp of certain misunderstood aspects of their history. These have been passed over in silence by writers who have described the Moroccan mellahs and their inhabitants or published accounts of their travels in the country.

What must be noted is the polarization of Moroccan rabbinic culture on halakhah and the hegemony of jurisprudential law. As Georges Vajda so rightly stresses in his book *L'Amour de Dieu dans la théologie juive du Moyen Age,* "the realm of legislation . . . is that area where the Jewish faith is essentially manifest." In the last analysis, halakhah became the goal of all the literary genres cultivated by the Moroccan scholar, as it was for his counterparts in other Diaspora communities. Whether the genre was biblical and talmudic exegesis, midrash and preaching, theosophic interpretation of scriptural texts in the mysticism of kabbalah, or poetry (liturgical or didactic *piyyuṭ*), all had close links with halakhah and served its cause. The works are a reflection of this culture, which was wholly religious in its ultimate goals, and the intellectual itinerary of the Moroccan scholar invariably and unfailingly led him toward halakhah and the composition of works of legal doctrine or jurisprudential compilations.

### *The Role of Custom*

Moroccan authors produced a considerable number of halakhic works that show varying degrees of talent and originality. In form (titles, subjects dealt with, classification of material), the works reproduced the classical genres and categories of writings on halakhah: collections of *dinim* (rules and laws), *pisqe dinim* (legal decisions), *teshubot* (responsa), *taqqanot* (ordinances), *ḥiddushe-halakhot* (novellae), *nimmuqim* and *shiṭṭot* (notes and comments, methods), *perushim* and *quntṭresim* (commentaries and documents), *liqquṭim* (collections and compilations), *qiṣṣurim* (summaries), *maftehot* (concordances), lists of precepts, summaries of methodology, and so on.

We have chosen five of the works that we have been able to consult for quasi-exhaustive treatment and will refer to others for supplementary information. These five books are a collection of *taqqanot,*[1] two collections of responsa,[2] a compilation of legal decisions (*liqquṭim* and *pisqe dinim*),[3] and a halakhic concordance.[4] The last two items only play a subordinate role in this study; priority is given to the first three.[5]

As a result of careful study of the texts, it is possible to show the relationship of Moroccan decisionary literature to the diverse trends in general halakhah, to reveal the dominant trends and the constant factors in the evolution of Moroccan rabbinic law, and to define the authors' conceptions and the principles on which they based their legal decisions.

Two conceptions, two influences, dominated Moroccan rabbinic law in the four centuries following the expulsion from Spain in 1492.

The first, represented by the school of Asher b. Yeḥiel (fourteenth century) covered a relatively short period, approximately the sixteenth century.

The doctrine of Asher b. Yeḥiel was a heritage of the Spanish school which the Castilian rabbis brought with them after the expulsion. The writings and works of the sages of Spain were well known in megorashim circles and inspired the thought of the intellectual elite of Castilian origin. This elite provided both the spiritual leaders of the large Moroccan metropolises and the authors of the *taqqanot,* who wanted to preserve the institutions, practices, and customs of their Spanish ancestors for their exiled communities.

This state of affairs lasted for nearly a century until the thought of

1. *Sefer ha-Taqqanot,* the register of the ordinances of the Castilian rabbis who settled in Fez after the exile from Spain. Several copies are extant (Bibliothèque S. D. Sasoon;, *Ohel David* I, 715; V. Klagsbald Collection, and others), one of which was used by Abraham Anqawa for the edition of *Keren Ḥemer* II (Leghorn, 1871).

2. (a) Jacob Aben Sur (1673–1752), *Mishpat u-Ṣdaqah be-Ya'aqob,* responsa, 2 vols. (Alexandria, 1894 and 1903). (b) Yosef Al-Maliḥ bar 'Ayyush (d. 1823), *Toqfo shel Yosef,* responsa, 2 vols. (Leghorn, 1923 and 1855).

3. Abraham Qoriat (d. 1845), *Berit 'Abot* (Leghorn, 1862).

4. Saul Serero (1566–1655), *'Urim we-Tummim,* MS in the British Museum, Or.6357.

5. On legal thought as a whole, see the inventory of works (both printed and in manuscript) composed by the rabbis of Morocco between the end of the fifteenth century and the beginning of the twentieth in Haïm Zafrani, *Les Juifs du Maroc, vie sociale, économique et religieuse: études de taqqanot et responsa* (Paris, 1972), pp. 243–64.

Joseph Qaro (Spain, 1488–Safed, 1575) made its appearance. It spread very rapidly in Moroccan rabbinic circles of all origins, among both megorashim and toshabim, who welcomed them as a new revelation from Sinai.

The work of Joseph Qaro, represented by his *Ṭur bet Yosef* and *Shulḥan ʿAruk*, accompanied by his commentaries, thenceforth exercised immense influence on the teaching of halakhah in yeshîbôt, on the jurisprudence of the rabbinical courts, and on the legal literature to which this jurisprudence gave birth.

The choice of the Moroccan rabbinate, which coincided on this point with that of oriental and Sephardic Jewry in general, was clearly based on historical factors. It can also be explained by the different conceptions of doctrine and rite which the Sephardi masters and their Ashkenazi counterparts held.

In the sixteenth century, the two protagonists of halakhah, Maran (Joseph Qaro) and Moram (Moses Isserles, 1520–1572), champion of the legal tradition and ritual of Ashkenazi Jewry, were closely associated in Moroccan rabbinic jurisprudence. It constantly compared them, unhesitatingly adopting the opinion of the first and automatically rejecting that of the second, except on non-contentious issues or when Qaro had nothing to say about a particular problem.

These dominant tendencies in Moroccan rabbinic law were themselves crossed by countervailing forces, by constants that no authority swayed and which were impervious to all influence. Not even the influence of the author of the *Shulḥan ʿAruk* could alter them, though Moroccan scholars worshipped him almost as a god. These constants were loyalty to the ancient customs and practices sanctioned by the *taqqanot,* and the attachment to the traditions transmitted by the "fathers" and to the personal teaching of local masters.

The primacy of custom over law in the Moroccan rabbinate, in certain areas of law, can be illustrated by the case of one of the most illustrious figures in Moroccan Jewry. R. Ḥayyim b. Attar, whose commentary on the Pentateuch, *ʿOr ha-Ḥayyim,* is a classic of traditional exegesis, took it upon himself to stigmatize the local customs concerning *nefiḥah* (testing for adhesions or lesions in the lungs by insufflation) in the case of an animal to be ritually slaughtered, and the consumption of locusts and grasshoppers. He immediately came up against the hostility of the Moroccan rabbinate, who rejected his pretensions to authority on questions of dietary prohibitions, denying his writings the immense reputation they had acquired with the Ashkenazi and Sephardi Jews of the Orient.

Another constant of Moroccan rabbinic law was the almost automatic reference to the Talmud, accompanied by Rashi's commentary and the tosafists' glosses. This constant return to talmudic sources was essentially an academic exercise and caused no major upheavals in the structures of Moroccan rabbinic law.

### *The Content of Juridical Literature*

Irrespective of doctrinal problems and the sources they shed light on, the purpose of our methodical analysis of certain works of rabbinic law was to discover the preoccupations of Moroccan legal scholars during the last four centuries. The legal questions that these scholars had to answer extended to every area of public and private life. They concerned the family and personal status, the social and economic structures of the community, its method of administration and its institutions, the reform of customs by what I have called the sumptuary laws, and the relationships with the surrounding Muslim environment, with countries overseas, and with the Palestinian communities in particular. Contained in them is important information on the Jewish languages of Morocco, Jewish onomastics, and some allusions to the history of events. Matters relating to religious life and ritual properly speaking, which form the customary material of the first two divisions of Qaro's Code, occupy a relatively small place in Moroccan *taqqanot* and responsa. The documents are mainly devoted to problems related to the law of persons and property and obligations, traditionally dealt with in the last two divisions of Qaro's Code. Of the 239 *taqqanot* known as Castilian, only six concern questions of ritual, notably the slaughter of poultry and animals. Of the 554 responsa contained in the book by Jacob Aben Sur, only fifty-six, or 10 percent of the total, are devoted to religious life properly speaking (dietary prohibitions, liturgy, laws of purity, etc.). In the collection of responsa by Joseph bar Ayyush Al-Maliḥ, only one of fifty-nine relates to this theme. We tried to find an explanation for this phenomenon and proved that, although these problems (of ritual life) occupy a more important place in countries where the Ashkenazi rite prevails, it is no less true that questions of civil and commercial law take pride of place in all legal literature and rabbinic jurisprudence.

We have no intention here of covering the themes dealt with by this important literature. We will only refer to a few specific points that have already been mentioned in earlier chapters.

In matters of family law, for example, we have noted two phenomena. In the first place, we saw the persistence up to the seventeenth century of some traces of the practice of *ṣadaq,* concluded before the Muslim *qaḏi* and *ʿudul* and at times substituted for the traditional ketubbah. Second, we encountered the institutionalization of the system of the legal community by the Castilian ordinances, and also of monogamy, a matrimonial system that seems to have been applied without any difficulty, at least among the Spanish immigrants, for almost a century, before resistance from public opinion eventually succeeded in securing a return to toleration of bigamy.

It is these *taqqanot* and responsa that enable us to look inside and see the face of the community lit up: its structure, its method of administration and its institutions; the dominant influence of the immigrant element of Spanish stock in the economic and social sphere, even in the realm of rabbinic knowledge itself; the leading role of the ruling class, which was mainly recruited from the educated elite; the important part played by the notables and their leader, the *nagid* or *shayk al-yahud,* the organ of liaison between the official authorities of the country and the community, whose council, or *maʿamad,* he presided over, and which legislated and administered through ordinances or *taqqanot.*

The question of the exercise of justice and the organization of judicial power, and the problems of resort to non-Jewish jurisdiction and denunciation, frequently associated with it, constantly demanded the attention of Jewish legal scholars, anxious to avert any outside interference in the affairs of the community and any violation of its internal autonomy.

Apart from problems of education and teaching, one of the subjects dealt with most frequently in Moroccan rabbinic jurisprudential literature is taxation. All aspects are involved, including delicate questions posed by the distribution of the heavy fiscal burden which weighed on the communities, taking into account certain legal imperatives and also the custom concerning the exemption from taxes which the learned class and certain lay figures enjoyed.

The texts that contain the richest information of every sort—as valuable for jurists as they are for ethnologists and linguists—are the sumptuary regulations. Written in Hebrew, Arabic, and Castilian, these texts contain endless detail (still unpublished) on the costume, feminine finery and jewelry, ceremonial, customs, and rites that at one time marked family celebrations, especially marriage.

The vast majority of the texts concern economic life and property law and obligations. Here it must be noted that all this literature formed of *taqqanot* and responsa reflects the internal life of Jewish society. Except for the odd incidental item, there is, therefore, only very sparse and fragmentary information—on the occasion of a lawsuit about an inheritance, for example—on the Jews' important role in the Moroccan economy and their not inconsiderable influence on the structures of commercial and artisanal urban life.

What the *taqqanot* that governed the collectivity, and the legal debates of the responsa, designed to settle daily disputes between individuals, basically conjure up, therefore, is the organization of economic life within the boundaries of the mellah.

Note too the texts that concern relations with the Palestinian communities and the role of the emissary/tax-collector rabbis in the spread of rabbinic knowledge, migratory movements (internal and external) of the Jewish populace, and their geographic distribution within Morocco, the Jewish languages, onomastic data, and the scarce documents that provide a few occasional and summary facts about the Moroccan history of events and the world outside the mellah.

The theme of religious life and ritual in some ways forms the link joining juridical thought and the law applied to the other branches of rabbinic knowledge, on the one hand, to the diverse areas of Jewish thought where the intellectual life of the community developed, on the other.

We said above that religious life and ritual, properly speaking, occupied a limited place in Moroccan legal literature. In the *taqqanot* and responsa devoted to this subject, problems of kashrut (dietary laws), which constituted the major concern of all the members of the community, hold pride of place, followed by the laws of purity and various other prohibitions. In texts that deal with the liturgy, talmudic scholarship is sometimes coupled with esoteric knowledge. Halakhah then takes on another dimension; theosophic interpretation underlies the search for the motives of the elementary prescriptions of the law and extends biblical and talmudic exegesis. However, to claim to mark the boundaries of the world of legislation in relation to the world of Jewish thought and its diverse modes of expression would be illusory. As G. Vajda emphasizes in his *Introduction à la pensée juive du Moyen Age,*

All this literature is entirely religious as far as its ultimate intentions are concerned. Everything in it combines to organize the life of the Jew in the direction that the Torah requires, life according to the revealed law being the ineluctable duty, the instrument of sanctification of the individual and the community and, finally, the means of gaining eternal salvation.

## *The "Poetic Chain"*

Poetry is one of the richest modes of expression and one of the most important aspects of the literary production of Moroccan scholars. If legal thought is a mirror reflecting the social, economic, and religious life of the community—in short, the external manifestations of the group's collective existence—poetry is the expression of inmost thought. It is the outpouring of the soul, the emergence at skin level of a sharpened sensitivity, where joy and grief can be read like an open book. It sings of optimism in good times, and mourns, in grief, the wounds of the past and the bitterness of the present.

### *Resort to Tradition*

Methodical examination of this mode of expression and systematic study of the basic works that represent it reveal the links which attach Moroccan poetry to traditional Jewish poetry. This "poetic chain" is made up of the ancient poetry of the Bible, the Palestinian *piyyuṭim* of the first seven centuries of the present era, and the medieval works of the great masters of the oriental and Sephardi world up to the sixteenth century. It is a whole series of messages and traditions transmitted from school to school, a collective memory from which the Maghrebian scholar, like his counterparts in other diasporas, drew the basic materials and ingredients of his poetry. It is a reservoir of already formulated thoughts from which he took his inspiration, and of models and paradigms that he imitated, interpreted, deepened, and constantly brought up to date.

Moroccan authors chose the Spanish school, in particular, for their references. Most of them were descendants of the Castilian megorashim, and they all claimed spiritual kinship with the glorious Andalusian Golden Age and laid claim to its heritage. The literary and poetic inheritance that it represented was looked on as a model, and it was considered a point of honor to imitate its patterns and match up to its works. The solidarity between Spain and the Far Maghreb, cemented over several centuries by constant and productive cultural exchanges and the stubbornly held memory of that period of intellectual pride and material prosperity, are the fundamental reasons for the predilection of Moroccan scholars to that particular "link" in the chain of Jewish poetic tradition. They also in some way justify the title, *Poésie juive en Occident Musulman,* which we chose for the second panel of our tetralogy dedicated to Jewish intellectual life in Morocco from the end of the fifteenth to the beginning of the twentieth century.[6]

The links maintained by the scholar-poet of the Maghreb with universal Jewish tradition and the local cultural landscape are perceptible at every level of analysis. They are visible in the authors' poetic consciousness, their basic motivations and preoccupations, the intellectual itinerary of the scholar-poet, the conceptions of the art of poetry, its doctrinal bases and current practice. They are evident in the actual poetry created, the themes, genres, and construction techniques, the language and style, the problem of the inspiration and poetic creativity of the dream. They are apparent in the relationships with the corpus of Jewish humanities, with legend (midrash and aggadah), the Talmud and its hermeneutics, halakhah, mysticism and kabbalah. And, lastly, they are to be found in the liturgy and song with which poetry was closely associated and whose constant assistant and inseparable companion it was.

But it is not always easy to separate the diverse literary ingredients that make up a work of poetry. For example, internal analysis of the texts can barely separate the mystical component from the talmudic, halakhic, aggadic, and ethical elements. Nevertheless, there is poetry which is predominantly mystical, essentially kabbalistic, where classical esotericism is combined with numerology, even magic, just as there is didactic poetry or poetry written for special occasions, with themes referring primarily to halakhah, the Talmud, the midrash, musar, and other modes of expression of Jewish thought.

## *Moroccan Jewish Poetry and the Bible*

Diverse religious trends run through Moroccan Jewish poetry. For the moment, we will concentrate on its relationship with the biblical world—the influence of scriptural literature on minds, the fascination

6. Haim Zafrani, *Poésie juive en Occident Musulman* (Paris: Librairie Orientaliste P. Geuthner, 1977).

and charm that the poetry of the Bible exercised on Jewish authors and audiences in every period. A good illustration of this trend is a little-known anonymous piece of verse inserted in the special liturgy for Shabbat Beshallaḥ, when the pericope *Beshallaḥ* (Exodus 13:17–17:16) is read in public, and for the eighth day of the festival of Pesaḥ. The poem was usually sung, in a few isolated Sephardi synagogues, as a prologue to the Song of the Red Sea, called the Song of Moses (Exodus 15:1–18). It can, however, only be found in a book of ritual and a collection of *piyyuṭim* designed for communities in the Islamic East and West. The poem expresses, with natural and spontaneous simplicity, even a certain naiveté, its author's impulse to sing like the great heroes of biblical history, and his yearning to match the stirring fervor of their songs.

I will sing as Moses sang,
A song which will never be forgotten;
Then Moses sang
The words of the song. (Exodus 15:1)

. . . . . . . . . . . . . . . . .

I will sing as Miriam sang
On the brink of the waters;
And Miriam answered, echoing
The words of the song. (Exodus 15:21)

. . . . . . . . . . . . . . . . .

I will sing as Joshua sang
On the mountain of Gilboa . . . (Joshua 10:12–14)

. . . . . . . . . . . . . . . . .

I will sing as Deborah sang
On the mountain of Tabor (ah). . . . (Judges 5)

. . . . . . . . . . . . . . . . .

I will sing as Hannah sang
Joined by her husband Elkanah. . . . (1 Samuel 2:1–10)

. . . . . . . . . . . . . . . . .

I will sing as David sang
Gathering his melodies . . . (2 Samuel 22)

. . . . . . . . . . . . . . . . .

The day his mother capped him with a crown (Song of Songs 3:11)

. . . . . . . . . . . . . . . . .

I will sing as Israel will sing
The day when its redeemer comes;
Then Moses will sing
And the sons of Israel.

The author of this poem borrowed from the Bible and the midrash, taking some liberties with the texts. In fact, according to the midrash, the Israelites dedicated a series of nine hymns and songs to their God in the course of their history. The first was in Egypt on the night that their freedom from Pharaoh's yoke was proclaimed and their long captivity ended; the second, at the Red Sea; the third, the Song of the Wells, in the desert; the fourth was the Testament of Moses, a song which the legislator bequeathed to his people before his death on the threshold of the Promised Land; the fifth was sung by Joshua after his victory over the five Amorite kings; the sixth was the war-song Deborah and Barak sang after the defeat of Jabin, king of Hazor, and his general, Sisera; the seventh is the psalm of thanksgiving that David sang after God had saved him from his enemies, particularly Saul; the eighth is Solomon's song at the time of the dedication of the Temple; the ninth is the prayer that Jehoshaphat addressed to God before joining battle against the Moabites and Ammonites. A tenth and last song, the most powerful and most stirring, is the one that Israel will sing on the coming of the Messiah, when the hour of its future and permanent deliverance will strike.

What must not be forgotten is the predominant role that the study of biblical literature played in the traditional teaching of ḥeder and yeshîbâh and in the intellectual education of scholars generally. In fact, it took a leading part in forming the emotions of every Jew who was cradled from childhood in the recitation of the texts and their cantillation, its rhythms and its melodies, which are an amazing aid to memorization, retention, and recall of whole episodes and sequences that reappear in the literary work. Maghrebian authors, like their counterparts in other communities, drew the best of their inspiration from the poetic capital of the Bible. They also utilized its themes and genres.

### *The Hispano-Arabic Poetic Model*

The Hebrew poetry of Spain has long fascinated learned Jews and lovers of the *piyyuṭim.* Its great creations have withstood the test of time, and even today reading certain pieces or hearing them sung produces a sharp, deep-seated reaction that defies analysis and the canons of modern criticism.

This poetry spread very rapidly in the Mediterranean and oriental Jewish communities, which welcomed it whole-heartedly. Its great classic compositions were introduced into the ritual, and the synagogue opened wide its doors to them. Evidence of this includes the prologue to a piece of poetry entitled *Shir Ḥadash* ("New Song") written by a nineteenth-century Moroccan scholar, Raphael Moses Elbaz, who was born and died in Sefrou. The prologue traces the broad outlines of the history of Hebraic poetry, recalling the various trends that it passed through since its beginnings, or, in the flowery language of the original text, "since the sun of poetry has shone on the horizon and its majestic beauty has appeared on the surface of the earth."

After describing the nature of biblical poetry and its various genres, prophecy in particular, the author of this historical preamble moves on to the production of poetry in later periods: by the Palestinian school, on which he scarcely, or only very fleetingly, dwells; then by the Spanish school, to which he pays more attention.

> After the horrible tragedy [the destruction of the Temple in Jerusalem], when we all but foundered, in expiation of our sins, when the muses, overwhelmed with grief, were silent and inspiration returned to God who gave it, the sages of Spain began to wield new poetic techniques and compose pieces, as skilled craftsmen and artisans, submitting to the authority and the order defined by the laws of prosody, bending their shoulders to the yoke of the conditions and rules imposed by grammar and logic, and thus conforming to the knowledge of poetry taught by the Arabs. . . . They enriched our liturgy with *baqqashot* [invocations and requests], *seliḥot* [penitential prayers], *pizmonim* [compositions in verse with a chorus], and *qedushot* [sanctifications], filled our rituals with hymns and songs of every sort, thus contributing to the salvation of the Israelite nation [*sic*] and safeguarding its traditions.

## *Poetic Art and Techniques*

Problems of form, notably the function of prosody, were also of quite considerable importance and deep significance, because of the strength of their impact on the mind and emotions. If the form was not always the expression of the content, it was its stimulus. In addition, in certain circumstances it took on a magical dimension and spellbinding strains, precisely through the workings of the rhythm and devices of prosody. "Verse must have a magical character or not be," said Paul Valéry.[7] It is the mainstay of prayer and song in Maghrebian

7. Paul Valéry, *Oeuvres,* I, p. 449 (Pléiade).

Jewish society, closely linked to the liturgy and folklore, the collaborator and inseparable companion of their many and varied manifestations. In the poetic canon and verse writings of Maghrebian Jewry, the focal element is the prosodic schema; its suitability for music and song is a fundamental requirement. That is the explanation of its close attachment to construction techniques inherited from the Spanish schools or imported later from the Orient.

Like all the postbiblical generations of Hebrew poets, including the poets of the Palestinian school of the *piyyuṭim* and of medieval Spain, Maghrebian writers borrowed from the Bible, and especially from its poetry, apart from the literary substratum and linguistic corpus apparent in the abundant references and quotations from the text via the devices of collage and textual mosaic, and such techniques as the acrostic, parallelism, and the pseudo-strophic structure of the simple *pizmon.*

The Maghrebian poets also seem to have tried to imitate the fifth- to seventh-century Palestinian *piyyuṭ* and its composition processes. But it was to the Andalusian heritage, the cultural heritage formulated in the Hispano-Maghrebian Golden Age, that this poetry owed the essential elements of its prosodic technique. It was, in fact, at the *'adab* school of Arabic linguistic knowledge and humanities that the Hispano-Maghrebian Jewish poets served their poetic apprenticeship. They remained faithfully attached to it.

The Hebraic poetry of the Maghreb bears the stamp of the prosody, style, and construction techniques of Arabo-Hispanic poetry more than any other visible influence. The reading of Hebrew was modeled on that of Arabic, adopting, with the quantitative distinction between long and short vowels, the other characteristics of the dominant language. The Jews were also attracted by the melody of the Arabic meter and adopted its rules, despite the disturbance in the structure of Hebrew verse this caused and the constraints thus imposed on its rhythm and meter.

External analysis of this poetry reveals another widely exploited tendency. Music and song, auxiliaries of poetry (and vice versa) became its favored platform, particularly with the birth of new genres, such as the *muwashshaḥ.*

Prosodic techniques continued to develop in the Orient and Italy after the exile from Spain. Very probably, only the influence of the kabbalistic school of Safed worked its way into the Maghreb, where the models that the poetry of Israel Najara seems to favor were more readily imitated than others.

As for the Muslim sociocultural environment, the only influence it exerted on the Hebrew poetic output of the last four or five centuries was through the medium of local Arabic dialectal literature, the *qaṣida* and *malḥun,* the oral apprenticeship in the Andalusian musical corpus. Their poetic texts were memorized, as Jews only very exceptionally had access to the noble genres belonging to written Arabic literature because of their ignorance of the classical language, an ignorance which increased in the fifteenth and sixteenth centuries. They also knew a large number of Spanish melodies in the Castilian dialect and imitated their prosodic schemas. This Arabo-Hispanic influence is seen in the indications of the *laḥan* in Arabic and Castilian (written in Hebraic characters) inscribed at the top of a large number of poetic pieces. The *laḥan* is not only a musical sign indicating the type of melody to be followed in setting the poem to song; it also designates a restrictive prosodic schema (meter, rhyme, and sometimes verse structure) belonging to an Arabic or Castilian piece of poetry which the author knew by heart, chose as his model, and mentions as the line *incipit.*

## *Andalusian Music and Song*

Song and music give the poetic message a dimension and a significance over and above its content, endowing it with resonances that add to the written words. They are the main manifestations of poetry. One might say that a hymn is the exceptional moment when the genius of poetry and music enter into a symbiosis.

Our research into Mahgrebian Jewry's contribution to the diffusion and preservation of Andalusian musical traditions is based, first, on an analysis of Moroccan anthologies of poetry, printed or in manuscript form. These include poems used by the associations and brotherhoods of the "guardians of the dawn" during the Sabbath vigils known as *baqqashot;* and many others not exclusively intended for this use. They all bear musical and prosodic indications of the *no'am* and *laḥan* (melodic themes borrowed from ancient or contemporary compositions), and of mode (*maqam, tab',* and *nawba*). With a few rare exceptions, these indications are expressed in the language and terminology of Arabic music and Andalusian song. They demonstrate a perfect knowledge, most frequently gained orally, of the theory and practice of *'ala,* "the Andalusian art of music" and of the contents of collections like *Al-Hayk,* which is still the bible and bedside reading of the perfect Moroccan musician, both amateur and professional. But the knowledge of the Moroccan Jewish singer went beyond the limits of the *Hayk.* He borrowed genres and modes inherited from an older tradition known as *ṭriq qdîm,* which drew either on Andalusian melodies elsewhere forgotten but perpetuated in the mellahs and synagogues, or on musical themes of ancient Palestinian origin or imported more recently from the Orient, circulated by emissary/tax-collector rabbis, those commercial travelers of culture and Jewish knowledge who regularly visited the most remote Diaspora communities.

In the Maghreb, and especially in Morocco, the Muslim and Jewish populations religiously preserved the memory of the Hispano-Arabic music that had emigrated with them from the Iberian cities they had been forced to leave. They both appreciated it and loved it with a passion that at times approached veneration. In both Spain and Morocco, the Jews were keen supporters of Andalusian music and the zealous guardians of its old traditions. On many occasions, when a prince took it into his head to apply to the letter the strictures of the Muslim law that prohibited this music, it was Jews who ensured its safekeeping. With the result that after a period of eclipse, when a sultan wanted to renew connections with tradition and reconstitute the palace orchestra (*sitâra*), it was often from the mellah that he recruited new musicians.

Moroccan Jews continued the Andalusian musical tradition in two ways. At weddings and other family ceremonies, the *musammi'în* played it and sang the most popular "series" and programs, without altering the poetic texts in classical Arabic and Andalusian dialect specific to it, the original *muwashshahât* and *azjâl.* In addition, Moroccan Jewry, like its counterparts in other Maghrebian and oriental communities, adapted the Andalusian music to *piyyuṭim,* poetry in the Hebrew language, liturgical or intended for the celebration of the major events in life. The result was a synagogue counterpart to the *sama'* of mosque and *zaouia,* a religious song that glorified the Prophet Mohammed in laudatory poems, exalted Islam in edifying cantilena, and which, like synagogal *piyyuṭ,* allowed no instrumental accompaniment.

The Moroccan Jew's loyalty to Andalusian song appears in the technique of substituting the Hebrew text for the original Arabic text, the first conforming to the prosodic laws of the second, bending to the requirements of its metrical system and even complying with the location of the vocalizations of liaison (*yala-lan*) and nanization (*na-na-na*). The two musical versions are in perfect accord, the melodic lines match exactly. But as far as subject matter is concerned, the two texts are in no way interchangeable. The Jewish poet was concerned with the faith, the liturgy, and the practice of legal prescriptions. The compositions he adapted were of a secular nature, conveying the commonplaces of laudatory, erotic, or bacchic poetry.

The same phenomenon appears in the bilingual poetic genre called *matrûz* ("embroidered piece") in which Hebrew and Arabic verses or stanzas alternate. We print below the first verse of a composition, which is a good illustration of this type of adaptation, of the marriage taken to its ultimate point. Here, Hebrew and Arabic stichs of the same iso-syllabic meter are interwoven. In the first, the poet exalts the greatness of God, deplores the vagrancies of the soul. The second evokes, by allusion in this first verse, more openly in those that follow, lost love and separation from the beloved. The poem is one of the items in the audio-archive we collected in Morocco some twenty years ago. It was sung by Rabbi David Bouzaglo, who gave an outstanding performance of it in the *al ḥgaz al-msarqi* mode (Andalusian music). The following is the translation:

1. Let every mouth exalt the name of God. (Hebrew)
2. My heart has fled, and no one is there for me to turn to. (Arabic)
3. My soul has scarcely found a place to shelter, not even a swallow's nest. (Hebrew)
4. You drew near, my soul, but have no strength to bear the burden. (Arabic)
5. Barely did my heart fall victim when I felt it writhe in my breast. (Arabic)

### *A Family of Moroccan Scholar-Poets*

The poetic works of Jacob, Moses, and Shalom Aben Sur are collected in one volume, printed in No-Amon (Alexandria) in 1893, through the efforts of a rabbi-emissary from the Maghrebian community in Jerusalem. They are entitled, respectively: *'Et le-Khol Ḥefeṣ* ("A Time for Everything"), *Ṣilṣele Shama'* ("Ringing Cymbals"), and *Shir Ḥadash* ("New Song").

*Genres and Themes*

The work of the Aben Surs shows the same inspiration, the same pre-occupations and motivations, the same genres and themes as all the poetry produced by Moroccan scholars. It contains the same series of *baqqashot*(invocations) *teḥinnot* (supplications and exhortations), *ahabot* (declarations of love for God), *ge'ullot* (hopes of redemption and evocations of the messianic era), *shebaḥot* (praises), *kinot* (elegies and funeral laments), and *reshuyot* (preludes). The influence of the dominant religious factor in all this poetic production has already been mentioned many times. It reaches its highest point in the liturgical function and emerges in the references to major events in Jewish history, commemorated by special ceremonies, as well as in ritual, folkloric practices, and the music and singing sessions that accompanied family ceremonies. It can be seen in the laudatory pieces themselves, dedicated to various personages and composed in the most diverse circumstances.

The following compositions, taken from our book, *Poésie juive en Occident Musulman,* belong to these diverse and varied poetic genres.

BAQQASHOT

*Baqqashot* are hymns and elegies, and may be regarded, in essence, as lyrical poetry. This is a genre that the Spanish poets and the poets of the kabbalistic school in Safed made considerable use of. Some of these compositions are integrated into the daily liturgy, as well as into the liturgy for Sabbaths and festivals, and are sung at dawn in the synagogue or simply at home, as individual prayers or simple meditations. This genre is related to lyrical poetry. Like lyrical poetry, it is closely linked to the emotive function of the theme and emphasizes the first person. Its monologues revive the biblical psalms in which the author expresses himself without reserve, breathing out his thoughts and feelings, freely communicating the essence of his relationships with God, the world, society, and mankind. Like the psalms, the *baqqashot* "share the characteristics of a hymn and an elegy, a combination which achieves a remarkable alliance between collective feelings expressed lyrically and those which arise from the innermost depths of the person and the faith." The Spanish and Palestinian *baqqashot* included in the Maghrebian dawn liturgy include the following, which we cite by their *incipit* lines:

Open your gates to me, O Lord of grace, when I knock.
Oh my [evil] inclinations, why do you thus so constantly pursue me?

Using the same themes and often the same prosodic techniques, Jacob Aben Sur composed the *baqqashot* that open his *diwan*.

The exordium of the first evokes the motif of the gates of heaven, where the poet knocks and waits on the threshold for them to open to his prayer.

Oh, my creator, see the servant who comes knocking at Your gates.
Let him cross the threshold of Your dwellings.

He lifts up his eyes to You. Let the breath of the entreaties
That he murmurs in Your house reach Your ears.

Accept his prayers, take them as sacrifices,
Burnt offerings and perfumed smoke on Your altars.

In the morning he rises, and very soon his silent word proclaims Your praise;
He breathes out the perfume of the offering before Your majesty.

Strengthen his arms [like] rock, for with all his heart
He yearns to shelter in Your great shadow.

Alone as is the bird caught in a trap, be pleased to break his chain;
Grant him the peace, the freedom of Your deliverance.

### Teḥinnot

Six pieces are collected under the heading of *teḥinnot,* or supplicative poetry. All of these compositions evoke the distress of the Jewish community, which, its spirit broken, asks God for remission of its sins, the restoration of Zion, and the redemption of the people of Israel.

Everlasting God who dwells above,
Living God, creator of the worlds,
When You sit in judgment on the peoples and the nations,
Remember us [and inscribe us in the book of] the living.
. . . . . . . . . . . . . . . . . .
Comfort the weak and needy,
Revive the breath of the humble.

Who then is equal to You amongst the gods,
Our king who delights in life?

### ʻAhabot

The poems in this category are inserted in pieces that are actually called by the name *ʻahabot* (singular, *ʻahabah,* "love") and are recited immediately before the Shema', "Hear, O Israel." Exploring the theme of God's love for Israel, joined to that of choice and the idea of redemption, Jacob Aben Sur uses the motif of the dove as a symbol of the community of Israel. We reprint below the first and last verses of one of his *ʻahabot:*

Dove, hold back the tears from your voice,
It is I who will release your sons,
Rejoice, for it is I who will come
And seal your stones with stucco.

Noble maiden of the righteous race,
Your throne forever will hold firm.
I will recall for you your youthful grace,
The love of your betrothal.

### *A Mystical Prelude*

This mystical prelude to a liturgical piece for Shabbat is a long composition with strong mystical overtones. Its twenty-six lines, corresponding to the numerical value of the tetragrammaton YHWH (one of the ineffable names of God), refer to the ten sefirot and the holy names attributed to them. In this didactic type of poem, Jacob Aben Sur condenses kabbalistic teachings drawn from various sources, including the Zohar, the Lurianic theories, and older works by authors from Provence and Catalonia.

My mouth will sing the praises of the everlasting God.
I will give thanks to Him in words clear and pure.

He is one; He gave life to all living beings
And was before all was conceived and created.

I pine with desire for the mystery of the Infinite (*en-sof*),
At the beginning and at the end, when I pour forth my prayers.

The primordial light, the clear light, and the transparent light
Shine there, and a glorious brilliance they display.

I will glorify the name EHYEH while yet I live,
In the mystery of the Crown (*keter*) where the secret of dominion is hidden.

The name YAH is in the mystery of primordial Wisdom (*ḥokhmah*),
Supreme, hidden, unexplorable.

The letters YHWH, punctuated, represent the name Elohim
In the mystery of perfect, pure Intelligence (*binah*).

They are the name El; on the right-hand side, I see their foundation,
In the mystery of the brilliant light of Mercy (*ḥesed*).

Elohim, on the left side, faces him,
It is there that Fear and Strictness (*paḥad*) is, and the secret of the attribute of Power (*geburah*).

YHWH is on the mid-way line, He it is who judges
And decides from the right-hand side of benevolence.

In Beauty (*tif'eret*), like a betrothed, He is adorned
With a magnificent diadem; and it is there that stands the stem of the menorah.[8]
In the Lord of Hosts (*Adonay Ṣeba'ot*) is the secret of the channels and the springs,

In the mystery of Eternity (*neṣaḥ*), whose name is Jachin.
In *Elohim Ṣeba'ot* is the mystery of the prophecies;
It has been passed on to Boaz with the attribute Majesty (*hod*).[9]

And in the name All-Powerful (*Shadday*), and the name just and living God (*El*),

Lies the mystery of Foundation (*yesod*), wherein is written the covenant of peace (and the power of the male).

---

8. The menorah is a mystical candelabrum with seven branches symbolizing the seven seraphim.

9. Jachin and Boaz are the names which King Solomon gave to the two columns in front of the Temple; they symbolize the two thighs of primordial man and the two sefirot, Eternity and Majesty.

The attribute of Rulership (*adnut*) is in the mystery of the Royal
Presence (*malkhut-shekhinah*), Which incorporates Justice (*ṣedeq*),
and also in that of Crown (*a'tarah*).

This last is like a perfect bride,
Sumptuously adorned, majestic.

Such are the holy sefirot.
In their rise and in their fall, they number ten.

But in truth, they are set apart by their oneness,
United like the flame with burning coal.

Within them, swarm a host of mysteries and secrets,
Concealed in the precious witness [of law and Tradition].

Conveyed by allusion in the form of the letters and the adornments
which crown them,
The cantillatory accents and punctuation marks.

They are found in the hearts of the sages,
Of the man of discernment and righteous intelligence.

My son, you will reflect on this, and you will understand, but you will
keep silent;
You will hold your peace, and your lips will be sealed.

But on the literal, homiletical, and allegorical senses of the text,
You may open your mouth; you will study them and teach them
openly.

Whether [the text] be aggadah, Talmud and mishnah,
Hagiographa, Prophets, or Pentateuch.

Your words will shine like the light, and you will rejoice
With the perfect joy of the souls.

You will proclaim the praises of the Soul of souls,
For He is great, powerful and terrible.[10]

10. Chapter 6, "Ritual and Religious Life," contains compositions of other types (hymns and elegies, canticles and laments) dedicated to other liturgical occasions, celebrations, and mourning.

*Natural Wonders; Bacchic Poetry*

When he left the narrow horizon of the mellah to travel, whether within the country or abroad, the Jewish poet observed nature and described the regions he passed through in the course of his peregrinations. Sometimes he composed moving portraits of the landscapes that met his eyes, and sang of the wonders of Creation in which he saw "the works of the hands of the everlasting God."

Some typical examples of this descriptive genre, which, to be honest, is very uncommon, can be found in the work of David Ḥassin (Meknès, eighteenth century). At the head of one of them, he writes:

> I composed this poem on my way to Tafilalet, a town built on the edge of the Oued Zig. There I saw wondrous things: tall plantations of trees, majestic palms, growing at the edge of waters, multiplying by thousands, by myriads.

The poem itself begins as follows:

> I tell of your wonders, O Holy King, whose home is in eternity
> You have stayed with your servant to his journey's end;
> You have led him to the city of the palms.
> . . . . . . . . . . . . . . . .
> The rivers and their streams delight the desert and dry lands.
> From Zig comes their prosperity, the fertile land, the corn and barley.

David Ḥassin composed another poem of this genre during an ocean voyage. "I found myself," he wrote, "on a boat in the middle of the ocean, looking at the wonders in its depths."

> Go and see the works of He whose home is in the heavens,
> It is the vast expanse of the immense ocean.
> . . . . . . . . . . . . . . . .
> The wind blows on the surface of its waters;
> Lining up for battle, they run to the four points of the compass.

To the best of my knowledge, the bacchic genre is poorly represented in Moroccan anthologies because it smacks of secular poetry. However, a poem by David Ḥassin refers to a work by another Maghrebian poet who sings of wine and intoxication. The libations that marked the celebration of the festival of Purim and often gave rise to an abundant production of verse can be attributed more to religious motive.

The absence of ordinary historiographical sources confers not inconsiderable documentary value on the large number of compositions that refer to happy or unhappy events: natural catastrophes like the flooding of wadis, famines, and epidemics, for example, or popular uprisings and tribal rebellions during interregnal periods whose first victims were most often the Jewish communities.

### *Honoring the Living, Glorifying the Dead*

The series of poems which David Ḥassin entitled "The Honor of the Living" and "The Glory of the Dead," and the laudatory poems and elegies included in the poetic works of the Aben Sur family, all form a source of precise information on Jewish society and its environment. They throw light on certain personalities who played a leading role in the history of Morocco, great agents of the sultan who reached the peak of power and honor, or high officials disgraced or assassinated. They make it possible to identify with certainty other notable figures, men of learning and authority. They enable us to follow the peregrinations of the emissary/alms-collector rabbis who came from Europe and the Orient, and whose graves, now places of pilgrimage, mark out their itineraries across the country where many of them disappeared, caught unaware by natural or accidental death.

Judeo-Moroccan poetry in the Hebrew language is represented by a considerable number of authors. In fact, every scholar was a poet on occasion. Apart from the Aben Surs, one or two other poets whose compositions have gained acceptance in the Sephardi world of the Orient and the West deserve to be recorded: David Ḥassin, *Tehillah le-David* (Amsterdam, 1807); Jacob Berdugo, *Qol Ya'aqob* (London, 1844); Jacob ben Shabbat: *Yagel Ya'aqob* (Leghorn, 1881).[11]

### *Cantors*

At this point we should mention a few Moroccan cantors whom we have had the opportunity to know in various capacities. Our memory

11. We refer to Zafrani, *Poésie juive*, chap. 8, pp. 397–424, for everything concerned with the inventory of nearly two hundred poetic works (anthologies, *diwans*, collections of every sort, and individual pieces) composed by Moroccan scholar-poets between the end of the fifteenth century and the beginning of the twentieth.

of one of them, Rabbi David ben Barukh, known also as R. David Iflaḥ, is all the more emotional as it dates from childhood and adolescence. Shîkh Dawid, born in 1867, was still the "doyen" of the Mogador community in the 1930s and 1940s, and led the services and sessions of *baqqashot* in the town's two largest synagogues. It was said that he was often summoned to the court of the sultans Moulay Youssef and Mohammed V, at the palaces in Rabat and Marrakesh, to accompany the *sitâra,* the royal orchestra. Rabbi David Alqayim was not only a musician, poet, and preacher, but also an engraver and sketch artist (in particular, he illustrated magnificent ketubbot). Rabbi David Buzaglo, who lived in Morocco until about 1970, died in Israel a few years later. A remarkable cantor, he was one of the great masters of *'âla,* "Andalusian music" and synagogal singing. His reputation in matters of musical tradition went beyond the limits of the Jewish community, and he was very often called in to arbitrate in doctrinal or technical disputes. In Fez, in 1963, we knew and recorded the voice of a talented synagogal cantor, Nissim An-Naqqâb, who also emigrated to Israel and ended his days there.

Not all synagogue cantors had the ability of those we have just mentioned. Some were less knowledgeable and gifted with less virtuosity. All had to have a good and pleasant voice. The cantor was designated by the word *payṭan,* as distinct from the poet (*meshorer*), although he too could occasionally write verse.

The *payṭan* was very often a poet and a scholar. He enjoyed public respect and esteem, exactly like the rabbi, the judge, and the other synagogue officials. He was a personage who played a very important role in Moroccan Jewish society. He knew a large number of pieces which he had memorized in the course of numerous musical sessions and vigils, spent in the shadow of one or several talented masters of regional or national repute. He had a role to play in the proceedings of the synagogue service, frequently interrupted on particular days (special Sabbaths, major religious and family festivals) by the chanting of poetry. He entertained the guests at ritual meals at weddings, circumcisions, *bar-miṣwah,* the young boy's first haircut. He mourned the death of a loved one in a *kinah* (funeral lament). He was present at the ceremonies that closed a cycle of talmudic study or dedicated a synagogue or a scroll of the law, and at the jollifications that marked the periodic pilgrimages and seasonal visits to the graves of local saints. He sang at meetings and processions organized by every sort of group and association (brotherhoods of readers of the Zohar, of the Psalms, etc.), at birthdays, jubilees, inaugurations, and commemorations.

When the *payṭan* was a professional cantor, he very frequently received a *nedabah,* or voluntary gift, from a member of the congregation on these diverse occasions. This was sometimes supplemented by a payment which it was the practice to provide for his participation in such-and-such a ceremony.

### *Artistic or Rhyming Prose*

The Hebraic *meliṣah* utilizes a rhetorical language comparable to Arabic artistic prose. The *meliṣah* is rhythmic prose, with assonance, cut up into short formulas. Like poetry, it makes more frequent and more concentrated use of the technique of *shibbuṣ* ("embroidery, plaiting"), a "mosaic" of centos, a "collage" of scraps from the Bible and quotations from the rabbis.

The Maghrebian Jewish scholar used the rhymed prose of the *meliṣah* in his epistolary exchanges with his colleagues in the form of *iggerot* (epistles); in the prolegomena to his books (*haqdamot*); in the *haskamot,* or laudatory prefaces or letters patent that a scholar handed a colleague; in the prologue or argument that generally introduced a homiletic lesson, or *drashah,* which was actually called a *meliṣah.*

## ***Kabbalists and the Mystical Life***

An example of the close relationships that could exist between a literary creation and the kabbalah is the profession of mystical faith embodied in the text, written in 1712, that Moses Aben Sur, a seventeenth- to eighteenth-century Moroccan author, placed at the top of his *diwan, Ṣilṣele Shama'* ("Resounding Cymbals"). These preliminary pages are a lesson in the art of poetry based essentially on the teachings of the kabbalah. They are also outstanding evidence of the preoccupation of Maghrebian scholars with the esoteric. The text is a masterly explanation of the impulses and motivations to sing of God. It lays particular stress on the mystical role and functions of poetry and song, and on the justification for poetic creation by its contribution to the re-establishment of the perfect unity of the sefirotic world and to the "act of unification" (*yiḥḥud*) of the Shekhinah, or Divine Presence, with its Master, to the process of the *tiqqun* (restoration) of the unity of the ineffable Name, broken by sin. This restoration would be marked by the simultaneous ending of the exile of the Shekhinah and of the people of Israel, and eventually by the achievement of the universal harmony.

The synthesis of the dominant mystical trend (here the zoharic and Lurianic Kabbalah in particular) with the other homiletic components (biblical, talmudic, and midrashic) is easily and judiciously achieved through processes of exegesis and textual interpretation, and the manifold methods and artifices (numerology, cryptography) that hermeneutics offers the skilled scholar who generally knew how to put them to excellent use. As anyone reading our study can see,[12] the literary devices employed are sometimes genuine masterpieces of rabbinic dialectic and talmudic casuistry.

Such, in brief, are the contents and inspiration of a prologue to a simple anthology of poetry. What makes it perfectly in keeping with its author's intellectual itinerary and works are the prevalence of religious preoccupations and the steadfastness and density of a train of thought which is explained by the kabbalistic training he received within a society of scholars attracted by the teachings of the Zohar and its commentaries, and entirely won over to the doctrine of Isaac Luria and his Safed school.

## *Kabbalistic Works by Moroccan Scholars*

Mystical literature as a means of expressing ideas was not the preserve of an initiated elite, the aristocracy of knowledge and intelligence in the large towns (Fez, Marrakesh, Meknès, Salé). Apparently the main centers for the teaching and spread of esoteric studies were situated in the south of the country, in the Sous, the Drâ, and the Saharan borderlands (Taroudant, Tamghrout, Aqqa, Tafilalet, etc.), which were the scene of great mystical excitement and considerable and fertile kabbalistic activity.

The primordial role of the Zohar in the intellectual and religious life of the Jewry of eastern and southern Morocco for two millennia is well known. The Zohar was there raised to the dignity of a holy book like the Bible and Talmud, and several passages from it were integrated into the liturgy. Its night-time study everywhere was safeguarded by brotherhoods bearing the name of Bar Yoḥay, who was regarded as the undisputed author of this "Book of Splendor." These

12. See Zafrani, *Poésie juive*, pp. 21–41.

brotherhoods had their centuries-old rites and traditions, as in those communities in the Todgha in the Upper Atlas where, so a legend tells, this book was actually revealed to the world for the first time, after having been hidden until just recently. According to the legend, recounted by the illustrious kabbalist Abraham Azulay in the preface to one of his famous commentaries on the Zohar, *'Or ha-Ḥammah,*

> The Zohar had remained hidden in a grotto in Meron, in the mountains of upper Galilee. An Ishmaelite found it and sold it to itinerant merchants who used it to wrap up their spices. A few sheets fell into the hands of a rabbi from the Maghreb, who sought out and collected all the pieces. This rabbi, a native of a Moroccan town called Todgha, brought the book with him to his homeland.

The greater part of Moroccan kabbalistic writing is little known and unpublished. It is remarkable because of its volume and variety, its documentary importance, and its cultural substrata, rich in remote and valuable references, despite the isolation of the centers of study and the difficulties of every sort that beset the scholar-writers, rich or poor, at the time.

This literature, spiritually on a higher level than writings deriving from other schools of thought, embraces diverse, though interdependent, fields: commentaries on the Bible, the liturgy, the Zohar itself, and the Lurianic Kabbalah, as well as poetry. Ecstatic mystical experiences may have been the prerogative of an elite minority, and study of the texts themselves necessarily restricted to limited circles of the initiated, but in contrast, certain aspects of the kabbalah—its manifestations and means of expression, which border on magic—had a vast audience and immense popular prestige. This genre, known as practical kabbalah, teaches the use of such instruments of meditation as the manipulation of the ineffable Names of God, multiple combinations of the letters of the alphabet, angelology, astrology, and other occult sciences that rabbinic orthodoxy very often condemns.

Using a variety of catalogues, we have drawn up a list of just over a hundred titles of works on various kabbalistic subjects composed by authors of Moroccan origin or adoption. Some are printed, others still in manuscript form; they range from voluminous large-scale treatises to modest notebooks. The writings themselves are dispersed in libraries in Israel, Great Britain, the United States, and elsewhere. We have consulted a number of them that will eventually form the subject of a separate study after more detailed examination.

Here it will be enough to mention a few works by way of example and to highlight a few major figures.

- Araham Sabba', an émigré from Spain, wrote his *Ṣeror ha-Mor* in Fez between 1498 and 1501. A commentary on the Pentateuch which rapidly became a classic of kabbalistic exegesis on the Torah, it was printed several times in Venice (1523, 1546, 1567) and elsewhere.
- Simon Labi, known to the Sephardi Jewish world through his mystical poem *Bar Yoḥay,* which entered the Sabbath eve liturgy, lived in Fez after the Castilian exile. He mentions various Fez customs in his *Ketem Paz,* partially printed in Djerba four centuries later. The book is a monumental exegesis on the Zohar, the only one, moreover, not written under the influence of the kabbalistic school in Safed, and consequently remaining very close to the original meaning of the text.
- Abraham b. Mordechai Azulay, who settled in Hebron at the beginning of the seventeenth century, was born in Fez, where he received a traditional and kabbalistic education. He composed a considerable number of commentaries, super-commentaries, and glosses indispensable to the study of the Zohar, republished several times in Europe and Palestine.
- Shalem Buzaglo (eighteenth century) produced a large quantity of writings that took their substance from the teaching he received from Abraham Azulay (not the man of the same name mentioned earlier), his theosophy master in Marrakesh.
- Moses b. Mimum Albaz, from Taroudant, in the Moroccan South, was the author of *Hekhal ha-Qodesh,* an esoteric commentary on the prayers, printed in Amsterdam in 1653. His disciple, Jacob b. Isaac Bu-Ifergan, was forced to leave Taroudant and took refuge in Akka, on the borders of the Sahara, where he composed a considerable number of kabbalistic commentaries on the Pentateuch, collected in one large unpublished volume, entitled *Minḥah Ḥadashah.* An autographed copy, dated 1619, is in the Liverpool museum. The work is of outstanding value because of its many precise references to the great masters and the fundamental doctrines of all the schools of kabbalah in every previous period.
- Several treatises on doctrinal and practical kabbalah are attributed to David Halevi. It has never been possible to ascertain the exact identity of this author. He is only known to have been a native of Debdou (northeastern Morocco), who died in an odor of sanctity and was buried in Tamghrut (in the Drâa), where his grave became an object of veneration and a place of religious pilgrimage for all the Jewish

communities of the Moroccan South. One of his works, *Sefer ha-Malkhut* ("The Book of Kingship"), was printed in Casablanca in 1930, at the expense of the brotherhood which bears the name of the Saint of Tamghrut. It has an added interest for us in that it contains an esoteric commentary on a book on ritual attributed to a kabbalist from the Moroccan South, Rabbi Mordechai de Dar'sa, who seems also to have been the author of *Ma'syenot ha-Ḥokhmah* ("The Springs of Knowledge"), a work which the kabbalists have caused to disappear, probably because of the "forbidden mysteries" it reveals.[13]

• Isaac Luria Ashkenazi (1543–1572), known as the *Ari* ("Lion), founded the Safed school. His famous disciples included scholars from the Maghreb, attracted, like so many others, by the teachings of the new kabbalists Yosef Ibn Taboul, Mas'sud Azulay the blind, S. Abuhanna Ma'arabi, for example. There was still great kabbalistic activity in the Islamic West in the nineteenth century and the beginning of the twentieth, represented by Abraham Anqawa in Salé (Morocco) and Mascara (Algeria), Jacob Abiḥsera and his circle in Tafilalet, and others.

By listing all the books and examining some of them it is possible to see the continuity of thousand-year-old traditions of world Jewish thought, to note the nature of the links which attached Moroccan esoteric literature to all the major trends in Jewish mysticism, and to assess its range. The scholars of Fez and Marrakesh, and even more certainly those from Taroudant or Tafilalet, had a perfect, unsuspected knowledge of all the kabbalistic writings available in their day, from those of the early postbiblical centuries found in certain midrashim up to contemporary kabbalah—from apocalyptic esotericism, the mysticism of the *Merkabah* of the *Hekhalot,* the *Ma'aseh Bereshit,* the *Sefer Yeṣirah,* the *Sefer ha-Bahir,* the Ḥasidei Ashkenaz in the Rhineland, the kabbalah of the Gerona school and the other schools of Provence and Spain, up to the expulsion of 1492, and obviously that of the Palestinian schools of Safed and Jerusalem.

Following the example of their masters in other countries, Moroccan scholars shared in the history and expansion of mystical thought, including certain deep-seated messianic movements that periodically shook oriental Jewry. Sabbatianism, for example, spread in the large cities of Morocco at the end of the seventeenth century and left its traces in certain liturgical texts and various still unpublished writings.

13. On this author and the works attributed to him, see the refinements made by Efrayim Gottlieb, *Miḥqarim be-Sifrut ha-Qabbalah* (Tel Aviv, 1976), pp. 248–56.

Gershom Scholem devoted an important study to Luria's disciples in which a Moroccan, Ibn Tabul, follower of the famous Ḥayyim Vital, plays a major part. One of his works, *Sefer Hefṣi Bah,* was printed (accidentally, as it were) at the top of another treatise on kabbalah in 1921 in Jerusalem, where the manuscript had been brought in the luggage of a rabbi-judge from Mogador, Rabbi Yehudah ben Moyal.

## *Preachers and* Drashot

### *Homiletical Discourses*

The pedagogy of the Bible at the elementary level of ḥeder teaching and the more elaborate, "academic" level of the yeshîbâh was followed, at a later stage, by a different approach to the Holy Writings. This was the function of the *drashah* or "sermon," a means of public education which ensured continuous and constant adult education. The homiletic signified that the *drash,* which belonged in some ways to the world of legend, midrash and aggadah, extended the textual, literal and commonsense (*pshaṭ*) study of the scriptural—historical, as it were, signifier.

Since history, according to tradition, ceased with the national tragedy (the destruction of the Temple in Jerusalem by the Romans, and the disappearance of the state), and would only resume its course with the coming of the Messiah, imagination carried the *darshan* (preacher) back to the past. But it also bore him toward the future; to be precise, to the messianic era which it was hoped would bring redemption and a return to the magical prestige of the beginnings.

The homiletic approach to the Bible, particularly aggadah, pushes everyday reality and present actuality aside in order to depict the imaginary world—at least in some of its expositions. It breaks the barriers of time and space, sometimes erupting in the glorious and distant past, in the ancient world of the patriarchs, judges, and kings, sometimes in the future, showing it in a fascinating light, describing, with a wealth of detail, the happy times to come, the messianic world and its miraculous metamorphoses of men and nature.

As we have seen, the introduction to the homily began at a very early age with the *bar-miṣwah* ceremony; the twelve- or thirteen-year-old adolescent was subjected to the ordeal of preaching on the very day he reached his religious majority.

During the ceremony, the boy wore tefillin (phylacteries) and the tallit (prayer-shawl) for the first time. He had, in addition, to conduct the service and give a *darush,* a genuine sermon, beginning with a *melișah,* or prologue in rhyming prose, and expanding into a long dissertation on a biblical verse related to the event, supported by talmudic texts and illustrated by homiletic narrative, stories, and legends.[14]

The studies of childhood and adolescence continued to a mature age, a lifetime in the case of the confirmed scholar. Their purpose was the long and difficult assimilation of traditional knowledge and mastery of rabbinic dialectic and casuistry. From the beginning, homiletic discourse, didactic in its very essence, was intended to cover the liturgical year and to be part-and-parcel of synagogal ritual. Dealing principally with biblical subjects, it was devoted to the scriptural lessons of the holy days, the Sabbaths and festivals. Using the customary process of exegesis, the *darshan* chose a verse and subjected it to several analyses, interpretations, and speculations. In addition, he left room for contemporary concerns, the hopes and aspirations of the community, associating them, by means of parables, symbols, and allegories, with the deeds and events of the past, written in the Bible, which thus became a mirror in which the picture of the present was reflected.

The preacher, like the poet, the exegetist, or the jurist, found examples for his own (homiletic) creation in the traditional works. Moreover, his sermon only became meaningful insofar as it drew its inspiration from this reservoir of already formulated thoughts. It would have been a sin, if not a disaster, to ignore or forget the contents of this "collective memory." What is more, the imitation of models or paradigms, hallowed by tradition, was not translated into an endless repetition of the same. The message received (and transmitted) was constantly renewed and more closely examined, so that new perspectives were constantly opened up and new creations generated.

### *Homiletical Writings by Moroccan Scholars*

The written transmission of this mode of expression and communication of Jewish knowledge was ensured principally, if not exclusively, in Hebrew. Almost all of the Maghrebian, mainly Moroccan, homiletical literature that we know of is a written transposition in Hebrew of sermons delivered verbally, probably in local dialects (Judeo-Arabic,

14. See our *bar-mișwah* discourse in Haim Zafrani, *Littératures dialectales et populaires juives en Occident Musulman* (Paris, 1980), pp. 274–98.

Judeo-Castilian, even Judeo-Berber). Nevertheless, a few pieces written in the first two of these dialects (in Hebrew characters, obviously) have been preserved, and we collected others orally during our research in Morocco and from Moroccan communities that have emigrated to Israel.

Judeo-Arabic discourse, in particular, was able to combine and connect Hebrew, Aramaic, and the local Arabic dialect, with a remarkable sense of rhythm and proportion. The preacher used the language with which his audience was familiar as a linguistic base, an infrastructure of sorts. He made use of their traditional cultural substratum in Aramaic and Hebrew either to introduce scholarly references (biblical, talmudic, and rabbinic) judiciously into his sermon or as a dialectic support, taking from it the linguistic tools of talmudic ratiocination, the discussions and debates familiar to the yeshîbâh student versed in the subtle mechanisms of hermeneutics and the great laws of the art of homiletics.

In this area, as in others, the Maghrebian scholar-preachers had learned the lesson of the Babylonian and Palestinian schools. More particularly, they followed the example of their Spanish ancestors, whose spiritual heirs they proclaimed themselves and whom they referred to in every situation. They are one of the links in the chain of creative communicators, and they fit admirably into it. Their homiletical work conforms to the models of their oriental and Andalusian masters and responds to the same concerns. Nourished on the same thought, they drew from the same sources, whether they referred directly to the traditional texts of classical literature and faithfully reproduced them or changed them to suit the geographical and human environment and local conditions of existence. Thus they rewrote ancient midrashim, reinvented myths, imagined new parables and legends in order to satisfy the demands of their literary creation.

The homiletical production of the Moroccan scholar-preachers is too large to be described in detail here. We have listed a total of 235 collections of homilies, 102 printed and 133 manuscripts, in public and private collections. These works cover the liturgical year (scriptural lessons for Sabbaths and festivals) and include sermons for specific occasions (celebrations or mourning).

The following are a few titles of printed works:

*Berit 'Abot* (Leghorn, 1862), by Abraham b. Yehudah Qoryat.
*Bet ha-Uzzi'eli* (Venice, 1604), by Yehudah Uzzi'el (II).

*Bin'ot Deshe'* (Amsterdam, 1735), by Salomon b. Mas'sud ad-Daahhan.
*Derekh ha-Qodesh* (Husiatyn, 1908), by Vidal-Ha-Sarfati.
*Doresh Ṭob* (Jerusalem, 1884 and 1965), by Jacob Abiḥsera.
*Ḥesed 'El* (Leghorn, 1826), by Ḥasday Elmosnino.
*Ḥesed we-'Emet* (Leghorn, 1806) (printed following *Milḥemet Miṣwah*)
*Me-Menuḥot* (Jerusalem, vol. 1, 1901; vol. 2, 1942), by Raphael b. Mordechai Berdugo.

### *Biblical and Talmudic Exegesis*

The exegesis of Bible and Talmud was pursued for the same reason as the other modes of expression. Here again, the number of works of certain value is too large to describe or to attempt to analyze within the parameters of this book. One name must be enough. Rabbi Ḥayyim ben Attar is one of the most famous figures in Moroccan Jewry, and his writings enjoy an immense reputation in Ashkenazi and Sephardi Jewry. His commentary on the Pentateuch, *'Or ha-Ḥayyim,* a classic of traditional exegesis printed in various editions of the Bible (see *Miqra'ot Gedolot*), has been unanimously acclaimed by Jewish scholars in the Orient and the West. In about 1739, Ḥayyim ben Attar left Morocco to go to the Holy Land, accompanied by a group of disciples whose numbers grew at every stage of the journey. His itinerary took him through Italy, where he found a source of finance that permitted him to found the Yeshîbâh Knesset Yisrael in Jerusalem. He died there in 1743, shortly after his arrival. This brief sojourn in Italy was enough to turn our Moroccan scholar of the law into an Italian rabbi in the eyes of the learned contributors to the *Jewish Encyclopedia* (vol. 6, p. 275), who state that he was born in Sale, near Bescia, Italy. May we be allowed to restore this author to his origins and to his Moroccan family in order to save the numerous users of this valuable reference work from glaring error.

Note that the authors of the *Jewish Encyclopaedia* subject the identity of another Moroccan rabbinic personality, Yosef bar 'Ayyush Almaliḥ, to the same fate. This great scholar-jurist from Rabat-Salé becomes "Almalia Joseph, an Italian Rabbi of the Beginning of the 19th Century." They are nonetheless familiar with his collection of responsa, *Toqfo shel Yosef,* and they also mention its dates and place of publication (*Jewish Encyclopedia,* I, p. 426). A glance at the preface and at a few signed and dated texts would have informed them on this author's origins, his duties at the Rabat-Salé rabbinic court, and the subjects of his legal consultations, which exclusively concerned Maghrebian Jewry.

Works of the scope of *'Or ha-Ḥayyim* were born in Morocco; some of the unpublished ones deserve to figure among the masterpieces of world rabbinic literature.

We list below a few works of biblical and talmudic exegesis, commentaries and super-commentaries, taken somewhat at random from our files:

*Mlekhet ha-Qodesh* (Leghorn, 1803) by Moses Toledano.
*Mishmeret ha-Qodesh* (Leghorn, 1825) by Ḥasday Elmosnino.
*Dibre Shemu'el* (Amsterdam, 1699) by Samuel Hassarfati.
*Magen Gibborim* (Leghorn, 1801–1805, 2 vols.) by Eliezer Davila.
*Mor Deror* (Izmir, 1730) by Mordechai 'Attia.
*Rosh Mashbir* (Leghorn, 1840) by Moses Berdugo.

## ORAL, POPULAR, AND DIALECTAL LITERATURE

### *The Written and the Oral*

If literature in the Hebrew language generally concerned written knowledge, the elitist knowledge of a learned society, made up almost exclusively of men, literary work in dialect was addressed to everyone, to the classes of the population who had inadequate knowledge of how to read and write or were only poorly taught, and especially to women and children. Moreover, both types of literature were engaged in communicating knowledge, customs and practices, and fulfilled the same initiating, pedagogic, and liturgical functions, though at different levels and to different degrees. The second was also the faithful guardian of unwritten traditions; it formed an ideal instrument for conveying information, and, in addition, in certain of its lay and secular aspects, possessed a remarkable ability to act as an integrating and socializing force, as certain compositions show.

However, it is impossible to escape the impression that something approaching a divorce existed between the Hebraic "written" and the dialectal "oral." Hebrew, the language of the Book and the ritual, served for communicating with God. It was in Judeo-Arabic and in Judeo-Berber (in *haketiya,* "Judeo-Spanish," in Spanish-speaking societies) that a person communicated with others, his parents, and those close to him, and dialectal literature was the mirror in which he looked at himself. It was the expression of the inner soul, the secular, even religious, manifestations of daily life, of all sorts of things which it was forbidden to speak of, or which could not be said, in the holy language.

Dialectal literature is essentially oral literature. If some of it was written down, this was done as a secondary consideration and on occasion. It was reproduced from memory, by chance circumstance, by the Muslim scribe in Arabic characters and by the Jewish copyist in Hebraic script.

Oral literature is an immense subject and difficult to define. It concerns folklore but also comes under the head of sociology, ethno-anthropology, and even history. Everything that has been said and then gathered up by the collective memory belongs to this vast domain. Generally described as popular, it is constantly enriched by the work of scholars and very rapidly assimilates it. It is therefore legitimate to infer from this that popular literature preserves and transmits the creations of historic civilizations as well as the heritage of prehistoric cultures. However, its survival and transmission conform to certain rules and are subject to the operation of popular mentalities. The similarity of the mental structures of the Jewish and Muslim—Arab and Berber—populations gave birth in the Maghreb to a literature and a folklore where the Jewish cultural substrata and the Arabo-Berber heritage were united in an original creation.

Note here that the great historical pieces of oral literature in dialect—the prophetic chronicles of the Jewish aggadah and the Muslim *qiṣaṣ*—belong to the collective memory of the Semitic world, which gathered up many and varied versions of them and molded them from a written tradition. Examples of this can be found in the legendary accounts of the life of Abraham, the story of Joseph, the death of Moses, and the misfortunes of Job which are in circulation in the Orient and the Maghreb, in diverse Ethiopian, Coptic, Arabic, Moorish, and Berber dialects.

Examination of works of poetry and other written pieces reveals a virtually unlimited power of suggestion, dense thought, an accumulation of emotions, a tight network of references, of formulas tending toward the greatest possible concentration of meaning, of connotations going beyond the frontiers of the text to a highly allusive, symbolic, and allegorical world, to literary traditions and cultural landscapes that it is a delight to uncover. Every element, every word of this internalized culture is an echo responding directly or allusively to an appeal, to a need for speech and self-expression.

What also emerges is the concern to adapt the exotic, sometimes mythical, element to the Maghrebian landscape and the traditions of the surrounding area, the wish to carry out its ethnicization in some way, to integrate an event and a foreign personage into the local world, so as to make the story more familiar. This can be seen at work with the exemplary heroes of the Bible or the Palestinian saints and miracle-workers in our Judeo-Arabic pieces from Morocco, (the Mordechai in our *Mi-Kamokha,* the Job in our historical chronicle, the *Bar-Yoḥay* in our *qiṣṣa* from Tinghir, etc.). It is also evident in the iconography of the Haggadah for Pesaḥ (the popular imagination sometimes turns the simple verbal form *shefokh* into a legendary holy old man, sometimes into a demonic figure). The translations of the Bible are themselves an autochthonous vision of the holy scriptural texts, a personal way of reading, conceiving, and interpreting them, integrated as they are into the framework of existential life and the linguistic and socio-religious environment, into a geopolitical area.

All the texts, in their own way, tell a story. The dominant religious theme, whose hold over all of Hebraic poetry has been noted, comes to the surface here in pedagogical and didactic genres, produced as aids to academic, biblical, and talmudic teaching, that extend into adult education via preaching and ethical and homiletical literature; it culminates in liturgical compositions.

The interest in events taken as human history is quite remarkable. In addition to the pieces labeled "historical," the laudatory and hagiographic compositions and, even more clearly, the laments, are based on a certain historicity. But historical reality is very rapidly transformed by the collective memory; metamorphosed by the popular imagination, it ends up in the realm of myth and legend after a period of time.

Chronology is the first to pay the price of this mythicization, with the confusion of periods and dates. Like other compositions, our "History of Job" swarms with anachronisms. The biblical hero is made a contemporary of the patriarchs, a councilor at Pharaoh's court at the time of Moses; he is said to have known the reigns of David, the queen of Sheba, or even Ahasuerus; he returned with the exiles from Babylon and founded an academy in Tiberias.

All this literary production, even the type known as "folkloric," which only seems to aim at entertaining and amusing (the parodic Purim pieces, for example), aimed to educate its audience and contribute to its initiation. The initiatory function was, in fact, primordial. It suffices to recall the scenario of the juvenile betrothal of the *kuttab,* and the grave and solemn *bar-miṣwah* ceremonial and its essential component, the sermon given by the adolescent promoted to religious majority.

It also happened, and more often than imagined, that Jewish literary work in dialect left the domain of the holy to indulge in other genres and other themes, less polarized on religion and liturgy, belonging to a popular literature common to Jewish and Muslim societies, and in which nothing visibly recalled religious or ethnic origin.

In a way, this literature was the favored meeting-place of the two communities, who achieved a genuine symbiosis in this specific cultural domain. This literary genre is living proof of the permeability of religious and sociocultural frontiers. Through its agency, easy communications were established between the popular masses, and a mutual fertilization of folklores was brought about. Dialogue between the cultures replaced confrontation of (national) ideologies and religious consciousness. The two societies certainly lived in religious opposition, jealous of their identity, intransigent in their faith, but they came together in the same mode of expressing thought, in a fusion of mentalities, and, on the whole, co-existed peaceably.

### *Themes and Genres*

This type of intellectual activity had an important place in the cultural landscape of Moroccan Jewry. We have given some idea of this in various publications on orientalism and, more particularly, in the study, written in collaboration with P. Galand, on the hitherto unknown thousand-year-old Judeo-Berber heritage,[15] as well as in our last work devoted specifically to Jewish popular and dialectal literature in the Islamic West.[16]

In the ocean of literature in dialect it is possible to distinguish multiple modes of expression corresponding to different functions, types of discourse, and works created for different occasions, as well as var-

15. Haim Zafrani with P. Pernet-Galand, *Une version berbère de la Haggadah de Pesaḥ, texte de Tinrhir du Todrha,* Supplement to the Proceedings of the GLECS, 2 vols. (Paris, 1970).

16. Zafrani, *Littératures dialectales.*

ied genres and themes. All of them enjoyed, though to different degrees, a certain favor in scholarly circles and among the general public and the masses.

Of exclusively Jewish interest, we can mention the Judeo-Arabic and Judeo-Berber (Judeo-Castilian in Hispanophone societies descended from the Spanish megorashim) translations of the Bible and of mishnaic tractates (more particularly, the Haggadah for Pesaḥ and Pirqe-Abot, "Ethics of the Fathers"); liturgical compositions; hagiographical pieces glorifying Palestinian saints (Rabbi Shimon Bar Yoḥay and Rabbi Me'ir) or the numerous local santons who were extolled by ḥillulas and seasonal pilgrimages; panegyrics; the songs and laments that punctuated family life and proclaimed celebrations and mourning; whole treatises on halakhah (practical law and jurisprudence); the paraenetic and homiletic literature of popular preaching; the satiric and parodic pieces that were part of the folklore of the festival of Purim or the ritual of other ceremonies.

We move on to the secular and lay world of a culture which knew no religious frontiers and was, as it were, symbiotic, where Jews and Muslims met, shared the same preoccupations, and were moved by the same impulses. Here one finds Berber and Arabic poetry, the *qiṣṣa* and the *malḥun,* the ballad and the ritornello (*'arubi*), the great compositions in oriental, Hispanic, or local Arabic. The last category includes the many works associated with classical Andalusian music, including all the ones, both ancient and modern, indicated in the *laḥans* at the head of various compositions, which served as models for the creation of Hebrew poetry and for the sacred and secular Jewish music of the *piyyuṭ* and popular song. They bear witness to the vast Mediterranean, oriental, and Maghrebian culture which the Jewish communities in the large cities and the remotest mellahs of the Atlas and the Saharan borderlands bore with them.

Add to all this the marvelous and fascinating world of story and legend, the scholarly or playful world of proverbs and popular sayings, of epistolary literature, the minor arts which Jews and Muslims without distinction pursued, and which were held in particular favor in female and juvenile society: *as-slâmât* (greetings, billets-doux, and other bittersweet messages), *al-laghza* ( "enigmas"), *al-ḥujjaya* (riddles), *al-ma'sâni* (word and language games), *al-ma'syâr* (reprimands), *al-a'ayyu'* (songs for specific occasions, generally improvised, humorous and sarcastic), *lă-ghna* (comic songs, lullabies, skipping songs—*maṭesha* to the Muslims, *sabuka* to the Jews, and those accompanying other games) *ad-d'a* (invocations to God, the angels, biblical heroes, Palestinian saints, and local santons), various types of short stories (*khrâfât* and *ḥkâyât*), songs of a polemical and political nature composed in wartime or during struggles against various invaders of the country, and so on.

### *Some Representative Pieces*

#### *Mi-Kamokha*

The poem presented here is the Judeo-Arabic version of a poem by Judah Halevi, poet and philosopher of the Andalusian Golden Age, born in 1085. *Mi-Kamokha* (Hebrew, "Who is like unto Thee?" from Exodus 15:11) is a liturgical piece that was read in the synagogue service on the Saturday morning before the festival of Purim. In it, the author tells the biblical story of Esther in his own way. Apart from the distich of the Hebraic prologue, the composition consists of a total of eighty-two quatrains, and the fourth metric line of each quatrain is a biblical cento. The version that we have published emphasizes the nature of this reference to the scriptural texts and the interpretation put on it by our Judeo-Arabic texts.

The following is a translation of quatrains 6, 38, and 48:

6. This happened in the time of Ashtaschir [Ahasuerus],
King, ruling over dukes and princes,
Most lofty, most exalted of any king or monarch;
God gave him victory.

38. Esther's ladies told her of the event:
"We heard a cry as of an ostrich in the desert;
Mordechai passed by in sackcloth clad,
We know not what had come to pass with him."

48. "Most beautiful of women, green branch of the anemone.
What is your wish? Everything is yours, at your mercy."
"That the king and one-eyed Haman come," she answered,
"To the feast I have prepared to honor him."

#### *Qiṣṣat Sidna 'Iyyub*

The "History of our Lord Job" is also a quasi-liturgical composition, generally recited during the mourning period that precedes the commemoration of the destruction of Jerusalem, the ninth of Ab. It consists of eighty quatrains in Judeo-Arabic.

The character of Job occupies pride of place in Jewish biblical and postbiblical literature (Book of Job, Talmud and Midrash, Testament of Job, etc.), and Muslim writers expanded the few verses the Koran devotes to it into copious commentaries or marvelous legends, largely inspired by rabbinic writings. Our Judeo-Arabic version tells the story of Job, drawing its inspiration both from Jewish literature and local and Arabo-Islamic traditions. It describes in succession the legendary figure of Job, prototype of the Bedouin prince; the campaign waged by Satan against this righteous man; the character of Raḥma, the faithful and devoted wife; a discreet intervention by Job's friends; the sufferings of Job, with emphasis on the episode of the worms (vermin that eat flesh and bones); and finally, the "return" of Job, the object of providential benevolence, who recaptures youth, fame, and fortune (doubled in the event), with his children, the daughters, enjoying favored treatment in our version.

Verses 29, 35, and 38, reprinted below, show some of the features of the character of Raḥma (absent from the biblical text):

> 29. Raḥma, his wife, was a noble lady.
> She worked for a wage carrying wood,
> Or begged from the Bedouin girls.
>
> 35. They saw her enter, sparkling like the light of the crescent moon.
> One said, "What splendor!
> Sell me some of your braids,
> And I will give you bread and a measure of dates."
>
> 38. "Alas, I have torn out that matchless hair.
> The women have shared it to make into braids
> That they set on their heads, but the braids will not stay,
> Flying off like birds."

As for Job's three daughters, they are described as follows in the epilogue (verses 72–74):

> Beautiful and generous,
> They had not their like in all the land.
> To the first gave he [Job] the name of Sun and Moon,
> The second called he Cinnamon Bark and Amber,

The third he named Gazelle's Horn, rounded.
Their beauty had no match! Oh, you who hear me!

*Two Parodies*

These two pieces, one of which is a marriage contract (*ketubbah*) for Esther and the other a requiem (*hashkabah*) for Haman, are associated with the festival of Purim and intended primarily for the entertainment of the masses. Nevertheless, they display a not inconsiderable amount of knowledge of the most ancient Jewish legends relating to the story of Esther, and they paraphrase, amplify, and sometimes travesty its scriptural, talmudic, and midrashic sources in order to adapt them to local circumstances and conditions. They provide information on certain customs and practices with which this central episode in Jewish history was formerly commemorated in Morocco.

*Nimrod and Abraham*

Although significantly altered and abridged by the narrator, this version of the legend of Nimrod and Abraham, recounted in the Arabic of the Jews of Debdou, still has some interest because it is a further confirmation of the influence in Jewish circles—rabbinic, in particular—of a legend partly composed of elements borrowed from Islamic literature.

*Qiṣṣat Yosef Aṣ-Ṣaddiq*

"The Story of Joseph the Just" is a poetic composition where the biblical story is extended and enriched by a host of elements taken from Jewish legend (midrash and aggadah) and Muslim *qiṣaṣ* (histories) of the prophets, themselves based on surah 12 of the Koran. This is a popular portrayal of a revered figure in the holy writings, the story of Joseph and his brothers. It exists in several versions, transmitted orally by storytellers or set down in writing, either in unpublished texts or printed on loose sheets in Hebraic characters for distribution to Jewish societies in the Orient and Maghreb, and in Arabic script for more limited Muslim circles.

It would be interesting to look further than the obvious disparities between the scriptural stories (biblical and koranic) and the popular versions (Jewish and Muslim, even oriental Christian), and subject all the texts to a structural analysis on the lines illustrated by the work of modern writers. This sort of comparison could provide useful information on the Semitic foundations and the genesis of signification in biblical and koranic discourse.

### *The Death of Moses*

The subject of the death of Moses is widely dealt with in Jewish homiletical literature (midrash and aggadah). It is treated in numerous Palestinian Hebraic *piyyuṭim* describing his last moments, his struggle against death, and his vehement challenge to the fatal decision that prevented him from completing his work and entering the Promised Land. There are many references to Moses in the Koran, and for Muslims, the great biblical prophet is a glorious figure who captured the imagination of storytellers and poets. A host of legends in prose and verse are devoted to him. The theme of the death of Moses is dealt with in many compositions in Maghrebian Arabic dialect. Jewish versions exist, and we have collected them, both orally or in manuscripts written in Hebraic characters. All of them sensitively recount the last moments of Moses' life.

### *Lament on a Tribal Raid*

The Judeo-Arabic lament on a raid against Fas Al-Jadid by the tribe of the Oudaya is a *kinah* that describes briefly, and laments, in a way, one of the frequent rebellions by the Oudaya against the central government at the beginning of the nineteenth century. The rebellion was the occasion of a raid by the men of this tribe on the Jewish quarter of Fez—on the whole, a fairly commonplace episode in the history of its inhabitants.

The substance of the poem conveys a certain number of facts about the rebellion of the tribes, the flight of the sovereign, the anguished wait for his return, the siege and bombardment of the town, the shortage of certain commodities like soap, the scarcity of foodstuffs, the material condition of the Jews, the usual prosperity of the affluent class of notables in normal periods of peace and tranquility, the distress of the besieged population, the forced labor that weighed on it, and so on (verses 4–26).

The following are a few extracts from the poem (verses 9, 12, 18, 22):

9. The Oudaya burst in and cried: "Now we have them in our grip!"

12. On Saturday, we sat and waited, all the men of quality and wealth,
Eyes fixed on heaven. Nothing was heard but plaintive cries, ah! Ah!

18. Supplies of fats and oil no longer reached us. Filth covered us,
And soap unobtainable. Where is it? Who saw it?

22. What sadness for the Jews of Fez, for man and woman!
Those one saw living a perpetual marriage feast,
In dwellings always hung with sumptuous draperies!
Have burrowed into cisterns, or shut themselves away with a double turn of the key,
Imprisoned in their homes.

### *Two Original Judeo-Muslim Poems*

*Al-Maḥbub* ("The Lover") and *Al-Qaftan* ("The Caftan") both come under the head of dialectal and popular Moroccan literature, common to Jews and Muslims, and containing no references to religious or ethnic origin. Jews and Muslims met here to be amused, to sing of feminine finery, to exalt love and strong, intoxicating drink.

*Al-Maḥbub.* The piece devoted to the caftan is more distinctive because of some unusual Jewish Hispanicisms, but the composition dedicated to the distant lover, the theme of separation, and the absence of the messenger is marked by none of the features usually noted in the Jewish languages of Morocco. Very strangely, there is no sign of Jewish Hebreo-Aramaic idioms, no trace of the elements of foreign, especially Castilian, origin, frequently found in other texts. Its author was none other than 'Abd-Al-Qader Al-' Alami, known as Sidi Qaddur, a popular Moroccan poet of the eighteenth and nineteenth centuries. Two versions of the text have reached us, both unpublished, one in Arabic, the other in Hebrew characters, with some textual variations between the two.

Like a large part of the secular poetry of the *malhûn,* and like several erotic and bacchic pieces, this *qaṣida* is interpreted metaphorically as an allegory referring to the prophet Mohammed. The following is the chorus, called by the Arabic word *harba* ("spear"), of the Arabic version, which consists of nine verses:

How to console the one separated from a lover,
Who has lost her reason and remained alone in the desolation of her dwelling.

How has the beloved of my heart cruelly abandoned me, leaving me nothing but his face, his features, his silhouette.
May I ever see the image of his dazzling beauty in the resplendent orb of the full moon!

The Jewish poet seems to have reproduced the *qaṣida* of Sidi Qaddur in Hebrew characters, from memory, having heard it sung in that symbiotic Maghrebian society where poetic traditions and popular song (*malhûn*) and the classical (Andalusian music and song) were transmitted orally. The following is the first of the four verses he retained:

I found nothing to say when my companion left me.
My whole being collapsed in stupor, and my tongue grew heavy,
Lord! Lord!
The nerves of my body have loosened,
And my eyes flood with tears.
Hardly did his fire touch me than I was filled with passionate burning.
He greeted me with vows of peace, and I began to sweep the places where he was wont to sit.
Seeing me carefree and joyous, he closed his eyes and said:
"I am separated from you, O Lord, after having abandoned me to my fate."
Thus did he possess me; my mind has flown into a passion, and he has gone.

*Chorus:*
May I ever see the image of my beloved in the resplendent orb of the full moon!
How beautiful are the features of his profile, the shape of his face, and the line of his silhouette!

*Al-Qaftan.* The second composition, mainly devoted to the caftan, is a sort of ballad-ritornello belonging to the Maghrebian poetic genre called *'arûbi,* a strictly female work which usually exalts love and passion. The townspeople formerly sang the *'arûbi* on their great spring outings to gardens and the countryside.

The piece consists of seventeen verses (one tercet, ten quatrains, and five quintains) and a chorus of three lines ending with the words *'ud* ("lute") and *maḥbub* ("beloved"). The central theme of this ballad is the caftan, its various forms and colors, its symbolism and mythology.

The caftan is a traditional component of the male wardrobe. But it is more especially an item of feminine finery. In brocaded silk, embroidered with gold thread, velvet, and brocade, enhanced with gold and silver braid, it is sumptuous and superb; in fine linen, decorated with multicolored filigree, it is more modest and more simple. It is always the ceremonial dress, whether for grand public receptions or intimate meetings. It forms the finery of the young girl, the new bride and the wife, the lover and the beloved. It is said that virtue and vice lodge in the vast folds of its gold and brocade cloth. Fastened by a thousand and one buttons sewn on with silken thread, it is the rampart of chastity, modesty, and sworn fidelity. Left negligently unbuttoned, it seduces, excites the impassioned heart and delights the lover, intoxicated with the dizziness of the eager desire that it suggests. It must also be noted that the color, richness of fabrics, and decorations vary with the seasons, fashion, and purpose of the caftan. All in all, this is an allusive, even symbolic and allegorical world where things have names like "Let me adore you," "Snow on the mountain," "Mr. Mohammed's beard," "O pretty pigeon," "The cuckold's foot on the stair," and "The axe in the mother-in-law's head."

The following extract includes the chorus and the first four verses:

The doves of the winds  
Have taken flight and flown  
To Salé, seeking fresh seas.  
The young unwed are bathing there.  
The young unwed are bathing.  
  Take me away, teach me the lute!  
  Boy, teach me the lute!  
  So that the lover's glass will please me!

Doves of love!  
O you, the little fool!  
The flowers are at the window,  
The roses in the ewer,  
And the betrothed are bathing.  
And the betrothed are bathing.  
  Take me away, teach me the lute!  
  Boy, teach me the lute!  
  So that the lover's glass will please me!

A violet caftan,  
My beloved will put on,

And will come to my house,
A fortnight [he will stay there].
A fortnight [he will stay.]
    Take me away, teach me the lute!
    Boy, teach me the lute!
    So that the lover's glass will please me!

A striped caftan,
My neighbor will dress in,
And will come to my house,
A fortnight [he will stay there].
A fortnight [he will stay there].
    Take me away, teach me the lute!
    Boy, teach me the lute!
    So that the lover's glass will please me!

### *Two Hagiographic Tales*

The first tale tells the miraculous story of what happened to Rabbi Jacob Halevi ben Shabbat, who was born in Mogador and died in an odor of sanctity around the middle of the nineteenth century. The text was collected in Hebrew in an anthology of poetry compiled by the hero of the tale himself. The anthology, entitled *Yagel Ya'aqob* ("Jacob Will Rejoice"), was printed in Leghorn in 1881. Versions in Judeo-Arabic were circulated in various popular publications.

Once upon a time, Rabbi Jacob was traveling in the south of Morocco with a large caravan composed of nearly three hundred Ishmaelite [Muslim] and Israelite [Jewish] men. The caravan was traveling to a far-off town situated at fifteen days journey from its starting-point, passing through places frequented by highwaymen and infested by legions of wild animals. The travelers escaped all these dangers, which threatened them at every turn, until one Friday, the eve of Shabbat, at around mid-day. Rabbi Jacob informed the whole caravan, and more especially the Jewish travelers, of his decision to stop on the road and of his duty to welcome the holiness of Shabbat.

His Jewish companions tried in vain to dissuade him, convinced as they were of the danger of separating themselves from the caravan and making a halt in an unsafe place. Faced with his stubbornness, they continued on their way, abandoning him to his fate. When he was left alone, he took refuge in a grotto and prepared some light food for the ritual Shabbat meal. Before sunset, he lit two candles in honor of the holy day, then he began the evening prayer, 'Arbit. Standing up for the 'Amidah [customarily said standing], he saw a gigantic lion facing him some dozen cubits away. An immense fear filled his heart and stirred his spirit, so much so that he interrupted his prayer.

At that moment, a figure with the face of a man appeared to him and said: "Why has fear entered your heart? Do not be afraid. It is to protect you from all harm, to ensure your safety, and to bring you safe and sound to the place where you are going." His spirit calmed as soon as he heard the voice, and he waited calmly and peacefully for the end of Shabbat and the appearance of the stars.

Then the lion came to him, crouched down next to him, and signaled to him to mount its back. Rabbi Jacob sat astride the lion, and in the twinkling of an eye, he was borne to the entrance to the town which he was bound for. The people of the town were surprised to see him on a Saturday evening, well before the expected date of the caravan's arrival, [his co-religionists] even suspecting that he had violated the Sabbath and profaned its laws.

He told them his story, and it was learned a long time afterwards that the caravan had been attacked by brigands and completely decimated, the travelers murdered, and the Jews too. Then they understood the meaning of the miracle of Rabbi Jacob, who, being called Halevi, added *ben Shabbaṭ* ["son of Shabbat'] to his family name.

Note that the lion, *as-sba'*, king of the beasts, symbol of supreme power, plays a very important role in hagiographic literature in general, and especially in that of the Jews of the Maghreb. Rabbi Simon Bar Yoḥay, the great saint of Tiberias, bears the attributes of the lion, and the Rab of Tlemcen, Efrayim Anqawa, in the fourteenth century, rode on a lion.

The second tale recounts one of the miraculous deeds attributed to Rabbi Jacob Nahmyas, also called *Moul Anmay,* a santon and miracle-worker who practiced in the south of Morocco during the nineteenth century. Collected in Judeo-Arabic dialect, this tale was printed in a modest booklet, together with others in the same vein, in Tunis in 1915.

The incident occurred in the *zawiya* of Siddi Rahhal, situated in the province of Marrakesh.

Sidi Rahhal was already the object of worship and adoration by the *goyim* [*sic*] inhabiting the country in his lifetime. People pledged devotion to him, obeyed him implicitly, knowing that he made use of magic, charms, and sorcery.

Siddi Rahhal had a son who was known to the Jewish population of

Marrakesh for his violence and godlessness; he even had designs on a Jewish woman of the locality. One day the woman went to draw water from the spring situated outside the town. The wicked lad seized her, despite her resistance.

At that moment Rabbi Jacob left the town and happened to witness the attack. Seeing the wicked fellow continuing his misdeed and the woman struggling, he came up to him and said: "You do wrong, let the woman go." The boy answered the rabbi with abuse.

Realizing that any word of remonstrance would be vain, the rabbi struck him down with a glance and the boy collapsed, metamorphosed into a heap of bones scattered on the ground. The rabbi returned to the town accompanied by the woman, thus delivering the oppressed from the hands of her oppressor.

The *goyim* arrived on the scene and found the corpse of the "ungodly." The news reached the father, who immediately decided to exterminate the Jews, even before burying his son. As the corpse had been found in their special domain, the crime was imputed to them. Rabbi Jacob went to see the father and said to him: "I will revive your son; he himself will bear witness and will tell you who killed him."

And so it was. The saintly rabbi touched the corpse with the tip of his thick cane and cried out: "Rise, ungodly man, and do what is needed to save Israel!" The corpse came back to life, rose to his feet, and spoke these words: "It was not the Jews who killed me. It was God who killed me!" Then he began to utter abuse against the Ishmaelite [Muslim] faith. The rabbi immediately commanded him to return to dust. Seeing this miracle, the father begged pardon of the saintly rabbi and of the Jews, to whom he henceforth granted his favors.

## *A Judeo-Muslim Chronicle from Safi*

The story of the rabbi and the *fqih* (Muslim scholar) takes place in the medina of Safi, where Jews and Muslims lived peacefully together. In fact, a street there was called *Derb-l-ihudi* ["the street of the Jews"]; it was inhabited mainly by Jews, and most of the synagogues were situated there. The story was told me by Mr. Levy and Mr. Barchechat, former leaders of the community in the town.

Rabbi Abraham Siboni, a merchant and a great scholar, was friends with the Muslim notables of the city. One of these friends, a *fqih,* often criticized him for drinking *maḥya* [local brandy]. One day, Rabbi Abraham dipped his index finger into a glass full of this liquor, set fire to it with the flame of a candle, and then wiped his finger without having felt the slightest burn. When his Muslim companion appeared surprised, he said to him: "If a Jew takes brandy, it is in order to saturate his body with it, so that the fires will not attack him on his passage to purgatory and he will reach paradise safe and sound." The *fqih* immediately requested: "Give me something to drink."[17]

17. The Jewish scholar probably had Isaiah 43:2 in mind: "When thou passeth through the waters, I will be with thee, . . . when thou walkest through the fire, thou shalt not be burned."

# Chapter 6

# *Ritual and Religious Life*

## DAILY LIFE UNDER DIVINE LAW

The Jew lives under the sovereign authority of the law written in the Bible, expounded at first by oral tradition, and then collected in the Talmud. A juridical doctrine was built up around the Talmud, and, as accessory to the Bible, took form in a wide-ranging literature (commentaries, codes, responsa, *taqqanot,* "ordinances," etc.). This doctrine, formulated in minute detail, enters into the tiniest interstices of public and private Jewish life, regulates every detail of the individual's existence from birth to burial, and requires unconditional submission to, and strict observance of, the precepts of the law. The divine origin of this doctrine explains the extent of its (legislative) domain and the legalism with which it is imposed. One of its fundamental dogmas holds that during the revelation on Sinai Moses received, not only the Pentateuch, or written Law, but also the Oral Law, which was handed down to all subsequent generations through an unbroken chain of leaders and teachers.

The readjustments made to adapt the revealed texts to the needs of communities or the ineluctable requirements of circumstances retain the character of inspired law. In the religious perception of Judaism, even the most recent prescriptions, born of the changing necessities of life, derive from the revelations on Mount Sinai.

All the extra-scriptural work of legislation that has accumulated over the centuries derives from this theocratic conception of law—

from the tannaitic period to the generations of Joseph Qaro (sixteenth century) and his successors, forming the source par excellence of rabbinic law. All this legal material is called halakhah, a term derived from the Hebrew verb *halakh,* "to walk," therefore, "a step, a rule to follow," a word comparable to the Arabic *shari'a.* "straight path, rule of conduct, law of divine essence."

### Custom and Practice

The dominant trends in Moroccan rabbinic law are expressed in terms of universal halakhah, represented here by the schools, first, of the old Spanish masters, then, later, of Joseph Qaro (Safed, sixteenth century). These trends themselves were subject to countervailing forces, by constants that no authority swayed and that were impervious to all influences, even the influence of the author of the *Shulḥan 'Aruk,* who was worshiped almost as a god by Moroccan scholars. These constants were loyalty to the ancient customs and practices sanctioned by the *taqqanot,* attachment to the traditions handed down by the "fathers," and the personal teachings of local masters.

In their juridical literature, Moroccan authors very frequently refer to old mishnaic and talmudic adages relating to *minhag* (custom): "everything must be in accordance with the custom of the land"; "custom goes beyond law and annuls it." This is the source of the considerable role of custom, designated here by the Arabic term *'ada,* informing local rabbinic law and domestic practice.

### Ashkenazim and Sephardim

Two sixteenth-century protagonists of halakhah, one Sephardi, Joseph Qaro, the other Ashkenazi, Moses Isserles, were closely associated in Moroccan rabbinic jurisprudence. It constantly compared them, almost automatically adopting the opinion of the first and rejecting that of the second, except in certain uncontentious situations or when the Sephardi master had nothing to say about a particular problem.

The choice of the Moroccan rabbinate, coinciding here with the choice of oriental Jewry as a whole, was clearly based on historical factors. It can also be explained by the different conceptions of halakhah and ritual as conceived of by the Sephardi and Ashkenazi masters.

The Ashkenazim tended to be strict in matters of prohibitions, of legality and legal things, while the Sephardim supported a more liberal and flexible interpretation of the law.[1] Conversely, in questions concerning relationships between Jews and gentiles, the Sephardim were stricter. These divergences arose from the nature of the relationships that the two communities maintained with gentiles: in Islamic lands, social relationships between Jews and Muslims were not marked by the violent hostility which characterized relations between Jews and Christians in Ashkenazic lands, where there was consequently no danger of assimilation and symbiosis. This was by no means the case in Muslim countries. Thus, Sephardi scholars felt it necessary to erect barriers in certain fields where Ashkenazic scholars felt no need to add to the severity of the law. Furthermore, the latter were anxious not to deepen the divide that separated them from their neighbors by emphasizing discriminatory rites, which would have aroused additional hatred.

## *Tell Me What You Eat and I Will Tell You Who You Are*

Despite a certain caution in their attitude to custom, a caution that sometimes turned into open hostility, the rabbinic authorities were in many cases forced to yield to custom. The majority set as much store by the law as by its practices and customs, which derived from a common fund of magic and mythology belonging to all the local ethnic groups irrespective of faith. This was especially true of certain dietary rites and of the consumption of couscous (accompanied by poultry or dairy products) on the evening before and the day after Sukkot (Tabernacles), Kippur (the Day of Atonement), and even Pesaḥ, despite the danger represented by the presence of *ḥameṣ* (food liable to ferment), which had to be eliminated from every Jewish house by the following day.

It was also true of the consumption of locusts. Rabbi Ḥayyim ben ʻAttar (eighteenth century), one of the most famous figures in Moroccan Jewry, was declaring war on his colleagues' liberalism and expressing scorn for local customs hallowed by long and ancient practice when he forbade anyone to touch what he called "impure insects." Boiled or variously prepared, locusts had always been a much appreciated delicacy in both Jewish and Muslim circles in southern Morocco,

1. Nevertheless, it appears from an examination of the laws of the *Shulḥan ʻAruk*, particularly those dealing with *nesekh* wine (wine forbidden because it has been, or is suspected of having been, handled by an idolater) that Qaro, usually more liberal on questions of dietary prohibitions, is stricter than Moses Isserles.

especially in periods of famine. Despite his immense authority, no one listened to him, and his condemnation of the consumption of locusts remained a dead letter.

He likewise encountered the hostility of the Moroccan rabbinate when he took it on himself to stigmatize the test of insufflating the lungs (*nefiḥah*) of an animal to be ritually slaughtered in order to reveal adhesions or lesions. The Moroccan rabbis rejected his claims to strictness and to censure in matters of dietary practice.

All Moroccan legislation concerning the ritual slaughter of poultry and animals is based on customs and practices specific to the various local communities. Over the last four centuries these have been the subject of a flourishing literature, the authors of which very often deviate from the prescriptions on this matter in Joseph Qaro's code, the *Shulḥan 'Aruk*.

In the area of forbidden foods, difficult circumstances often forced Moroccan authors, like their colleagues in other Diaspora communities, to apply the law with a certain degree of liberalism, in accordance with a general principle of rabbinical law based on the notion of greater injury: "In a period of distress and in every case where the fulfillment of a legal rule must entail a greater injury, actions forbidden in normal circumstances are declared permissible." The legislator makes his decision on the basis of the situation. He is empowered to take account of its leniency or harshness, evaluate the extent and the breadth of the injury, and personalize it if need be. Thus, certain dietary prohibitions can be lifted in a period of hardship or of a considerable rise in prices, but strict observance of the law is restored as soon as the economic situation improves.

Problems related to kashrut, the dietary rites, are the major concern of every strictly observant Jew, and particularly the woman of the house, responsible for the household and guardian of tradition inside the home. On the communal level, providing the population of the mellah with kosher food, in accordance with the legal and ritual rules, was a daily preoccupation of the rabbinical authorities and community leaders. Either directly or through their representatives, called *shliḥim* (emissaries) and *muqaddemin,* they supervised very closely the practice of certain professions related to foodstuffs (bread ovens, milk, wine, fish and meat suppliers), being extra vigilant in the case of butchers and small restaurants.

We will not go into the details of *sheḥiṭah* (ritual slaughter) and *ṭrefot* (meat unsuitable for consumption) or the position of the *shoḥeṭ,* the official ritual slaughterer. It will suffice to cite some of the evidence on the subject.

Jacob Aben Sur, a Fez rabbi of the seventeenth to eighteenth century, allowed a cereal called *anili,* a Berber term designating a type of millet, to be eaten on Passover. On the other hand, he recommended that people refrain from eating what he called *trid,* a thin galette that the Jews of Fez used to eat at Passover.

R. Yosef Messas, a rabbi from Meknès, called to act as judge at Tlemcen between 1924 and 1940, recounts the following incident from his rabbinic mission:

> I had a great deal to do in the matter of kashrut. I began by assembling all the restaurant owners and merchants of grilled liver, meat, spleen, and sausage. I came to the conclusion that they were not advised of the laws relating to the processes of the ritual salting and cleansing of meat and did their grilling in a utensil that was not pierced with holes. I taught them the elementary notions of the law relating to this process and warned them against any transgression in this respect. Once a month I went and inspected their restaurants and preached them a sermon.
>
> All the inhabitants of the town mixed meat and spleen in the same cooking pot during cooking, particularly when preparing the "Saturday dish," in Arabic, *dafîna* or *skhina.* I warned them against such practices. In addition, the butchers had an imperfect knowledge of the rules concerning the forbidden fats. Twice a week I went to inspect their abattoirs.
>
> At the time when the *maṣot* [unleavened bread] were manufactured, there was a great deal of work: ritual cleansing of the mills and ovens and their daily supervision, drawing water at the prescribed time, strict supervision of the dough, sale of *ḥameṣ,* scrupulous observance of all the other commandments relating to Pesaḥ.
>
> The new generation of men gave me serious cause for concern. I had all the trouble in the world making them give up prohibited foods, unclean varieties of fish, forbidden mixtures (milk and meat), etc.

Custom and practice were the compromise zone, as it were, between universal rabbinic law and the world of the Judeo-Muslim social imagination.

## *The Divine and Holy in Daily Life*

Every action in life is accompanied by the ritual blessing "Blessed art Thou, O Lord our God, King of the universe, who has sanctified us by

Thy commandments and commanded us to . . ." It is legally prescribed in the Mishnah and the Zohar that a blessing formula is to be pronounced on the occasion of both a happy event and a misfortune. This obligation, says Maimonides, is based on the following reasoning: "The commandment bidding us have great love for God implies that man gives thanks and praises God joyously even when he is suffering."

Every action receives a fragment of the divine, even the sexual act. The relations of a man with his legitimate wife, sanctified by the seven marital blessings, become a religious obligation, a *miṣwah,* to which the Zohar also gives a magical meaning and a mystical dimension.[2]

### *The Mystical Dimension of Ritual*

The eruption of the divine into daily life can be seen more specifically in the way the mystical dimension enters into the fulfillment of every *miṣwah* (precept), every prayer, every blessing, to strengthen its halakhic (and legalistic) motivation, under the increasingly dominant influence of esoteric doctrines, more particularly the Zohar and the kabbalah. In accordance with these doctrines, every action is carried out with a view to union with the Holy One, blessed be He, and his Shekhinah (Presence), in fear and love. Its fulfillment is accompanied by a mystical prayer which the liturgy incorporated into many rituals, inspired by the kabbalah of Isaac Luria and his disciples of the Safed school, who included several Moroccan scholars.

The irrational and esoteric entered increasingly into religious life and ritual in a period dominated, perhaps more than any other, by the burden of the exile. Mediterranean and oriental Jewry at that time adopted an attitude of withdrawal, or retreat and isolation, in expectation of the imminent advent of the messiah. This was precisely the attitude evoked by the kabbalistic doctrine of *ṣimṣum* as defined by Isaac Luria, that is to say, a self-willed/volitional act of contraction through which the *Kabod* (divine glory), which embraces everything, has been restricted.

### *Mysticism and Prayer*

The liturgy, the world of prayer, is one of the favorite spheres of kabbalah. Mysticism here finds its most classic expression, either in the

2. The evocation of the Divine Name by an appropriate formula is intended to banish the demon Lilith, Adam's first wife, before the fulfillment of the act which, once sanctified, contributes to the restoration of the divine unity and the re-establishment of universal harmony.

large number of pieces by authors who were mystics themselves, or by way of the esoteric interpretation of the ordinary liturgy, fixed long since by law and tradition. The influence of kabbalah is mainly crystallized in several overlapping and interdependent notions: the mechanism of *kawwanah,* which may be defined as "deep purpose" or "mystical meditation," for example, or the processes of *tiqqun,* the restoration of heavenly harmony, and *yiḥḥud,* the act of unification. Examination of them will help us to reach a better understanding of the preoccupations of the scholar-mystic accustomed to a discourse and dialectic whose deep meaning was known to a limited circle of initiates.

## Kawwanah

*Kawwanah,* the orientation and concentration of the individual's spirit, has a privileged place in mystical prayer as its dominant psychological component. The Ḥasidei Ashkenaz, the medieval pietists of the Ashkenazic countries, combined an absolute demand for *kawwanah* with scrupulous respect for the established texts, counting their words, even their letters, to discover theosophical mysteries in them by way of cryptographic procedures. In the Lurianic kabbalah, this aspect of prayer is even more central and is colored with other subtleties. Through the process of *kawwanah,* the personal element and the contemplative activity of the worshiper acquire a considerable power in prayer. The kabbalah answers the Talmud's question, "How do we know that God Himself prays?", in the following terms: "Through the medium of mystical prayer, an irresistible force draws man toward the heights, and he is absorbed into the mysterious and dynamic life of the divinity, with the result that God shares in the act of prayer that he is fulfilling."

"Prayer," it repeats, "is like an arrow that the worshiper shoots toward heaven with the bow of *kawwanah.*" A Moroccan kabbalist, Abraham Azulay, defined *kawwanah* in terms of attraction toward the base of the divine spiritual light which thus lights up the letters and words of the ritual in order subsequently to ascend to the highest levels.[3] Prayer means more than a free outpouring of religious feeling. Nor is it simply the codified acknowledgment and praise of God as

3. See Haim Zafrani, *Poésie juive en Occident Musulman*, pp. 196 ff., which refers to the books by G. Vajda and Gershom Scholem.

Creator and King by the religious community in the ordinary liturgy. It is a vehicle for the soul's ascent to God. And the aim of *kawwanah* is the discovery of the various stages in this ascent.

## *The Act of Unification*

Lurianic prayer reserves a special place for *yiḥḥudim,* acts of unification that comprise meditations on the combinations of the letters of the Tetragrammaton or on the other ineffable Names of God. The *yiḥ-ḥudim,* like similar practices in other mystical meditation systems, were instruments intended for the soul's elevation. They were sometimes used as a means of communication with other souls, particularly those of departed *ṣaddiqim* (righteous men and saints). Consequently, these exercises in mental concentration on the holy names of God and the angels show a tendency to associate prayer with magic and many other practices in order to reach the Holy Spirit. The messianic element, linked to the notion of *tiqqun,* is also intensely present in this contemplative activity, and it is in no way surprising that at the peak of the era of messianic tension, which was also nourished from other sources, the Lurianic Kabbalah gave birth to the Sabbatean movement, which deeply and sometimes tragically marked Jewish history and consciousness in the seventeenth and eighteenth centuries.

## *The Restoration of Cosmic Harmony*

*Kawwanah* in prayer and the fulfillment of the precepts of the law, combining *yiḥḥud* and *tiqqun,* thus contribute to unifying the Name of God and restoring cosmic harmony. This discourse and dialectic obviously eluded the common run of worshipers, who sometimes recited the texts of their prayers mechanically and repetitively. But for the worshiper, prayer is most often a simple individual or collective communication, rising from man to God. Covered with his ritual prayer-shawl (ṭallit), he prays in the composure of his solitude, but also within the *community* of worshippers (*'edah*), the quorum of ten (*minyan*), and in order to bear witness (*'edut*). Prayer is simultaneously worship, intense communication, testimony, and a privileged relationship with one's fellows.[4]

4. Compare Kafka, *Préparatifs de noce à la campagne*, Gallimard, Folio, 1957, pp. 64–65 and 135.

## TIMES FOR LITURGY AND MAJOR CEREMONIES

Daily life is punctuated by privileged moments, commemorations, ceremonies that obey the laws of the universal Jewish code (halakhah) or are incorporated in customs and practices hallowed by old and long-standing observance. What we are looking at is a fundamentally religious and ritual calendar that also bears the marks of historical and national influences, the imaginary world of legend, the mystery of the mystical dimension, and even of contemporary events.

The day, from dawn to sunset, is divided by the three major prayers: Shaḥrit in the morning; Minḥah (literally "offering") in the afternoon; and ʿArbit at sunset. Meals are made sacred by the grace that concludes them, and even the night is broken up by special liturgies: Tiqqun Ḥasot, the midnight supplication, and Seliḥot, the supplications in the month of Elul and in the period between Rosh Hashanah, the New Year, and Kippur, the Day of Atonement.

The week is marked by the recurrence of Shabbat, distinct from other days as the sacred is distinct from the profane. The month is inaugurated by the special liturgy for the neomenia, Rosh Ḥodesh and the blessing of the new moon, on the seventh day. The year is divided by the three pilgrim festivals (*shalosh regalim*): Pesaḥ, Shabu'ot, and Sukkot, respectively, Passover, Pentecost, and Tabernacles, and the historical commemorations, Ḥanukkah and Purim. These joyful days alternate with "undesirable moments," as the Moroccan poet Jacob Aben Sur called them. These are occasions to recall a painful past, the destruction of the Temple in Jerusalem, the exile and the dispersion, the days of mourning, fasting, and lamentation on the ill-fated days of 9 Ab, 17 Tammuz, 3 Tishri, 10 Ṭebet, and 13 Adar.

All these liturgical moments, all these ceremonies and commemorations, will not be described in detail. The need, dictated by time and space, to restrict this chapter to a reasonable size prevents the lengthy expositions that they merit. They will only be mentioned in connection with factors that seem to distinguish the Moroccan communities from their counterparts in the Diaspora, over and above their general and universal structure; factors that make for their identity and display their specific personality. To this end, some significant rites and actions will be picked out here and there, some customs and practices noted, which have now been lost or lie dormant. Their existence can only be confirmed by someone who has lived inside the Jewish life of these communities for so long ignored, who has known from internal and personal experience the intellectual and spiritual itinerary of the learned elite and the more relaxed cultural space of a Jewish society that was broader, more easily open to the influence of the Arabo-Berber and Muslim environment.

## SHABBAT

The Written Law (Bible) and the Oral Law (Mishnah and Talmud), law and jurisprudence (halakhah, responsa, and rabbinic ordinances, *taqqanot*), homiletical literature, Jewish legend (midrash and aggadah), and kabbalah all speak at length of the pre-eminence, sanctity, and delights of the Sabbath (*shibḥe Shabbat,* that which make it a very special day, distinct from the other days of the week. The contribution of local custom and practices must be added. Only three privileged moments of this unique ceremony will be mentioned here: the *baqqashot* vigil, and the coming in and going out of Shabbat, as they are celebrated by the vast majority of traditionalist Moroccan families. We know this celebration from personal experience. But written evidence will also be mentioned: the documents provided by Moroccan literature itself and the references to certain zoharic texts that are known here by tradition and are regarded as the foundation of the commandment relating to Shabbat.

### *Mystical Observances*

*The royal table.* If the ten commands whereby God created the world correspond to the Ten Commandments of the Torah, these are ten prescriptions which have to be fulfilled on the occasion of Shabbat, according to a zoharic text (Zohar III, 272b–274a). The text is more particularly concerned with the Sabbath meals, called the "royal table." The prescriptions are: perform ablutions, prepare two loaves of bread for each meal, consume the three meals prescribed by the ritual, light the lamps to illuminate the table, bless the glass (of wine) that inaugurates the meal, discourse on the Torah, prolong the meal, make the last ablutions, say grace after meals, bless and drink the last glass of wine.

But it is the commentary that reveals the deep esoteric significance of these ten actions which fulfill a function and a role in the reconstitution (restoration) of the holy mystery of the ten sefirot (the ten mystical entities), which include the Shekhinah (Divine Presence), the "table" of the Holy One, blessed be He.

Ablutions are prescribed because the hands carry impurities and are therefore unsuited to the blessing that integrates the force of the divine Name, which is numerically identical to the twenty-eight phalanges, and only descends on pure hands.

The two loaves of bread for each Sabbath meal are the two tablets that were given on the Sabbath day, in one single pair, representing the Written Law and the Oral Law. On Shabbat, man has the benefit of two souls, the everyday one, and an additional one (*neshamah yeterah*) special to the day. Spirits and souls leave and descend in pairs on that day, and no satan or demon has any hold on them or on the world. Gehenna itself is at rest, and its fires do not burn on Shabbat.

The author of the Zohar amplifies the legend, found in the Talmud and aggadah, that the torments of the wicked stop on Shabbat. All the forces of evil are rendered powerless on that day, he declares; all judgment activity in the heavenly courts comes to a halt; harshness is banished from the world from top to bottom, and mercy alone rules everywhere.

The three ritual meals, with the seven blessings (eulogies) of the prayer, are the sefirotic tree of the ten divine entities constituting the mystery of the "delight" (*'oneg*). Without these three meals, it would become *nega'* (a pestilential wound). Note the permutation of the *'avin* root, and it is also said: "Then shalt thou delight thyself in the Lord" (Isaiah 58:14).

To illuminate the table with the light from the lamps is the fourth commandment. This rite presupposes a table laid with the best linen, the most beautiful cutlery, the tastiest dishes, and the most delicious wines, a table surrounded by embroidered cushions and rich hangings. In fact, Shabbat must be distinguished from ordinary days by increased sumptuousness, by singing hymns and canticles composed for the occasion, and welcoming it with the same joy as a bridegroom welcomes his bride, because Shabbat is queen and bride.

We will pass over the rest of the commandments except for the seventh, which decrees that the meal must be prolonged, not only because the Torah has to be discussed at table but also to give the poor time to come and share in it. Developing the well-known verse "righteousness [charity] delivereth from death" (Proverbs 10:2), the Zohar adds a paradoxical idea to the usual commentaries which seems to contradict many other biblical and rabbinic texts. It says,

> The Holy One, blessed be He, could find no better quality to give to Israel than poverty. . . . Every other people and nation, if it so happen that they be starving, grows angry, curses their king and their God, and turns against heaven (Isaiah 10:21). As for Israel, it adheres to its God through the quality of poverty and does not deny Him, and it is by this quality that it will be delivered.

*Sabbath queen and bride.* It is told that the sages of the Mishnah, in the last centuries of the Second Temple period, ceremonially went forth from their towns on Friday afternoons to welcome Shabbat, saying: *Bo'i kallah, Bo'i kallah,* "Come bride, come bride." The kabbalistic movement, born in Palestine around Isaac Luria and his disciples, reinstated this welcoming ceremony at Safed and Tiberias in the sixteenth century. They gave it great impetus, matching it with a mystical significance which enjoyed an immense success throughout the Mediterranean basin and most especially in the Maghrebian communities. This was largely due to the blossoming of an original genre of poetry, chiefly represented by the Sabbath hymns and canticles of Isaac Luria himself and his companions, who thus spread the new esoteric doctrines by way of liturgical song. Pride of place must go to the famous poem composed by Salomon Halevi Alqabeṣ. This Sabbath hymn, which combines mystical symbolism with messianic hopes, enjoyed immense success in every Jewish community in the world and is still sung to welcome in Shabbat at today's Friday evening service in synagogues of all affiliations. This is the chorus:

> *Lekha dodi ligrat kallah . . .*
> Come my friend, to meet the bride;
> Let us welcome the presence of the Sabbath.

The second verse begins as follows:

> Come, let us go to meet the Sabbath,
> For it is a well-spring of blessing.

The piece ends with a last call to the bride:

> Come in peace, thou crown of thy husband,
> With rejoicing and cheerfulness,
> In the midst of the faithful of the chosen people,
> Come bride! Come bride!

The celebration of Shabbat is thus surrounded by quite exceptional solemnity. It is steeped in an atmosphere dominated by doctrines relating to man's role in the restoration of the cosmic universe. It is enriched by the symbolism of the marriage of the King and Queen celebrated in the mystical hymn by Salomon Alqabeṣ, and by the recital of the Song of Songs and of chapter 31 of Proverbs, which are the object of meditations on the Shekhinah in her role as God's mystical wife.

Remember here that to the mystics, the magnificent portrait of the woman of valor depicted by the author of Proverbs does not represent the lady whose praises he intended to sing when he originally composed the biblical text. In their view, this eulogy is addressed to the Shekhinah. Then again, this scriptural piece, an alphabetical acrostic, contains the same number of verses as there are letters in the Hebrew alphabet, these twenty-two letters symbolizing the twenty-two channels of the blessing and abundance that emanate from heaven. Woman also represents the Torah.

*Welcoming Shabbat under the prayer-shawl.* Echoes of the mystical celebration of Shabbat can still be found in Moroccan rabbinic literature of the past four centuries. For example, a responsum describes a rite that Jacob Aben Sur observed in Fez at the beginning of the eighteenth century.

In this document, Jacob Aben Sur explains to his correspondent in Salé, Meir De Avila, the "reason for and esoteric meaning" of a practice that De Avila had seen him observe in Fez. The practice in question consisted of covering oneself with a ṭallit on Friday evening in order to welcome Shabbat.

> You ask me whether I learned this practice from my father or whether it came to me from my reading. . . . In actual fact, every Shabbat evening, my father used to make his ablutions in hot water, take off his everyday clothes, purify himself by the prescribed immersion in forty measures of water, dress himself in his Shabbat clothing, cover himself with a ṭallit, recite the Song of Songs, say the Minḥah prayers, chant psalms, go to the synagogue for the ʿArbit prayers, return to the house, read the Tiqqun Shabbat [special liturgy for Shabbat] according to the rite of Isaac Luria, remove the ṭallit, and eat his dinner. . . . He never explained the reason for this practice to me. but I nonetheless observed it after his death, fulfilling the maxim: "They grasp the works of their fathers in their hands." However, I found some basis for this practice in the Talmud: "R. Judah said, in the name of Rab, that on the eve of

Shabbat, Judah bar El'ay . . . made his ablutions and covered himself with a [prayer] shawl." Maimonides, for his part, explicitly recommends that face, hands, and feet be washed in hot water . . . in honor of Shabbat, and that the man wrap his ṭallit around him and await in meditation and humility the time to welcome the face of Shabbat as he would await a visit from a king. The early sages, he added, gathered their disciples on the eve of Shabbat, and all of them, wrapped in the ṭallit, cried: "Come, come out to meet the Shabbat king."

You also ask me whether this custom has esoteric meaning. Although I have seen nothing of that sort in the books on kabbalah that we possess, I have, on the other hand, found the following text in an old manuscript: "Know that the Torah was given on the day of Shabbat, and it behooves us to devote ourselves to its study, to glorify its precepts when Shabbat comes in and, if possible, to fulfill them all simultaneously. That is why it is fitting to cover oneself with a ṭallit at the time when Shabbat comes in because all the precepts of the law rest on this last act."

. . . The precept contained in the verse "Spread therefore thy skirt over thy handmaid" (Ruth 3:9), that is to say, the flaps of the ṭallit, must also be fulfilled. Whosoever fulfills this precept sees the hostile and unclean forces depart from his soul when it leaves the body; for they recognize him as someone who delighted the bridegroom (*ḥatan*) in his beloved *kallah*. . . .

I learned from Rabbi M. ben H. that the obligation to don the ṭallit on the eve of Shabbat is essentially based on this teaching of our sages: At that time, the Holy One, blessed be He, wraps himself in his ṭallit, like an officiating minister, pronounces the passage from the Scriptures, "On the sixth day, the heavens were completed" (Genesis 1:31 and 2:1). The first letters of this form the Tetragrammaton YHWH, which, as we have shown, has the numerical value of *ṣiṣit* ["fringes" of the ṭallit]. Then he says: "Stretch over us the tabernacle of peace," as we ourselves have stretched out the flaps of our ṭallit. . . .

I will add another explanation according to the Kabbalah of R. Isaac Luria. His disciples have written that the ṭallit is the mystical symbol of the "enveloping light" and of the shadow mentioned in Psalms 39:7, "Surely man walketh as a mere shadow." The "enveloping light," in fact, preserves man from evil, and whosoever wraps his ṭallit around him with *kawwanah* is rescued from exiles and the forces of evil.

We know some families from communities on the Moroccan coast who customarily ate a light meal consisting of fish and brandy on Friday evening before going to synagogue, immediately the Shabbat lights were lit. This meal was given the Hebrew name *bo'i kallah,* which thus entered the Judeo-Arabic colloquial language.

### Baqqashot *Vigils*

In the larger Moroccan communities, associations of a primarily religious nature brought together lovers of Andalusian song and Jewish music for vigils held after midnight on Shabbat and during the six months between Sukkot and Pesaḥ.

These associations were placed under the patronage of King David and claimed kinship with his name or with one of his characteristics, calling themselves Brotherhoods of King David or Brotherhoods of the Singer of the Psalms of Israel. Each association had its own repertoire, generally consisting of twenty-four "series" of melodies (*nawba,* "mode," or *triq,* "way") corresponding to the weekly scriptural lessons from the Pentateuch. Additional series were provided for embolismic years, comprising the four intercalary weeks of the month of Adar II. The *moqaddem,* or principal singer, directed the ceremonial of the vigil and assigned the roles.

The most popular of the repertoires of songs and collections of *piyyuṭim* is an anthology entitled *Shir Yedidut* ("Song of Love and Friendship") compiled by two Mogadoran cantors, David Iflaḥ and David Alqayim, with the help of a fellow citizen, Ḥayyim Afryat. An extract from the preface describes the nature of this anthology and its editors' preoccupations:

> This book is in accordance with the practice of Moroccan communities, where it is the custom to keep vigil from midnight to morning on the night of Shabbat, during the winter season, to glorify and sing the praises of our God by reciting the Psalms of David, the Song of Songs of King Solomon, and then by hymns and songs which authors of old and new generations have composed at various moments in our history. . . . The pieces presented have been collected and classified by professional artists and singers with long experience of the techniques of Arabic music.

The Marrakesh rabbis who wrote the preface add the following information:

> The custom of these Sabbath vigils dates from a remote period; the memory of this tradition goes back to times when people knew how to

sing the holy melodies like angels and in the pure tongue of the seraphim. But because of the burden of the exile and the worries of existence, many things were forgotten, disappearing forever, as knowledge was passed on exclusively orally. . . . That is why the illustrious masters of the town of Essaouira [Mogador], with the chief rabbi's agreement, have undertaken to collect the poetic compositions in this *diwan,* following a sequence in accordance with the weekly scriptural lessons and with regard for the accepted musical traditions.

A second piece of evidence comes from Meknès. It concerns the practice of poetry and song on the day of Shabbat, insofar as that practice remained closely linked to spiritual, even mystical, experience. This evidence is written on the title page and preface of an anthology of poetry collected by the Brotherhood of the Prophet Ezekiel:

"We were accustomed to rise at midnight in order to study the psalms and lauds of King David and say the blessings, read the Song of Songs by Solomon his son, particularly on the night of Shabbat, keeping vigil with song until the light of dawn, thus glorifying the addition to the soul which distinguishes the holiness of the Sabbath King. When Shabbat goes out, when this addition to the soul departs the body and returns to the place whence it came, a remnant of the Sabbath holiness is retained by studying the Mishnah [because the letters of this word also form *neshamah,* "soul"], and by hymns dedicated to the prophet Elijah, the redeeming angel, and to our lord-king-messiah, David. . . . Thus we exult at the arrival of Shabbat and rejoice when it goes out.

## *The Close of Shabbat*

The rite of Habdalah, the "separation" of the sacred from the profane, takes place at nightfall, after evening prayers. It is preceded and followed by a special liturgy accompanied by songs of gladness recalling the redemption. The four actions that comprise the rite are signaled by their basic objectives, namely, in succession: the blessing over wine; the blessing over *besamin* (aromatic species), which in our countries are myrtle branches from the lulab kept after the festival of Sukkot; the prayer over fire, or more exactly, over the light fire gives; and lastly, the eulogy that hallows the separation of the sacred from the profane, the Shabbat from ordinary days.

Developing the theme of this ceremonial in one of his poetic compositions, David Ḥassin, who lived in Meknès at the end of the eighteenth century, used the initials of the Hebrew words that designate the four objects in the Habdalah rite, integrating them in the word *YBNH* (pronounced *yibne*), "He [God] will build," which evokes the theme of the restoration of the Temple in Jerusalem in the messianic era. Worth noting is a practice observed in Mogador (Essaouira) at the end of this ritual. It consists of a sort of *dikr* ("mention") of the name of the prophet Elijah while touching the phalanges in succession as many times as there are phalanges in the fingers of both hands.

Note here that tradition closely associates the prophet Elijah with the close of Shabbat. It makes this biblical character, metamorphosed into an angel before he had even come to the end of his earthly career, into the precursor of the messiah, the herald of redemption—dominant themes, of which he is the archetype, in the liturgy for that evening. He is the mythological figure glorified in the thousand and one popular compositions and songs which poets of every generation have dedicated to him in the diverse Jewish languages. He is the hero whose story is told in a thousand and one legends of folklore and homiletical literature (aggadah and midrash).

The practice of singing Elijah's praises at the end of the Sabbath is specifically based on one of these legends. It tells that at that precise moment, Elijah is seated beneath the Tree of Life, busily noting down the works of pious souls who have scrupulously observed the laws of Shabbat. In addition, it is he who takes the souls of sinners out of gehenna on the eve of Shabbat and returns them on the morrow, when the day of rest has ended. It is he, too, who leads these same souls to their place of eternal bliss when they have expiated their sins.

The prayer over fire is accompanied by an action that tradition explains in numerous ways. While it is recited, the four fingers (not the thumb) of the right hand must be bent and held up to the light of the flame, while the eyes must be fixed for quite a long time on the fingernails. The mystics, and the Zohar in particular (II, 207b and 208b), give this action an esoteric dimension. They consider this the moment of transition from the sacred to the profane, the transmission of power from the holy fire of the divinity to the fire of the angels who govern the ordinary days. At this moment, four chariots and four legions appear down here below in order to receive the light of the blessed fire, and they are what is called "the luminaries of fire." My grandfather thought it enough to tell me: "If you look hard, you will see the image of the prophet Elijah." I looked in vain but the prophet Elijah hid from my gaze.[5]

## THE PILGRIMAGE FESTIVALS

The pilgrimage festivals originated in the biblical period. In those days people traveled to Jerusalem three times a year to visit the Sanctuary, where ritual sacrifices were performed and offerings made, as the scriptural text commands (Exodus 23:14–17).

> Three times thou shalt keep a feast until Me in the year. The feast of unleavened bread shalt thou keep; seven days thou shalt eat unleavened bread, as I commanded thee, at the time appointed in the month Abib—for in it thou camest out of Egypt; and none shall appear before Me empty; and the feast of harvest, the first-fruits of thy labors, which thou sowest in the field; and the feast of ingathering, at the end of the year, when thou gatherest in thy labors out of the field. Three times in the year all thy males shall appear before the Lord God.

The first festival is Pesaḥ (Passover); the second is the festival of Weeks (Shabu'ot, Pentecost), which coincides with the presumed date of the Giving of the Law on Mount Sinai; the third corresponds to the festival of Tabernacles (Sukkot).

The three festivals hallowed three seasons: spring, summer, and autumn, and three essential phases in the agricultural calendar.

In both the Holy Land and the Diaspora, these festivals have taken on a liturgical, even a mystical, significance over the past two millennia, while keeping their character as commemorations of historical events. Superimposed on this is the folkloric dimension wherein local custom, social imagination, and the essence of the place are expressed, and which plays a major part in the manifestations marking these three major festivals.

### *Passover*

In the Moroccan communities the festival of Passover (Pesaḥ) was the occasion for long and detailed preparations. In fact, they began the

5. The belief in the appearance of the image of a spirit of or an angel on a reflective surface is at the basis of various magical practices. In Judeo-Moroccan society, bowls filled with water were employed for this purpose (hydromancy), as were shiny gold and silver lamina (lecanomancy), so-called magic mirrors (catophonancy), or more simply, the oiled and polished surface of the fingernail (onycomancy).

summer before, when the wheat that would be used to make the unleavened bread was harvested under special supervision and carefully preserved from humidity, far from any object capable of making it unsuited for Passover use.

The preparations intensified some thirty days before Passover, and the production of the *maṣot* (unleavened bread), or *arrghayef* as it is familiarly called, was a series of complicated operations. The women (sometimes the children) sieved the wheat through their fingers to eliminate grit, grains of barley, and weevil-eaten grain. Then came the ritual cleansing of mills and ovens, the drawing of water at a propitious time (sunset), to be stored in the prescribed manner (new jars covered with muslin), the strict supervision of the dough, and the immediate baking of the "galettes" before the slightest suspicion of fermentation.

In addition, a considerable number of rules and precepts had to be scrupulously observed and fulfilled according to a ritual fixed by law, custom, and practice, especially those concerning the cleanliness of the house. Walls were washed with lime, woodwork scrubbed, kitchen utensils replaced, held over a flame, or immersed in boiling water, and so on. Everything had thus been through the sieve of the laws of kashrut (*takshir* in Judeo-Arabic) before Passover was welcomed in (in new clothes) at the solemn occasion of the first evening.

### *Seder and Haggadah*

Passover is celebrated from the fourteenth to the twenty-second of Nisan, eight days, the legal duration of the festival in the Diaspora (seven days in the Holy Land). However, it is the first evening, Seder night, which constitutes the essential moment, the privileged liturgical instant, when the Jew is obliged, in accordance with a quite specific ceremonial, to commemorate a vital event in Jewish history, the exodus from Egypt and the liberation of the Hebrew people from Pharaoh's oppression (see Exodus 12), by reciting the Haggadah (history of the exodus from Egypt). The Seder ("order") is a compendium of the fourteen rites of the Passover evening, arranged in *order* according to a ceremonial prescribed by the code. The recital of the Haggadah is the fifth rite, which in fact dominates this ceremonial. The miracle of the exodus from Egypt actually occupies an eminently important place in the Holy Writings, which connect it with the most remarkable events in the history of the Hebrews and make it the fundamental basis of the principal precepts of the law and the foundation of the great moral values of Judaism. The ideas of liberation and redemption, which give this festival its moral and spiritual dimension, are thus added to the historical thread of the biblical story and the legally ordained ritual that surrounds it.

The Passover ritual, in the form of Seder night, has one unusual characteristic. As a general rule, and for the major religious celebrations as a whole, worship, to be valid, takes place in the synagogue amid the holy congregation. The Seder service, on the contrary, and despite its importance, is strictly a family ceremony. The children are the leading actors, and it is held in the intimacy of the home, which becomes a genuine sanctuary for the occasion, with the Seder table as its altar. The head of the family, taking the role of priest and preacher, conducts the service and inculcates the teachings connected with the miracle of the exodus from Egypt into his children.

This family character is probably at the origin of the numerous myths, customs, and practices that surround the Seder ceremony and the rites accompanying it.

To meet the needs of women and children who did not understand Hebrew, the language of the liturgy, the Haggadah was translated into the dialects of every country, in both East and West, where a Jewish community was established. The religious authorities in the Diaspora (and even in Palestine, where Hebrew was no longer a language of communication) first began to recommend this didactic procedure in the early centuries of the present era.

Translations of the Haggadah exist in German, English, Arabic, French, Italian, Spanish, the Slavic languages, and many others.

In Morocco, we know of several oral versions in Arabic and old Castilian (brought by the exiles from Spain in 1492), one in Berber from Tinrhir, and others in Chleuh from Susa. There are very many translations printed in Arabic and Spanish, generally accompanied by the Hebrew text.

In fact, it was customary in every Jewish home on the Passover evening to follow the reading of each paragraph of the Hebrew text by its translation into the local dialect. This was common practice even in certain families where the dialect was no longer in daily use. As happened with the teaching of biblical texts, the need for translation became a sacred rite and then simply a custom as far as the Haggadah was concerned.

The Haggadah is supreme over all other liturgical collections because of its immense popularity and its wide diffusion among the Jewish masses.

### *Some Local Customs*

The text of the Haggadah begins with the words: "In haste did we leave Egypt." It was the custom in Essaouira and elsewhere, while reciting this verse, to thrice turn the Seder plate, on which unleavened bread, bitter herbs, and a lamb's bone (symbolic of the paschal lamb) were arranged in a prescribed order, over the heads of those present. In Tafilalet and the Atlas, a simulation of the hasty exodus from Egypt was performed: The men left their houses carrying bundles knotted to the end of sticks, running, and calling out: "This is how our ancestors left Egypt."

In Morocco, when it came to the fourth rite of the ceremonial, which consisted of breaking one of the three *maṣot* on the Seder plate, it was customary to recite the following passage exclusively in Arabic, simulating the parting of the waters of the Red Sea:

> It was thus that God divided the sea into twelve paths, when our ancestors left Egypt, through the medium of our master and prophet, Moses son of Amram, when he saved and delivered them from servitude to [give them] liberty. So will He save and deliver us from this exile, for [the love] of His great and terrible name.

The master of the house handed half of the *apikomen maṣah* to a member of the family, who hid it in a secret place until the end of the meal, the time prescribed for its consumption (the eleventh rite of the Seder ceremonial).[6]

The hungry and needy were then invited to come and eat the bread of affliction and celebrate Passover. That is why it was the custom to leave the doors open and say, before the meal: "Let all who are hungry enter and eat," the text of this first paragraph ending with a millenarian wish: "Next year in Jerusalem."

"Why is this night different from any other night?" the text continues. This is the first of the Four Questions which the child asks his father in order to learn the significance of the Passover service. They originated in the Bible. To be understood, the first question needs to

6. In some families this rite occasioned a little "hide-and-seek" drama in which the protagonists were the father and one of his male children.

be placed in the period when it was written, the talmudic era, when it was not the custom to eat raw vegetables dipped in salt water or vinegar before the meal. To distinguish this night from other nights "we dip twice": celery in saltwater and bitter herbs in *ḥaroshet* (a special fruit mixture symbolizing clay). The other three questions concern the consumption of unleavened bread and bitter herbs and the position to take during the meal; instead of sitting, the participants must lean to the left on cushions, as free men, and only on this night which commemorates the liberation from slavery.

The following custom was associated with the reading of the ten plagues: As each plague was announced, the head of the household threw a drop of wine, and the mistress of the house a drop of water, into a utensil that was then emptied down the drain or outside the door of the house (a rite to expel the evils which had just been named, or an expression of compassion for the Egyptian victims?).

After an interruption for the meal, the reading of the Haggadah continued with the recitation of Hallel (Psalms 115–118, the psalms of thanksgiving), followed by *Ḥad Gadya,* the parable of the goat, and various songs in Hebrew, Arabic, Berber, and Castilian. When the ritual resumed, the door of the house was left open in order to let the prophet Elijah enter (or to let it be seen that no child's body was hidden—material proof of the ritual murder accusation to which Jews in Christian countries were subject in the Middle Ages).

### *The Mimuna*

Like everything that on other occasions (birth, marriage, or death) touches on the major manifestations of the Judeo-Maghrebian social imagination, here too there is a dual ceremonial, a double polarity, as it were, with an additional complication: the vague origins and the obscure history of the Mimuna. Rabbinic orthodoxy strove to retrieve it in some way by making it a religious ceremony, allotting it a special liturgy and legitimizing it on grounds contained in traditional Jewish literature (biblical texts, talmudic and homiletical legends, etc.). We think that it belongs more to the Maghrebian social-cultural landscape and to the immediate local environment. This is shown by almost all the popular manifestations, rites, practices, and customs which mark its celebration. They seem to derive from ancient autochthonous folklore, that symbiotic area where Jews and Muslims happily meet and where the expression of a common destiny on the land which both have inhabited from time immemorial, and to which they are attached, is confirmed in a certain way and on certain special occasions.

The term Mimuna which designates this ceremonial has given birth to diverse, mostly fantastic, etymologies, most frequently adopted in order to provide a basis for attributing an ideological role to this celebration. One example is the relationship—no more than superficial—between the name Mimuna and the Hebrew *'emunah,* "faith and belief." If Passover commemorates the historical deliverance from the Egyptian yoke, it also celebrates "faith and belief" in future deliverance, in the end of the exile and the messianic return of the Jewish people to its land. This, moreover, is the meaning that rabbinic tradition gives to the ritual of the last two days of Passover, which comprises the reading of the song that Moses sang with the children of Israel after the crossing of the Red Sea (Exodus 15) and the prophetic text of the visions of Isaiah (chaps. 10 and 12).

The reference to Maimonides is also fantastic. Moses Ibn Maymun, or Maimonides, who seems to have lived in Morocco after his flight from Cordova at the time of the Almohade persecutions (mid-twelfth century), left a deep impression on the memory of Maghrebian Jews. This episode gave birth to fabulous stories and legends circulated throughout the Jewish world.

The essentially religious aspect of the Mimuna is seen in the special liturgy for the evening that brings Passover to an end. It incorporates biblical texts (Proverbs), mishnaic texts (Ethics of the Fathers), and didactic poems which anticipate the ritual of Shabu'ot (Azharot). It is also apparent in the ritual following the prayers the next morning, which is called *Birkat ha'-Ilanot,* "the blessing of the trees." People go to one of the gardens situated at the gates of the town and generally carry out the prescribed ritual at the foot of a fig tree whose fruit is still green (in Mogador) or an olive tree (in Marrakesh). The ritual is based on a talmudic tradition (Berakhot 43b) which recommends going to the fields in the month of Nisan to recite prayers and give thanks to God for the gift of the trees and their benefits.

The Judeo-Maghrebian social imagination and the local folkloric dimension of the Mimuna are more extravagantly expressed in the multiplicity and variety of popular manifestations and rites that will only very briefly be mentioned here. But essentially they refer to the return to nature, to re-creation and renewal, to relationships with other ethnic and religious groups, to the interventions of supernatural powers, and so on.

The central theme is connected with the popular meaning given to the term Mimuna, "good fortune." The reference to the patron of that "blessed" night (*mabruka*), called in fact Lalla Mimuna, "Dame Fortune," is expressed in the wishes *tarbhu u-tsa'du,* "May you succeed in what you undertake and rejoice," exchanged whenever one encounters someone during the many visits and social events throughout the evening and the following day.

If Mimun is king of the spirits, the supernatural power who irrevocably determines destiny and whose blessings are beseeched, Lalla Mimuna is the saint who intercedes, even the divinity who distributes fertility, success, happiness, and plenty. Moreover, both are invoked by the two neighboring religious groups. Jews and Muslims.

At this season, happiness and plenty are associated with the re-creation of the world, with renewal. The symbol and the substance of it can be seen in the houses decorated with greenery, in the "prepared table" which the mistress of the house has arranged for this exceptional night: fish, ears of barley and corn, stems of beans, lettuces, fruits and cakes, milk and dairy produce, fresh butter and honey, bowls overflowing with wheat flour and vessels full of pure oil, in which sparkle jewelry and gold and silver coins. Most often this has all been given by Muslim neighbors, as a concession to custom, a token of friendship, and also in exchange for the presents that it was the practice to give one another on numerous occasions.

When the father of the family, or the grandfather if he was still alive, returned from the synagogue after 'Arbit, he performed the first rite, blessing each member of the family. He placed his left hand on each head and with his right gave each a lettuce leaf dipped in honey and a sip of milk. This was followed by a rite of re-creation and renewal which featured the myth of the eternal return and was in some way represented by making a new leavened dough, *la-khmira.* This dough was left to rise for several days and reach the normal level of fermentation without the help of any yeast whatsoever, even if it had to be eaten unleavened or had not risen sufficiently in the interim. The flour and water were mixed in a large earthenware or copper bowl, everybody dipping in their hands and throwing in a jewel or a gold or silver coin. All this took place amidst an immense hubbub created by the men singing canticles in Hebrew, Arabic, Castilian, or Berber and the women ululating (*zgharit*) with ear-splitting cries of joy. The whole mixture was then covered with wool and silken kerchiefs.

*'Ada*, "custom and practice," decreed that the evening meal consist of pancakes (*mufleta*) with butter and honey, and the uninterrupted stream of invited guests and chance visitors were served cakes made of almonds and raisins (*massapans* and *ḥalwa* in Essaouira, *mrozeya* in Meknès, etc.). Indoors, the women wore the married woman's sumptuous traditional costume *al-kaswa la-kbira*, the young girls their most beautiful finery. In fact, the evening of Mimuna, an evening pervaded with a sense of destiny and *mazel-tov*, was the evening chosen for exchanging promises of marriage. Again, it should be noted, custom recommended that milk be spread on the thresholds of rooms and that children be allowed to whip their fathers with branches of greenery or old swords.

Outside, it was all carnival and great parade. Lively groups of young people roamed the streets of the mellah, the girls' multi-colored dresses competing with the men's fancy-dress. Youths and adults alike dressed up as women on this occasion, or even more often donned Muslim costume, cheerfully wearing fez, turban, or red chechia, the colored *djellaba* or unbleached linen *farajiya* with silk buttons, and white or yellow babouches.

This disguise, this effort to look in some way like their bourgeois Muslim neighbor, shows a deep-seated wish for social and political liberation, a wish that in this case coincided with religious and messianic redemption. However, this carnival-type celebration seems to have borne some relationship to the Muslim festival of the Sultan of the Tolbas, which, curiously enough, was celebrated in Fez student circles around the same time. It commemorates the victory of the king who in the seventeenth century founded the Alawite dynasty over Ibn Mesh'al, the leader of the Jewish tribe, who terrorized Muslims in the Taza region.[7]

The festivities continued late into the night. Preparations began very early the next day for visits to gardens, trips to the country, with a ritual halt near a water point (spring, wells, or river), and picnics on the grass. Jews in the coastal towns preferred the sea: toes were dipped in the water and meals eaten on the rocks or the beach. People sang and danced. This too was a way of celebrating renewal. It was an erup-

7. See Pierre de Cenival, "La legende du Juif Ibn Mech'al et la fête du Sultan des Tolba à Fez," *Hespéris* 2 (1925), pp. 137–218.

tion into the open air, into radiant nature, so cruelly absent from the closed field of the mellah, a temporary breaking down of its thick walls, as it were. It was also an affirmation of living, in a certain way, like other people despite the normal conditions of existence, of expressing attachment to the land and to the work of the Creator. It also signified a convergence toward the cultural environment, apparent in similar customs, popular manifestations, of Muslim Arabo-Berber society. The water rites (and at other highpoints in the year, the fire rites) are amazingly similar. As will be seen, Jews repeat these water rites (compulsory bathing and sprinkling) at the festival of Shabu'ot, which coincides with the Muslim festival of 'Anṣra, which calls for both fire and water rites.

The Muslims did not eye this eruption by Jews into their fields with disapproval, nor yet their halt by the water points situated in them. They considered these visits, in the circumstances, as bearing *baraka*, that is, as a guarantee of a rainy year and abundant harvest. Sometimes, these excursions were even arranged in advance, and Jews were invited to the estates of Muslim friends and neighbors to celebrate their country festival, the Mimuna, and to indulge in their revels and libations, as shown by evidence collected at Marrakesh, Quezzane, Sefrou, and Essaouira, in the Tafilalet, and elsewhere. Racy legends and stories tell of occasions when Muslims dug sources of water to be reserved for the Jews' libations at the Mimuna. Let the following chronicle suffice:

> A Muslim potentate by the name of Al-Mjudi had a very beautiful daughter. One evening, seized with passion, he raped his daughter. The next day he realized the extent of his crime and consulted the sages of the tribe and the country as to how he might redeem himself and be pardoned. He received the answer: "It is fitting that with your own hands you hollow out a water channel (*sagya*) four days' march long. On this condition your sin will be expiated." Al-Mjudi began the task of digging the *sagya* and completed it. This water channel and the spring at which it emerges supply the town of Essaouira, which, as is well known, has a sizable Jewish population. It is to this spring that the Jews go for their excursions at the Mimuna if they do not go down to the sea.

One inevitably concludes that the ceremonial at the end of the Jewish Passover is ambivalent, that the celebration called Mimuna had a dual nature. On one hand, it shows the affirmation of the historical, messianic, and redemptive dimension that makes it a Jewish religious festival. On the other, it demonstrates the wish to be identified with the socio-cultural environment, an attachment to the local spirit, the land, the horizons, and the natural landscape familiar to the people of the country.

Muslims very often appeared as partners in the celebration of the rites that characterized this ceremonial. They could make a considerable contribution to the preparations for the festival and its procedures and sometimes stood at the center of a ritual in which they were the protagonist, even the archetype and model.

Like all the folkloric manifestations enacted by Maghrebian Jewry and, moreover, all Jewish popular and dialectal literary work in the Maghreb, the Mimuna is an integrating and socializing factor within the Jewish community and, at the same time, in the wider framework of the population, irrespective of race or religion.

Despite orthodoxy's desire to Judaize the celebration, the Mimuna remains an affirmation of the deep links which attached the Jewish minority to the Muslim majority. It was evidence of the existence of an area of convergence that must be taken into consideration where the two groups found each other and met—both here and in similar festivities marked by similar rites and reciprocal influences. It constituted one of the elements in a remarkable symbiosis and a mainly peaceful co-existence that lasted for nearly two millennia on the hospitable soil of the Maghreb.

Note, finally, that the Mimuna was the only local Jewish celebration that the disrupted Maghrebian community took with it and transplanted when it settled in new places in France, Canada, and the South American continent. The emigrants carried the memory of it with them and celebrate it sumptuously everywhere. In Israel, it has even assumed the nature of a national celebration, and the Ashkenazic establishment has adopted it, not without an ulterior political motive.

### *Shabu'ot*

A distinction must be made between the religious ceremonial of Shabu'ot (Pentecost), with ritual and liturgies that give the festival its Jewish universal nature, and the customs and practices that drew their inspiration from the local spirit and their nourishment from the sources of the social imagination, giving it a local Judeo-Maghrebian character. Clearly, religious ceremonial and folkloric ingredients were closely linked in the celebration of the festival. The major themes and dominant motifs to be considered here are Shabu'ot's character as the festival of the giving of the Torah, with its mystical symbolism and special liturgies, some dietary customs, and the popular water rites and lustrations associated with the reading of the 'Azharot.

*The Giving of the Law*

Themes relating to the giving of the Torah, God's revelation on Mount Sinai, and the great manifestations associated with it will be discussed here, as well as the covenant made between God and His people on "that day of 6 Siwan in the year 2446 of the Creation."[8] Like the major part of postbiblical literature, we will leave aside the seasonal nature of the festival, the place in the agricultural calendar that the Scriptures assign to it, both as the festival of the first fruits and a harvest festival. Moroccan authors themselves (poets, exegetes, and preachers) barely seem to concern themselves with these considerations. They draw their inspiration from postbiblical literature, principally from the Mishnah, and from the symbolism of the Zohar and the Lurianic Kabbalah, in accordance with traditions established since the esoteric knowledge and mystical writings laid hands on the scriptural texts and liturgy on which to stamp their imprint. (Nevertheless, note must be taken of the restoration of biblical traditions and the revival of the agricultural significance given to this festival by the pioneers of the kibbutz since the end of the nineteenth century.)

A Moroccan poet from Meknès named a "series" of pieces he dedicated to Shabu'ot in the second half of the eighteenth century *We-Qol ha-Tor,* a term with multiple echoes. Literally, it means "the voice of the turtle," as in Song of Songs 2:12. But, says the author, it is also the Voice of the Holy Spirit which was heard on Mount Sinai, dictating the Ten Commandments and revealing the Torah, this word containing within itself the *tor* of the title. The halt at the foot of Mount Sinai was also the sign of the mystical union of God and the Community of Israel, and consecrated the faithfulness of their mutual love, which the turtle specifically symbolized.

8. Historians date the scene on Mount Sinai in the thirteenth century B.C.E. The chronological precision, cited here, belongs to legend. It is borrowed from *La Ketubbah de Shabu'ot* ("The Pentecost Marriage Contract"), by Israel Najara, a sixteenth-century Syro-Palestinian poet; see his *Zemirot Yisrael* (Venice, 1599), fol. 114a,

An earlier Moroccan poet from Fez, Jacob Aben Sur, gives the following description of the scene at Mount Sinai:

My Rock appeared resplendent on Sinai when He gave the Law.
His Name blessed, with love, the soul of the survivors of my people.
From the heights of His heavenly abode, He bent the firmaments of his glory,
He rose up, spread clouds over the mountain where He chose to stay.
On stone tablets He fixed a Law of fire for a unique nation.
Come to His gates with grateful songs, my brethren
The race of men who share my faith!

In another piece Jacob Aben Sur takes an idea that is, on the whole, fairly original as compared with other traditions, and develops it with even more simplicity of expression than the legends that inspired it. When the Voice from heaven was heard on Sinai instructing the Israelites to obey the law that would be handed to Moses, they demanded, in no uncertain terms, the presence on the spot of God Himself, rejecting any human intermediary.

We quote below the prelude-injunction from this long verse piece of the *muwashshaḥ* genre, and also the last lines of the following two verses that answer it:

All of you, my brothers, sons of our covenant,
Hear
The Law of our God!

They answered: "From the mouth of a man like us,
We wish to hear nothing, if it be not from the mouth of the Rock of our power."
"It was not this we requested," they repeated;
It is our King we wish to see."

The poet develops the notion of primordial Torah in another canticle intended to be sung when the scrolls of the law are taken out of the holy ark. The Torah is represented as "draped in power and majesty . . . existing before all the works of the Creation, cherished child of the primordial God. . . . Its delicious honeyed words, sweeter than nectar from the flowers, more precious than pearls, exude drops of myrrh."

A verse piece with a chorus, a didactic tone, and an ethical conclusion glorifies the Torah and prescribes its teaching. It was designed to be sung while the scrolls of the law (*sefarim*) were being carried round. It borrows its melodic line from a Spanish song which begins with the following words: *Florida estaba la rosa,* "The rose was in full bloom."

Repeating the themes of the previous poem, a melody in Judeo-Spanish was associated with it and accompanied it in the synagogue rite, in accordance with a long-established tradition in megorashim communities of Castilian origin. We have reproduced the full text of this cantilena, a song comprising a prelude-ritornello and seven quatrains, in our book *Poésie juive en Occident Musulman* (pp. 353–54).

### *Mystical Symbolism*

There are favored moments for carrying out mystical rites. One example is the institution of vigils, night-time sessions devoted to mystical readings: the midnight vigil (*tiqqun ḥasot*) which referred to the exile of the Shekhinah, the vigils on Hosha'anah Rabbah, on the seventh night of Pesaḥ and on the first night of Shabu'ot, which were also marked by a *tiqqun,* a special liturgy, a ceremonial of "repair" or a procedure for the restoration of heavenly harmony. This was one aspect of the influence of the Kabbalah of the school of Isaac Luria and of the spread in the Maghrebian communities of teachings, customs, and practices born in Palestinian circles in Safed. In local jargon it was called the reading night, *lilt al-graya.* Vigil was kept until dawn, in the synagogue or a private house, reciting a selection of extracts from the Bible, the Mishnah, and the Zohar, and also singing songs. This was a very popular rite: even the children were in some way initiated into it by sharing in the small feast which accompanied it, because tea and coffee, dried fruit and sweetmeats were served right through the night.

For kabbalists it was only a short step from the idea of God's covenant with the community of Israel to the idea of union and marriage. The Zohar tells that Rabbi Simon Bar Yoḥay and his companions gave a mystical dimension and an esoteric significance of the greatest importance to the first night of the festival. On that night the bride prepared herself for the marriage, which took place the following day. These are the terms in which the zoharic texts speak of it (Zohar I:8a):

> Rabbi Simon was sitting and studying Torah on that night when the bride was preparing herself to be united with her master. For we have been taught that all the companions of the sons of the bride's palace

must stay close to her throughout the night when she makes ready to join her master under the marriage canopy on the morrow and delight with her in the finery that she is preparing for herself, that is to say, devote themselves to study of Torah, passing from the Pentateuch to the Prophets, from the Prophets to the Hagiographa, expounding the verses and examining more deeply the mysteries of Wisdom. These, in fact, are her preparations, her jewels and her finery. The bride then enters with her followers and stays at their head; she decks herself and rejoices in them all that night; and on the morrow no one enters beneath the marriage canopy except in their company. They it is that are called by the name of "children of the wedding." As soon as the bride enters under the canopy, the Holy One, blessed be He, calls them, blesses them, and adorns them with the bride's crowns. Happy is their lot! Rabbi Simon, and all the companions with him, glorified the Torah with hymns and canticles, each of them giving a new meaning, an unknown dimension, to the words of the law. Rabbi Simon was happy, he and all the other companions.

According to an interpretation of Isaiah 3, the bride's finery is made up of twenty-four objects which, says the Zohar, are none other than the twenty-four books of the Bible. Whosoever devotes that night to reading a selection of texts from the twenty-four holy writings, and to their exegesis as applied to the mystery of the festival of Shabu'ot, shares in dressing the bride and thus proves himself worthy of sharing in her joy.

*The marriage contract.* The conception of the union of God and Israel by marriage found such an echo in the Jewish soul, and especially among the kabbalists, that it was fascinatingly expressed in a concrete way in the ritual of the first day of Shabu'ot, the morning after the night of the *tiqqun*, by the reading of the *ketubbah* (marriage contract) in its right and proper form as prescribed by the rabbinic code.

Mention has already been made of the lyrical and mystical paraphrase of the *ketubbah* that Israel Najara composed for the celebration of the allegorical and symbolic wedding of the *ḥatan* (bridegroom), God, and the "virgin Israel." This piece, still sung in Sephardi synagogues today before the reading of the Ten Commandments, in front of the open ark of the law, is conceived as a formal contract establishing the terms and conditions of that union.

In Moroccan synagogues, this text was not felt to be enough. On the second day of the festival, other, similar *ketubbot* were read, poetic works by local scholars, in particular one composed by Rabbi Raphael M. Elbaz on the model of Israel Najara's.

The reciprocal duties of the couple and the contributions of both partners are meticulously stated, listed, specified, and certified. There are some illuminating discussions of this theme in the Maghrebian homiletical literature.[9] One author says in substance:

> From the moment that He chose the Community of Israel as His bride by entrusting it with the Torah, God fulfilled a husband's obligations to her, in accordance with the prescriptions of the halakhah [rabbinic law.] There are ten in all: to feed her, clothe her, join with her in marital union; the others consist of the duty to care for her when she is ill, to ransom her from her abductors if she is taken prisoner, to bury her when she dies, to provide her with decent accommodation, to assure the subsistence of her and her daughters, if the husband himself dies, to provide a reserve to endow the male children. . . . In fact, Israel is given the name of *kallah* [bride, future wife] ten times in the scriptural texts; six times in the Song of Songs; and four times in the writings of the Prophets.

All this ritual revolves around an event of crucial importance: the revelation of God on Mount Sinai, which, for the kabbalists, means no less than the mystical union of God and Israel.

However, in order to keep alive the nostalgic memory of the ancient Shabu'ot, the ritual has given this festival a rural flavor. The passages read from the scrolls of the Torah concern the offerings of the first fruits. The book of Ruth, which describes the life of the ancient Hebrews at harvest time, is then read aloud. True, the pastoral idyll of Ruth, the Moabite, and Boaz, the Lahmide, is also a hymn to love. True, too, that it gives the genealogy of King David, himself a descendant of the union of Ruth and Boaz, who died on Shabu'ot according to tradition, and will father the king-messiah, author of future redemption. But the presence of greenery in houses and synagogues, the dietary practices, the lustrations and the water rites recall remote history and local myth.

---

9. See especially the book by Azaryah ben Efrayim Pigo, an Italian rabbi of the sixteenth to seventeenth century, *Binah la-'Ittim* ("The Understanding of Liturgical Moments"). It includes a group of homilies dedicated to Shabu'ot bearing the meaningful title *'Et-Dodim* ("The Time of Loves"). Every Maghrebian scholar had this book in his library.

### *Dietary Practices*

It is customary to eat foods that contain a good proportion of milk and honey, symbols of the Torah. A more refined traditional dish (at least that is how I personally remember it) consisted of a special concoction made from vermicelli. A week before Shabu'ot, the dough was spun in the same way as wool, in order to weave a lacework of vermicelli over sieves. This was left to dry in the sun and unraveled on the eve of the festival. The next day, it was cooked in a lamb sauce and served at the midday meal, sprinkled with cinnamon and crowned with a topping of fried onions and raisins.

### *'Azharot and Water Rites*

The 'Azharot (singular, *'azharah,* "warning") belong to the genre of didactic *piyyuṭ,* poetry in the service of the law. They systematically catalogue the 613 precepts of the Torah, divided into orders (positive commandments) and prohibitions (negative commandments). This genre of rhymed series was cultivated in medieval Spain by poets like Solomon Ibn Gabirol, Judah Halevi, and Isaac ben Reuben of Barcelona, and was accepted into the liturgy for the festival of Shabu'ot. Mahgrebian, particularly Moroccan, ritual adopted the 'Azharot of Isaac of Barcelona and incorporated them into the liturgy for Minḥah, the afternoon prayer. Each of the worshipers read one verse, and anyone who made the slightest mistake in his reading was immediately called to order by the whole congregation shouting: "Repeat, repeat, repeat. . . . you don't know anything!" and splashing him with water. Unlucky the man whose fate it was to read the last verse. He was literally soaked. Everyone brought along a jug, even a bucketful; pails and jars stood by, waiting for the prayers to end. The participants in this type of poetic joust had a hard time avoiding the compulsory shower that marked the end of the ritual. The victim was very often chosen in advance. Everyone knew who he was. The accomplices winked at one another, employing calculations and ruses so that he would be given the last verse. All the same, the fun ended in happy hubbub, the scapegoat receiving a cash gift for his pains.

Lustrations were not confined to the synagogue. The popular water rites that marked the Mimuna were repeated at Shabu'ot. In this case, they coincided with the similar rites for the Muslim festival of the summer solstice, 'Ansra, observed at the same time of year, by the splashing of water and the forcing of baths upon reluctant participants. Much could be said about the etymology of the word *'ansra* itself, attributing its derivation, as some philologists suggest, to the Hebrew *'asara/'aseret,* which designates the "convocation," or gathering of the people, for the celebration of a religious ceremony, Shabu'ot, in this case, or the eighth day of Sukkot (Shemini 'Aseret), as is shown by the exegesis of a rabbinical text dating from the talmudic period (fifth century C.E.).

In the streets of the mellah, all the children were armed with simple little squirts, crude white iron syringes (*rashshashat*) mass-produced by craftsmen on the eve of the festival and sold for ten sous. They had water-fights, squirting each other with their *rashshashat,* and went home soaked to the skin. The rite took on another dimension when the brotherhood of "watered waterers" moved into the patios of houses. People rushed to the balustrades of the upper stories. The "brethren" spread water over the ground from hollow bulls' horns. Jugs of water were emptied over them, but they were also thrown a loaf of bread and some coins.

### *Sukkot*

The festival of Sukkot commemorates the Hebrews' sojourn in the desert under the fragile roofs of tabernacles (*sukkot*) after they had left Egypt and until their entry into the Promised Land. At least this is the biblical meaning of the festival. As with all the other festivals, other meanings have been added to its first, "historical" significance, and it has acquired rites, practices, and customs in the course of time that were, necessarily, borrowed from the environment and local mythology.

#### *The* Sukkah *and the* Lulab

As soon as the fast of Kippur is broken, on the evening of that awesome day, the circumference of the *sukkah* is outlined with a knife on the terraces or patios of houses. The next morning at first light, preparations to build it begin. At Essaouira (Mogador), people went to Bab Doukkaia, where merchants selling *qsob* (reeds) and *rtem* (genista) were waiting at the ramparts. The *lulab,* a plaited bunch of the four species, had also to be prepared: a palm branch decorated with multicolored silks, three myrtle branches, and two of willow, and also a clean and unblemished citron.

Detailed descriptions of the "tabernacle" can be found in local rabbinic literature, and even in the poetry of David Ḥassin and Jacob Aben Sur. Its construction has to fulfill certain very precise conditions given down to the last detail in the code. This temporary and fragile dwelling must be "decorated with valuable fabrics and contain a comfortable, rich, and downy bed, so that people can live in it, and eat the fourteen statutory meals there for the seven days that the festival lasts, rest and study there . . . fulfill *miṣwat lulab*, that is to say, shake the ritual bunch of four vegetable species, the flag of victory and symbol of triumph."

The universal dimension of this festival is evoked, on the one hand, by the recall of the ritual of the Temple in Jerusalem, where seventy oxen were offered as sacrifices, this number corresponding to the seventy nations of the world; on the other hand, in the allusions to scriptural texts referring to the priestly vocation of the Jewish people, the sole basis for its selection. Unlike Shabu'ot, the agricultural aspect of this harvest festival has not been ignored. Here, as elsewhere, authors borrowed their literary material from the basic foundations of rabbinic culture, the Talmud, the midrash, and the halakhah.

The mystical symbolism of the festival and its ritual is indicated in a large number of other texts. A poetic work composed by the Meknès poet David Ḥassin and dedicated to this religious ceremonial depicts a remarkable cosmic drama. It features the figures of the Seven Holy Guests, seven biblical heroes transformed, metamorphosed, by the Zohar and kabbalah into mystical archetypes. They take turns in living in the earthly *sukkah* for the seven days of the festival, in which they are the leading actors, or take turns in receiving the heads and dignitaries of the seventy nations in the celestial *sukkah*, in the presence of Rab Hammuna Saba, who controls protocol, and at the side of the Master of the Worlds, whose attributes they bear, incarnated in seven sefirot.[10]

The mystical note appears again, heavily emphasized, in the

10. The seven holy guests are the three patriarch, Abraham, Isaac, and Jacob, plus four other high-ranking biblical figures, in the following order: Moses, Aaron, Joseph, David. As for Rab Hammuna Saba: a mysterious figure from the Zohar, and pseudo-grandmaster of esotericism, he often appears to the companions of R. Simon b. Yoḥay as a simple, common ass-driver. The companions always end up acknowledging the profundity of his knowledge.

description of the *lulab,* the sefirotic symbolism of its components and the esoteric basis of the biblical precept which is the reference for it (Leviticus 23:40).

### *Hosha'anah Rabbah*

The readings of the night of Hosha'anah Rabbah, which continue until the morning of the seventh day, with its *tiqqun* like those of the Shabu'ot and Pesaḥ vigils, was instituted by the kabbalistic school of Safed in the sixteenth century and observed in the Maghreb as elsewhere. The children also participated, keeping vigil like their elders. From time to time, they left the company of the adults to go outside and scan the sky to catch the moment when the sky would open up to receive their wishes. Happy the child who was so lucky!

The next day a special liturgy followed the morning prayers; it was accompanied by beating the ground with the branches of *'araba* (willow).

The women kept vigil at the kitchen stove, preparing a special dish for the day. It varied depending on family customs and practices: couscous for some, that traditional food already served to inaugurate the *sukkah* on the first night of the festival; others had a more original dish, less widespread among residents of the large towns, but well known in the Berber environment, *talekhsha,* a thick paste of beans moistened with *argan-or* olive oil and accompanied by hot, succulent wheat galettes.

### *Simḥat Torah*

The "Festival of the Law" constitutes the real ending of Sukkot (the ninth day in the Diaspora, the eighth in the Holy Land). It is in some ways a repetition of the festival of Shabu'ot, with less serious ceremonial and more demonstrations of joy and exaltation: places of prayer decorated with fairy lights; *haqqafot* (processions) around the synagogue dais (*tebah*); dancing with the *sefarim.* (Torah scrolls) and children raised in the air; the accompaniment of a special liturgy and various songs in Hebrew, Judeo-Arabic, Berber, or Castilian; the distribution and throwing of sweetmeats and dried fruit. It is also the day of the *ḥatanim,* the "newlyweds" of the year and the two privileged readers of the Torah, the man who reads the last *perashah,* the closing pericope of the Pentateuch, and the man who inaugurates the annual cycle of weekly lessons.

The law is magnified and tribute paid to the mass of worshipers at the synagogue, adults and children, who are all called up to the Torah on this day and read a section of the Scriptures.

The ritual observed on this day, as on many similar occasions when the law was honored, was in many respects reminiscent of a marriage ceremony. The ceremony that accompanied the dedication of a scroll of the Torah (*ḥinnukh sefer torah*) is an example of this. After the dedication meal, the *sefer* was borne like a bride from the house of the donor to the synagogue for which it was destined. The procession, led by the rabbis and dignitaries of the community, moved through the Jewish quarter, chanting hymns in Hebrew and songs in the local dialect.

### Taberyanut

*Taberyanut* ("bonfires") is the Berber-sounding term which in Essaouira designated a fire rite practiced on the last evening of the festival of Sukkot. (In Marrakesh, the word used was *Tamezzergut.*) The *sukkah* was dismantled, and its roof of palm or genista branches provided the raw material for a bonfire which the father made his children leap over, to the accompaniment of many a prayer and incantation.

The Berbers of the Upper and Anti-Atlas, like other autochthonous Maghrebian societies, also have a bonfire ritual and observe it at the solstice. Fires made of aromatic plants that give off considerable fumes (thyme, thuya, etc.) were lit in courtyards, at crossroads, in the fields. People, children in particular, exposed themselves to the fumes. They leaped over the fire seven times and walked around it, thus also fulfilling a type of rotatory rite, comparable to the religious circuits of orthodox Muslim pilgrimage (the *ṭawaf* around the *Ka'aba*).

The rite is also similar to the Jewish *haqqafot,* the circular processions (circumambulatory rite) mentioned above and in connection with the ceremonial accompanying the burial of pious men. An eleventh-century Jewish author mentions a custom marking the spring equinox, consisting of an entertainment called in Aramaic (the language of the Talmud) *meshawarta de Pura,* "the leap on to the Purim" stirrup. At Kairouan, he says, large fires were lit on the eve of Purim, as was done in Babylonia and Persia, and people leaped over the flames. In the Second Temple period until the beginning of the common era, a water rite known as *simḥat bet ha-sho'ebah,* "the rejoicing of drawing and splashing," was observed on the last days of Sukkot. Nowadays, these days are marked by another ritual, the rogations for rain.

### *Rogations for Rain*

The special liturgy for the last day of Sukkot is called *tiqqun hageshem,* "prayers for rain." As the winter season is commencing, a special request is made to the "living God to open the treasury of the heavens to fertilize the land."

Prayers for rain are also said during the winter and in the spring in case of drought. They take place at the same time as the *salat al-istisqa'* observed by Islam, in the same circumstances, and are accompanied by a ritual fixed by orthodoxy, and also by a popular local pantomime, a dramatic ceremonial whose details vary in the different regions that form the Maghrebian complex and the populations that inhabit them. One of the central ideas of the ceremonial is that the earth receives rain thanks to the virtues of righteous men, an idea also found in ancient and modern rabbinical documents as well as in Muslim homiletical literature. The great intercessor saints and the cohorts of local santons (Jewish and Muslim) have therefore to be approached from the very start to make rain fall.[11]

## TWO COMMEMORATIVE FESTIVALS

### *ḤANUKKAH*

The name Ḥanukkah, which designates the festival, literally means "dedication." This historical and religious ceremonial commemorates the victory of the Maccabees over the Greeks, and the dedication of the Temple of Jerusalem, restored to the worship of the God of Israel after having been sullied by idols and pagan rites. It is also the "festival of lights," because of the occurrence of another miracle: A tiny vial contained sufficient pure oil to light the holy candelabrum for the

---

11. In the discussion of circumcision (above, Chapter 2), see the invocation of the holy Jew of Sefrou in periods of drought, and the blood rite accompanying the prayer addressed to him.

eight days of the festival—a sort of multiplication of oils; such, at least, is what the texts passed down by tradition tell and what Jewish memory has retained for two thousand years.

The festival of Ḥanukkah is celebrated with special dietary rites, rejoicing, and entertainments that take their substance from the sources of the imagination, custom, and practice observed in the Diaspora. Maghrebian Jewry has its own.

### *A Historical and Religious Festival*

The historical and religious dimension of Ḥanukkah can be seen in the poetic works of a great seventeenth- to eighteenth-century Jewish scholar from Fez who has been frequently referred to in this book. Jacob Aben Sur composed seven poems to commemorate this historical and religious festival. Whatever its dimension, each of them is invariably constructed on the same scheme. Within the framework of a prologue and a peroration, containing the familiar subject matter of these two elements of the text, the main body of each piece, the *narratio,* successively develops two essential themes, with predominance passing from one to the other for no apparent reason. On one hand, the poem gives a brief account of the Hasmonean period; on the other, it describes the commemoration of the festival by means of actions perpetuating its memory: the eight-fold rite of the lights that the law prescribes, the special liturgy for great religious ceremonies, lastly the folkloric manifestations and rejoicings that accompanied the festivities.

The following is a piece with a chorus. It borrows the verse structure of the Arabic poetic genre known as the *muwashshaḥ.*

*Prelude*
I will sing beautiful songs
to Him who dwells in the heavens.
He has brought victory to the priestly dynasty, the Hasmoneans.

*1st verse*
The mighty ones attacked me,
all the armies of Antiochus.
They sought to annihilate me,
the lords and princes.
But the Rock, my shield and my protector,
made them drink the poisoned cup.

They wandered blindly as wild beasts
floundering in darkness.

*Chorus*
He has brought victory to the priestly dynasty, the Hasmoneans.

*2nd verse*
So it is that the masters have commanded that the lamps be lit.
But we must not make use of them, these are lights to be looked at only.[12]
At the entrances [to the houses] and at the gates [of the town]
they will form lines,
To bear witness to the miracle and the marvels,
for the eyes of the crowd [and the people].

A slightly longer piece gives a more detailed account of events. It refers to the decrees of Antiochus, the death of Nicanor, the defeat of the Syrian army, the victory of the Hasmoneans, the purification of the Temple, and the festival of dedication. This is the first verse:

Your lovers, God, are the sons of a simple man.[13]
When the merciless tyranny of the Greeks beat down on them,
You stood by their side at the time of their distress,
You led their battles and fought their cause.

### *Fritters with Honey, Games, and Entertainments*

At least once during the eight days of Ḥanukkah, it was the custom to eat fritters with honey in every Jewish home in Essaouira (Mogador) and other agglomerations on the Moroccan coast. The major activity was, therefore, the preparation of this delicious food in sufficient quantities for the consumption of the family, for distributing to relatives and friends, and also for giving to the poor and to the schoolchildren by way of *ma'ruf* (religious gift).

A sack of pure white wheaten flour (*al-khalṣ*) and a large drum of oil had been waiting in the kitchen for several days. The batter was very carefully prepared in large earthenware or copper bowls (*qaṣriyya/qṣari*) and left to rise for a long time covered with a muslin cloth. Watch was kept over it for one night and frying began at dawn in large

12. The law prohibits the use of these lights, especially for illumination.
13. This epithet is applied to the patriarch Jacob in Genesis 25:27.

pans over great charcoal stoves (*mjamer*). The rounds of batter sizzled, swelled, and turned golden in the boiling oil. To ensure the success of this delicate culinary operation, a professional, a *seffaj,* of high repute, was sometimes engaged. Once the platters of fritters were ready with pots of honey by their side, they were taken round from house to house by the eldest of the children, and male and female servants.

Ḥanukkah was also the occasion for games and entertainments for the children. Master coppersmiths manufactured the statutory *ḥanukkiyot,* special lamps with nine cups to hold the oil and the wool or cotton wicks, but they also made smaller or simpler ones for the children, who were often quite happy to model them out of clay or *zegmuna.* This paste is well known to everyone in the Moroccan south. It is the residue which sticks to the millstones after the golden, sweet-smelling oil from the crushed fruit of the argan tree has been collected. Games were also played with tops and with batteries of characters and strange objects made out of white metal or colored green or red, bought for a few sous from the local tinsmith.

### *Purim*

Purim, or the Festival of Lots, on the fourteenth of the month of Adar, commemorates the episode recounted in the biblical book of Esther. Queen Esther, the wife of Ahasuerus, and her relative Mordechai saved the Jews from a plot woven by Haman in Persia twenty-five centuries ago.

A special liturgy is recited on the Saturday before the actual day of Purim, known as Shabbat Zakhor, "The Sabbath of Remembrance." It includes the *Mi-Kamokha* by the medieval Spanish poet, an epic composition which the Moroccan communities habitually recited during the morning service in its original Hebrew text and also its Arabic version.[14]

The ritual reading of the biblical book of Esther (*qeri'at megillah*) was included in the liturgy for 14 Adar and also in the vigil in the evening. The historical event was also remembered in the grace after meals (*birkat ha-mazon,* "blessing over food") and especially after the great traditional jollification which had to take place before sunset.

14. For the literature on this preliminary ceremonial and also on the preliminary ceremonial for Purim, see Haim Zafrani, *Pédagogie juive en Terre d'Islam*, p. 121; *Poésie juive en Occident Musulman*, pp. 343–46; and *Littératures dialectales et populaires juives en Occident Musulman*, pp. 195–206 and 405.

Note the centuries-old institution of the Purim cup (*tasa de Purim*), still in force a few years ago. This bowl was passed round the congregation during the morning service, everyone dropping in a coin: coins dedicated to the *nistarim*, the anonymous poor whose identity was not revealed; coins designed in olden times for ransoming prisoners, not to mention the demi-réal, the equivalent of the half-shekel prescribed by the Bible, that was collected for the benefit of the Maghrebian communities in Palestine who regularly sent itinerant rabbis to receive the proceeds of this special collection. Professional beggars also took up their stance at the doors of the synagogue to receive their due share of charity.

The streets of the mellah were very lively on Purim. The craftsmen were out in force, hawking their stocks of crudely made, noisy toys at the tops of their voices. People crowded round the multicolored displays of cake-sellers and the tables of card and dice players. On Purim, the Festival of Lots, games of chance are especially encouraged. Meanwhile, inside the houses the great feast was being prepared.

Over the years, the festival of Purim was the occasion for a fertile outpouring of literature. This took place on two levels. Corresponding to scriptural knowledge and rabbinical learning, there were poetic works in Hebrew and Aramaic, while in the areas of oral and popular knowledge in dialect, there were burlesques, satires, and parodic pieces in Arabic, Berber, and Castilian. This literature shows the religious, even mystical, dimensions of the festival and a ritual which derives form local practice, custom, and folklore.

*Mystico-Religious Dimensions*

For the first of these aspects we will refer to a poem by Jacob Aben Sur which gaily associates the sumptuousness of the feast that marks the ending of Purim with religious and mystical preoccupations. The author himself specifies its aims and meaning in a brief preamble: "I composed it," he writes, "in the language of the Targum [Aramaic], in accordance with a popular dictum whereby 'the drunkard only expresses himself in the language of the Targum.'" Purim is especially the time of the Minḥah *se'udah*, the meal that ends the festival. It is the time par excellence of drunkenness and inebriation. Apart from the prelude, which serves as chorus and ritornello, the poem consists of fifteen verses, a number corresponding to the numerical value of the divine name YH (*yah*), represented, according to the Kabbalah of

Isaac Luria on the mystery of the festival of Purim, in the words *'akylh styh* (*'akhilah shtiyah,* "eating and drinking"), which, if the letters *y* and *l* in *'aklyh* are transposed, is metamorphosed into *'akl yah* (*'akhal yah,* "God has eaten") and *sht yah* (*shat yah,* "God has drunk"), processes which symbolize the outpouring of the forces emanating from the brain.

Jacob Aben Sur is here referring to the Lurianic doctrine of the *tiqqun,* as expounded in *Sha'ar ha-kawwanot,* in the chapter *Derushe ha-Purim,* article *Miṣwat Se'udat Purim* (Salonika edition, 1852, fol. 158d). In the *tiqqun* procedure and its symbolism, the mystical meal helps to ensure the outpouring of the three forces of the brain hidden in the *ze'ir 'anpin* ("small face"). The three potentialities represented by Ḥokhmah (Wisdom), Binah (Intelligence), and Da'at (Knowledge) are thus joined in perfect union with the rest of the sefirotic universe. Mystical preoccupations and theosophical speculations are no strangers to the festivities of Purim. We must not lose sight of the doctrines deriving both from halakhah and kabbalah that attribute religious significance and a spiritual dimension to the most commonplace act. It is accomplished "in honor of the union of the Holy One, blessed be He, and his Shekhinah, in awe and love, in order to unite *YH* and *WH* in a perfect union."

The obligation to rejoice, eat plentifully, and drink to the point of drunkenness is one of the features of this festival. And people scarcely stinted themselves in the Moroccan communities, where, on this occasion as on so many others, excessive use was made of alcoholic beverages, particularly the local brandy (*maḥya*). By so doing, they were conforming, excessively, to a rabbinic prescription on a talmudic sentence (Megillah 7b): "Each man has a duty to get so drunk at Purim that he cannot tell the difference between 'cursed be Haman' and 'blessed be Mordechai'."

Wine, says Joseph Qaro, author of the rabbinic code (*Shulḥan 'Aruk*), was the instrument through which the whole miracle of Purim was brought about. Vashti was dismissed at a feast where wine was served (Esther 1:10) and Esther took her place. The fall of Haman was likewise decided at a feast where wine was served (ibid. 7:2, 7–8). That is why the sages prescribed drinking to the point of drunkenness.

The prelude to the piece by Jacob Aben Sur makes reference to another melodic composition, with themes describing music and song, love and wine. It is actually written in Aramaic and begins with this significant formula: "We are forbidden to drink water during the festival of Purim."

The historical account is told in four verses, the rest being devoted to a detailed description of the banquet, the foods and the wines. The bitterness of the exile is remembered even at the height of inebriety, and a vow made that it will end with "the ascent to the land of holiness and love."

The days of Purim are the days
when it is man's duty to get drunk.
These days are the days of Purim.
They recall the time when the living God
caused miracles and wonders,
and the signs which He called on us to witness.
He had pity on us and delivered us
from our slanderers and our detractors.
He challenged our enemies
and cut them to pieces.
Before Haman could vent on us
the fury of his oppression,
our eyes saw in him our revenge.
He was hung from the gallows that he
built, from a beam, straight and sturdy.

And against each of his ten sons,
God burst out in fury;
on them were the curses fulfilled,
the excommunication and the anathema.
For love and favor,
we have been permitted to indulge in rejoicings,
to prolong the meal by a plenitude of food,
and by the pleasures of drunkenness too.

Fat braised meat,
stuffed pigeons,
turtle doves and other poultry,
bone-marrow and brains.
Wines and spices in profusion,
quail, partridges, and pheasants
stewed with cereals,
seasoned with peppers and aromatics.
[Meat] roasted without water,
accompanied by delectable wines and sparkling liqueurs.

Grace after meals to the glory
of the Lord who, in His bounty, showers down His blessings.
You will break and crumble a piece of your bread,
mix it with wine, and, the height of your drunkenness reached,
when you cannot distinguish between "curse" and "bless,"
as the sages prescribe.

### *Parody and Folklore*

The oral, popular, and dialectal literary work produced in Morocco, and throughout the Maghreb, included a large number of parodic and satirical compositions belonging to the folklore of Purim and centered on the characters of Haman and Zeresh. A parody of their marriage took the form of a satirical *ketubbah,* and their deaths were mourned in a burlesque requiem.

This literary component of Purim folklore belongs to an old tradition which seems to go very far back in Jewish history. It is one of the favorite themes of Jewish parodic literature.

Three parodies written at the beginning of the fourteenth century, between 1319 and 1332, made this form of expression into a genuine literary genre: *Massekhet Purim* by Kalonymos ben Kalonymos, and *Megillat Selârîm* and *Sêfer ha-Baqbûq ha-Nâbî,* attributed to Levi ben Gerson. These poems represent the first time that scholars of great repute ventured to use talmudic literature for jesting and entertainment. The multiple anecdotes and diverse customs attached to the festival of Purim were translated and interpreted in the serious, solemn language of the Talmud.

Thirty-two parodies from Provence appeared in the first half of the fifteenth century, consisting of ordinances and decisions decreed by King Purim, supreme master of the "Community of the Vine." This ephemeral monarch was also a member of the cast of an anonymous *Massekhet Purim,* probably written in Provence in the fifteenth century. According to this talmudic parody, every Jewish city elected a King Purim a month before the festival, investing him with absolute power over his subjects' lives and property. The appearance of this character in Jewish parodic literature and the manifestations that accompanied it are perhaps comparable to the more recent festival of the Sultan of the Tolba, which took place in Fez in spring, and where the Jews' participation by way of a burlesque *hadiya* ("present, offering") must be noted.[14]

---

15. The festival was instituted after an incident at the beginning of the reign of Moulay Rashid, the first Alouite sultan (1660–72), studied by P. de Cenival (see n. 7 above).

Burlesque wills and requiems multiplied in the seventeenth and eighteenth centuries, including a collection of parodies composed by David Raphael Polido, published in Leghorn in 1703, and a *Mémorial de Purim* by Malachi Colorni of Modena in about 1781.

There were also some in Judeo-Spanish. These are the pieces which the memory of Maghrebian Jewry has preserved and which very recent generations were still performing. They deal with a burlesque subject and meet a need alien to the holy domain of religion or hagiolatry. Their construction is unpolished, and they are written in language more related to living local speech, the everyday and heterogeneous language of the masses in the mellah. The authors of these pieces may have wished to instruct the masses to some extent, but their primary purpose is to entertain them and make them laugh. The frequently coarse and violent content of their works were often condemned by the rabbinical establishment on ethical grounds or simply out of concern for prudence and discretion.

Moreover, none of these pieces has any intellectual pretensions, and they barely deserve to be described as literary creations.

Essentially they consist of a flood of anathemas and curses, insults and gibes, hurled at the head of Haman, symbol of oppression and hatred, who is overwhelmed with scorn and opprobrium. As the Arabic vocabulary of the authors is not very rich in sufficiently violent and forceful epithets, they borrow them mainly from Hebrew. A predilection for assonance and a marked preference for paronomasia free the authors from any exercise in reflection, original thought, intelligent imitation, or healthy humor.

But although all these compositions are defective from a literary point of view and represent the laborious efforts of mediocre minds, they nevertheless demonstrate a not inconsiderable knowledge of rabbinic teaching and of the most ancient Jewish legends relating to Purim. Its biblical, talmudic, and midrashic sources are paraphrased here, amplified, sometimes travestied to adapt them to circumstances and ecological conditions. In addition, these pieces provide information on certain customs and practices in Morocco that once commemorated this crucial episode in Jewish history.

It is obviously the latter aspect, copiously described in this literary genre, the popular celebration of the festival, that we have taken special note of here.

In the Jewish communities of Morocco, as indeed everywhere else, Purim festivities were marked by over-indulgence in the pleasures of the table. Pastry cooks and housewives vied in ingenuity and imagination to create recipes for the preparation of delicacies, particularly cakes with honey (*maqrud, shabbakiyya, ḥalwa*), numerous varieties of brightly colored nougats and caramels, cooked dishes (chicken and lamb with truffles), everything abundantly laced with brandy and wine.

The favorite diversions were games with dice and cards for the adults. A few coins, the *grâda,* were distributed among the children, who bought themselves rowdy toys (crude flutes, *zuwwayat,* deafening rattles) from the Jewish tinsmith in the mellah, and everyone took pleasure in stamping their feet or banging the wooden handle of the *megillah* every time Haman's name occurred when the book of Esther was read.

In the Moroccan countryside, notably in the Sous, in the region of Imintanout from where we received first-hand information, a sort of fantasia was performed.[16] The long Moroccan musket, the *mkoḥla,* was rarely the weapon used; more often, it was a wide-barreled blunderbuss. These displays took place after the evening meal eaten before sunset, when a quantity of brandy had been consumed. They sometimes ended tragically. They ceased shortly after the Protectorate was established, bringing peace to these southern zones through the prohibition or control of the carrying of firearms.

## *Special Purims*

As Purim became, in time, a symbol of salvation, the Moroccan communities, like those in other countries, had "special" local Purims with names of their own, in addition to the festival celebrated every 14 Adar to commemorate the events described in the biblical book of Esther. Purim Sebastiano, also called Purim d-en-Nṣara or Purim de los Christianos, was instituted after the battle of the Three Kings and the victory of Sultan Moulay Abd-al-Malik over Don Sebastian, the king of Portugal, on 4 August 1578 at Al-Ksar Kebir (Alcazarquivir), on the Qued Al-Makhazin. The event is celebrated every year, particularly in Tangiers, Tetuán, and Fez, by giving charity and by a special ritual that incorporated some very significant poetic works and a *megillah* telling of the event.

---

16. An equestrian entertainment staged by horsemen who carry out various maneuvers at the gallop, shooting into the air and shouting.

There were also Purims in Tangier, including the memorable Purim de las Bombas observed on 21 Ab every year as a reminder that on that day in 1844, the Jewish population was spared when the French fleet bombarded the town. Meknès also had its local Purim, Purim d'Al-Ma'gaz, which commemorated the defeat in 1862 of the rebel Al-Jilali al-Mu'jaz, common enemy of the Jews and the Alaouite sherifs. Beginning in 1943 the Jews of Casablanca also celebrated a Purim Hitler on 2 Kislew to celebrate the American landing in North Africa. Lastly, remember the Algiers Purim, or Purim-Edom, fixed on 4 Ḥeswan, which commemorated an episode in the Spanish-Algerian war at the beginning of the sixteenth century, the defeat of Charles V and the sinking of his fleet off the city. It is said that if he had triumphed, Charles V intended to have the Jews baptized.

Judeo-Muslim cultural interrelations clearly emerge in the epilogue of one of the parodic pieces in Judeo-Arabic, the *Ketubbah de Haman,* which associates other "utterly godless men" in the Bible—Pharaoh, Balaam, and Balak—with Haman's ill-omened plan. Legends on this subject abound in Arabic and Hebrew literature, which influenced each other here. According to the Islamic sources, Haman was a member of Pharaoh's court, where he was involved in various episodes in the history of the Hebrews, particularly those that preceded the exodus from Egypt and are described in the first pericopes of the book of Exodus. For example, in the Koran (40:24–25), Haman is found in the company of Pharaoh and Koraḥ (Qoraḥ); Haman and Koraḥ slander Moses and try to destroy him, together with his flock, the children of Israel. Note here that the biblical episode of the Korahite revolt against Moses is told in chapter 16 of the book of Numbers. Sura 29:38 of the Koran states: "We have annihilated Koraḥ, Pharaoh, and Haman." The association of Koraḥ and Haman is also mentioned in Jewish homiletical literature (Genesis Rabbah 31:2, 33:5; Numbers Rabbah 10:7, and particularly 22:6), where the two colleagues, seen as very wealthy and very arrogant, end up destroyed by their pride and wealth. According to a Muslim tradition, reported by the historian-exegetist Al-Tabari (839–923) in his *Jami' al-bayan fi tafsir al-Qur'an,* Haman was Pharaoh's grand vizier. Pharaoh instructed him to build an immense tower to be used to mount an assault from the sky in order to reach and kill the God of Moses.

The last verse of this *ketubbah* gives some indication of the aim of this satiric composition, principally intended to entertain rather than instruct. Its author also solicits his audience, making a discreet appeal to their generosity and inviting them to obtain the text of his *qasida* (so that he too can suitably celebrate the miracle of Purim):

> Hear my *qasida,* my brethren, laugh and enjoy yourselves! May each one of you hold it in your hands while you rejoice. Give praise and love to Mordechai and Esther, who have saved us.

### *Days of Ill-Omen*

Side by side with days celebrating happy events, there are days of ill-omen, joyless days or, as a Moroccan poet from Fez called them, "undesirable days," in contrast to the "desirable days and festivals."

The undesirable days mainly relate to the major events that determined the fate of the Jews two and a half millennia ago, leaving a mark on their existence ever since: the destruction of the first and second Temples in Jerusalem, by the Babylonians and Romans respectively, the disappearance of the Jewish state, and the resulting exile and dispersion, especially following the Judeo-Roman war at the beginning of the common era. Despite the passage of time, the memory of these national catastrophes stubbornly lives on in the heart and memory of the Jews. This is particularly the case in Orthodox and traditionalist communities, which commemorate these tragic episodes in the history of Judaism on the Ninth of Ab by mourning, fasting, and a special liturgy, dominated by the *kinah,* since its lamentations and plaints express the depth of grief and affliction.

#### *The Three Weeks of Grief*

The ninth of Ab is the culmination, the end of a three-week period of ill-omen which begins on the seventeenth of Tammuz (*tes'a sghira*). It is known as a period of grief, which the Hebrew term *ben ha-mesarim* actually defines, and which the Judeo-Arabic dialect designates by its two extremes, *tsa'i,* the two days of fasting, mourning, and lament: *tes'a la-kbira* and *tes'a sghira.* During this eminently somber time, hostile, natural, and supernatural powers are unleashed. The burning dog-days of summer and the ill winds of winter are supplemented by the redoubled activities of demons (*jenoun*), carriers and perpetrators of evil. The belief is that they operate in complete freedom at this time of mourning when mankind—more especially its children—is highly vulnerable. Moreover, it is forbidden to inflict corporal punishment on children in this period. During these three weeks, adults are also threatened by all sorts of dangers to their health and their businesses. That is why people are vigilant and suspicious.

The slaughter of animals for consumption ceased during the first nine days of Ab. The ritual slaughterers "put up" their large knives and laid them on the shelf. This practice was called *rfud as-sakkin.* The housewife kept her knives out of the children's reach. No meat was eaten during this long week, except on Shabbat. During this period the population of the mellah fell into three groups depending on their dietary rites and practices. "Fresh" meat was permissible for families called *ṭriyyin* ("clean" people); the *khanzin* ("dirty" people) ate only canned meat, acceptably high or preserved in fat (*khli'*); the *mzeyytin* did not accept either type of meat and cooked exclusively in oil (*zit*). The origin and significance of these rites gave rise to various legends relating to the destruction of the Temple in Jerusalem and the exodus from Egypt. As will be seen, these two major events in Jewish destiny were joined together in laments that developed the themes and reasons distinguishing the joyful nights of Passover from the ill-omened evening of the Ninth of Ab.

The meal that sealed the fast was a sort of funeral meal, consisting of lentil soup and hard-boiled eggs. Some people dipped the eggs in ashes instead of salt. At the evening service in the synagogue, the lights were put out and the benches were turned over. People prayed by light from night-lights, sitting on the bare floor or on mats. The biblical scroll of Lamentations was read, and sad songs and laments were sung. The next day, neither tefillin nor ṭallit were worn at the morning service; the adornments of the *sefer torah* were turned round and the *yad,* the silver "hand," was not used to follow the reading of the scriptural text on the scroll. The beadle threw a few ashes over the scroll, and the congregation also put ashes on their heads.

The women whitewashed the graves of their close relatives and of saints and santons at the cemetery, while professional mourners wailed and lamented. The men of the holy brotherhood, the *ḥebra qaddisha,* were there at dawn to carry out the burial of the synagogal archives in the genizah. They had spent the evening in every place of prayer and study, gathering up all the old Bibles, any books of ritual in very poor condition, every printed or manuscript page in the Hebrew language, any writing whatsoever, whether amulet, personal or business letter, and so on, that contained even one letter of the holy alphabet. All these papers, stored away in boxes or wall cupboards over the year, were assembled on the Ninth of Ab to be rightly and properly buried in the town cemetery, in the same way as a *ṣaddiq* and a saint were buried, with a special liturgy and the honors due to the Holy Writing.[17]

In the streets of the mellah it was the custom to fight by throwing handfuls of green jujubes, the fruit in season, at one another. (In Ashkenazi countries, people whipped themselves with branches of nettles or brambles.) As on Purim, charity was given to the poor, *grada* (silver coins) and toys to the children, and people played cards.

The fast was broken, or rather *hell as-syam* ("opened"), as the local dialect put it, at nightfall, beginning with soup made of ground corn (*hrisa* or *hshuwa d-al-qamh*), then, mint tea, accompanied by a special nougat made from sesame seeds or cubes of pastry with syrup (*ḥalwa d-al-'jin*), followed by a late dinner of pumpkin and onions cooked with the remainder of the high or preserved meat.

## *Liturgy for the Ninth of Ab*

In addition to the ordinary weekday ritual, with emphasis on the supplicative and penitential texts for the day, the liturgy for the Ninth of Ab comprised the reading of the book of Job and the prophetic texts (*hafṭarot*) for the occasion, which were translated into Aramaic and the local dialect (Arabic, Castilian, or Berber). The liturgy was dominated by the genre of poetry called *kinah* ("lament," "threnody," "elegy"), which referred, in essence, to the sorrowful events in Jewish history mentioned above (the destruction of the Temple in Jerusalem) and also to the tragedy for the Sephardic Jews of the expulsion from the Iberian peninsula in 1492/98. This was regarded as the third *ḥorban,* the conquests by Nebuchadnezzar and Titus.

The most famous *kinot* are the so-called Sionides by Judah Halevi, which Sephardi and oriental synagogues have incorporated into their

---

17. This is a hidden treasure, inexhaustible and still little exploited by researchers in Jewish archives. The genizah in Old Cairo is one of the most famous examples. A repository of documents was discovered there around the end of the nineteenth century, consisting of hundreds of thousands of pages of manuscript in Hebrew and in Arabic written in Hebrew characters, preserved over the centuries. It was an extraordinarily important discovery, probably comparable in its impact on Jewish studies to the stimulus given to biblical and postbiblical knowledge by the later discovery of the Dead Sea Scrolls. In fact, this documentation is related to the history and medieval civilization of the entire Mediterranean world, as shown in the monumental work by S. D. Goitein, *A Mediterranean Society*, 3 vols. (University of California Press, 1967, 1971, 1978).

ritual, and the elegies by Eleazar Kalir, which have entered the Ashkenazi liturgy. Jewish authors in Morocco enriched this branch of poetry with a large number of compositions. Each community, and sometimes every synagogue, had a collection, formed of works by local poets, that custom and tradition had turned into an additional liturgy for the ill-omened period between the seventeenth of Tammuz and the Ninth of Ab. Jacob Aben Sur contributed a series of 125 pieces to this elegiac production. They are collected in his *diwan* under the heading "For the joyless days."

Very often, of course, these compositions are slavish imitations of models and paradigms hallowed by tradition, borrowing their literary substance from the reservoir of thoughts and formulas built up from similar works in the recent or ancient past. Nevertheless, they remain the sole mode of expression of a semi-morbid awareness of the individual and collective wrongs and sufferings inflicted on the community of Israel, of past misfortunes and present calamities. The current situation very often had the bitter taste of the lamentations of Jeremiah and of Psalm 137. Past and present blend in elegiac poetry; the *kinah* is the genre that best expresses the grief felt by Jewish hearts, torn by historic tragedies that are still mourned and by the grief of everyday living. Strains of deep and intense emotion run through its mournful songs; some are movingly sad, sometimes calm and serene, sometimes resounding with violent cries of grief, anger, and hatred; they all invariably end on a note of hope expressed in the reiterated themes of the usual perorations of Jewish poetry: redemption, the reconstruction of the sanctuary in Jerusalem, the restoration of the ancient city of Ẓion and of the national glory of Israel.

In respect to form and construction technique, some of the *kinot* borrow the slow, monotonous rhythm of the *qasida* or the verse pieces with long, sing-song phrases, broken up by choruses or punctuated by echoes and responses. Others adopt the shorter, quicker schemas of a prosody that utilizes verses with multiple rhyming segments and the Arabic metric models of the *mutagârib, khafîf,* and *basît,* linked to the accelerated cadence and the quick, brisk movement of the funeral chants (*tamrurim,* sing. *tamrur*), to which the author refers in the heading of his elegies.

The language of the *kinot* is Hebrew here, except for the first, which is written in Aramaic. The author exploits all the resources that could contribute to the expression of the lament, to the poetic development of the rhyming lamentations that accompany the ritual actions of the professional mourners around the funeral bier. This preoccupation with style can be seen in the unusual frequency of certain types of expressions and linguistic signs, in the significant recurrence of thematic unities and lexical and syntactical models, in the sometimes excessive use of homophony, alliteration, assonance, and antithesis.

Jewish poets generally excelled in this genre of poetry, perhaps because it reflected the wounded soul of the Jew so sorely tried by fate, the perpetual agony of a human group that had not been spared persecutions and calamities over the centuries and had struggled constantly to safeguard its identity and for its physical and spiritual survival. The story is told of a sultan who invited Jewish and Muslim singers to participate in a poetic and musical contest. The Muslim artists equaled their Jewish rivals in the multiple genres of Andalusian poetry and song. Disappointed at seeing victory slipping through their fingers, the Jews turned to the *kinah*; this ensured their success and enabled them to beat their Muslim rivals.

The *kinot* of Jacob Aben Sur borrow their melodic themes from the elegies of the set liturgy for the Ninth of Ab. The author also refers to local musical traditions, and more especially to laments in the Castilian language, mentioning them in the *incipit* verse at the top of the elegiac compositions and serving as their *tamrur,* "lament to the tune of . . ." We have noted a few Castilian *tamturim* in this series, transcribed in the text in Hebrew script, including the following:

*Qué mal qué mali* [sic]
*Qué dolor tan grande.*
*Qué mal señoras la muerte.*
*Ah soduras*
*Como se desparte.*
*La una de la carne*
*Ansi se desparte.*
*El novio de su nobia*
*Qué dolor tan grande.*

What evil, like my evil!
What grief immense!
What evil, my ladies, [as] death!
Ah! How hard are [these griefs]! How to wrench out
The nails from the flesh,
so to wrench
The bridegroom from the bride.
What immense grief!"

Two of the twenty-four compositions that Jacob Aben Sur wrote for the ill-omened Ninth of Ab mention the grievous fate of Judean princes and free men who fell at the hands of their enemies. These are the same compositions in which the author indulges in the literary devices of homophony and homography. One word with multiple meanings, generally incorporated in a biblical quotation, serves as a rhyme, repeated in the last lines of two successive verses.

As an example, we have taken the following two lines, the final lines of the third and fourth verses, from the first piece:

> They fell into the abyss of prisons,
> into holes in the earth and rocky *caverns* (*hurim*).
> They floundered in the ditch of exile,
> princes together with *patricians* (*horim*).

In a series of elegies entitled *Zekher la-Ḥorban* ("In Memory of the Destruction"), Moses Aben Sur, a contemporary and close relative of Jacob Aben Sur, also laments the bi-millenary tragedy of the downfall of Jerusalem and the annihilation of the Jewish state. In a note at the top of this series of elegies, which also includes some laments and funeral eulogies, the author explains:

> Here I have arranged some *kinot* that I composed on the *ḥorban* [destruction], on the exile of the Divine Presence (Shekhinah) and on our own exile, which still continues, on the growing poverty of the people, on the weight of the fiscal burden, taxes, and forced labor, and on the grief of the nation of Israel. May God bring it to an end by sending our messiah without delay, by hastening the restoration of the House of our God and of our glory.

On the model of some *kinot* belonging to the liturgy for the Ninth of Ab and imitating an equivalent genre used by the authors of the Palestinian *piyyuṭ*, the Moroccan poet exploited all the resources of antithesis to compare the contrast between the sad commemoration of the Ninth of Ab and happy events like the festivals of Pesaḥ and Sukkot.

Even in the title of the first group of elegies, Moses Aben Sur metamorphoses the names of Pesaḥ and Sukkot (*ḥag ha-massot* and *ḥag ha-sukkot*) into Festival of Fasts (*ḥag ha-sumot*) and Festival of Calamities (*hag ha-suqot*) by a play on words and letters that uses the cryptographic devices of notarikon and gematria. The same technique is adopted to transform *hag ha-pesaḥ*, "Festival of Passover," into *ḥag has-pesha'*, "festival of sin," by substituting one laryngeal (*'ayin*) for another (*ḥet*).

This is a very old technique. It originated in the methods of exposition peculiar to the Talmud and Midrash, from which the fifth- to sixth-century Palestinian *piyyuṭ* had already borrowed its rhetoric.

We know the role that talmudic hermeneutics and the rules of rabbinical interpretation played in the explication of the law in halakhic and aggadic literature. Once these essentially logical schemas were refined and removed from their prosaic shell and their dialectic strictness, designed for halakhah and jurisprudential language, they provided the authors of *piyyuṭim* with valuable material. They employed it to fashion original instruments of stylistics which responded to the needs of poetic discourse and to aesthetic requirements.

We will take the *kinah* as an example to illustrate our hypothesis. An examination of its structures reveals close relationships with the midrash and *piyyuṭ*. To mourn the misery of the national body and the destruction of the Temple in Jerusalem, the Palestinian poet resorted to the literary techniques of the midrash, finding its rhetoric and its various methods of expounding ideas suited for expressing the grief of Jewish hearts torn by the immense tragedy. The *kinah* uses stylistic features which are very common in the midrash, and uses them happily and successfully, if one can say that in this context.

One of these features, antithesis, is, as it happens, a particularly fertile mode of expression. It compares two events, two situations, that are completely different in nature, proceedings, and consequences. The comparison between Pesaḥ and Tish'ah be-Ab, for example, shapes a whole series of *kinot*. The procedure is sometimes very simple; it consists of the juxtaposition in one distich of two antithetical biblical verses: Exodus, 14:30 followed by Lamentations 1:14, and so on right through the piece. The procedure can become more elaborate, more complex. For instance, the themes of the exodus from Egypt and the departure from Jerusalem for exile in Babylon are grippingly summarized, and the characters of Moses and Jeremiah, each in his own way a hero of one of these major events in Jewish history, are brought into the action in word pictures where heavy shadows and dazzling light rub shoulders. The piece is sometimes an unbroken succession of distiches, sometimes a long series of verses of three or four rhythmical lines, both forms at times using rhyme and alphabetical acrostics.

Returning to the poetic work of Moses Aben Sur, his *kinot* are variations on the themes usually developed in this poetic genre. The *kinot* by his cousin Jacob Aben Sur have been mentioned. Despite the relationship between the two poets and the fact that they lived in the same period and the same sociocultural environment, there are marked differences in their works.

A very talented preacher and an eminent jurist, Jacob Aben Sur is distinguished by a sort of classicism imposed on him by his functions, his relationships with his colleagues in the rabbinate, and the authority he exercised over the Jewish masses in the Moroccan communities. He was a powerful personality who left a mark on his own times and the generations of scholars who succeeded him.

Moses Aben Sur did not have the same rabbinic fame and probably did not follow a spiritual itinerary identical to that of his relative. He was in some ways an innovator because of the exclusively mystical orientation he gave to the whole of his intellectual work, although the work of his contemporaries was not devoid of kabbalistic esotericism. With him, traditional talmudic intellectualism seems to give way to a deep sensitivity that becomes apparent in a sort of surrealism avant-la-lettre, in the abstruseness of a highly allusive, dense, even obscure mode of expression. The terminology, made up of hapax legomena, is difficult. The selection of stylized expressions, the choice of figures of speech and images, the language, style, and construction techniques themselves, all these literary components certainly display the customary erudition and rabbinical knowledge. But the work nonetheless shows a certain originality and is stamped with the seal of a mind and personality that are in many respects attractive.

We have chosen the following verse from the first lament in this category of *kinot:*

In that day shall there be a great mourning,
as in the mourning of Hadadrimmon (Zechariah 12:11).

My entrails moan,
and the walls of my heart roar.
Tremors spread through me,
as spreads cumin (Isaiah 28:25).

Oh that my head were waters, and mine eyes a fountain of tears:
(Jeremiah 8:23).
I will make myself master cup-bearer;
I will fill the glasses without cease, and my cup would run over.

The poetic genres of the *teḥinnot* (supplications), *widduyim* (confessions), and *tokhahot* can be linked to the *kinot.*

Moroccan authors also wrote a large number of these works. Borrowing the melodic and rhythmic style of the Spanish sentimental song and the Castilian cantilena, the pieces in the *diwan* of Moses Aben Sur are sometimes evocations of messianic times, sometimes prayers to hasten deliverance, sometimes examples of the struggle against the temptations of the evil inclination (*yeṣer ha-ra'*) or a dialogue between the soul and the body, the two protagonists taking turns to pour out their confessions and supplications. The author gives the following explanation in a preamble written at the head of one of these prayers:

> Today I am arranging some *kinot, teḥinnot,* and *tokhahot* which I composed for myself and for people of my generation in order to fulfill the words of the Scriptures: "Take with you words, and return unto the Lord" (Hosea 14:3). Arm yourselves with prayers and supplications. Perhaps the obstacle formed by the heart of stone which is in our flesh will be broken, and "Let the wicked forsake His way, and the man of iniquity his thoughts; and let him return unto the Lord, and He will have compassion upon him, and to our God, for He will abundantly pardon" (Isaiah 55:7).

This poetic work by Moses Aben Sur reverberates with a mystical echo from the Orient, especially from the kabbalistic school in Safed. Evidence of this is the frequent reference to the models of Israel Najara, the marked preference for the themes of his poetry and his favorite motifs, the frequent symbolism of the dove, as in the following example:

> Dove, floundering in the slumber of exile;
> Break free of the dust.
>
> Chant songs and praises;
> Celebrate the living God by melodies.

### *The Six-Day Fast*

A more recent "exhortation," composed around the middle of the nineteenth century by Judah Aben Sur a member of the Tetuán branch of the Aben Sur family, is dedicated to a pious scholar of that town. The note at the head of the piece explains that this scholar observed the unbroken six-day fast, the *ta'anit hafsaqa.* The poem develops the theme of the temptation of the *yeṣer ha-ra'* which the fast destroys. It begins as follows:

> My friends, brethren, close ones,
> Mourn with me my many sins.
>
> The evil counsel of the implacable enemy from the north[18] made me stray;
> Like a bird I fell into the traps he set me,
> No one came to aid me.

We mention this exhortation here because it describes a little-known rite observed by pious people, called the *ta'anit hafsaqa* in Hebrew. The Judeo-Arabic designation, *settiya* ("six-day period") is more meaningful. The fast actually consisted of total abstinence from food and drink for six consecutive days, including nights. The fast began at dawn on Sunday and ended on Friday evening at sunset with an appropriate ceremonial and a special liturgy (see above, pp. 66–67).

## *The Days of Awe*

The cycle of the liturgy reaches its culminating point in the ten Days of Awe (*yamim nora'im*), also known by virtue of the role they play as the ten days of self-appraisal, of penitence (*'aseret yeme teshubah*). This is an eminently solemn period which begins at Rosh Hashanah ("head of the year"), the festival of the New Year, and ends with Yom Kippur, the Day of Atonement, a day of confession, fasting, and penitence.

### *Forty Days of Austerity*

Rosh Hashanah is the culmination of an austere period which lasts for the whole of the preceding month, Elul, the last month of the year,

18. The north (*ṣafon*)is the favored place of evil, the origin of impurity. See Gershom Scholem, *Origin of Kabbala*, pp. 170, 310. Compare Jeremiah 1:14, "Out of the north the evil shall break forth," an allusion to the invasion by the Assyrians and Babylonians, countries in the north and enemies of Israel and Judah. See also Joel 2:20, "I will remove far off from you the northern one."

called the "month of mercy and penitential prayers" (*ḥodesh ha-raḥamin we-ha-seliḥot*). According to a Maghrebian text, the close relationship between God and man is embodied in the word Elul, which designates it because it incorporates the initials of the beautiful declaration *Ani le-dodi we-dodi li,* "I am my beloved's and my beloved is mine." The text is borrowed from the Song of Songs; its allegorical and mystical import must here be restored to it.[19]

From the neomenia of Elul, people begin to prepare themselves for the great and terrible day of judgment, the day when men's actions are assessed by the holy court. This period, which lasts until Yom Kippur, is the occasion for revived zeal in observing the precepts of the law. It is also the time for Seliḥot, nighttime sessions of penitential prayers. Every day, in the hours before dawn, during what is called the third watch, the mellah came awake and sprang to life. The synagogues filled with adult and adolescent worshipers, giving up their sleep to participate in this ritual.

In the year after my religious majority, I used to go and wake up my school and yeshibah friends, running through the dark streets of the Mogador medina (where Jews and Muslims lived peacefully together), knocking on the doors of houses, holding a lantern (*fnar*) containing a lighted candle. Once a week, the vigil lasted for the whole night, and was devoted to a special liturgy called *tiqqun karet,* intended to spare participants from the violent death (*karet*) that punished certain types of serious sin.

## *Annulment of Vows and Kol Nidre*

The morning service on the eve of Rosh Hashanah and Yom Kippur was followed by the ritual of the annulment of vows (*ḥattarat nedarim*). Neighbors and friends sought reconciliation; disputes that had remained unsettled during the year were resolved. This ritual was solemnly repeated at one of the culminating points of the liturgy for Yom Kippur, during the serious and moving ceremonial of Kol Nidre. Absolution from vows, promises, and pledges made during the year was publicly proclaimed three times in front of the opened Holy Ark by the three oldest members of the synagogue, qualified by their piety and learning. Clad in white, wrapped in their prayer-shawls, they recited the consecrated formulas with constricted throats, tears in

19. The Hebrew initials of the four words are *'lwl* (read as Elul).

their eyes. It was the custom in our Moroccan communities to read a special prayer for the well-being of the king and the peace and prosperity of his kingdom immediately after Kol Nidre

### *Flagellation and Purification Bath*

On the eve of Yom Kippur, pious people arranged to have themselves whipped. The ritual flagellation was carried out by one of the rabbis from the synagogue, in accordance with precise rules fixed by the code. It was inflicted with a special lash and consisted of thirty-nine blows applied to the subject's bare back. This figure corresponds to three times the thirteen words of the biblical text which evoke the divine attributes of clemency and mercy (Psalms 78:38). The person who had been whipped went to the ritual pool immediately afterwards to take a purification bath. It is necessary to prepare oneself to "live the life of an angel," says a talmudic text.

### KAPPAROT

*Kapparot* is the ransom for sins committed during the year, in short, the price of redemption actualized by expiatory "sacrifices" of chickens which are substituted for the sinner. This was common practice in almost all Maghrebian families and went very far back in their socio-religious memory. An ancient midrashic text cited by Moroccan authors mentions this custom, adding that the chicken is regarded as a substitute for the scapegoat sacrificed in Temple times in expiation of the sins of Israel.

Around midnight on the day before the eve of Yom Kippur, the *shoḥeṭ* went from family to family to carry out the operation. A cock was sacrificed for every man or male child, a chicken for every woman or girl. After having examined the bird, the rabbi held it firmly in his right hand and whirled it around above the head of the person named. Then, before slaughtering the bird, he recited the following formula: "This is your ransom, your substitute, the price of your redemption; this cock [or hen, as the case might be] is slaughtered so that you can live a long and peaceful life." The blood was then covered with ashes or earth, as the rite prescribed. The slaughtered chicken was eaten by the family; one of the sacrificed cocks was generally donated to a needy person.

*Dietary Practices and Rites*

It is the rule to mortify the soul, fast, and afflict oneself with all manner of penitence at Yom Kippur. Rosh Hashanah, on the contrary, is a time for eating, drinking, and rejoicing, as prescribed by law and custom.

In actual fact, the food is rich in auguries and symbols. This is evident from the dietary rites that mark the first meal on the eve of the festival. Its manifold meanings are written into the ritual which follows the Kiddush (sanctification) and the *moṣi* (blessing over bread). Evidence is found in what was very appropriately called "the leaf of honey," in Arabic *al-warqa d-al 'asel.* In the past, this arrived from the Holy Land with New Year greetings. The inscription "May the year begin with blessings," the last line of a liturgical poem sung in the synagogue at the evening service every Rosh Hashanah eve, was often stamped on it locally in Morocco.

To begin, it must be noted that the Kiddush wine had to be white wine made from white grapes which the woman of the house had pressed with her own "white" hands. Red wine was banned from the table on this evening. The color red is a symbol of harshness, whereas white stands for mercy. The bread for the *moṣi'* was dipped in honey and not in salt, as was usually the case. Honey played a vital role in the food for this evening. It is, in fact, the mystical symbol of grace and bounty and good augury.

The items that had to be eaten before the meal figured in a prescribed order in the "leaf of honey." Each was a symbol and a portent. The name of each food served a predetermined function and possessed a specific quality of considerable import. The literal meaning and sound of the name, the prayers said before eating the named food, all combined with the actual act of consumption to give the rite its full significance, its spiritual, mystical, even mythical and cosmic, historical dimension.

Thus a segment of apple was dipped in honey and the following said: "May it be Thy will, O Lord our God . . . that this New Year from beginning to end be to us as good and as sweet as honey." This formula is associated with a kabbalistic meditation on the ineffable name of God.

These words were said when eating dates from the new harvest: "May it be Thy will, O Lord our God . . . that we blossom like the palm; let an end be made to our sins, the hostility and hatred that our enemies and adversaries (essentially our evil inclinations) nourish against us." Note here the association of *tamar* ("palm") and the notion of making an end, annihilating, expressed by the verb *yit-tammu.*

The following wish was expressed on swallowing a few pomegranate seeds: "May it be Thy will, O Lord our God . . . that our virtues and merits multiply like the seeds of the pomegranate." Esoteric meditation had its place here, as elsewhere, in view of the mystical interpretation that Moroccan kabbalists themselves gave to the text of the Song of Songs, which several times mentions the pomegranate.

The same procedure was repeated with sesame seeds, fenugreek, and vegetables with Hebrew and Arabic names laden with allegorical and mystical significance: pumpkin (*qera/qara',* "to tear, pronounce judgment"), leek (*karti/karat,* "to cut"), and the stalks and leaves of beet (*salqa/salaq,* "to eradicate").

A sheep's head was produced at the end of the ritual. Everyone present swallowed a bit of it, at the same time remembering the testing of the patriarch Abraham when called by God to sacrifice his son Isaac on the altar, where he is eventually replaced by a ram caught in the thicket (see Genesis 22). This is the occasion to voice the wish "to be at the head and not at the tail."

Note that the vegetables used in the ritual are among the "seven vegetables" (*sba' khdari*) that accompanied the couscous. This was the traditional dish par excellence at this time of year, when festival follows festival in quick succession. It was eaten on Rosh Hashanah, the eve of Yom Kippur, and Sukkot.

### *Liturgy and the Shofar*

Apart from the standard ritual made up of prayers fixed since time immemorial, the Jews of Morocco, like most of their co-religionists in the Sephardi, Mediterranean, and oriental world, inserted into the liturgy for Rosh Hashanah and Yom Kippur a considerable number of poetic works composed specifically for these major festivals by the great authors of the Hispano-Maghrebian Golden Age with whom they proudly claimed kinship: Judah Halevi, Solomon Ibn Gabirol, Moses Ibn Ezra.

These compositions include a poetic genre called *'Aqedah,* ("binding") which commemorates the great testing of Abraham, the "sacrifice" of his son Isaac. Special mention must be made of the *'Aqedah* composed by Judah ben Samuel Ibn Abbas Al-Maghribi, a scholar and poet who lived in Fez, Spain, and Baghdad in the twelfth century. On the surface, this prayer, which was accepted into the liturgy of the Jews of the Islamic East and West, is no more than a paraphrase of the biblical account of the binding of Isaac, filled out by elements belonging to the legendary world of the midrash. But in reality it is a moving elegy in which the author, an unhappy father, expresses his deep grief at the spiritual death of his son, who had embraced Islam.

Only a few other quite typical components and moments in the body of the ritual will be mentioned here.

The "sacrifice" of Isaac is also recalled in the reading from the Torah scroll. The biblical text dedicated to the New Year is chapter 22 of the book of Genesis, which tells of this testing of the patriarch Abraham.

Rosh Hashanah has various names in biblical and post-biblical literature, including Yom Teru'ah ("Day of Remembrance and Memory") and Yom ha-Din ("Day of Judgment").

*The sounding of the shofar.* When I was young I was always fascinated by the way the shofar was made, starting from a ram's horn chosen from the many that my grandfather brought home from the abattoir one day in the month of Elul. I watched him for hours on end. The process was long and, I still think, very complicated, taking account of the rudimentary tools at his disposal. He held the horn over the fire, carefully hollowed it out, cleaned it, shaped it, polished it, and pierced it in order to give it what he used to call a "thin mouth." After a thousand and one metamorphoses and numerous attempts, it became, in his skilled hands, a valuable instrument which entered the ranks of religious objects. At those culminating moments of prayer on the Days of Awe, it would play the role of intercessor between men and their Creator, since it is the medium through which the three series of sacred sounds, the *teqi'ot, shebarim,* and *teru'ah,* reach the heavens, and the very foot of the divine throne.

Following Saadya Gaon of Fayoum (Egypt, tenth century), the Maghrebian rabbis assigned various functions to the sounding of the shofar. They gave this precept, ordained in the Bible, some crucially important motives in the eyes of the believer. It proclaimed the sovereignty of God on the anniversary of the creation of the world, which, according to the Talmud, was completed on Rosh Hashanah. It recalled the appearance of God and the revelation of the Torah on Mount Sinai, the messages of the prophets, the memory of the "sacrifice" of Isaac and the destruction of the Temple. It was a reminder of the day of the last judgment, the redemption, and the sounds of another shofar that would be sounded by the Messiah on the day of the resurrection in times to come. Further, the sound of the shofar made hearts tremble and incited men to repent.

### *The Musaf Prayer*

A important part of the service, following upon Shaḥrit, was the Musaf. The Rosh Hashanah Musaf 'Amidah was dominated by three important themes that can be expressed in three key words: *malkhuyot* ("kingship"), *zikhronot* ("remembrance"), and *shofarot* ("sounding of the ram's horn"). Each of these themes was copiously illustrated by biblical texts taken in succession from the Pentateuch, the Prophets, and the Hagiographa. The texts on the *malkhuyot* proclaimed God's sovereignty: "The Lord hath established His throne in the heavens; and His kingdom ruleth over all" (Psalms 103:19). Those of the *zikhronot* exalted divine providence and its intervention in the destiny of the world: "You remember all actions, You recall all beings created from time immemorial. Nothing remains hidden from Your eyes, nothing is forgotten before Your throne of glory." As for the texts of the *shofarot,* they referred more specifically to the scene of God's revelation on Mount Sinai and the grandiose manifestations which accompanied it: "There were thunders and lightnings and a thick cloud upon the mount, and the voice of a horn exceeding loud. . . . And when the voice of the horn waxed louder and louder, Moses spoke, and God answered him" (Exodus 19:16, 19). Obviously these texts were also a reminder of the duty to sound the ram's horn.

### *The Expulsion of Sins*

On the afternoon of the day of Rosh Hashanah, small groups of people went down to the seashore if they lived in the coastal towns, or to wells or a watercourse if they did not, and carried out the ritual of *tashlikh* for the expulsion of sins. It was accompanied by a special liturgy which contained the invocation "Thou wilt cast (*we-tashlikh*) all their sins into the depths of the sea," a reference to Micah 7:19. Some object or other was thrown into the sea, most often a stone; people turned out their pockets, shook the skirts of their djellabas, and returned, relieved of their sins.

### *Seder ha-'Abodah*

The Musaf prayer on Yom Kippur contained an eminently important component, regarded as the fundamental element in the liturgy for this most awesome day. This was the *Seder ha-'Abodah,* a collection of texts in rhyming prose and verse that described in detail the divine ritual of the Day of Atonement (*Yom ha-Kippurim*), that is to say, the sacrifices, rites, and actions that the high priest used to carry out in the Temple in Jerusalem. The mishnaic texts, which prosaically expound this theme in tractate Yoma, are here elevated to the most noble rank of poetic literature, because when Palestinian authors of the first century C.E. and their Spanish successors in the Golden Age composed a genre of poetry specifically called *'Abodah,* they borrowed the prosodic trimmings from this source.

The *'Abodah* is a sort of epic hymn which sings of the unfolding of the sacred service and expresses nostalgia for a period that is past, the hope and desire of finding again the immemorial times of a distant glory which disappeared specifically with the destruction of the Temple and the interruption of the divine service. It is believed that history itself ceased with this national tragedy, and would only resume its course with the advent of the messiah. The poet travels back to the past and exalts its legendary memory. His imagination also takes him into the future with the hope of redemption and a return to the magical prestige of the beginnings.

The *'Abodah* begins with a brief account of the creation of the world, contrasting images of light and shade, expressed by a choice of paronomastic pairs, and echoing the first pages of the book of Genesis: *tohu* and *bohu,* heaven and earth, day and night, air and water, fauna and its various species, the visible world and the hidden universe. It continues with the creation of man, the progress of mankind to the patriarchs, the birth of the people of Israel and its history until the investiture of Aaron and his descendants with the priestly function.

The periodic renewal of the world in the Jewish religion, says Mircea Eliade in *Aspects du mythe,* "consisted of a cultural scenario, the principal rite of which symbolized the reiteration of the cosmogony, the enthronement of Yahweh as king of the world, the representation of his victory over his enemies, both the forces of chaos and the historical enemies of Israel. The result of the victory was the renewal of creation, of election and of the covenant."

Wensinck, in *The Semitic New Year and the Origin of Eschatology,* shows that "the ritual scenario of the New Year, by which the transition from Chaos to the Cosmos is signaled, has been applied to historical events like the exodus and the crossing of the Red Sea, the conquest of Canaan, the Babylonian captivity and the return from the exile."

Gershom Scholem finds the same theme and the same motives in the kabbalistic literature.

It will be noted that one of the typical features of the *'Abodah* is its universalist tone. The service of the high priest, designated by the term *'Abodah,* takes place against an epic backcloth in which, curiously, images of Jerusalem, Eretz Israel, and the Jewish society living there barely appear. It is as though the descendant of Aaron were operating in the name of all mankind.

The liturgy for Rosh Hashanah and Yom Kippur, like the world of prayer in general, is one of the favorite realms of kabbalah. The mystical finds its most classic expression there, whether through the large number of liturgical compositions actually written by mystics or through the esoteric interpretation of this liturgy.

The hymns and canticles of the so-called heavenly liturgy were composed for the ceremonial of the Days of Awe. The most famous of them is the alphabetical litany called "The Song of the Angels." It begins with the words "Majesty and fidelity are to the eternally living . . ."

All this literature also uses a highly fertile system of symbolization, complicated because it calls on a deep knowledge of rabbinic learning. When the fifth- to sixth-century poet Yosi b. Yosi recounts world history from the creation until Aaron's priesthood in his *'Abodah,* he does not call the characters by their own names, the ones the Scriptures give them. Instead, he uses a series of formulas made up of specific attributes and paraphrases, whose relationships with the protagonists and heroes of biblical history can only be perceived by initiates in biblical, talmudic, and midrashic literature. The same is true of concepts like heaven, earth, water, law, serpent, and hell.

In this symbolic terminology, the patriarch Abraham, for example, is sometimes designated by the phrase "tested father," sometimes by "father of a multitude [of nations]," "native or tree trunk," or "righteous, foundation of the world"; the patriarch Isaac by "foliage produced [born] in old age"; the patriarch Jacob is the "simple man." "Heaven" is replaced by "seat," "residence," "fine linen"; for "earth," we have "footstool," "place of forgetfulness"; for "water," "measured [quantities]"; for "gehenna," "leech"; for "law," "teacher and pupil"; and for the "community of Israel," "chosen object," and so on.

The moment awaited most impatiently on the day of Yom Kippur was the time when "the sun touched the treetops." It was at that precise instant that the ritual of Ne'ilah ("closure") commenced. It was specially marked by the solemn recital of the priestly blessing and by a double sounding of the shofar which the congregation listened to fervently, covering their children with their prayer shawls. It announced the end of the penance and the breaking of the fast.

### *Tu-Bishbat*

Judaism has another new year, the New Year for Trees, which falls in mid-winter on the fifteenth of the month of Shebat, and is therefore called Tw/Tu-Bishbat (the numerical value of the letters *t* and *w* is 15). Its origin goes back a long way, since it already appears in the first chapters of the mishnaic and talmudic tractates of Rosh Hashanah. They say, in substance, that "this date has been chosen because the great rains of the year fall before Shebat, and, as the trees generally flower shortly afterwards, they are considered [for the collection of the tithe due from them] as belonging to the coming year." When this reason later became anachronistic and pointless, the New Year for Trees attracted the attention of the sixteenth-century kabbalists of the Safed school. Isaac Luria and his disciples gave it esoteric meaning, keeping the date of 15 Shebat in order to make it a liturgical moment designed to bear witness to the participation of man in the joy of the trees, a day marked by the consumption of the largest possible number of different fruits and cereals. These latter are so many symbols, interpreted by a mystical ritual known from a few publications, such as *Ḥemdat Yamim* and *Peri 'Eṣ-Hadar,* which also tell the history and legend associated with custom and practice.

Tu-Bishbat is certainly not a remarkable ceremony, nor a festival meticulously observed by everyone. However, in some Moroccan families it assumed the character of a festivity marked by abundance and richness. This abundance and richness was signaled by the variety of foods displayed on a sumptuously laid table: the seven species celebrated and sung of in the Bible as a reminder of the Promised Land, "land of wheat and barley, and vines and fig-trees and pomegranates; a land of olive-trees and honey" (Deuteronomy 8:8), some thirty other species of cereal and grilled vegetables, and more especially, seasonal fruits—or unseasonal fruit that was carefully kept the whole year for this special moment (from oranges to apples, from ripe jujubes to sugary pods from the carob tree), loaves of wheat and barley bread, galettes made of maize, red and white wine, brandy made from wax or figs, cakes, and so on. The children had a part in the festival, and also the poor, because good care was taken to prepare individual packets for them containing a little of everything displayed on the table, over which a prayer has been said and a wish made.[20]

20. Quoting from memory, there is the New Year of the Kings, which, in the Bible, coincides with the first of Nisan, the month of Passover and the exodus from Egypt. Another new year occurs on the first of Elul, the date when the tithe on cattle was collected. All in all, Jewish tradition, as embodied in the Talmud, knew four new years, two of which have currently lapsed.

# Epilogue

An epilogue is a recapitulation, the statement of a case and a judgment. It is also the outline of a project. This means that I should conclude this portrait of a Jewish society in the land of Islam that already belongs to history by going back briefly over some of its features to specify their meaning and range. I also need to extend my remarks by a rapid incursion into the present and an outline of my thoughts on what I call the historicity of the Judeo-Maghrebian cultural world.

## DUAL LOYALTY

The Maghrebian Judeo-Muslim societies prolonged a civilization, a way of life and a culture, which their ancestors had known from the end of the fifteenth century, after the collapse of the Andalusian Golden Age and the turning inwards of the country, up to the nineteenth century in Algeria and Tunisia, and the twentieth in Morocco. Four centuries passed by with hardly any notable changes either in men and the cultural landscape or in the socioeconomic arena and daily life. The pictures were eternal, the characters unchanging. A few decades ago there was a feeling of absolute stagnation in Morocco—more than in any other country in Islam, perhaps because Muslim traditionalism was augmented by Berber conservatism. And the conviction rapidly grew that often enough all you had to do to know what the country was like during previous centuries was to look around you; that an hour's walk was as rewarding as a day's research in a library. Jewish society seemed to have shared the same fate. The prosperity of the Hispano-Maghrebian Golden Age was followed by the poverty of later periods, particularly the most recent which preceded the advent of the West and the intrusion of its culture and civilization.

The relatively rapid decline of the Jewry in the Land of Islam had political, economic, and social causes that to a large extent involved the fate of the whole Muslim world. However, the situation of the Jewish communities of Morocco was particularly difficult for a variety of reasons. These included the isolation of the country itself, withdrawn from all Western civilization, as well as the confinement within the mellah and the degrading status of *dhimmi*.

Of course, the two societies, Jewish and Muslim, led different lives, jealous of their identity, intransigent in their faith and beliefs. However, looked at from the historical perspective of Jewish life in the country, it is possible to see areas of convergence where they met and co-existed, on the whole peacefully. There were privileged meeting-places where a genuine symbiosis between them came about in the intimacy of language and the similarity of mental structures. It can be noted at every point in this book that this symbiosis was created and achieved at the level of daily life, in economic affairs, at the major moments in life, in the social imagination and popular culture. These were zones which acknowledged neither religious frontiers nor the confrontation of "national" ideologies and religious consciousness. Certain customs and practices observed at the time of major religious festivals and family celebrations seem to show that even liturgical moments were marked by a not inconsiderable portion of syncretism.

Here, as elsewhere, we are dealing with a bipolar Jewish society, an original sociocultural identity, a complex Judeo-Maghrebian personality which manifested a dual loyalty. There was, first, this society's loyalty to world Jewry, with which it maintained a close and fruitful relationship, especially in the realm of thought, its major trends and the Jewish "humanities" in general. On the other hand, there was a loyalty to the local historical and geographical environment of which it was an integral part, to the sociocultural and linguistic landscape of the Islamic West and the old Hispano-Maghrebian world.

## A SHATTERED COMMUNITY

We will only describe very briefly what has for the sake of convenience been too summarily called the period of changes. In this case, it coincided with the introduction of the French Protectorate (1912–56), the intrusion of the West and its civilization into a semi-medieval society. Some students of this period have found it possible to talk indiscriminately about emancipation and uprootedness. As for the Moroccan Jew's contacts with European society, its way of life, its economy, and its culture, scholars have hastily and rashly concluded that it only resulted in the ambition to "live like a European" by adopting the external signs which distinguish the "colonial," a too hurried and too superficial westernization, a break with the past, tearing apart and loss of identity. The Jewish community of Morocco, it was said, found itself in a very uncomfortable position, solicited by trends of diverse types and going in conflicting directions, split between irreconcilable loyalties.

In actual fact, all this only concerned a tiny fraction of Moroccan Jewish society. It involved no more than a few families living in the large metropolises, who had always been privileged, and whose children had been able to obtain a high level of education and find comfortable positions in the economy and the liberal professions. The great masses were only slightly disturbed by the problems resulting from westernization and acculturation which worried the cultured and wealthy elite minority. Unaware of the controversies and polemics that filled the columns of the Moroccan Jewish press or were displayed in other, not always disinterested, publications, the great majority remained untouched by the solicitations of the West, and attached to the values, and loyal to the hopes, of traditional Judaism. When the time came, it was prepared to emigrate en masse to Israel, unaware of considerations related to the current political situation, but responding to messiano-spiritual impulses and thus realizing a millennial dream.

Behind the visible but misleading exterior that the uninitiated witness is tempted to take for profound reality, the Moroccan Jew succeeded in living an inner life which lacked neither serene joy and optimism nor even spirituality. It consoled him for the disappointments of existence and led him to say with the psalmist, "This is my comfort in my affliction" (Psalms 119:50). As for his readiness to return to the land of his fathers, authentic documents and a large body of autochthonous literature demonstrate that Moroccan Jewry as a whole, in its expectation of the messianic era, was better prepared for the penetration of Zionist ideology than the Jewries of Western, Central, or Eastern Europe.

After the creation of the State of Israel (1948) and the independence of Morocco (1956), the community was shattered and almost all its population emigrated. A society settled in the country for nearly two millennia, in its famous metropolises and in the rural areas of the coastal plains, the Atlas valleys, and the borders of the Sahara, was henceforth condemned to disappear without recall. Of the 250,000 individuals who in 1950–60 populated the mellahs, living side by side with Muslims in the medinas of certain towns and with Europeans in the new districts of the big cities, fewer than 20,000 remain, most of them concentrated in the economic capital, Casablanca.

Some chose France, Canada, and Latin America as host countries. The vast majority were taken to the Promised Land or went there of their own volition. In Israel, in company with Jews originating in other countries of the Orient, they constituted a society apart, distinct from the Ashkenazi community which had come from Central and Eastern Europe. Theirs was the society of the proletarians and "blacks" of the "second Israel," as opposed to the "whites" of the establishment, from which the ruling and political class, the wealthy and cultured elites, had been recruited since the days of the British Mandate.

How did the extinction of Moroccan Jewry come about? What were the major reasons for individual or collective departures, for the great waves of emigration?

Oral rabbinic literature and recent events provide much interesting information on the extraordinary mobility and the motivations of the Moroccan Jews. Individually or in compact groups, Moroccan Jews were always leaving the country in the past, moving primarily toward the Orient. Even internal migrations had not been solely determined by the inexorable social and economic laws which govern population movements in developed or developing societies.

The flow of emigration to Palestine had never ceased over the centuries, fed by the movement of students sent to yeshîbot and pilgrims going to end their days in the Holy Land. The pursuit of wealth, hopes for greater security and for social and legal emancipation led hundreds of Jews to leave Morocco in the nineteenth century. Their travels did not take them solely to the traditional destinations, Jerusalem, Safed, and Tiberias, but also to places as far away as the United States, Argentina, Brazil, and Peru. Most of the emigrants hardly needed to go so far. Most often they settled in the neighboring country, Algeria, under French rule since 1830, or in Gibraltar, hub of British trade with Morocco. The African and European peripluses of two rabbis from the Moroccan south have been described above and their adventures and peregrinations recounted.

Emigration to the Holy Land was negligible during the first five decades of the twentieth century, a period which saw the establishment of the French Protectorate in Morocco (and the British Mandate in Palestine). However, Zionist groups existed in Tangier, Tetuán, Mogador, Fez, and Marrakesh from the beginning of the century, and much later in Casablanca. On the creation of the State of Israel in 1948, the different kibbutz movements and the Israeli political parties were represented in Morocco by emissaries who brought their rivalries and their struggles for influence with them. Casablanca was the seat of Kadima, the office which quasi-officially organized emigration. Large contingents were supplied by the disinherited masses from the towns. But a clear preference was shown for *ʻaliyat ha-noʻar*, "youth aliyah," and also for aliyah by populations from the Moroccan south and the Atlas mountains, considered better equipped than city dwellers to found agricultural colonies.

The implementation of departures from the communities of the Atlas and the Moroccan south between 1952 and 1956, and in the following years, was a response to specific objectives and carried out by well-tried methods. The populations of these areas, far removed form the large urban centers, did not set off of their own accord and hardly crowded the offices of the Jewish Agency to put their names down on the departure list, as some people have found it possible to believe and claim. They waited where they were in their isolated mellahs for someone to come and transfer them over the Moroccan frontiers en bloc, after a short stop in Casablanca or Marrakesh. The operation was prepared down to the last detail and did not take more than one night, or two in certain specific cases (purely by chance, I witnessed the "unexpected" departure of the population of Amizmis, in the Upper Atlas).

These populations, very typical of Moroccan Jewry, had remained almost on the margin of Western civilization, despite the educational efforts of the Alliance Israélite Universelle in these areas. They were transplanted without any transition to the Promised Land. It would be interesting to follow them more closely in the country of welcome so as to recount their reactions to their new living conditions, if there were time enough and space to describe this fascinatingly interesting adventure.

### *Vichy and the Jews, the Statute governing Jews*

As in Metropolitan France, the versions dated October 3, 1940 and June 2, 1941 of the statute governing Jews constituted the cornerstone of anti-Jewish legislation. This statute was to be applied to French Jews, to foreign Jews residing in the country and also to indigenous Moroccan Jews through adjustments relating more to the exclusively religious factor than to the degree of belonging to a Jewish family. A Moroccan Jew who had converted to Islam (and by the way, the same rules applied to Jews in the Tunisian Protectorate) was no longer a Jew in the eyes of the law, even if the person had four grandparents of the Jewish "race." However, a person was considered to be a Jew even if he had only a single grandparent of the Jewish "race."[1] The legislation of the French Protectorate subjected Jews to several incapacities under both public and private law and provided for the Aryanization of education and property.

In addition to legislation and the ordinary implementing texts, the new regime could utilize, for the purposes of propaganda and its extrajudicial activism, the services of the French Legion of Combatants, which was responsible for disseminating the principles of the New Order and the Legionnaire Order Service (S.O.L.) recruited from within the Legion. This so-called revolutionary elite body—equivalent to the Nazi S.S.—made the following oath: "I swear to combat democracy, Gaullist dissidence and Jewish leprosy," and was in charge of carrying out special jobs and the most heinous tasks. The worst was not accomplished for want of time. In Casablanca, the S.O.L. and the P.P.F. (Parti Populaire Francais) were openly preparing a pogrom in the *mellahs* (Jewish neighborhoods) for November 15, 1942. Anti-Jewish posters covered the walls of large towns and, on November 8, the main mouthpiece of the local press, *Vigie Marocaine,* published the first of a series of violently anti-Semitic articles designed to prepare public opinion for that sinister event. But a miracle occurred. The Allies landed in North Africa on November 8 and, after three days of combat with General Nogues' troops, the Americans entered the town. The great pogrom was nipped in the bud and, with the exception of some local unrest and minor incidents aimed at the Jews—

1. The Sherifian (or Moroccan) *dahirs* (decrees) implementing the statute governing the Jews of Morocco appeared in the Official Bulletin of Morocco of November 9, 1940 and August 8, 1941. Two important remarks are necessary in this respect. The first concerns the procedure for the publication of *dahirs.* The Resident General alone had real, effective authority: his offices drafted the texts of the *dahirs* in French; his signature gave them legal effect; the texts were then translated into Arabic and sent to the Royal Palace for the King to initial and affix his seal. The second remark related to the scope of these laws: The Jews who were affected by their content were those who had adopted the French lifestyle and way of thinking, in other words, a tiny minority.

encouraged by the way by the French Administration as yet unpurged—the thirst for violent direct action against Jews ended to the detriment of those who had hatched the deadly plot and their deeply disappointed troops.

Until 1945, Moroccan Jews were subjected to the strictures of rationing, which continued to be based on racial criteria—a situation shared by Muslims—with the distribution of food and items to meet basic needs (white cloth and other fabrics) favoring people of European origin, Jews and non-Jews alike.

## *Jewish Refugees in Morocco*

After the Armistice, as early as July 1940, a rather large number of foreign Jewish refugees living in Belgium and France, who had originally come from Germany and Central and Eastern Europe, reached Morocco by various means, either having sailed from Marseilles or having crossed Spain. Those whose papers were in order and who were only in transit were cared for by local aid communities or by international relief organizations (HIAS, AJDC, HICEM) in Casablanca and Tangiers until their departure to the Americas or other more distant destinations (Australia, British colonies in the Indian Ocean). Others were spared internment, thanks to a remarkable effort of solidarity. Reception homes were opened in Tangiers. Other refugees were taken in by the communities in Fez, Marrakesh, Mogador, Safi, and Mazagan . . . or by private individuals whose generous assistance proved highly effective. The more than one thousand refugees who were interned were held in camps in Eastern Morocco and in the Sahara in very harsh conditions comparable to those in a prison. They, too, received relief and assistance until the internment camps were closed.

## *The Sultan of Morocco, Mohammed Ben Youssef, Moroccan Muslims and Jews*

The Muslim nationalist extremist circles, which were attracted by Hitler's Arab policy but at the same time the victims of its contradictions, had little hold over other Muslims whose pro-German sentiments were diffuse and inoffensive. In Morocco (as in Algeria and Tunisia), there was no leader comparable to Al-Amin Al-Husseini who, because of the special political circumstances in Palestine, had turned these same sentiments into the ferment for an uprising against both the Jews and the colonial presence. During the darkest period of the reign of Vichy laws, from July 1940 to November 8, 1941 when the Allies landed in North Africa, there was scarcely any open revolt against French authority, on the one hand, or any violence or marked extortion directed specifically against Jews by their Muslim compatriots, on the other hand, despite the overt incidents or those stated, admitted or concealed by European sources, coming from the P.P.F. (Parti Populaire Francais) and other Fascist political movements or local anti-Jewish groupings, both official and unofficial.

The personal attitude of the Sultan of Morocco, Mohammed Ben Youssef, deserves careful consideration.

We had occasion in November/December 1985 to deliver before the Academy of the Kingdom of Morocco a document discovered in the Archives of the Ministry for Foreign Affairs, Quai d'Orsay, in Paris. This document confirmed something which was already known and which many Moroccan Jews had experienced and witnessed. It was an AFI telegram dated May 24, 1941, sent by Rene Touraine to Vichy entitled "Dissidence" concerning the attitude of the Sultan of Morocco towards the Moroccan Jews.[2]

A second document from the National Archives in Paris belonging to the "Maurice Vanikoff Papers" (72 AJ 594, Morocco) refers to the census taken of Jewish property in Morocco in 1941/42 and the statements made by His Majesty the Sultan to delegations from the Jewish communities in connection with this tragic affair (Annex II).

These documents are included in the annex.

## ANNEX I
## DISSIDENCE
## May 24, 1941
## AFI Telegram

"Change in Attitude of the Sultan of Morocco Towards the French Authorities"
by Rene Touraine

"We have learned from a reliable source that relations between the Sultan of Morocco and the French authorities have been quite tense

2. Archives of Foreign Relations, Paris, Quai d'Orsay, 1939/45 war series, Vichy-Morocco, file 18, Jews (general), binder 665, diplomatic corps series (Annex I)

since the day when the Office of the Resident General applied the decree concerning the 'measures against the Jews,' despite the official opposition of the Sultan. The Sultan had refused to distinguish among his subjects, saying that all were 'loyal.' Annoyed at seeing his authority thwarted by the French authorities, the Sultan decided to show publicly that he rejected the measures against the Jews: he waited for the throne festival to do so. On that occasion, it was the custom for the Sultan to hold a great banquet which was attended by French officials and distinguished individuals from Moroccan circles. For the first time, the Sultan invited representatives of the Jewish community to the banquet and placed them most obviously in the best seats, right next to the French officials. The Sultan had wanted personally to introduce the Jewish individuals present. When the French officials expressed their surprise at the presence of Jews at the meeting, the Sultan told them: 'I in no way approve of the new anti-Semitic laws and I refuse to be associated with any measure of which I disapprove. I wish to inform you that, as in the past, the Jews remain under my protection and I refuse to allow any distinction to be made among my subjects.'

"This sensational declaration gave rise to lively comment within French and indigenous communities."

## ANNEX II

### STATEMENT BY HIS MAJESTY THE SULTAN OF MOROCCO TO DELEGATIONS FROM THE MOROCCAN JEWISH COMMUNITIES

According to an ancient Moroccan custom (the *Dbiha*), subjects of the Sultan whose property or lives were threatened could invoke His Majesty's protection by uttering the customary prayers and burning a few head of cattle. The Moroccan Jews therefore proceeded to sacrifice four bulls. Following this ritual ceremony, a delegation of eminent Jews, composed of Messrs. Elie Danan, El Alouf, Isaac Cohen—all three from Fez—and Mr. Mardoche Dahan of Casablanca, was received by His Majesty who, referring to the various *dahirs* promulgated with respect to the Jews, stated: "Rest assured, I will sign nothing else concerning Moroccan Jews. I consider you to be Moroccans in the same capacity as Muslims and your property, like theirs, will not be touched. Should you hear bad reports concerning the Jews, come and let me know." The delegation then pointed out that the census to which the Jews had been subjected contained a detailed statement of all their assets: cash, bank accounts, jewelry, furniture, and property. Surprised, the Sultan stated: "That is not what I intended to sign; the obligation was to apply only to immovable property." The delegation left with the impression that, in allowing the *dahir* subjecting the Jews to a census, His Majesty wanted 1) only a count of such persons, and 2) only a statement of "property" in the sense of goods and property, that is, exclusively immovable property and not the broad meaning given by the Administration.

A second meeting took place on June 26, 1942 between the Sultan and the three eminent individuals from Fez mentioned above. During that meeting, His Excellency confirmed the statements he had made at the previous meeting.

On Monday, July 13, a great reception was held by the Sultan at the Imperial Palace in Rabat to celebrate the circumcision of the young princes. A delegation of Jews from Fez had officially been invited by the Pasha of Fez. The delegation was composed of four representatives of the community, four eminent individuals and two rabbis. Messrs. E. Danan, El Alouf, and I. Cohen were again included among these ten persons. Just as the delegation was withdrawing and preparing to leave the Palace after presenting its wishes and congratulations, His Majesty, who had recognized the three latter representatives, asked for them to be called back and received them in his private chambers . . . He reiterated the assurances given twice before and kindly added: "My Palace is open at all times for you to come and find me when you hear something unpleasant about yourselves." He was so good as to ask personally that his steward serve them tea and traditional cakes.

On the same occasion of the circumcision of his sons, the Sultan came to Casablanca on Thursday, August 6, to receive tribute from distinguished personalities in that city. Again, a Jewish delegation composed of two rabbis and Messrs. Isaac Pinto, Mardoche Cohen, and Moses Nahon was presented to him by the Pasha of Casablanca in one of the chambers of the Palace. After the delegation had presented its congratulations and customary wishes, Rabbi Abichsera gave a blessing in Hebrew. The text of the blessing, written in Hebrew and translated into Arabic, was then placed in the hands of His Majesty who told the Jews: "Be like your ancestors. Remain dignified and no one will trouble you. I have not failed to recommend you to your

Pasha. Even though you belong to a different religion, I consider you to be equal to other Moroccans, without any distinction."

In 1940, Mohammed V had already opposed the implementation of the anti-Semitic legislation of Vichy on sherifian territory. Independent Morocco, through its sovereign, gave the Moroccan Jew equal legal status with the Moroccan Muslim and granted him access to citizenship with the same rights and duties. In the past, this would have surpassed all his wishes and satisfied his deepest aspirations. But complete implementation of the statute very soon proved impracticable, at least in certain fields.

In addition, the open hostility to Israel resulting from Morocco's solidarity with the other Arab countries and the Jew's natural sympathy for Israel, of which he was a potential citizen, combined to create a climate of suspicion and mistrust that did not facilitate normal relations between the two elements of the population, Jews and Muslims.

Moreover, it was hard for the Jew to come to terms with Morocco's gradual movement toward the economy of an underdeveloped (or developing) country, since his traditional role of intermediary agent was now less and less necessary. His dynamism summoned him elsewhere, all the more so as the risks of international political fluctuations and the fear of a possible change of attitude toward him on the part of the authorities were hardly favorable to his rootedness, the stability he yearned for so strongly. He was therefore condemned to seek more clement climes.

The emigration movement, which mainly affected the disinherited sectors of the Jewish populace during the first years of independence, gradually extended, by contagion, as it were, to the classes with relatively higher living standards, and imperceptibly reached the wealthiest families.

The Jewish community of Morocco certainly dwindled more slowly than other Maghrebian or oriental Jewish communities. But will this not lead it to suffer inexorably the same fate?

Let us recapitulate some of the landmarks in the disintegration process in the first decade following the proclamation of independence.

The emigration to Israel must seem at first glance a natural phenomenon. The Moroccan Jews, like their brethren in other Diaspora countries, had been flowing to Israel since the creation of the state. The movement continued during the last years of the Protectorate, its rhythm dictated solely by the organizations that represented the Jewish Agency locally, particularly the office of Kadima. When Morocco regained its independence, the movement accelerated for almost six months, then was checked because of the establishment of the new order and even more by pressure put on the sherifian authorities by the Arab League, to which Morocco would afterwards belong and pledge solidarity. Nonetheless, movements from Morocco to Israel and vice versa by various means did not cease (the movements from Israel to Morocco involved a few permanent returns, but primarily concerned tourism and family visits). Members of the same family, neighbors from the same house or the same street, necessarily felt the need for reunions whatever the obstacles.

The political aspect of the phenomenon overlaps with the psychological aspect, and it is hard to separate the two. In the climate of confidence and euphoria created in the first days of independence by the declarations of equality and liberty repeated many times by His Majesty King Mohammed V and by the leaders of the political parties, the integration of the Jewish community into the greater Moroccan family was believed to be possible and even desirable. This integration was not confirmed by the facts. It had become a myth despite the efforts of some well-wishers who attempted to bring about a rapprochement between the two elements of the Moroccan population in a short-lived association called Wifaq ("entente"). The centuries of life on the same soil, the affinities of language and custom did not succeed in outweighing the mistrust, the incompatibilities of every sort, the interests and, over and above all else, the problems created by the existence of the Jewish state and the unanimous hostility of the Arab states, bound together in respect of Israel. Moreover, this hostility was kept alive by the propaganda of the oriental ambassadors established in Morocco and even by the national radio.

In addition, in respect to the problem[3] posed by the freedom of movement—an infinitely sensitive one in the eyes of the Jewish community—it must be admitted that the attitude of the Palace and even

---

3. The Jewish-Arab conflict quite obviously had a part in the events which made up the history of independent Morocco. The wars of 1947/48, 1956 and 1967 did not facilitate coexistence between a small Jewish minority and the dominant Muslim group. The most serious unrest, probably fomented from abroad, broke out in the mining center of Djerada, a few kilometers from Oujda in eastern Morocco, during the Protectorate. In the night of June 7 to 8, 1948, the small local Jewish community was surrounded and attacked by a wild mob, which spared neither children nor old people. Thirty-nine people died and 30 were gravely wounded. The Army and the police responsible for maintaining order intervened only very belatedly without any haste to put an end to the massacre.

more of the local authorities charged with distributing travel documents was not always consistent. Periods of restriction alternated with periods of considerable liberalism. These fluctuations, which corresponded to general political considerations, had repercussions on the state of mind of the Jewish population: anxiety followed hope, and vice versa. This system ended up by disorientating and disappointing even the least mistrustful individuals until they too reached the point of envisaging a plan to leave.

In the difficult periods, and especially those marked by unexpected stopping of free emigration, clandestine movements took over. Departures were organized in such dangerous circumstances that they were sometimes followed by tragic accidents, as, for example, the shipwreck of the *Pisces* in January 1961. The loss of the forty-three people aboard aroused very strong emotions, both in Morocco and in the Jewish world. It was following this painful episode and deals made under pressure from American Jewry that the Moroccan government authorized the resumption of official emigration.[4]

After the accession of Moulay Hassan II, the apprehension that marked the beginning of the reign rapidly dissipated. Moroccan Jewry lived in a state of tranquility, even euphoria, barely dreamed of a few years earlier, however benevolent His Majesty Mohamed V, and which it could not have expected after President Nasser's famous visit to Morocco.

In fact, in the eyes of his Jewish subjects, the person of King Hassan is the sole guarantee of the freedoms written into a constitution which Moroccan Jewry voted for unanimously, notably the freedom of movement to which it attaches primordial importance. Under the rule of King Hassan II, the Moroccan Jew leaves the country and returns as he wishes. What once was the major obstacle, obtaining a passport, has for practical purposes been eliminated. The Jews have their elected members on the representative organizations: a deputy and municipal councilors in the urban agglomerations, vice-presidents and members on the boards of chambers of commerce. The government ministries use the abilities of several Jewish high officials.[5] Even the man in the

4. Some of these shipwreck victims were collected and buried not far from Tangers. His Majesty Hassan II decided in December 1992 to authorize the transfer of the bodies to Israel, thereby acceding to the request of the families and the communities. The Moroccan Government took charge of transporting the bodies.

5. Mention should be made here of the recent appointment of Mr. Serge Berdugo, President of the Council of Jewish Communities of Morocco, to the post of Minister of Tourism. It should also be recalled that, after the independence of Morocco, H.M. Mohammed V had named the late Dr. Leon Benzaquen to head the Ministry of the Post

street, the simple Jewish citizen, seems to have lost all his complexes and leads a peaceful life while waiting for possible departure. The contrast with the periods of anxiety in the not-so-remote past is so striking that one half-expects to hear someone say that Morocco is the country where the Jew is king, all in all a genuine Promised Land.

The Israeli-Arab war of 1967 and the Six-Day War may have accelerated departures, but life resumed its normal course shortly afterwards, disturbed from time to time by events inside or outside the country, marked by alternating anxiety and tranquility.

The situation has hardly changed in the last ten years.

## RECEPTION OF THE IMMIGRANTS

The wave of immigrants who flocked to Israel met enormous and manifold difficulties, as at the outset the young state had neither foreseen nor prepared the means to receive them properly. At first, they occupied houses which had been abandoned by their Arab inhabitants during the war. Then, the new *'olim* were taken to *ma'abarot* (transit camps). These were no more than tents, hutments, and shanty towns, pitiful dwellings, places of insalubrity and malnutrition, prostitution and criminality. They became living hells of mud or dust, depending on the time of year, of moral and material hardship. The immigrants only succeeded in leaving them after long and difficult stays of a few months or several years, depending on whether they were "white" or "black," powerful or wretches. The camps grew enormously in size. In 1952, there were eleven of them, housing 250,000 of the underprivileged.

Once the camps had disappeared, around the beginning of the sixties, the vast majority of their inmates, increased by new immigrants, were directed to development zones and towns (*'are hapituaḥ*) and immigrant cooperative villages (*moshabim*). Only 15 percent of them live in an urban environment, particularly in the three large Israeli cities, Jerusalem, Tel Aviv–Yaffa, and Haifa. The development towns situated in the Negev and the border regions (Beer-Sheba, Dimona, Kiryat Gat, Bet-Shan, Kiryat-Shmoneh, Ma'alot, etc.) were conceived as a means of relieving the congestion in the coastal plain, ensuring

---

Office and Telecommunications in 1956. May the memory of them both be for a blessing. Mr. André Azoulay is presently Counsellor of H.M. Mohammed VI and also member of the Royal Academy of Morocco.

the geographic dispersion of the population and, at the same time, guaranteeing the better defense of the country by a belt of settlements. The vast majority of their populations consist of Jews originally from the Maghreb, principally from Morocco. Maghrebians have also founded more than a hundred *moshabim* in the Negev, in Galilee, and on the borders of the country (Noam, Yashresh, Avivim, Deborah, etc.).

The reception and orientation of the new immigrants did not take place without difficulties; populating the development zones by the operation called "from the boat to the village" was not carried out without shouts and tears (The name Dimona, its earliest inhabitants say, derives from the Arabic and Hebrew *dim'a,* "tear"). People often refused to get off the trucks carrying them from the port to their settlement site, a desert area which town-planning officials envisaged turning into a village or town.

It is probably true that the social map of Israel is the result of the process by which it was populated and that the contours of what is known as the "Second Israel," the body of Jews described as "Sephardi and Oriental," were drawn in the living hell of the transit camps and the underprivileged districts of the large towns (Katamon in Jerusalem, Hatikvah in Tel Aviv, Wadi-Salib in Haifa). Moroccan immigrants and their numerous offspring form the bulk of the membership of the Second Israel. The large majority of them elected to live in Israel as the country of their choice and not as a refuge. They went up to Zion in messianic fervor and found no warmth in the welcome they received in the land of their fathers.

Government circles acknowledge the existence of wide disparities whose geographic or ethnic origin is manifestly hidden. There is awareness of a gulf in Israeli society where the Orientals are the misfits. People prefer to speak of backward social strata, large families, needy populations, assisted groups, and so on. If there is poverty in Israel, the poor, the badly housed, the malnourished are the Orientals.

The deficiencies in education and teaching which are the almost exclusive lot of the Oriental communities are obviously most serious in their consequences for the life of the individual and the collective. These communities scarcely feel themselves to be full partners in what is being achieved in the country. Except in wartime and the long periods of military service, when they are summoned to fulfill the same duties as everyone else, they have the impression of being regarded as second-rate partners.

## THE JUDEO-MAGHREBIAN AND ORIENTAL CULTURAL WORLD

It is not within our brief here to open wide the file on the Second Israel and its enormous social, economic, and cultural corollaries. This entails a whole mass of problems which embarrass or disturb public opinion in the Diaspora and even more in Israel, where, diverted at times from their real object, they are posed in terms of tensions and confrontations between communities. Our comments will be limited to the questions regarding culture, teaching, and education which face the Sephardi and Oriental Jew, particularly those of Maghrebian origin. The vital and irreducible needs of the individual must certainly be given their due place. But in the last resort, everything comes back to the necessity for information, education, and culture. Intellectual and spiritual pleasures are the greatest and purest for the poor—as they can be for those favored by fortune. It goes without saying that the fertile potential contained in the possession of knowledge, learning, and education are eminently capable of conferring the means of power, and constitute the real key to social promotion.

The Oriental and Sephardi Jew can define himself as a Jew in the same way that Kafka, in one of his letters to Milena, defined himself in relation to the Jews of the West. "I have to obtain everything," he said, "not only the present and the future, but also the past, that thing which all men receive their share of free; that too I must obtain, that is perhaps the hardest task; if the earth turns to the right—I do not know if it does—I have to move to the left to catch up with the past."

In the political and social context of present-day Israel, where the vast majority of the Oriental Diaspora has taken root, the thought and history of this Jewry, for a long time marginal, deserve to be known.

On this subject it is appropriate here to sketch a brief reflection on the historicity of the Jewish cultural world. If the history of most peoples and civilizations is inscribed in their national and municipal archives, in official chronicles and annals, the Jewish communities, dispersed among the nations and preoccupied with their religious, even physical, survival, were not able to bequeath us similar evidence. In order to write the history of Jewry in general, and of the Sephardi and Oriental world in particular, it is necessary to conduct a methodical documentary investigation into the ensemble of Jewish thought, seizing on any form of expression able to represent a certain existential content.

Written and oral literary work in Hebrew or dialect must not be regarded or studied for itself, having a value in itself, as an isolated essence, an ethereal entity, but as an integral part of the social whole, closely linked to the whole of history. All literary production, all thought, is a source of history. To "do history" is to examine all the forms of expression, the modes and genres, testing them by the currently accepted tools and investigation, analysis and criticism, and interpreting the results correctly. Juridical thought and its social, economic, and religious environment, especially as represented in the responsa and *taqqanot,* religious and secular poetry, exegetic, homiletical, even mystical and kabbalistic writing, popular literature handed down orally in the local dialects (Judeo-Arabic, Berber, or Castilian)—all this constitutes the fundamental basis of any global approach to Jewish existence, at every level of analysis. We have given evidence of this here and elsewhere, in relation to the Jewish actuality in the Islamic West—Moroccan Jewry, formerly considered as having no past, but whose collective memory, identity, and awareness of belonging to an ethnic category and a cultural landscape of its own within the constellation of cultures, ethnic groups, and mentalities which form the Jewish world are just beginning to be restored.

Steps have been taken, in Israel and elsewhere, to promote and develop studies and research into the last five centuries of this Oriental and Sephardi Jewry. One hopes that they will take immediate and concrete form. It is high time to bring out of the shadows those dark centuries of history and thought of the Oriental diasporas, a whole sector of the Jewish world and its culture left outside knowledge and research, excluded from study and education.

Moreover, the interest at present being shown in the Jewry of the Sephardi and Oriental world corresponds to a reality and answers a deep need.[6] Not so long ago the usual attitude was totally negative.

---

6. The First International Colloquium on the Jews of North Africa was convened by the Center for Research on the Jews of North Africa from April 5 to 8, 1977 at the Ben Zvi Institute in Jerusalem. Day-long study and research sessions on Judaism in Islamic countries and of Sephardic origin were organized by several institutes and establishments of higher learning. In addition, the University of Haifa designed and created, somewhat timidly, a chair of Jewish civilization of Islamic countries which I personally was asked to inaugurate during the first trimester of the 1977–1978 school year with courses in the history and literature of the Jews of the Muslim West for the period following the expulsion from Spain in 1492.

Furthermore, the Israeli Ministry of Education established its own "Commission for the Integration of the Sephardic and Eastern Cultural Heritage into the Curriculum . . .", and a new institution named *Misgab Yerushalayim* convened in Jerusalem from June 20 to 30, 1978 *the first international congress for the study of the cultural heritage of Eastern*

The European and Ashkenazi communities knew nothing of it, and the Oriental and Sephardi Jew himself, both elite and masses, exercised a sort of self-criticism, even self-destruction, in respect of his origins and culture. He erased his past and hid the values inherited from his parents and ancestors, thinking, through ignorance, unawareness, or shame at being what he was, that they were not worth being brought to light.

Today, there is an awakening Sephardi and Oriental awareness, an awareness of belonging to a different ethnic category and cultural landscape. This phenomenon is found in the daily life of the communities in Israel and the Diaspora. In addition, the search for a Sephardi and Oriental identity, at first regarded as a subversion and a desire for dissidence, is now seen as an appeal for the legitimacy of an institution.

If, at the level of disinterested and objective knowledge of the fate of social groups, we emphasize, in the area that concerns us, the necessity and urgency of undertaking and promoting, while there is still time, studies and research into the cultural heritage of Sephardi and Oriental Jewry over the last four or five centuries, it is because it is an integral part of universal Jewish thought, on the one hand, and because it contributes to a better knowledge of the Arabo-Islamic world and Mediterranean society, on the other. Moreover, there is awareness of this in the Maghreb itself where university and scientific circles, specialist reviews, and the press in general are showing a strong interest in work on Maghrebian Jewry and in the documentation being utilized, which certain Muslim Maghrebians now consider a not negligible source of their history, even as their own memory, especially when it is a question of oral, popular, and dialect literature, artistic creation, music, and song.

## JUDEO-MAGHREBIAN MEMORY

The fate of the Moroccan Jews in other host countries seems to have been very different. Whether in France, Canada, or Venezuela, they all formed remarkably vital communities, and their social and economic

*and Sephardic Judaism.* Since 1978, the number of international congresses, conferences, and colloquiums on the Sephardic world and the dialogue of cultures has grown considerably (see *The Jews of Andalusia and the Maghreb,* pp. 411–413).

integration is far more advanced than that of their co-religionists who emigrated to Israel. In France and elsewhere, they were required to adapt themselves to the culture of the host society, their desire for assimilation into French, Canadian, or South American life taking precedence, in the majority of cases, over regret for the past and the feeling of uprootedness. In this progress toward assimilation, a few points of resistance can be observed: The hold of the family circle still maintains a certain force, and the attachment to Judaism remains a reality. In France, the Maghrebian Jews certainly constitute the most religious and most traditionalist element in the country's Jewish community. Israel exercises a strong attraction for all these immigrant populations, but nonetheless a significant proportion of North African Jews see their settlement in France, Canada, or Venezuela as permanent.

The individual belonging to the Judeo-Maghrebian minority in France is associated with French culture and society by the use of the language, by the repeated acts of daily life, by what constitutes the "private life" of people, by his relations with his autochthonous next-door neighbor, his workmate in the workshop or office, his partner or competitor in trade and industry, his colleague at school or university, and so on. However, he remains rooted in his loyalty to Hebrew writing and world Jewish thought and, even more, is strongly marked by his Maghrebian origins and his ancestral participation in its Hispano-Arab-Berber culture.

All the same, there remains a Judeo-Maghrebian memory of two millennia of history on the hospitable soil of the Maghreb. Its echo still resounds in the uprooted soul of the immigrants; it rings through their music and song, their folklore and their rites, their celebration of the Mimuna and the *hillula,* their collective pilgrimages to the tombs of their local saints (Rabbi Amram Ben Diwan at Quzzane, Mwalin Dad at Settat, etc.). It can be seen even more among the immigrants settled in Israel: their homesickness for their country, their melancholy regrets, their bitter or nostalgic cries, their violent or restrained writings. It is more subtly expressed in Hebrew literary works, still very modest, by a few authors of Maghrebian origin, and in the sensitivity of young poets whose message renders, in a quite remarkable fashion, the bruised soul, the hidden or humiliated culture, and the hard and difficult conditions of life of a "second" diaspora whose fascinating face, moving warmth, joys, and sorrows we formerly knew on Moroccan soil.[7]

Thoughts on some of the past's lessons in wisdom, which might also concern today's world, will serve as a conclusion.

It might have seemed absurd just a short while ago, in the tragic circumstances of Jewish-Arab relations and more precisely in the torment and tension, the conflict and war being experienced for more than half a century in the Middle East so near and dear to us, to speak of places of social and cultural dialogue, of wisdom and spiritual transcendence.

As far as we are concerned though, we have remained faithful to our mission and convinced, for more than 30 years, that we must not reject the lessons of history, that we must try to see things from the inside, to break through the barriers of arrogance and to maintain distance in order to study and understand. There is no better future than one rooted in the past.

The events referred to as historic that are taking place before our eyes and the seeds of peace they contain justify the hope we place in other places of meeting and dialogue, of peaceful coexistence, friendship and cooperation, in short, places of wisdom. What had been a wish now bears the embryo of fulfillment. The reconciliation of the sons and descendents of Abraham can be glimpsed on the horizon, and a decisive step has been taken to put an end to the Israeli-Palestinian conflict.

History will retain the crucial role played by the King of Morocco, Hassan II, in the success of the negotiations; it will retain the tribute paid to the Moroccan people and its sovereign, a pioneer of the agreement reached, by the Prime Minister of the State of Israel on a visit to Morocco following the signing of that agreement in Washington on September 13, 1993.

Current events give us ground to examine the very special moments in the medieval history of the Land of Islam and to focus on places of wisdom, meeting places of ideas and civilizations, places that would be unimaginable without places of freedom and without that very high degree of cultural, legal, financial, and administrative autonomy which the laws of *dhimma* gave to religious minorities, including people of The Book.

---

7. I am thinking of Erez Bitton, of his "Offrande marocaine" (Moroccan Offering) and his "Livre de la menthe" (Book of Mint) and of Gabriel Bensimhon and his "Requiem pour le Messie, roi marocain" (Requiem for the Messiah, Moroccan King).

A full page in the newspaper *Le Monde* of March 17, 1980, was devoted to the report by two Moroccan writers, Tahar Ben Jelloun and Edmond Amram El-Maleh, on my book *Litteratures dialectales et populaires juives en Occident Musulman,* which had just appeared. Their article was entitled: "When Jews and Arabs sing together" and noted, among other things, that "for centuries Jews and Moslems in Morocco had recited the same poems and sung the same songs . . . (The author of the book) has gathered examples of this common culture . . . Jews and Arabs recognized each other and exchanged differences; they shared a common history and thus left their children a common memory and cultural heritage . . ." On the cover of the same book, I myself had reproduced an excerpt of a verse by Louis Aragon taken from his collection *Le Roman Inacheve:* "What has been will be, provided one remembers."

Reporting in *Matin du Sahara* on my book *Kabbale, vie mystique et Magie,* which appeared at the end of 1986, Mr. Allal Sinaceur, a member of the Academy of the Kingdom of Morocco and former director of the UNESCO Department of Philosophy, gave his article the following title: "This Judaism of Arabic Language and Civilization." An excerpt of his text continues: "History will return rightfully to its sources . . . because, if you scratch the surface, you discover even freedom and friendship. And without that, what is written is merely a semblance of history, history where demons are at work. . . ."

In fact, the past has sent us a message, a reminder that we owe it to ourselves to examine. The special moments of history must help us to get our bearings, and its places of wisdom must serve as paradigms for building the present and envisaging the future in regained peace.

These places of wisdom, like the gatherings of Fustat, Cordova, Baghdad, and Grenada, which are mentioned in the early chapters of my book, *Juifs d'Andalousie et du Maghreb,* all the places of meeting and dialogue of which we have described a few examples, all are places of cooperation among minds devoted in particular to things spiritual, thus creating a state of mind which could give birth to that *Societe des Esprits* to which Paul Valery referred some 60 years ago, the conditions for a genuine *Societe des Nations* (League of Nations) (UNESCO Courier, September 1993, p. 44, selected texts).

We fervently hope that the peace process initiated following the Oslo talks and the accords signed in Washington on September 13, 1993, will not be weakened, delayed, interrupted or compromised by the many obstacles in its path. The tragedies that have occurred in

Hebron, Jerusalem, Tel Aviv, and Cana, Lebanon, are but a few among others. Let us arm ourselves with greater determination, courage, and strength to defeat the monster of intolerance and fanaticism as well as policies gone astray and to ensure that political action goes hand in hand with a thirst for justice, generosity, and love.

# Bibliography


ABEN SUR, Jacob. *'Et le-Kol-Ḥefeṣ* (anthology of liturgical poetry). No-Amon, Alexandria, 1893.

———. *Mishpat u-Ṣdaqah be-Ya'aqob* (responsa). vol. 1, Alexandria, 1894; vol. 2, Alexandria, 1903.

ABITBOL, Michel. *Témoins et acteurs: Les Corcos et l'historie du Maroc contemporain.* Jerusalem, 1977.

ABITOL, Michel, *Tujjar al-Sultan, une élite judeo-morocaine au XIX^e^ siecle*, Jerusalem, 1994.

ADDISON, L. *The Present State of the Jews in Barbary.* London, 1675.

*Ahabat ha-Qadmonim* (Book of the ritual of the toshabim, of Fez). Jerusalem, 1889.

AL-FASI, M. "Introduction à l'étude de la littérature populaire marocaine." *La Pensée* (Rabat), no. 1 (1962), pp. 61–77.

AL-HAYK, Muhammad ben al-Ḥusayn. *Majmû'ât al-Ḥayk* (photo-copy of the manuscript). Maktabat al-Rishâd, Casablanca, 1972.

ANQAWA, A. "Ordonnances des rabbins de Castille." *Kerem Ḥemed* 2 (1871).

ATTAL, Robert. *Les Juifs d'Afrique du Nord. Bibliography.* Jerusalem, 1973, 1993.

AUBIN, Eugène. *Le Maroc d'aujourd'hui.* Paris, 1904.

BARGES, J. J., and GOLDBERG, D. B. *Risalat Yehudah ben Quraysh 'ila Jama 'ât Yahûd Madînat Fâs.* Paris, 1857.

BARON, S. W. *A Social and Religious History of the Jews.* first five volumes, New York and Philadelphia, 1958–76.

BELLOW, Saul. *Humbold's Gift.* Penguin, Harmondsworth.

BENAÏM, Yosef. *Malke Rabbanan* (bio-bibliographical dictionary of the rabbis of Morocco). Jerusalem, 1931.

BEN AMI, Issachar, *Saint Veneration Among the Jews of Morocco*, Jerusalem, 1984 (Hebrew), Paris, 1990 (French).

BENECH, José. *Essai d'explication d'un mellah.* Marrakesh, 1940.

BENSIMON-DONATH, Doris. *Évolution de judaïsme marocain sous le Protectorat français*. Paris and The Hague, 1968.
BERQUE, J. *Structures sociales du Haut-Atlas*. Paris, 1955.
———. "Al Yousi." *Problémes de la culture marocaine au XVIIIe siécle*. Paris, 1958.
BETTAN, I. *Studies in Jewish Preaching*. Cincinnati, 1939.
BIARNAY, S. *Notes d'ethnographie et de linguistique nord-africaines*. L. Brunot and L. Laoust, Paris, 1924.
BLAU, J. *The Emergence and Linguistic Background of Judaeo-Arabic*. Oxford University Press, Oxford, 1965.
BOURRILLY, J. *Éléments d'ethnographie marocaine*. E. Laoust, Paris, 1932.
BROWN, Kenneth L. *People of Salé*. Manchester University Press, Manchester, 1976.
BRUNOT, Louis. *Textes arabes de Rabat*. Paris, 1931 (texts), 1952 (glossary).
———, and MALKA, E. *Textes judéo-arabes de Fés*. Rabat, 1939.
CENIVAL, P. de. "La légende du Juif Ibn Mech'al et la fête du Sultan des Tolba à Fez." *Hespéris* 5 (1925), pp. 137–218.
CHOTTIN, A. *Tableau de la musique marocaine*. Geuthner, Paris, n.d., (Prix du Maroc, 1938).
COHEN, D. *Le parler arabe des Juifs de Tunis*. vol. 1, Paris and The Hague, 1964; vol. 2, 1975.
CORCOS, D. *Studies in the History of the Jews of Morocco*. Jerusalem, 1976.
D'ERLANGER, R. *La musique arabe*. vol. 5, Paris, 1949; vol. 6, Paris, 1959.
DOUTTÉ, Edmond. *En tribu*. Paris, 1914.
———. *Magie et religion*. Algiers, 1909.
DOZY, R. *Supplément aux Dictionnaires Arabes*. Leiden and Paris, 1927 (2nd edition).
DURAN, Profiat, *Ma'aseh Efod*. Vienna, 1865.
ED-DER'Y, Moïse b. Isaac. *Yad Moshe*. Amsterdam, 1809.
———. *Ma'aseh Nissim*. Amsterdam, 1818.
———. *An Historical Account of the Ten Tribes*. London, 1936.
EISENBETH, M. *Les Juifs d'Afrique du Nord. Démographie et onomastique*. Algiers, 1936.
ELIADE, Mircea. *Aspects du mythe*. Gallimard, Idées, 1963.
FERRE, D. *Lexique marocain-français*. Fédale Morocco, n.d.
FLAMAND, Pierre. *Un mellah en pays berbére: Demnate*. Paris, 1952.
FOUCAULD, Charles de. *Reconnaissance au Maroc*. Paris, 1888.
GEIGER, Abraham. *Judaism and Islam*. New York, 1970 (preface by Moshe Perlman).
GOITEIN, S. D., *Juifs et Arabes*. Paris, 1957.
———. *Sidre Ḥinnukh Mitqufat ha-Geonim 'ad Bet he-Rambam* (Medieval Jewish Education). Jerusalem, 1962.
———. *A Mediterranean Society*. vol. 1, University of California Press, 1967; vol. 2, 1971; vol. 3, 1978.

GOLDBERG, Harvey. "The Mimuna and the Minority Status of Moroccan Jews." *Ethnology* 17, no. 1 (January 1978), pp. 75–87.
GOULVEN, J. *Les mellahs de Rabat-Salé.* Paris, 1927.
ḤASSIN, David. *Tehillah le-David* (anthology of poetry: *piyyuṭim* and *qinot*). Amsterdam, 1807, and Casablanca, 1931.
HESSE, Hermann. *Glasperlenspiel.* 1943. Available in English in various editions under the titles *The Glass Bead Game* and *Magister Ludi.*
HIRSCHBERG, H. Z. (J. W.). *A History of the Jews in North Africa from Antiquity to the Sixteenth Century.* Brill, Leiden (2 volumes), 1974, Jerusalem (Hebrew), Paris, 1990 (French).
JOUIN, J. "La mort de Moïse. Poéme en arabe dialectal marocain." *Littérature Orale Arabo-Berbére.* CNRS and EPHE, 5th Bulletin de liaison (1971–72), pp. 153–59.
KAFEḤ, J. *Halikhot Teman* (the life of the Jews in Sanaa and the surrounding area). Ben-Zvi Institute, Jerusalem, 1961.
KUNDERA, Milan. *La Plaisanterie.* Gallimard, Folio, 1968. English trans. *The Joke.* New York: HarperCollins, 1992.
LAOUST, E. *Mots et choses berbéres.* Paris, 1920.
LAREDO, A. I. *Les noms des Juifs du Maroc.* Madrid, 1978.
———. "Les Purim de Tanger." *Hespéris* 25, pp. 193–204.
LEGEY (Doctoresse). *Essai de folklore marocain.* Paris, 1926.
LE TOURNEAU, Roger. *Fés avant le Protectorat.* Casablanca, 1949.
———. *La vie quotidienne á Fés en 1900.* Paris, 1965.
LEVI-PROVENÇAL, E. *Les Historiens des Chorfa.* Paris, 1922.
LOUBIGNAC, Victorien. *Textes arabes des Zaer.* Paris, 1952.
MAIMONÏDES, Moses.
MALKA, Élie. *Essai de folklore des Israélites du Maroc.* Paris, 1976.
MASSIGNON, L. "Enquête sur les corporations musulmanes d'artisans et de commerçants au Maroc. *Revue du Monde Musulman* 58 (1924) (2nd section), Paris.
———. *Le Maroc dans les premières années du XVIe siècle. Tableau géographique d'après Léon L'Africain.* Algiers, 1906.
MIEGE, J. *Le Maroc et l'Europe. 1830–1894.* Paris, 1961–62.
MIRSKY, A. "Ha-piyyut she-ba-tefillah." *Tarbut* 18 (1964).
———. *Reshit ha-piyyut.* Jerusalem, 1965.
———. *Shire Yishaq Ibn Kalfon.* Bialik Institute, Jerusalem, 1961.
MOYAL, Elie, *Le mouvement Sabbistaiste au Maroc, son histoire et ses sources,* Tel Aviv, 1984 (Hebrew).
OHANA, Raphaël. *Mar'eh ha-yeladim* (Medicine and magic). Jerusalem, 1900.
PELLAT, Ch. "Nemrod et Abraham dans le parler arabe des Juifs de Debdou." *Hespéris* 39 (1952), 1st and 2nd trim., pp. 121–47.
PERES, H. *La poésie andalouse en arabe classique au XIe siècle.* A. Maisonneuve, Paris, 1937 and 1953.

PEREṢ, Yehudah ben Yosef. *Peraḥ Lebanon*. Berlin, 1712.

QORIAT, Isaac. *Naḥalat Abot*. Leghorn, 1898.

SCHOLEM, Gershom. *Major Trends in Jewish Mysticism*. New York, 1946.

———. *Origins of the Kabbalah*. Jewish Publication Society, Princeton University Press, Princeton.

SCHIRMANN, H. Y. *Ha-Shirah ha-'Ibrit bi-Sfarad u-bi Probans* (Hebrew poetry in Spain and Provence). Jerusalem and Tel Aviv, 1954–56, vols. 1 and 2.

SCHWARTZBAUM, H. *Mimeqor Yisra'el we-Yishma'el*. ("The folkloric aspects of Judaism and Islam"). Tel Aviv, 1975.

SEMACH, Y. D. "Le Saint d'Ouezzan. Ribbi. 'Amram ben Diwan et les Saints Juifs du Maroc." *Bulletin de l'Enseignement Public du Maroc*. March 1937 (24th year), pp. 1–21.

SHROETER, J. Daniel, *Merchants of Essabura*, Cambridge University Press, 1988.

SLOUSCH, Nahum. "Étude sur l'histoire des Juifs et du judaïsme au Maroc." *Archives Marocaines*. Paris, 1905–6.

———. "Les Juifs de Debdou." *Revue du Monde Musulman* 22 (1913).

SONNECK, C. *Chants arabes du Maghreb. Étude sur le dialecte et la poésie populaire de l'Afrique du Nord* (I, Arabic text). Paris, 1902.

SOUSTELLE, Jacques. *La vie quotidienne des Aztèques*. Paris, 1955.

TADJOURI, R. "Le mariage juif à Salé." *Hespéris* 3 (1923), 3rd trim., pp. 393–420.

TAHAR, A. *La poésie populaire algérienne (malḥun). Rythme. mètre et formes*. Algeria, 1975 (Arabic).

TEARRASSE, Henri. *Histoire du Maroc*. Casablanca, 1949–50.

TOLEDANO, J. M. *Ner ha-Ma'arab* (History of the Jews of Morocco, Hebrew), Jerusalem, 1911.

———. *'Oṣar Gnazim*. Jerusalem, 1960.

VAJDA, Georges. *Introduction à la pensée juive du Moyen Age*. Paris, 1947.

———. "Un recueil de textes historiques judéo-marocain." *Hespéris* 12, Paris, 1951.

———. "Juifs et musulmans selon le Hadit." *Journal Asiatique* 229, pp. 57–127.

VALÉRY, Paul. *Cahiers*. Éd. de la Pléiade, 1974.

———. *Oeuvres*. Bibl. de la Pléiade, 1957.

VASSEL, E. *La Littérature populaire des Israélites Tunisiens*. Paris, 1907.

VOINOT, L. *Pèlerinages judéo-musulmans du Maroc*. Paris, 1948.

WESINCH, A. J. "The Semitic New Year and the Origin of Eschatology." *Acta Orientalia* 1 (1923), pp. 159–99.

WESTERMARCK, Edward. *Marriage Customs in Morocco*. 1914. Reprinted, Rowman & Littlefield, Totowa, N.J., 1972.

———. *Ritual and Belief in Morocco*. London, 1926 and New York, 1968, 2 vols.

YA'RI, Abraham. *Shluḥe 'Ereṣ-Yisra'el* (The Palestinian Emissary Rabbis). Jerusalem, 1951.

———. "Moses ben Isaac Edre'y and His Books" (Hebrew), *Kiryat Sefer* 33 (1958), pp. 521–28.

YELLIN, David. *Torat ha-Shirah ha-Sfardit* (introduction to the Hebraic poetry of the Spanish period). Jerusalem, 1940.

ZAFRANI, Haïm. "Langues juives du Maroc." *Que de l'Occident Musulman et de la Méditerranée* 4 (1967), pp. 175–88.

———. "Mi-Kamokha." *Journal Asiatique* 253, no. 2 (1964), pp. 97–104.

———. "Une histoire de Job en Judéo-arabe du Maroc." *Revue des Études Islamiques* 26, no. 2 (1968), pp. 279–316.

———. "La parodie dans la littérature judéo-arabe et le folklore de Purim au Maroc." *Revue des Études Juives* 178, no. 4 (1969), pp. 377–93.

———. "Notes sur G. Vajda. *Inscriptions Antiques du Maroc. Inscriptions hébraïques.*" CNRS, (1966, in *Revue des etudes juives* 127, no. 1 [1968], pp. 125–6.

———. "Une qessa de Tinghire. Hymne à Bar Yoḥay." *Revue des Études Juives* 127, no. 4 (1968), pp. 366–82.

———. "Les Communauté's du Todgha." *Revue des Études Juives juives* 133, nos. 1 and 2 (1964), pp. 191–98.

———. *Pédagogie juive en Terre d'Islam.* Paris, 1969.

———. *Une version berbère de la Haggadah de Pesaḥ. Texte de Tinrhir du Todrha* (Maroc). Supplement to the Proceedings of the GLECS, 2 vols., Paris, 1970 (in collaboration with Madame P. PERNET-GALAND).

———. "Abitbol, Saul Amor"; "Ankawa, Raphael"; "Arrobas, Isaac, and family"; "Hagiz family"; "North African Jewish Dialects": all in *Encyclopaedia Judaica.* Keter, Jerusalem, 1971.

———. "Judéo-berbère"; "Qissa"; "Mallâh": all in *Encyclopédie de l'Islam.* new edition.

———. *Les Juifs du Maroc. Vie sociale. Économique et religieuse. Études de Taqqanot et Responsa.* Paris, 1972.

———. *Littérature populaires et dialectales juives en Occident Musulman.* Paris, 1980.

———. *Poésie. juive en Occident Musulman.* Paris, 1977.

———. "Problèmes monétaires du Maroc dans la littérature juridique (Taqqanot et Responsa) des rabbins marocains." *Journal Asiatique* 262, nos. 1 and 2 (1974), pp. 37–46; *Revue Historique* 55 (July–September 1974), pp. 73–80.

———. *Kabbale. vie mystique et magie.* Paris, 1986, 1996.

———. *La version arabe de la bible de Sa'adya Gaon. L'éclésiaste et son commentaire "Le livre de l'Ascése."* Paris, 1989, in collaboration with André Caquot.

———. *Ethique et mystique (Judaïsme en terre d'Islam). Le comment'aire kab-*

*balistique du traité des pères de J. Bu-'lfergan (texte français et hébreu).* Paris, 1991.

———. "*L'irruption du divin, du sacré et de l'ésotérique dans la vie quotidinne de la société judéo-maghrébine*" dans Signes du Présent (revue scientifique et culturelle marocaine) n° 6, Fédala-Mohammadia, 1989.

———. *le livre de la Création ou la Kabbale des Origines (Sefer Yesirah),* Editions Art et Valeur, Paris, 1978, (Ouvrage illustré par le peintre viennois Ernst Fuchs).

———. *Los Judios del Occidente musulman Al-Andalus y El-Magreb,* Madrid, 1994.

———. *Traditions poétiques et musicales juives au Maroc, Centralité religieuse et fonctions sociales,* dans "Journal of Mediterranean Studies," vol. 6/1, 1996, p. 145–156.

———. *Juifs d'Andalousie et du Maghreb,* Maisonneuve et Larose, Paris, 1966, Madrid, 1944 (version espagnole), Rabat, 2001 (version arabe).

———. *Mille ans de vie juive au Maroc (Histoire et culture, Religion et magie),* Paris, 1983, version hébraïque avec un sous-titre: *Sefer home-querot,* Le livre des sources, Tel-Aviv, 1986; Rabat, 1987 (version arabe), Coracas (Venezuela), 2001 (version espagnole).

## ENCYCLOPEDIAS

*Encyclopédie de l'Islam,* 1st and 2nd eds., Leiden and Paris, 1913–42, 1954–.

*Encyclopaedia Judaica.* Jerusalem, 1971.

*Jewish Encyclopedia.* New York, 1901–9.

# Index

economic life, 5
existence, 5
expulsion from Spain, 6–7
Hebrew initials, 7
Reconquista, 6
*serarah,* 7–8
teachers of, 5
Spanish schools, 5, 172
sterility, 44–45. *See also* infertility
Sukkot
agricultural aspect, 253
ending of, 254
Hosha'anah Rabbah, 254
*lulab,* 252–253, 254
meaning, 252
mystical symbolism, 253–254
*Simḥat Torah,* 254
*sukkah,* 252, 253
*Taberyanut,* 255–256
sumptuary regulations, 135–138, 175–176
Sur, Jacob Aben, 84, 85, 115–118, 185–186, 247, 257–258, 260, 261, 270, 271–272, 274
Sur, Moses Aben, 185–186, 194, 272, 274–275
Sur, Shalom Aben, 185–186
*suwwaqa,* 17
synagogues
function, 129
major *miṣwot,* 130
Moroccan, 249–250
revenues, 130
taxation of officials, 133
as schools, 57

*taḥdid,* 46, 47–50
*taḥmîla,* 61
*ta'anit hafsaqah,* 67–68
talmid *ḥakham,* 164–170
Talmud
exegesis, 202–203
juridical doctrine, 219. *See also* halakhah
kabbalah, 225
prayer, 225
Tamghrut, 21
*taqqanah,* 124, 125
*taqqanot,* 139
Tausk, Samuel, 28
taxation, 175
assessing wealth, 132
direct, 131–132
fiscal immunity, 133
indirect, 132–133
for the welfare fund, 133
tax evasion, 131–132
teachers
attitudes toward, 62
status, 59
in the yeshîbot, 64, 65
teaching
basic principles, 53
biblical literature, 180
books, 58
discipline, 61–62
elementary, 56–57
language and, 60
and liturgy, 57, 60
methods, 60–61, 66
nocturnal, 69–70
oral transmission, 166
*piyyuṭim,* 70
premises, 58
programs, 54
reading, 60, 66
reform, 72
trades, 71–72. *See also* apprenticeships
tradition, 54
traditional, 72
writing, 61, 66
yeshîbâh, 65
*teḥinnot,* 187
tobacco, 147
Torah, 247–248
dedication of a scroll, 255
giving of, 246